AF823133

ZEW Economic Studies

Publication Series of the Centre for
European Economic Research (ZEW),
Mannheim, Germany

ZEW Economic Studies

Vol. 1: O. Hohmeyer, K. Rennings (Eds.)
Man-Made Climate Change
Economic Aspects and Policy Options
1999. VIII, 401 pp. ISBN 3-7908-1146-7

Vol. 2: Th. Büttner
Agglomeration, Growth, and Adjustment
A Theoretical and Empirical Study
of Regional Labor Markets in Germany
1999. XI, 206 pp. ISBN 3-7908-1160-2

Vol. 3: P. Capros et al.
Climate Technology Strategies 1
Controlling Greenhouse Gases.
Policy and Technology Options
1999. XVIII, 365 pp. ISBN 3-7908-1229-3

Vol. 4: P. Capros et al.
Climate Technology Strategies 2
The Macro-Economic Cost and Benefit
of Reducing Greenhouse Gas Emissions
in the European Union
1999. XIII, 224 pp. ISBN 3-7908-1230-7

Vol. 5: P. A. Puhani
Evaluating Active Labour Market Policies
Empirical Evidence for Poland During Transition
1999. XVI, 239 pp. ISBN 3-7908-1234-X

Bernd Fitzenberger

Wages and Employment Across Skill Groups

An Analysis for West Germany

With 45 Figures
and 28 Tables

Physica-Verlag
A Springer-Verlag Company

ZEW
Zentrum für Europäische
Wirtschaftsforschung GmbH
Centre for European
Economic Research

Series Editor
Prof. Dr. Wolfgang Franz

Author
Prof. Bernd Fitzenberger, Ph. D.
Department of Economics
Dresden University of Technology
01062 Dresden
Germany

ISBN 3-7908-1235-8 Physica-Verlag Heidelberg New York

Cataloging-in-Publication Data applied for
Die Deutsche Bibliothek – CIP-Einheitsaufnahme
Fitzenberger, Bernd: Wages and employment across skill groups: an analysis for West Germany; with 28 tables / Bernd Fitzenberger, ZEW, Centre for European Economic Research. – Heidelberg; New York: Physica-Verl., 1999
(ZEW economic studies; Vol. 6)
Zugl.: Konstanz, Univ., Habil.-Schr. 1998
ISBN 3-7908-1235-8

Cover design: Erich Dichiser, ZEW, Mannheim

SPIN 10735584 88/2202-5 4 3 2 1 0 – Printed on acid-free paper

To Angela

Preface

For some time, it has been debated whether a lack of wage flexibility is at the roots of the high and persistent unemployment in West Germany. In the presence of a skill bias in labor demand, which increases the relative demand for more highly skilled labor over time, there only seems to exist the choice between higher wage inequality or higher unemployment rates. This study scrutinizes whether and in what way this line of thought is consistent with empirical findings for West Germany. The analysis ranges from extensive descriptive evidence on wage trends to the estimation of a structural model of wage bargaining. As the most important database, I use the *IAB–Beschäftigtenstichprobe* from 1975 to 1990.

This study was accepted as a Habilitation thesis by the Department of Economics and Statistics of the University of Konstanz in October 1998. The only major change relates to appendix B on the block bootstrap procedure now summarizing the main aspects of the method. I am very grateful to my advisor Prof. Dr. Wolfgang Franz for his support, encouragement, and inspiration. From 1993 to 1997, he ran the Center for International Labor Economics at the University of Konstanz in such a way that it provided a fruitful environment for empirical research in labor economics. I am also indebted to Prof. Dr. Winfried Pohlmeier and to Prof. Dr. Gerd Ronning for undertaking the task to evaluate my Habilitation thesis.

I am grateful to the Deutsche Forschungsgemeinschaft for a Habilitation scholarship from October 1996 to September 1998. The scholarship allowed me to stay for some time as visiting scholar at Stanford University and at the University College London. I appreciate the hospitality of these institutions.

This study benefitted from the comments and the help of numerous people in addition to those mentioned above. I am very grateful to all of them. Here, I would like to mention Ralph Baumann, Stefan Bender, Thiess Büttner, Michael Burda, Ina Czekalla, Martin Falk, Isabelle Haggeney, Olaf Hübler, Bertrand Koebel, Nadine Leiner, Inge Mattern, Reinhold Schnabel, Werner Smolny, Viktor Steiner, Peter Winker, and Gaby Wunderlich. Obviously, all errors remain my own responsibility. Finally, I especially thank Angela for being with me during the time when this study was completed and my mother who supported me all through my life.

April 1999 Bernd Fitzenberger

Contents

1 Introduction

The European unemployment problem and the US inequality problem are two sides of the same coin.

Krugman (1994)

West Germany experienced a sharp increase in unemployment during the 70's and 80's. While real wages increased moderately during the economic recovery of the 80's, unemployment rates have remained on a high level ever since with the exception of the unification boom (1990–1992). The problem of high and persistent unemployment rates has been discussed intensively by the economic policy debate in Germany for many years, see the recent reports of the German Council of Economic Experts (1994, 1995, 1996). The discussion often points to the high level of wages in international comparison, the insufficient degree of wage differentiation, and the impact of labor market institutions and governmental regulations as the reasons for the dismal unemployment experience in West Germany, see Paqué (1995) or Siebert (1995a, 1997).

A fairly broad consensus exists that the West German labor market is too inflexible to allow for a substantial reduction in unemployment rates. Even though total employment increased considerably during the second half of the 80's and the early 90's, it is argued that employment of certain segments of the labor force could have been higher if it had been possible to employ these persons for lower wages. In particular, this appears to be the case for workers without formal occupational degree ("Ohne abgeschlossene Berufsausbildung") whose employment has decreased by 3.1 Million persons from 1976 to 1989, see German Council of Economic Experts (1996, pp. 321, 347). In contrast, employment of workers with an occupational degree ("Mit abgeschlossener Berufsausbildung") increased by 5.1 Million persons during the same period. Correspondingly, unemployment rates among persons without formal occupational degree have been considerably higher than for persons with formal occupational degree. Descriptive evidence on wage trends often suggests that relative wage differentials between these two skill groups proved fairly stable or even declined, see Abraham and Houseman (1995), OECD (1993, 1996), or Steiner and Wagner (1998). Contrasting the differing trends in employment with the trends in wages suggests that exogenous forces have caused a drastic shift in labor demand towards more skilled labor. This hypothesis is often referred to as the skill bias in labor demand and, in fact, it is argued that the fundamental causes of the shift in labor demand operate in the entire advanced world. Correspondingly, Freeman (1995, p. 15) argues

> *In the 1980s and 1990s, the demand for less-skilled workers fell in advanced countries. In the United States, this showed up primarily in falling real wages for less-educated men, ... In OECD-Europe, it took the form of increased unemployment for the less skilled.*

This quote by Freeman and the quote at the beginning by Krugman most clearly represent the so-called "two-sides-of-the-same-coin hypothesis"[1] which has played a central role in the academic discussion of the differences in labor market trends between the United States and Europe since the mid 80's. As a stylized view, the two-sides-of-the-same-coin hypothesis states that labor demand for different skill groups has experienced the same kind of autonomous shocks in the United States and in Europe but that the results have been strikingly different. At the cost of a large decline in the wage position of low-skilled workers, the United States experienced no secular increase in unemployment. At the cost of a secular increase in unemployment, which was particularly strong for low-skilled workers, wage ratios across skill groups remained fairly stable in Europe. The two-sides-of-the-same-coin hypothesis is based on the argument that, in addition to the wage level, also the flexibility of the wage structure exhibits a major influence on the unemployment trends in reaction to internal and external shocks. For instance, the increase in unemployment due to structural change involving a reallocation of resources across industries can be mitigated by a sufficient flexibility of wages across skill groups when the likelihood to find a new job after displacement is positively correlated with the skill level of the worker. Flexibility of the wage structure prevents the increase of unemployment for particular groups in the presence of labor supply or labor demand shocks which are non-neutral across different types of workers.

The different chapters of this study explore various aspects of the labor market developments in West Germany in light of the two-sides-of-the-same-coin hypothesis. The results obtained are contrasted with the international trends (mainly for the United States). As a fundamental working hypothesis in this literature, it is assumed that cross-country differences allow for a better discrimination among different economic hypotheses. This is the case because certain fundamental factors driving labor demand are ubiquitous at the international level while others are country-specific.

So far, I have put forward a labor demand perspective implying that aggregate unemployment is caused by the wage level being too high and that disproportionate unemployment among a group of workers is caused by the

[1] See also Beißinger and Möller (1998) for this terminology.

relative wage for this group being too high. This is a classical hypothesis in economics and, taking this perspective, it is possible to estimate the wage gap, i.e. the difference between actual wage levels (ratios) and wage levels (ratios) which are consistent with full–employment, see e.g. the recent treatment in Franz (1996, p. 375) or in German Council of Economic Experts (1994, pp. 259–260). At this point, I would like to add a few clarifying remarks to put this study into context: First, even though the shifts in employment might not be caused by changes in wages (e.g. trends towards wage compression) but by forces exogenous to wage setting, a sufficient flexibility of the wages could have prevented the emergence of unemployment. In this sense, unemployment is "caused" by a lack of wage flexibility. Second, this study focuses on changes in wages in order to influence employment. It is not investigated here whether government policies (aggregate demand policies, supply side policies in education, in research, or in the formation of infrastructure) can mitigate the adverse effects on labor demand. Third, having determined, what changes in the wage level or the wage structure can mitigate adverse labor demand trends, does not provide a strategy how to implement such changes. In fact, it remains to analyze why wages are set at the level they are even though unemployed workers would apparently be happy to take a job at a lower wage. While a large literature has provided rationalizations for wage rigidities in levels, rigidities in wage ratios are often introduced in a merely adhoc way, see Krugman (1995) and Landmann and Pflüger (1996). In order to understand the labor market trends, it is very important to analyze to what extent wage setting has reacted in response to increasing unemployment rates and why it might not have reacted sufficiently.

At this point, a discussion of the fundamental factors causing the purported prevalent skill bias in labor demand trends is in order. The literature discusses two main candidates which basically apply to all advanced industrialized (mainly OECD) countries: Skill biased technological change and increased globalization (integration) in international trade. An additional candidate is the so–called capital–skill complementarity hypothesis, which I view as being related to the first candidate. Still another candidate is the long–run trend in value–added and employment away from Manufacturing to service industries. In addition to the worldwide candidates, there are, however, country–specific changes which might very well affect trends in wages and in employment and some of which might go beyond a simple labor demand perspective as described above. These effects often relate to institutional differences. Countries like the United States and the United Kingdom have experienced a considerable decline in unionism to which some authors attribute partly the increasing wage dispersion in these countries, see Machin et al. (1997). Changing governmental regulations or increasing openess towards foreign trade in some countries might erode monopoly rents in certain industries, see Borjas and Ramey (1995). These rents used to be shared between the workers in the industry and the firms such that increased competition might hurt the wage position of the workers in these industries. As another important candidate, national policies to enhance the educational attainment of the population translate into a higher share of high–skilled persons among the younger birth cohorts. Further differences across countries relate to the trends in female labor force participation rates and to the timing of the Baby Booms. E.g., while the United States experienced its Baby–Boom during the 50's, the event took place in West Germany during the 60's.

The following discussion considers in more detail most of the different fundamental factors mentioned above. In particular, I discuss the following worldwide candidates

- Skill biased technological change
- Capital–skill complementarity
- Globalization (increasing international trade)
- Shift from Manufacturing to Service industries

and the following candidates referring to country–specific changes

- Skill composition of labor supply
- Institutional differences in wage bargaining
- Female labor force participation

The discussion starts with the worldwide candidates: ***Skill biased technological change*** implies a complementarity between technical progress and higher skill levels. Technical progress increases the relative demand for high–skilled workers relative to low–skilled workers. Put differently, technical progress is non–neutral such that it reduces disproportionately the necessary input of low–skilled labor. This is the case because new technologies often require more sophisticated labor services and, at the same time, provide a substitution for simple labor services. Empirically, technical progress is often measured by the residual time trend in factor inputs after everything else has been controlled for, see among many others Bound and Johnson (1992), Bergström and Panas (1992), Leamer (1996), Möller (1996), Betts (1997), or Fitzenberger and Franz (1998). There are two main versions of this approach: First, total factor productivity growth measures the additional output growth which cannot be accounted for by changes in factor inputs assuming a Cobb–Douglas production funtion with constant returns to scale (see chapter 4). Second, estimating a system of factor demand functions allows to measure how the level of factor input necessary to produce a given level of output decreases over time. The first version assumes implicitely that technical progress exhibits no factor bias within the aggregate considered (entire economy, individual industry). However, skill biased technological change can be viewed as total factor productivity growth being larger in skill–intensive industries, see Leamer (1996) and chapter 4, i.e. it is conceptualized in terms of the industry bias of total factor productivity growth relating to differences in factor usage across industries. The second notion of technical progress addresses directly the factor bias of technical change: Skill biased technological change implies that the necessary input of more highly skilled labor declines faster than for less skilled labor. When estimating a system of factor demand functions in chapter 5, I avoid the use of time trends as residual measures for technological progress since it has various problems. First, it is sensitive to a misspecification of the model. Second, the time trend is often correlated with the trends in wages, in capital, and in output, thus rendering the estimation of the coefficients on these variables more difficult. And third, the estimated time trends simply "fit" the observed reduction in the relative employment of less skilled workers without necessarily reflecting a causal relationship. Therefore, researchers have moved towards considering explicit measures (typically proxies) for technical progress, the most common one being R&D intensity, see Berman et al. (1994) or Machin et al. (1996, 1997). I will follow this strategy in chapter 5.

The notion of *capital–skill complementarity* is based on a similar view, see Hamermesh, 1993, for a general discussion and FitzRoy and Funke, 1994, for an analysis of West Germany. According to this hypothesis, the relative demand for more highly skilled labor increases with the installment of additional capital stock. This is likely to be the case because capital requires more highly skilled labor to operate and the installment of new capital often involves a substitution for low–skilled labor services. Recently, Krusell et al. (1997) suggest that the complementarity relationship differs depending on whether capital in form of equipment or in form of structures is involved. The results obtained by this study for the United States imply that the capital–skill complementarity hypothesis mainly involves structures but not equipment. Differentiating between the two forms of capital enables the authors to explain a much larger share of the skill bias in labor demand by increases in the capital stock compared to using only one measure of capital stock. However, since new technologies are often embodied in new capital stock, it remains an open question to what extent technical progress can be sharply distinguished from increases in the capital stock. As a final note on the notions of skill biased technological change or of capital–skill complementarity, it should be mentioned that it is conceivable that the impact of technical progress or of increasing the capital stock can very well be non–monotonic across skill groups. New technologies can simplify certain tasks such that less training is required to do the work while, at the same time, requiring more very highly skilled workers to operate the entire production process. Thus, it could be the case that the specific skills of workers with a specialized vocational training degree (medium–skilled workers) are no longer required.

Turning to *globalization* as the important alternative factor which is common across OECD countries, international trade grows considerably faster than output in the OECD and, at a global level, the OECD exhibits an abundance in more highly skilled labor compared to the rest of the world. According to standard trade theory, increasing possibilities for international trade (e.g. via tariff reductions) raise the skill differential in wages. Especially in popular discussions across OECD countries, increased trade with low–wage countries is believed to have deteriorated the labor market position of low–skilled workers in the OECD. Based on an estimation of the factor content of exports and imports for the United States, Wood (1995) provides evidence for this position. However, the evidence is closely linked to the increasing trade deficit for the United States during the 80's. Many trade theorists have attacked Wood's approach for another reason: Standard trade theory predicts that relative output prices are the important intervening variables for international trade to have hurt the labor market prospects of low–skilled workers. As the important empirical implication, the price ratio between goods whose production is intensive in more highly skilled labor and goods whose production is intensive in less skilled labor should have increased for OECD countries, see Lawrence and Slaughter (1993) as a seminal empirical study investigating this issue for the United States. For the case of West Germany, another problem arises for factor content calculations. The fact that West Germany has experienced a large trade surplus makes it even harder to calculate an adverse effect on the labor market position of low–skilled workers based on factor content calculations. Nevertheless, it could very well be the case that output price ratios on the world markets changed to the detriment of goods whose production is intensive in less skilled labor thus hurting the labor market position of less skilled labor also in West Germany. Chapter 4 will address these issues in detail.

For completeness, it should be mentioned that the discussion on the labor market effects of globalization in the literature is also concerned with increased capital mobility (see Baldwin, 1995) and with the impact of immigration (see Borjas, 1994). In the following, I restrict myself to a few comments. A further analysis of capital mobility and of labor migration is beyond the scope of this study. With increasing capital mobility, it becomes more difficult to sustain rents for workers in certain industries where producers exhibit market power, see Borjas and Ramey (1995). The primary example in the literature for this argument is the automobile industry in the United States. Until the advent of massive foreign competition in the 80's, low–skilled workers used to earn fairly high wages in this industry. In a simple demand and supply framework, the labor market effects of immigration depend upon whether immigration increases the relative supply of more highly or of less skilled workers. Both the United States and West Germany have experienced large inflows of fairly low–skilled workers during the 70's and 80's.

Turning to the final worldwide candidate, namely the long–run *shift from Manufacturing to service industries*: Total employment in West Germany (excluding self–employment) increased from 22.1 Mill. in 1970 to 25.5 Mill. in 1990, while employment in Manufacturing declined from 9.6 Mill. in 1970 to 8.6 Mill. in 1990, see German Council of Economic Experts (1994, p. 345). Among others, Sachs and Shatz (1994) point out that technical progress appears to be faster in Manufacturing and that the income elasticity for Manufacturing goods appears to be less than one. Both effects result in a decreasing share of Manufacturing in employment. The literature for the United States points out that there exists a higher share of "good" jobs (≡ well paid and stable jobs) for low–skilled workers in Manufacturing compared to services and that, during the 80's, the decline in Manufacturing coincided with a large increase in Manufacturing imports. Service industries are often believed to provide the necessary jobs for the low–skilled but there is concern that these jobs are predominantly "bad" referring to the famous example of "flipping hamburger". Such jobs are viewed as generating little income ("working poor") and as providing little stability for the employees. The stylized view in the economic policy debate for Germany is that wages for low–skilled workers in the service industry are too high preventing that a sufficient number of jobs are generated in this part of the economy. In chapter 5 of this study, it is investigated whether demand for low–skilled workers in service industries is sufficiently elastic to provide the necessary jobs for low–skilled workers in response to wage moderation. Chapter 2 also analyzes whether skill upgrading in employment occurs in the same way in this part of the economy as in Manufacturing. Also, wage trends are investigated separately for the two parts of this economy, one motivation being, that unions play a more important role in Manufacturing compared to service industries.

Next, the discussion turns in more detail to some of the developments mentioned above, which are possibly country–specific; namely, *trends in the skill composition of labor supply*, *changes in wage bargaining institutions*, and *trends in female labor force participation* rates. First, in West Germany university type education has been extended considerably since the early 70's, see the discussion in Möller (1996). An increase in educational attainment has, however, also been observed in other countries (however, in the United States college attendance has not increased further during the 80's). Such a policy results in an increasing relative supply of more highly skilled workers. At the same time, it is likely to change the unobserved ability distribution of the workers in the different skill groups. Regarding another aspect of skill formation, West Germany differs considerably in its system of vocational training from other OECD countries (again, in particular, from the United States and the United Kingdom). Also during the 70's and 80's, the share of workers with a vocational training degree still increased in West Germany. Nickell and Bell (1995, 1996) raise doubts about the two–sides–of–the–same–coin hypothesis based on the observation that relative unemployment rates for less–skilled workers in West Germany have increased fairly little (this finding is not confirmed in chapter 2) even though these workers earn twice as much as their counterparts in other countries. Nickell and Bell argue that low–skilled workers in West Germany are not comparable to their counterparts in the United States and the United Kingdom because the German educational system makes them relatively more productive, in fact, justifying their high wages. Second, trends in wage bargaining institutions differ considerably. Countries like the United States and the United Kingdom have experienced a considerable decline in union density and in union coverage while European countries like West Germany did not experience such a decline, see Machin et al. (1997) for an international comparison and Fitzenberger, Haggeney, and Ernst (1998) for a recent analysis of union membership in West Germany. Some authors attribute partly the increasing wage dispersion in the United States and the United Kingdom to these changes in wage bargaining institutions. Put differently, it is often argued that the stable wage bargaining institutions in West Germany have prevented the wages of low–skilled workers to fall in order to prevent increases of their relative unemployment rate. Third, female labor force participation has increased in all OECD countries but growth has been different across countries. Starting from a similar level in 1973, it grew by 18 percentage points until 1993 in the United States and only by 11 percentage points in West Germany, see Franz (1996, p. 24). Also labor force participation rates for men decreased in West Germany by 11 percentage points and only by two percentage points in the United States. Assuming that on average women are still less educated compared to men and that it is more likely that low–skilled men reduced their labor force participation rates in West Germany (e.g. due to early retirement plans or due to workers being discouraged by long–term unemployment), these trends implied that the relative supply of more highly skilled labor increased more in West Germany than in the United States.

After having set the scene, what are the issues covered in this study and where does it contribute to the debate presented above? The following discussion provides a short description of its goals and a short preview of its content. In addition, each chapter will link its specific analysis in more detail to the debate above. Before doing so, two additional remarks are in order: The first involves the general scope of this study and the second refers to the database put together for this study.

First, the focus of this study on the skill structure of wages and employment is primarily an empirical one. The study starts with a purely descriptive analysis in wage trends and then addresses various issues discussed above. In doing so, theoretical concepts are developed and used as far as necessary to undertake the empirical analysis. At first glance, it might seem awkward to start the analysis with purely descriptive evidence and to end with a structural model. However, given the controversies in the literature about the most basic facts in wage and employment trends (as will become clear later), it is appropriate to get first the stylized facts right and then to analyze empirically different aspects of the two–sides–of–the–same–coin hypothesis. When moving along, the study makes increasing usage of theoretical concepts to put a tighter structure on the empirical analyis. Leamer (1996, section 3)[2] very clearly points to the trade–off involved: Without a theoretical conception of reality, data will never be sufficiently informative to answer economic questions. However, at the same time, the theory should never be taken "too seriously" since, after all, it is only an abstraction of a complex reality and possibly the available variables in the data do not correspond exactly to their theoretical counterparts.

Second, to address empirically the issues discussed above, most of the international literature uses an industry dataset distinguishing different skill groups of workers. Given the emphasis in labor economics on wage differentials by age (experience), it is also important to control for age. It is natural to construct such a database from wage and employment data on individual workers and to aggregate that data to the industry level where it can be merged with data from national accounts and other aggregate statistics. In fact, this describes exactly what is done in this study which has only become possible with the advent of the IAB–Beschäftigtenstichprobe (I_ABS) as a large and representative individual wage and employment dataset for the time period from 1975 to 1990, see Bender et al. (1996).[3] The data appendix A.3 describes in detail the construction of the core database, which is used throughout this study, merging the I_ABS with national accounts data. Based on this dataset, the empirical analysis considers three skill groups (low–, medium–, and high–skilled) defined by the educational attainment of the workers. Unfortunately, the I_ABS dataset has three important limitations. First, the wage data is topcoded (censored from above), second, the wage data exhibit a structural break between 1983 and 1984 (see Steiner and Wagner, 1998), and third, the dataset does not provide information on hours worked. Considering the topcoding problem, the wage information for highly skilled workers is limited since censoring is quite severe for this group. I use censored quantile regressions to exploit the available information in the data. Regarding the second problem, I develop a correction method for the structural break in the data, see appendix A.3. Regarding differences in working time, the analysis in this study is restricted to wage observations for full–time workers.

Turning to the content of this study, the core analysis consists of five chapters. In addition, the study contains three appendices. The first two are concerned with econometric methods which are applied at various places in

[2]See quote at the beginning of chapter 4 in this study.

[3]I would like to express my thanks to the research institute of the Federal Employment Service ("Institut für Arbeitsmarkt– und Berufsforschung") in Nürnberg for having made this dataset available.

the empirical analysis. The third appendix describes the database used in this study.

Starting from the conventional wisdom in the literature and the economic policy debate that the wage structure in West Germany has been very stable in international perspective, chapter 2 scrutinizes wage and employment trends across skill groups (proxied by educational attainment) both for male and female full–time workers. The analysis also distinguishes between Manufacturing and Non–Manufacturing industries. The descriptive evidence in this chapter also shows the degree of censoring in wages which is especially severe for high–skilled male workers.

Since a proper analysis of trends in female labor force participation and wages is beyond the scope of this study, the subsequent chapters are restricted to wage observations either for males alone or for all workers together. Chapter 3 provides a cohort analysis of wage trends. The data is grouped by skill level, age, and time. Defining cohorts by year of birth, it is investigated whether a parsimonious decomposition of wage growth into age and time effects uniformly describes wage profiles across cohorts. Being able to accept this uniform wage growth hypothesis allows one to construct a uniform life–cycle profile and a uniform time trend in wages for each skill group. I show to what extent purely descriptive evidence on wage trends is plagued by certain composition effects. The analysis is performed for the entire economy and, separately, for Manufacturing and Non–Manufacturing industries. Also, a heuristic procedure is implemented to correct for selection effects due to changing unemployment patterns over time.

Turning to globalization and technical progress as the two major world-wide candidates explaining labor market trends across skill groups, chapter 4 investigates the impact of international trade and technological progress in West Germany. An empirical analysis of the relationship between trade and the labor market in West Germany is provided for the period from 1970 until 1990. Taking a closer look at the globalization debate, it is investigated whether the labor market trends across skill groups can be rationalized by the impact of trade. The analysis builds on relative product prices as the major transmission channel of trade effects on the labor market. The major part of the chapter consists of an extensive descriptive analysis. Then, building on Leamer (1996), a more structural analysis identifies empirically the qualitative effects of trade and total factor productivity growth.

Chapter 5 uses a structural model to estimate the determinants of the skill structure of labor demand as the major building block of the two–sides–of–the–same–coin hypothesis. The determinants of the skill bias of labor demand are estimated and a theoretical and empirical analysis of the importance of wage flexibility across and within skill groups for the structure of employment is provided. I estimate a translog cost function and share equations in order to determine the impact of relative wages and other variables on the structure of employment. The approach takes account of wage differences both across and within skill groups and it treats output, capital, and technical progress as given. Rather than using residual time trends as proxies for technical progress, I use various explicit technology indicators at the industry level. Also, I distinguish between equipment and structures as two forms of capital. Estimation is performed separately for Manufacturing and Non-Manufacturing industries.

Finally, the study turns to the determination of the wage structure itself. Inflexibility of wages is often viewed as being the result of the prevailing wage bargaining system in Germany. Therefore, chapter 6 develops a structural model of wage bargaining at the industry level with heterogeneous labor taking account of wage dispersion across and within skill groups. The union's objective function is of Stone–Geary form putting specific weights to employment, to average wages across, and to wage dispersion within the two groups of labor. Building on the "right–to–manage" assumption, wage bargaining is constrained by labor demand being determined at the firm level. In contrast to chapter 5, the modelling of labor demand has to take account of the output reactions to changes in factor prices. It is analyzed whether wage setting can be rationalized in light of the two–sides–of–the–same–coin hypothesis. The empirical estimation of the model investigates how wage bargaining weighs employment and wages and to what extent it reacts to increases in unemployment. Analyzing factor demand and wage setting at the same time, chapter 6 uses the tightest theoretical structure in this study to analyze the data. In order to keep the analysis feasible, I have to compromise on some of the complexities in the analysis of factor demand considered in chapter 5. Estimation is performed separately for Manufacturing and for Non–Manufacturing industries.

The appendices A.1 and A.2 are concerned with methodological innovations which are relevant to the econometric analysis in various chapters. As referred to above, the third appendix A.3 provides a comprehensive description of all data sources used for this study

Appendix A.1 is concerned with the computation of censored quantile regressions (CQR). The computation of the CQR estimate is quite involved since it amounts to the minimization of a non–differentiable and non–convex distance function. Various suggestions in the literature on how to calculate this estimator proved unsatisfactory. The appendix provides a short overview on the computational aspects of CQR's and describes the algorithm BRCENS developed by the author and applied in chapters 3 and 5. Simulation results obtained by the author and referred to in the appendix show the superiority of BRCENS over various algorithms suggested in the literature.

Appendix A.2 deals with the block bootstrap procedure to draw robust inference which is applied in chapters 3, 5, and 6. For the purpose of this study, the goal of robust inference amounts to estimate consistently the sample variance–covariance matrix of a coefficient vector in order to construct reliable test statistics when estimation is based on grouped data from time series of cross–sections. The estimate of the variance–covariance matrix should take account of fairly arbitrary heteroskedasticity and correlation of the error term. Analogous to the treatment in Fitzenberger (1998) for the pure time series case, it suffices in a linear method–of–moments estimation approach to establish the asymptotic validity of a block bootstrap procedure for the case of the sample mean. Building on Fitzenberger and MaCurdy (1996), the appendix defines the estimation problem and describes the block bootstrap procedure for inference.

2 Basic Trends in Wages and Employment Across Skill Groups

... the earnings distribution has continued to become more compressed in Germany.
OECD (1996, p. 63)

The stylized view of the labor market in West Germany during the 70's and 80's considers West Germany to be a high–wage and high–productivity economy with a fairly compressed wage structure and resulting insufficient employment growth. In particular, wage floors set by the prevailing wage bargaining system result in a lack of jobs for low–skilled workers (refer to the two–sides–of–the–same–coin hypothesis discussed in chapter 1). This view is "confirmed" by descriptive evidence showing that the distribution of wages has been stable or even "continued to become more compressed" in situations of considerable unemployment and imbalances in the distribution of unemployment across different groups of workers (see Abraham and Houseman, 1995, Kraft, 1994, Paqué, 1995, Pischke, 1998, Steiner and Wagner, 1998, OECD, 1993, 1996, or Fitzenberger and Kurz, 1997). This evidence is based either on aggregate data for different groups of workers or on micro datasets such as the German Socioecomic Panel or the Qualifications and Careers Survey ("Qualifikation und Berufsverlauf", data collected by the Federal Institute for Occupational Training (Bundesinstitut für Berufsbildung, BiBB) and the research institute of the Federal Employment Service (IAB). On the employment side, West Germany exhibited modest employment growth (small compared to the United States) with a continuous trend towards skill upgrading of the labor force (see figure A.1 in the appendix).

The above stylized view did not remain unchallenged. Based on the same dataset (IAB–Beschäftigtenstichprobe, $I_A BS$) as used in this study, a series of studies (Möller, 1996, 1997, Möller and Bellmann, 1996, and Beißinger and Möller, 1998) finds an increasing wage dispersion for full–time working males in West Germany during the 80's. The results in the earlier studies by Möller (1996) and Möller and Bellmann (1996) were questioned by Steiner and Wagner (1998) pointing to a structural break in the $I_A BS$ wage data between 1983 and 1984 (I will come back to this issue later and a correction for this structural break is developed in the appendix). Comparing the marginal wage distribution in the $I_A BS$ and the German Socioeconomic Panel, Steiner and Wagner show that this structural break results in a spurious increase in wage inequality between 1983 and 1984 (see also figures A.3 and A.4 in the appendix). However, even after accounting for the structural break, Möller (1997) and Beißinger and Möller (1998) as well as Fitzenberger (1996) and Fitzenberger and Franz (1998) still find that the wage dispersion for full–time working males in West Germany increases during the 80's. Fitzenberger (1996), Fitzenberger and Franz (1998), and, based on an earlier dataset for the time period from 1976 to 1984, Fitzenberger et al. (1995) show that various conflicting trends appear to be operating across the wage structure. Even though wage dispersion for full–time working males was increasing during the 70's and 80's, the wage differences narrowed between workers with and without vocational training degree while the difference between workers with vocational training degree and university degree increased. This U–shaped pattern in average wage trends across skill groups coincided with increasing wage dispersion within the groups with higher skill levels. The latter effect accounts for most of the aggregate increase in wage dispersion measured in the $I_A BS$ dataset.

Nickell and Bell (1995, 1996) forcefully questioned the employment side of the two–sides–of–the–same–coin hypothesis mentioned above. They argue that in international comparison, West Germany did not experience a disproportionate increase in the relative unemployment rates for low–skilled workers even though the relative wage of low–skilled workers did not deteriorate during the 80's to the extent as it was observed for the United States or the United Kingdom. Nickell and Bell view this as a challenge for the two–sides–of–the–same–coin hypothesis of a simple trade–off between increased wage flexibility or increasing unemployment for low–skilled workers. They consider low–skilled workers in West Germany to be more productive compared to their counterparts in the United States or the United Kingdom. Pischke (1998) and Beißinger and Möller (1998) provide evidence for this view using a similar framework as developed in Card et al. (1996). These two studies for West Germany form age–skill (–industry) cells of workers and contrast changes in wages and employment rates over the 80's with the wage level at the end of the 70's. Assuming a skill bias in labor demand trends, they take the wage level at the end of the 70's as a proxy for the skill level and therefore for the relative demand shock experienced by the respective group of workers. If the two–sides–of–the–same–coin hypothesis is correct, one expects for West Germany a positive correlation between the initial wage levels and the change in employment rates and no correlation with the changes in wages. However, the first correlation does not prove significantly positive. And the second is significantly positive in the study by Beißinger and Möller (1998) and negative in the study by Pischke (1998). This difference mainly appears to reflect the use of different datasets as pointed out above. Overall, in my opinion, it remains questionable whether changes in employment rates (or unemployment rates) suffice to capture the impact of wage flexibility (or the lack thereoff) in a situation of massive skill upgrading among the labor force both in the skill structure of employment and labor supply. Evidence on this point will be given in the following.

This chapter provides descriptive evidence on the basic trends in wages and employment across skill groups. Here and in the remainder of this study, I use a sectoral dataset combining national accounts data and data from the IAB–Beschäftigtenstichprobe ($I_A BS$, see data appendix A.3 for a detailed description of the data sources). In contrast to some of the literature mentioned above, this chapter contains wage trends both for male and female full–time working employees. As will be seen in the following, wage trends exhibit considerable differences across genders. These differences are likely to reflect selection and composition effects in female labor force participation behavior and (political) efforts to reduce the gender wage gap. Therefore, the analysis in the subsequent chapters 3, 5, and 6 will be restricted to wages for full–time working males under the assumption that wage trends for this group are representative for the price per "efficiency unit" of labor.

Before I present the basic trends in wages and employment over the time period from 1975 to 1990, some further remarks about the data used in this chapter are in order. Workers are grouped by their skills defined according to the following formal education levels given in the $I_A BS$:

(U) without a vocational training degree (low–skilled)

(M) with a vocational training degree (medium–skilled)

(H) with a technical college ("Fachhochschule") or a university degree (high–skilled)

The basic information in the $I_A BS$ dataset consists of social security insurance spells for which average daily gross wages are available. Wages in this dataset are topcoded (censored from above). Censoring is due to the threshold levels in social security taxation. Earnings above this level are not subject to the social security tax and therefore, in such a case, the $I_A BS$ dataset only records the fact that earnings lie above the threshold. The level of the threshold changes annually and is denoted as "CENS" for the graphical illustrations in the appendix of this chapter. Also, the dataset does not include any information on hours worked. However, one can distinguish between full–time and part–time employment. I will concentrate on wage trends for full–time working males and females in order to reduce the impact of participation changes and composition bias. As mentioned above, a further problem of the dataset lies in the structural break in wages between 1983 and 1984, cf. Steiner and Wagner (1998). In the appendix, I describe a heuristic correction for the problem. The trends in the marginal distribution for males before and after correction are depicted in figures A.3 and A.4.

Without referring to this every time in this study, real wages are deflated by the price index for aggregate private consumption.

Even though employment trends across skill groups and industries could be constructed from the $I_A BS$ dataset, it is important to recognize that the share of employment subject to social security taxes ("sozialversicherungspflichtige Beschäftigung") differs considerably across industries (see Bender et al., 1996, p. 10). Therefore, as described in detail in the appendix, I only obtain the employment shares by skill group and gender from the $I_A BS$. In a second step, I multiply these shares by total employment obtained from national accounts data in order to estimate the employment level for a skill group within a certain industry. Aggregate employment figures are then obtained by explicit aggregation across industries based on the industry specific estimates.

2.1 Employment Trends

Figures A.1 and A.2 in the data appendix depict aggregate employment and unemployment trends across skill groups for men and women together. From 1975 to 1990, aggregate employment increased by almost 10%. Nevertheless, aggregate unemployment was increasing from 1980 to 1983 and did not decrease considerably after this recessionary phase. These aggregate trends hide considerable differences across skill groups. The relative unemployment rate of (U) was increasing considerably after 1975 until 1984, whereas unemployment of (M) and (H) remains lower than the aggregate figure with the relative unemployment experience of (H) improving slightly during the course of the 80's. Employment trends differ even more. Employment of (H) almost doubled from 1975 to 1990 whereas employment of (U) decreased by almost 50%. Again, the trends for (M) are in between. Thus, there exists a strong trend of skill upgrading in employment.

Figures 2.9 and 2.10 in the appendix of this chapter show the differences in employment trends by gender and between Manufacturing (MAN) and Non–Manufacturing (NON–MAN) industries (see tables A.1 and A.2 in the data appendix for the industry classification). The trend of skill upgrading seems to be uniform for men and women and across parts of the economy. However, for female workers, it is even more pronounced than for male workers: the number of high–skilled female employees almost quadruples from 1975 to 1990 while it only doubles for male workers. Also, as it is well known, overall employment growth is larger in NON–MAN compared to MAN and for females compared to males.

Given the massive changes in employment patterns, it does not seem warranted to restrict the attention to unemployment rates or employment rates across groups of workers (as done by Nickell and Bell, 1995, 1996, and others) since the size and most likely the composition of these groups changes drastically over time. Most of the employment trends reflect changes in the supply of skills in West Germany and only a small part of the changes in the skill structure of employment is actually reflected in the increasing imbalance of unemployment rates across skill groups over time (see figure A.2). Therefore, the analysis of the skill bias in labor demand and the role of wage flexibility should focus directly on relative employment across skill groups in relation to the structure of wages (see chapter 5).

2.2 Wage Trends Across and Within Skill Groups

This section first presents wage trends for male workers which are then contrasted with the findings for females. Figure A.4 in the data appendix shows the evolution of corrected deciles of real wages of full–time working males over time. Whereas the 90%–Quantile is censored at the social security threshold in all years, the 80%–quantile is always uncensored. Real wages increase over time at all deciles and it is apparent that the growth of real wages is higher at higher quantiles, i.e. there is a trend towards higher overall inequality in wages. This is confirmed by figure 2.2 in the appendix of this chapter showing the trends in the log–difference between the 80%– and 20%–quantile and the decomposition of it into the difference between the 80%– and the 50%–quantile and the difference between the 50%– and the 20%–quantile. The pattern for all workers (Skill Group=ALL) exhibits an increase of the 80%–20% difference by around 12 log percentage points. While most of this increase is due to an increase of the dispersion above the median (the 80%–50% difference increases by around 9 log percentage points) there is also some evidence for increasing wage dispersion below the median during the second half of the 80's. These findings are in sharp contrast to findings in OECD (1993, 1996) for West Germany based on the German Socioeconomic Panel (see also Steiner and Wagner, 1998, and Möller, 1997). The OECD studies argue that, during the second half of the 80's, wage inequality had been slightly decreasing and this compression had continued into the 90's. My results are quite close in spirit to the cross–sectional findings in Blau and Kahn (1996) arguing that there exists substantially more compression of male wages at the bottom of the wage distribution in countries like West Germany compared to the United States. This finding is attributed to different institutional settings. From a dynamic perspective, it is conceivable that a trend towards higher inequality in West Germany is mitigated by the wage bargaining institutions in the lower part but not in the upper part of the wage distribution.

Considering male wages across skill groups, figure 2.1 shows how the wage deciles move over time for the three skill groups considered in this study. The wage distribution for skill group (U) is much more compressed compared to (M). Whereas the 10%–quantile is only 10 DM below the same quantile for (M), the difference more than doubles for the 80%–quantile. However, there is a large overlap of the within wage distribution. Between skill groups, there is a tendency that (U) gains relative to (M) over time. For instance, in 1975 the 40%–quantile of (M) corresponds roughly to the 70%–quantile of (U). In 1990, the 40%–quantile of (M) barely exceeds the median for (U). Skill groups (U) and (M) are not much affected by censoring whereas for (H) censoring is very severe. In 1975, almost 80% of the observations for (H) are censored and this number decreases to less than 60% in 1990, i.e. censoring becomes less severe over time. Due to censoring, one can only determine the relative position of the lower two deciles for (H). While the 20%–quantile for (H) lies above the 80%–quantile for (M) in 1975, it only lies slightly above the 70%–quantile for (M) in 1990. Thus, at least the relative wage position of the bottom part of the wage distribution for (H) has slightly deteriorated over time.

Figure 2.2 depicts the trends in quantile differences within skill groups (U) and (M). Due to censoring, the numbers are not available for (H). Whereas skill group (M) exhibits a clear trend towards higher within inequality, mostly in the 80%–50% difference but also in 50%–20% difference during the second half of the 80's, within inequality for (U) only seems to increase slightly during the second half of the 80's. In fact, until 1982 there seems to be a decline in within inequality in the bottom part of the wage distribution for (U).

Figure 2.5 presents time trends in wages for all male workers (All) and for males in the skill groups (U), (M), and (H) for the entire economy and for the three skill groups also separately for MAN and NON–MAN. The time trends for all workers and for the two lower skill groups concern the median of the marginal wage distribution. Due to the severity of censoring for (H), the time trend for the median cannot be calculated for this group (see figure 2.1 for the entire economy and figures 2.3 and 2.4 for MAN and NON–MAN, respectively). Since the degree of censoring decreases over time (while in 1975 about 80% of wages in the entire economy are censored, censoring is reduced to less than 60% in 1990, see figure 2.1) and since within group wage dispersion, as far as observable, seems to increase over time, I calculate for (H) the piecewise time trend for the highest uncensored quantile: For the entire economy, I use the time trend of the 20%–quantile from 1975 to 1979 and the time trend of the 40%–quantile from 1979 to 1990, where the latter starts in the 1979 value of the former. For MAN, the time trend is constructed analogously based on the time trend for the 15%–quantile from 1975 to 1976, for the 20%–quantile from 1976 to 1979, and for the 30%–quantile from 1979 to 1990. And for NON–MAN, the time trend is constructed based on the time trend for the 20%–quantile from 1975 to 1977, for the 30%–quantile from 1977 to 1983, and for the 40%–quantile from 1983 to 1990.

The time trends for males show that real wages for male workers grow on average by around 20% (in logarithms) from 1975 to 1990 for all skill groups in the entire economy as well as in MAN and in NON–MAN. However, there exists a U–shaped pattern across skill groups: Wage growth was higher both for (U) and (H) compared to (M). This is the case for the entire economy as well as in MAN and in NON–MAN. Wage growth in MAN was slightly higher than in NON–MAN, with the largest difference for (M) where median wages grow by around 20% in MAN and by around 16% in NON–MAN from 1975 to 1990. With increasing within group wage dispersion, the depicted time trends for skill group (H) are likely to underestimate wage growth for the median. Thus, the U–shaped pattern is likely to be even more pronounced for the unobservable median of (H). Finally, the trend for all male workers is strongest reflecting the trend of skill upgrading in employment.

Turning to full–time working females, overall wage trends across deciles (after a correction for the structural break between 1983 and 1984 analogous to figure A.4 for males) are such that the 90%–quantile is never censored (the graph is omitted). Figure 2.6 shows trends in the wage distribution for females across skill groups. It is evident that the wage distribution for females lies considerably below the corresponding one for males in figure 2.1 and, in contrast to males, the median for (H) is uncensored in all years. Also, compared to male workers, there seems to exist an even greater overlap of the wage distributions across skill groups. The 10%–quantile for (U) and (M) seem to coincide, the 90%–quantile for (U) corresponds to the 70%–quantile of (M) in 1975 and to the 80%–quantile for (M) in 1990, and the 30%–quantile for (H) corresponds to the 80%–quantile for (M) in 1975 and to the 60%–quantile for (M) in 1990. Apparently, overall wage growth is inversely related to the skill level which is confirmed by the time trends in figure 2.8 for female workers at the median being quite different from the trends for males. Since the median is uncensored for females in skill group (H) in the entire economy (see figure 2.6) as well as for MAN or NON–MAN (figures are omitted for these cases), median trends are available in all cases. The trend for all workers in the entire economy implies that median real wages for full–time working females grows by around 26% from 1975 to 1990 which is slightly higher than for males. However, the wage growth for females is inversely related to the skill level and the differences across skill groups are larger than for males. The wage growth is largest for (U) and smallest for (H) with very little wage growth for the latter group from 1975 to 1985.

Also, the trends in within dispersion for females depicted in figure 2.7 differ from those for males. The 80%–20% difference is considerably higher compared to males and remains fairly stable over time. Overall wage dispersion for (M) is larger than for (U) and it seems to decrease slightly over time. Differentiating between wage dispersion below and above the median shows further interesting differences. Again, the dispersion for all workers remains fairly stable over time. The wage dispersion above the median for females is higher than for males at the beginning of the sample period and of the same order of magnitude at the end of the sample period. Below the median, wage dispersion for females is considerably larger than for males (even at the end of the sample period). Differentiating by skill groups, the wage dispersion is larger for (M) than for (U) both below and above the median and fairly stable over time for (U). However, for (M) the trends differ considerably below and above the median: below the median, the wage dispersion decreases from 1975 to 1990 by almost 10 percentage points, and, at the same time, it increases by almost 5 percentage points above the median. These pronounced conflicting trends coincide with a stability of the overall dispersion for skill group (M).

2.3 Summary

Overall wage inequality for full–time working males rises continuously from 1975 to 1990. However, this rise in inequality is far from uniform and one finds some complex movements within and between the skill groups. The differential wage trends contrast sharply to the continuous trends towards skill upgrading in employment of male and female workers. The analysis in the next chapter tries to shed more light on the wage trends across and within skill groups for male workers. In particular, it is analyzed to what extent the aggregate trends can be explained by pure composition effects, for instance, the trend towards higher skill levels in younger cohorts and the differential unemployment trends across skill groups.

The trends for full–time working females are somewhat different compared to males. Skill upgrading occurs at an even faster rate and, starting from a considerably higher level compared to males, wage dispersion across skill groups and also within skill groups in the lower part of the distribution decreases strongly from 1975 to 1990. However, the wage dispersion for medium–skilled workers above the median tends to increase considerably. The (political) strive for a reduction of the gender wage gap might have led to the particularly strong wage growth for low–skilled female workers and to the reduction of within dispersion for medium–skilled workers below the median. It is for these workers that contract wages arising from collective wage agreements are likely to bind. The trends could be the result of the union policies to eliminate the low–pay groups in the contract. However, also the labor market behavior of women might have changed considerably with regard to the growing labor force participation rates. Given the strong skill upgrading among women, the rise in labor force participation might have overcompensated a skill bias in labor demand trends resulting in the low wage growth observed for high–skilled women. At the same time, labor market attachment behavior might have changed among the high–skilled women due to child bearing and rearing in such a way that average labor market experience or tenure effects could have decreased for the pool of high–skilled women. Overall, wage trends for women show fairly complex patterns and are unlikely to be explicable in the context of this study. Therefore, the analysis in the following chapters is restricted to wages for full–time working males (chapters 3, 5, and 6) or to wages for all full–time workers (chapter 4). However, the female component in total employment is also considered.

2.4 Appendix of Chapter 2

Figure 2.1: Distribution of Real Daily Wages for Full–Time Working Males

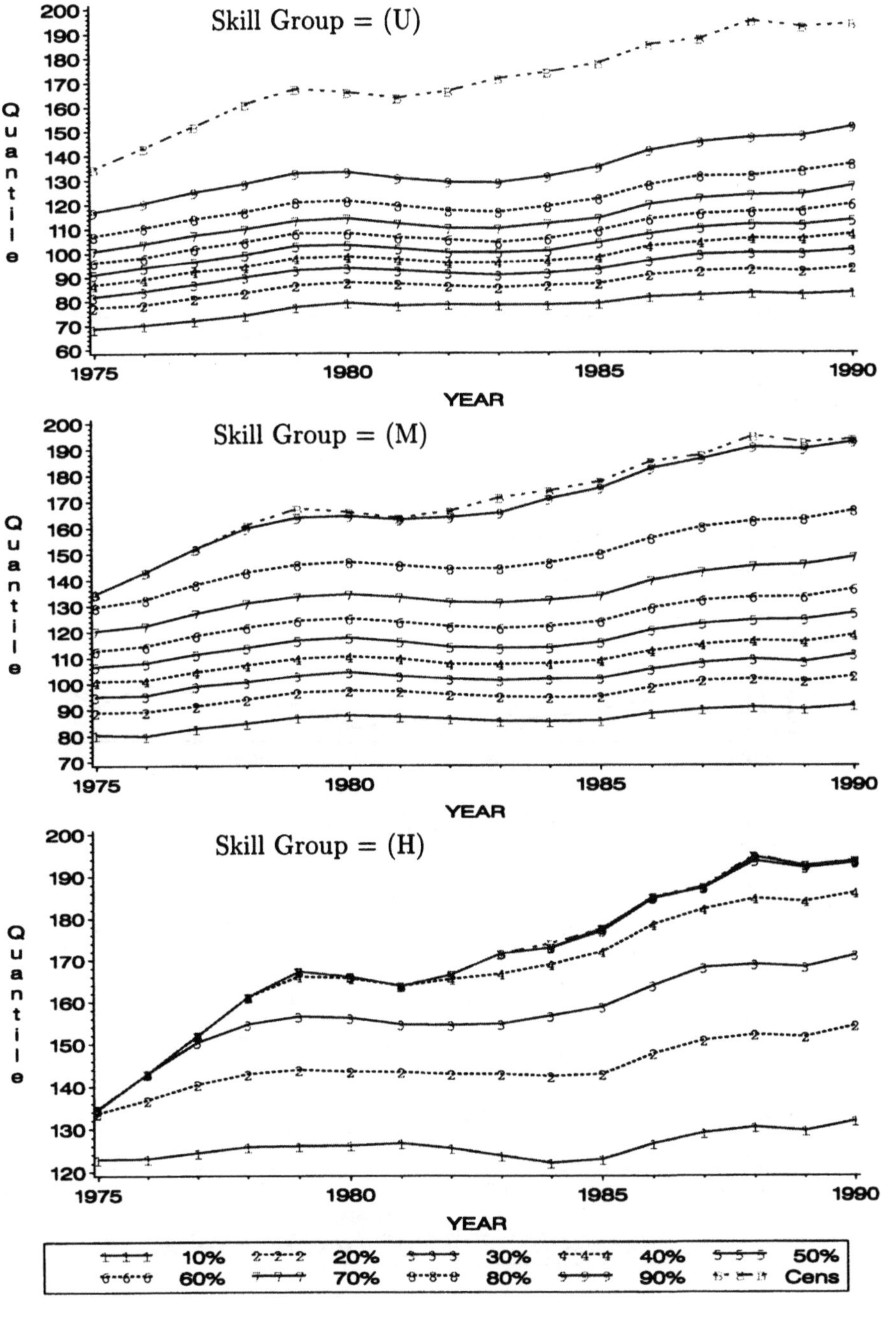

Figure 2.2: 80%–20% Difference of Log Wages for Full–Time Work. Males

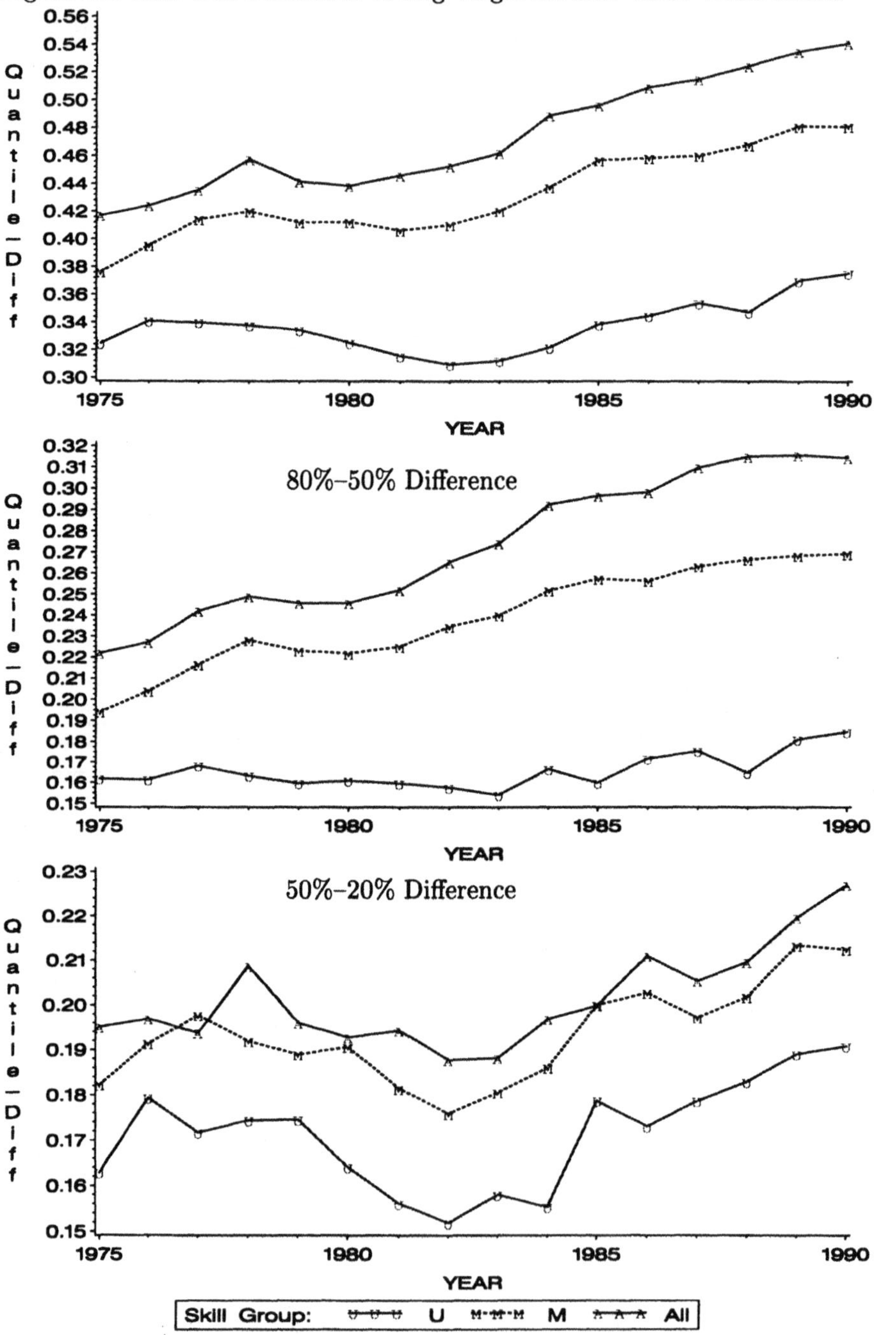

Figure 2.3: Distribution of Real Daily Wages for Full–Time Working Males of Skill Group (H) in Manufacturing

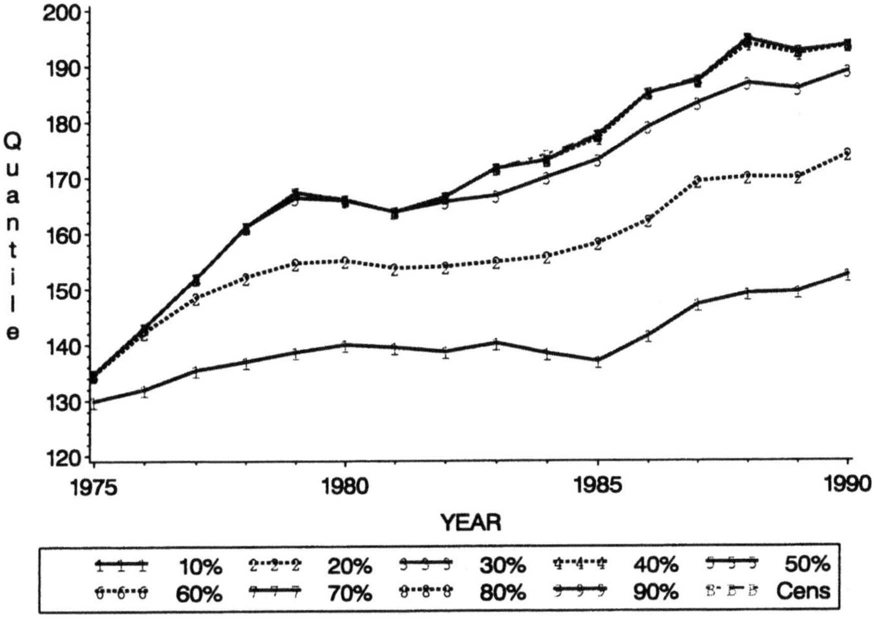

Figure 2.4: Distribution of Real Daily Wages for Full–Time Working Males of Skill Group (H) in NON–Manufacturing

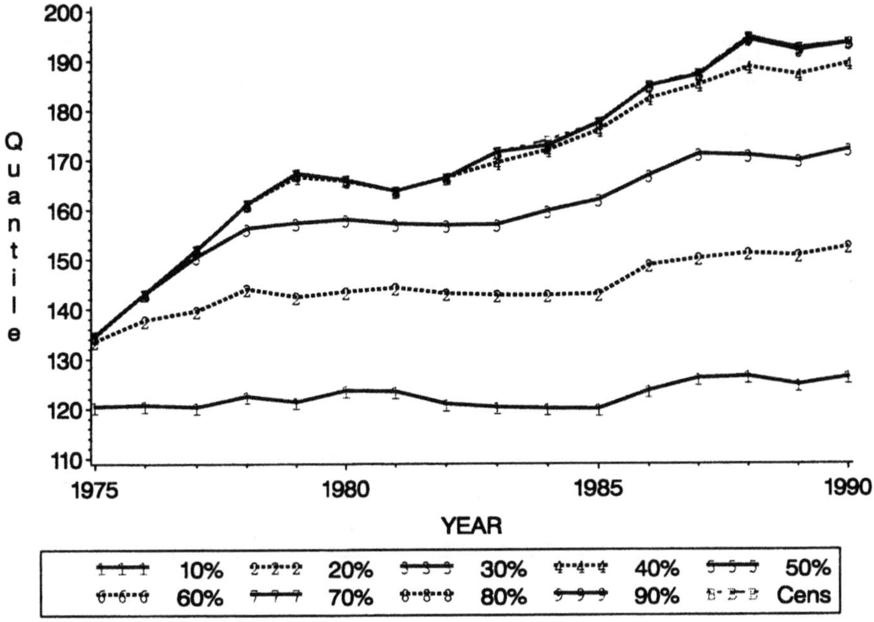

Figure 2.5: Trends in Median for (U,M,Total)/ 20%–40%–Quantile for (H) of LOG Real Wages for Full–Time Working Males (1975=0)

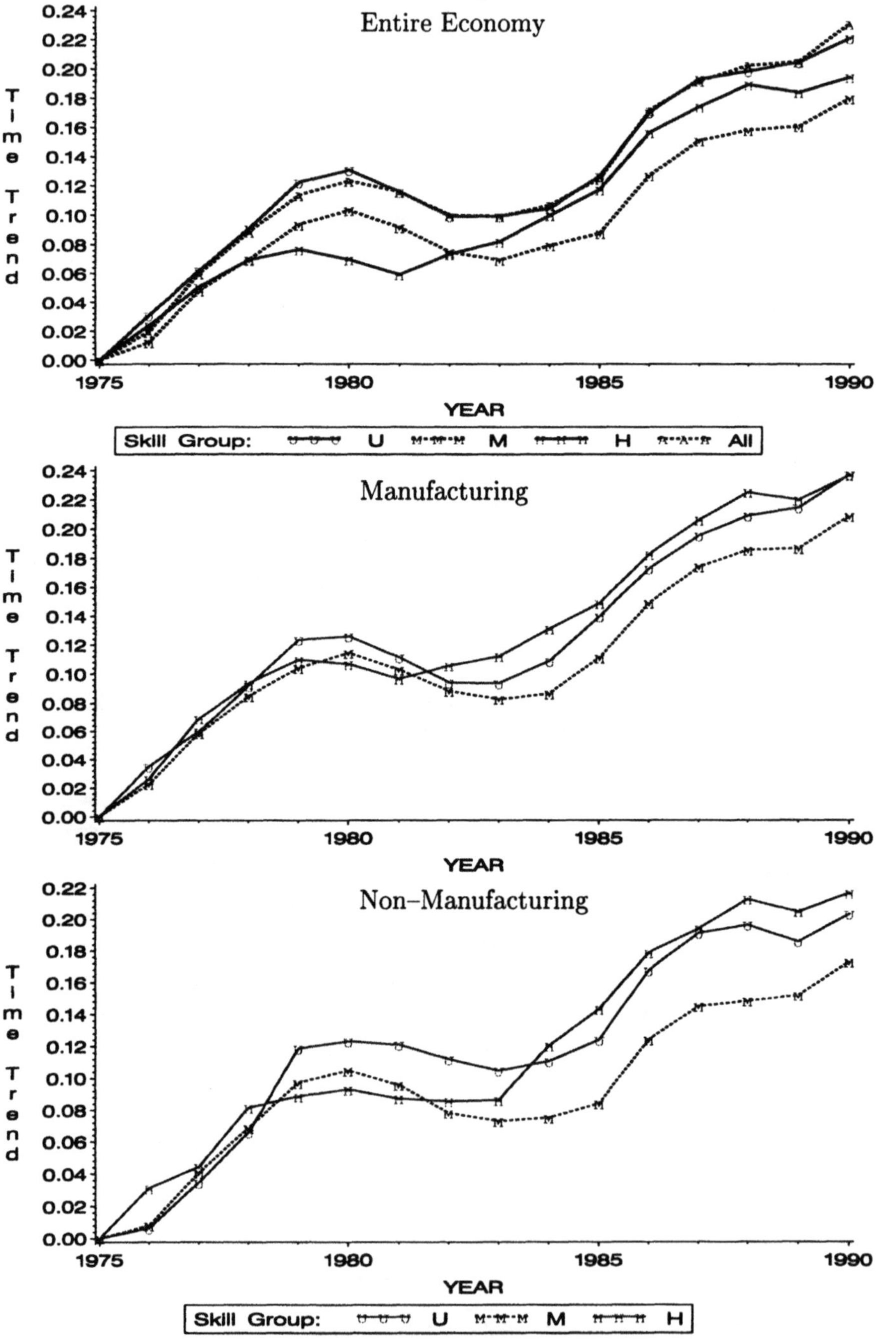

Figure 2.6: Distribution of Real Daily Wages for Full–Time Working Females

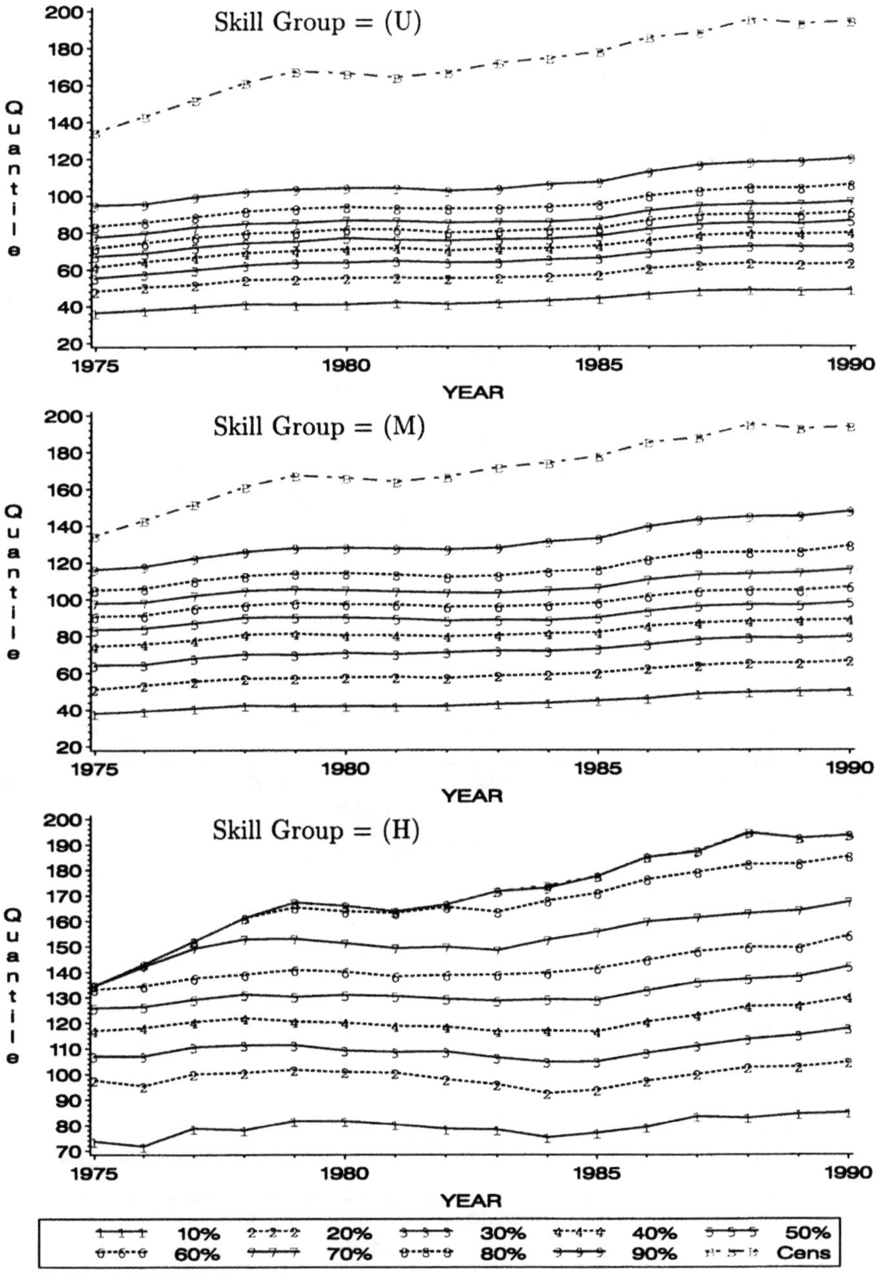

Figure 2.7: 80%–20% Difference of Log Wages for Full–Time Work. Females

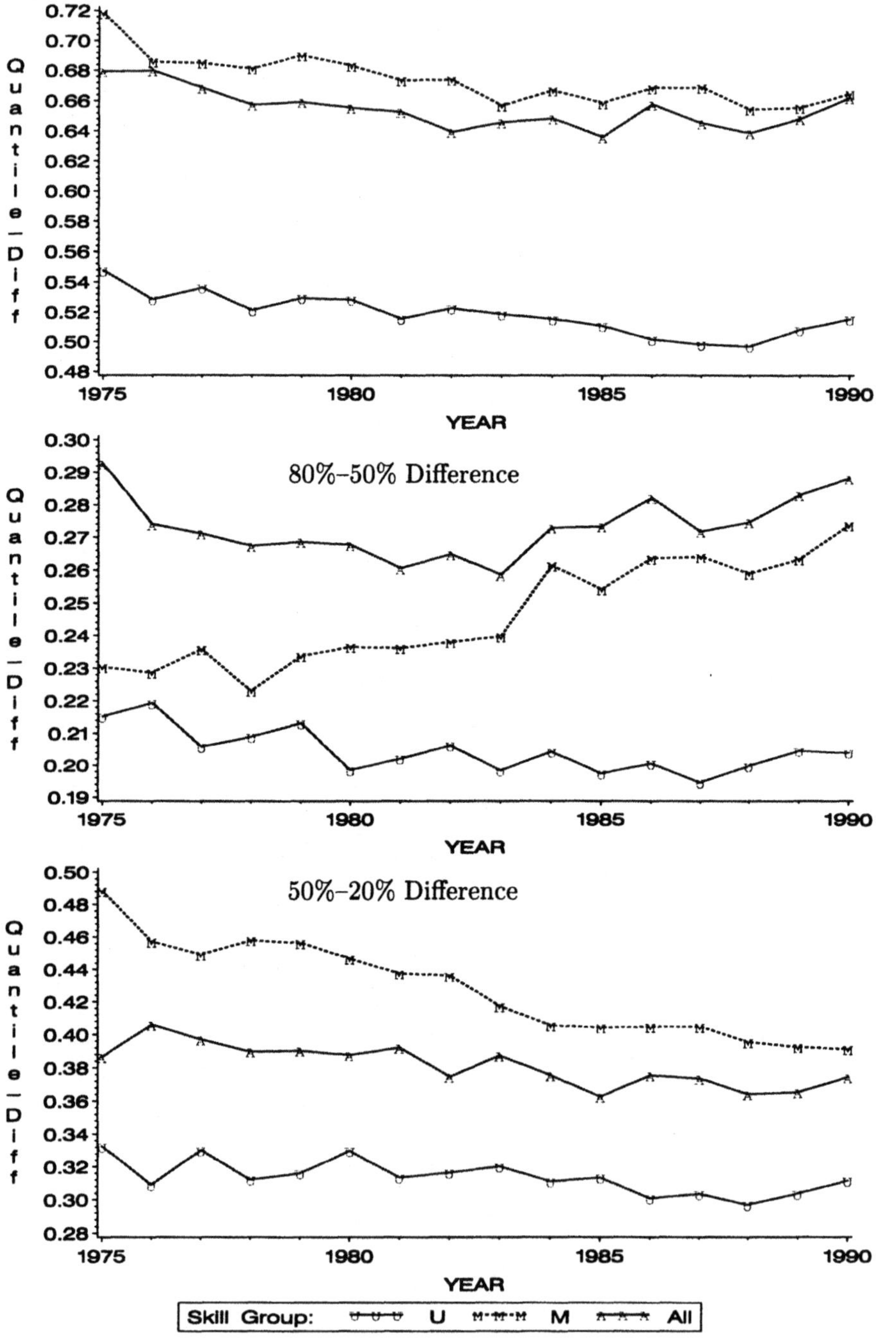

Figure 2.8: Trends in Median of LOG Real Wages for Full–Time Working Females (1975=0)

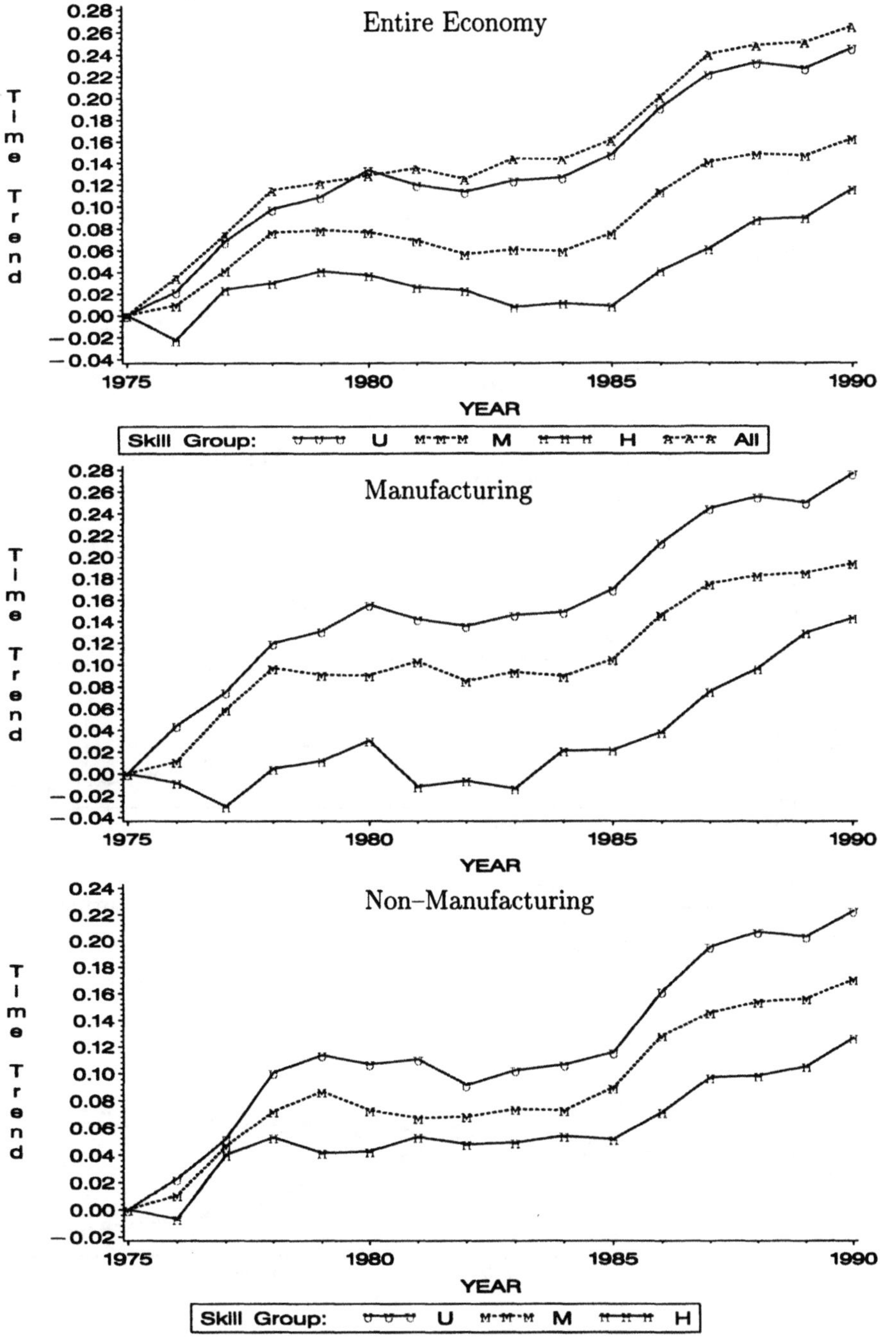

Figure 2.9: Employment Trends (1980=100) for Full–Time Working Males

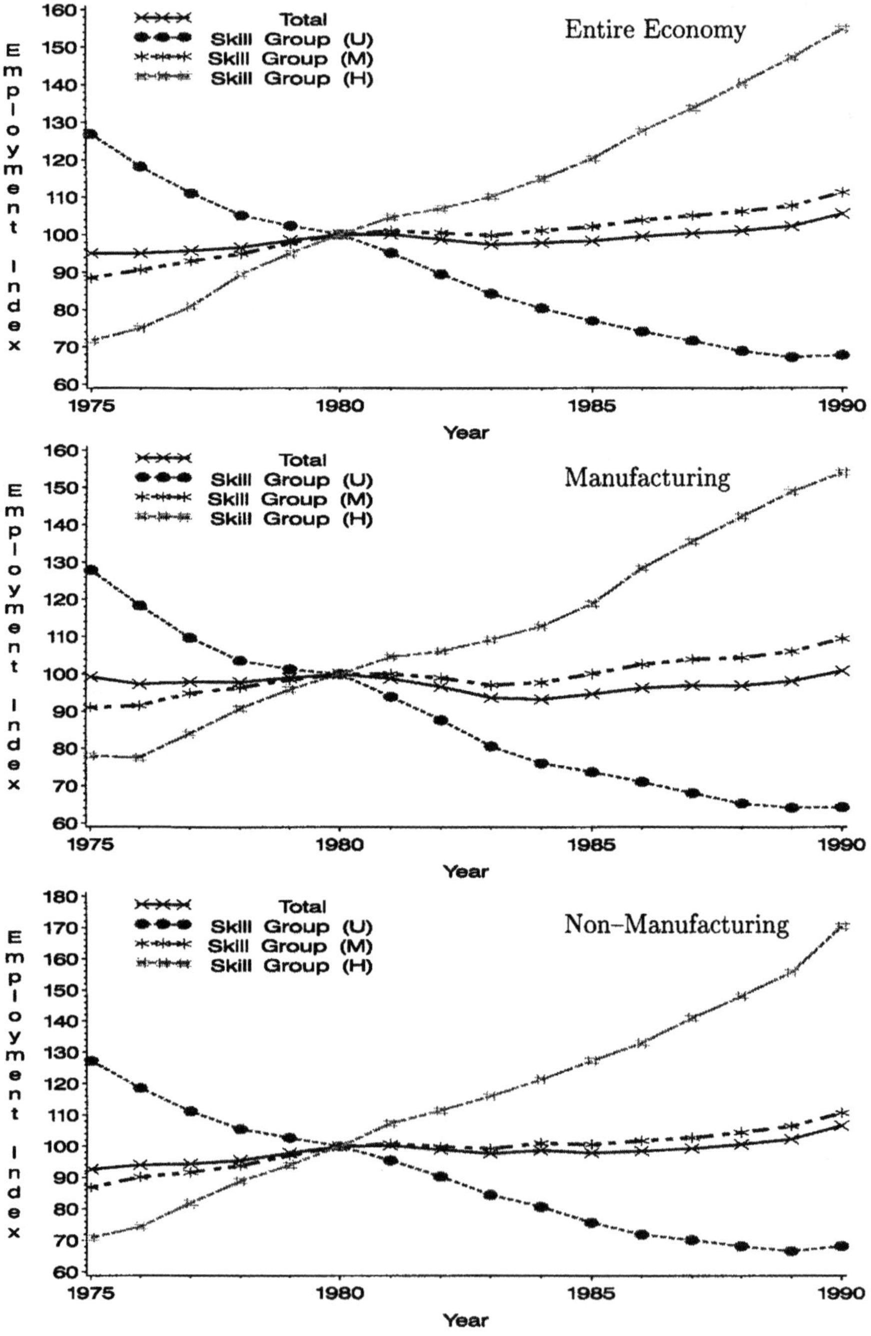

Figure 2.10: Employment Trends (1980=100) for Full–Time Working Females

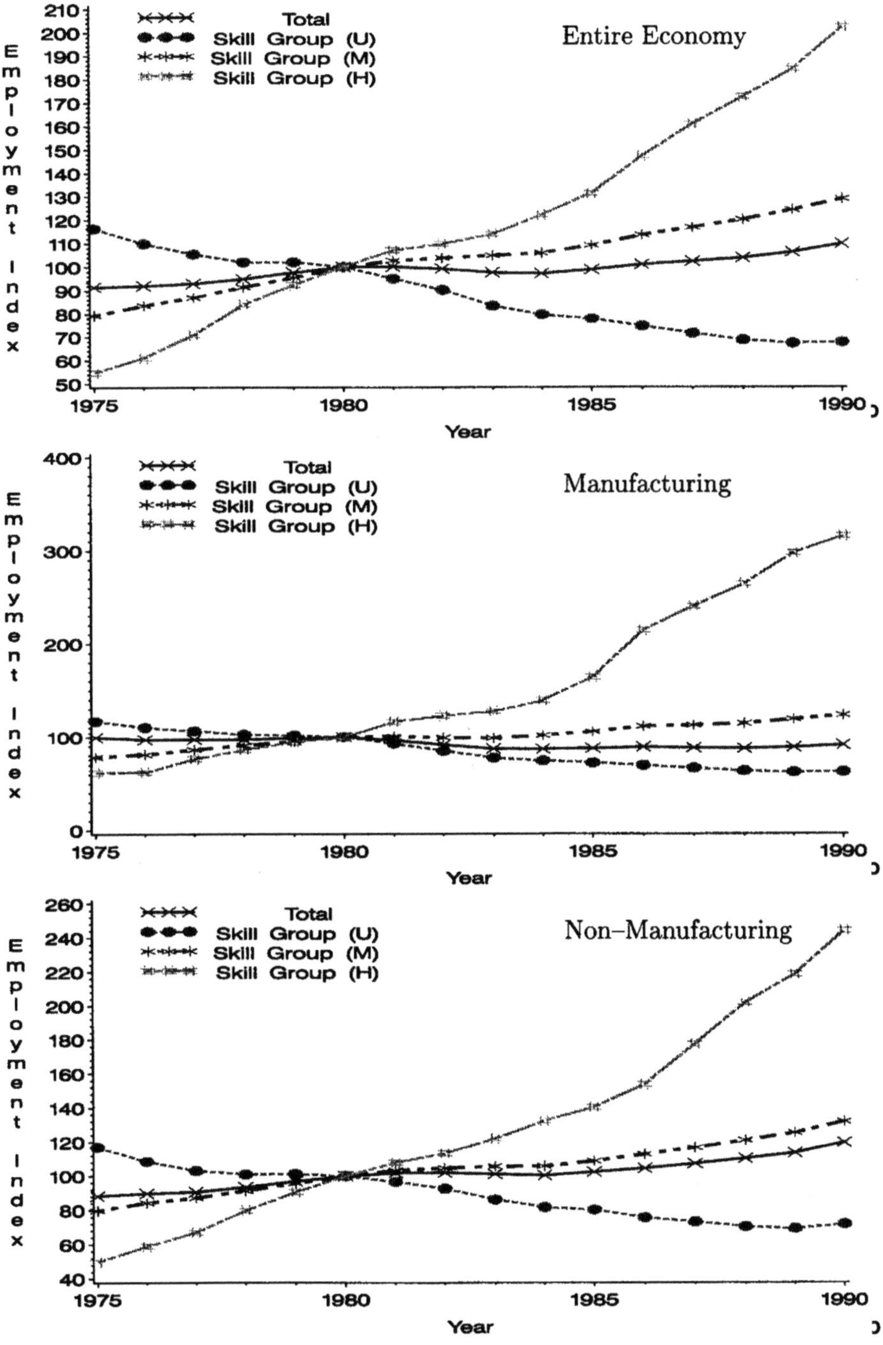

3 A Cohort Analysis of Wage Trends

This cross–section result might be due to cohort effects.

Remark Heard in Many Seminars

Many commentators view the wage structure in West Germany as particularly stable or even as becoming more compressed over time. The descriptive evidence in the previous chapter shows that such a simple view is not warranted in light of the fairly complex trends during the time period from 1975 to 1990. However, mere descriptive evidence on trends in wage dispersion provides only a limited basis for an evaluation of the two–sides–of–the–same–coin hypothesis that the lack of wage flexibility in West Germany has resulted in a disproportionate increase of unemployment among low–skilled workers. This is true because of prevalent composition and selection effects which are likely to influence aggregate wage measures. In this context, a typical composition effect could be that the share of low–skilled workers at older age increases over time, since younger cohorts tend to obtain higher education levels. Assuming an age–earnings profile with positive slope reflecting increased productivity at higher age, average wages for low–skilled workers might exhibit a disproportionate increase relative to other skill groups even though wage ratios between equally productive workers (after controlling for age) have not changed. This example can also be used for an illustration of two possible selection effects. On the one hand, if it is the case that abilities are equally distributed across generations and education as an investment in human capital is positively correlated with unobserved ability, a trend towards increasing education levels among the younger cohorts due, for instance, to an exogenous reduction in the cost of education is likely to imply that the average ability level among the low–skilled workers (if a low–skill level is measured by educational attainment) is decreasing for younger cohorts. On the other hand, a second selection effect emerges, if a lack of wage flexibility or an ongoing wage compression fosters a rise in unemployment among low–skilled workers such that the ability distribution among the low–skilled workers improves. This is the case if the likelihood of becoming unemployed is negatively correlated with the unobserved ability level.

Defining cohorts by year of birth of the worker and estimating age–

earnings profiles for a given cohort, this study attempts a comprehensive characterization of the movements in the entire wage distribution. A comparison of standard cross–sectional age–earnings profiles over time hinges on the assumption that workers of the same age are comparable over time. Taking a cohort perspective allows to investigate wage trends for well defined groups of workers over (a part of) their actual life–cycle.

As it is typically done in the literature, controlling for differences in the skill level and for the age (cohort) composition of workers allows to decompose aggregate trends into movements between and within these groups. However, here a broader characterization is attempted: Acknowledging the obvious fact that wages within groups (cells) of workers defined by their skill level and by their age differ across individuals (within distribution), the goal is to describe trends between and within these cell distributions by means of quantile regressions. Information about these trends can provide reduced–form evidence for the evaluation of certain popular hypotheses. At the same time, they might confirm or they might force one to revise simple interpretations of descriptive evidence as put forward in chapter 2. In order to derive a parsimonious description of actual wage trends, this study applies an empirical framework which builds strongly on the notion of uniformity. Two important forms of uniformity are: First, if wage growth is the same for all cohorts in a skill group over time after controlling for pure life–cycle growth, then wage growth over time can be designated as the overall (macroeconomic) time trend for this skill group and is likely to be caused by economic forces applying to the entire skill group. A second form of uniformity relates to the wage distribution within a cell. If the entire wage distribution is shifted in parallel fashion (uniformly) over time, then wage ratios within the cell do not change, i.e. the economic force behind the trend operates uniformly within the cell irrespective of the unobserved ability of the individual worker. Taking a cohort perspective allows one to compare wages for the same set of workers (or at least for the same synthetic cohort) over time. As a working hypothesis, I take uniformity of wage trends for different workers to imply that the economic cause for the wage ratio between the workers does not change. For instance, if it were the case that wage trends could be described by uniform shifts of a stable wage distribution within a skill group and these uniform trends differed across skill groups, then it would be natural to focus the economic analysis on the skill bias of wage trends, due e.g. to a skill bias in labor demand or in labor supply. Such a result would not be consistent with the argument that unions were successful in raising disproportionately the wages of low–wage earners. Of course, as pointed out above, such a conclusion hinges critically on having dealt appropriately with potential selection effects.

This chapter uses a novel empirical framework applied in MaCurdy and Mroz (1995) and Fitzenberger, Hujer, MaCurdy, and Schnabel (1995) to represent wage trends across skill groups and cohorts in a parsimonious way.

Acknowledging the fundamental identification issue involved when estimating age, cohort, and time effects, the analysis focuses on the empirical implications of uniformity of wage trends for different cohorts in a skill group across time. If such a uniform time trend is not rejected by the data, it is designated as the macroeconomic wage trend for this skill group and, at the same time, it is possible to construct a life–cycle age profile which is common across cohorts. In such a situation, a simple characterization of wage trends for the entire skill group is possible. Taking account both of wage inequality between and within cells of workers defined by the skill level and the age of the worker, the empirical analysis uses quantile regressions in order to obtain a comprehensive view of the entire wage distribution. If wage trends are uniform across quantiles, they describe uniform shifts of the within–cell distributions. In testing for uniformity across quantiles, the analysis in this chapter extends upon the earlier studies MaCurdy and Mroz (1995) and Fitzenberger, Hujer, MaCurdy, and Schnabel (1995).

The empirical analysis in this chapter uses wage data for the time period from 1975 to 1990 (which extends upon the available time period from 1976 to 1984 in Fitzenberger, Hujer, MaCurdy, and Schnabel, 1995). The data is taken from the IAB–Beschäftigtenstichprobe ($I_A BS$) as described in the previous chapter and in the appendix. The analysis is restricted to full–time working males in the age group 25 to 55 in order to minimize the possible composition and selection effects due to changing labor force participation behavior of women, due to early retirement patterns, and due to shifts in the division between full–time and part–time work. In addition, the analysis takes account of the following two composition and selection issues mentioned above: The first effect is concerned with the fact that wage trends themselves can change the composition of workers with respect to unobserved characteristics via their effect on unemployment. In order to evaluate the importance of this selection effect, the paper uses a heuristic correction for unemployment suggested by Card et al. (1996). The second issue relates to the possibility that wage and employment trends differ across Manufacturing and Non–Manufacturing. Differences across these parts of the economy are to be expected because of the growing share of Non–Manufacturing in total GDP, because of differences in the importance of wage bargaining institutions (on average union representation is smaller in Non–Manufacturing compared to Manufacturing), and because Manfucturing is much more exposed to international competition. Because of the above considerations, the analysis of wage trends in this chapter is performed for the following four different settings: (i) Entire economy, (ii) Entire economy using a selection correction for unemployment, (iii) Manufacturing, and (iv) Non–Manufacturing. Note that the cases (i), (iii), and (iv) consider wage trends in the actual sample of employees whereas in case (ii) changes in unemployment are taken into account. The empirical analysis builds on block bootstrap covariance estimates accounting for dependency of the error term in adjacent cohort–year cells in order to draw robust inference. This is particularly important when testing for the uniformity of wage trends.

The remainder of this chapter is organized as follows: Section 3.1 introduces the empirical framework to investigate the uniformity of wage trends and deals with the empirical implementation. The results of the empirical analysis are presented in section 3.2. Section 3.3 provides a summary of the main findings in this chapter and the appendix of this chapter (section 3.4) contains the details of the estimation results.

3.1 An Empirical Framework to Investigate Uniformity

This section presents the empirical framework to investigate the movement of the entire wage distribution for synthetic cohorts over time. A cohort is defined by the year of birth of the worker. The goal of the analysis is to provide a parsimonious description of trends in the entire wage distribution across cohorts for different skill groups. In order to decompose between– and within–shifts in the wage distribution, I estimate various quantile regressions. Testing for uniformity across cohorts and across quantiles for given cohorts, allows one to investigate, whether the entire wage distribution was shifted uniformly over time. Alternatively, it could be the case that wage trends differ across cohorts indicating the presence of "cohort effects" and by quantiles indicating a trend towards increasing or decreasing within group wage dispersion. Under certain conditions, as will be made precise in the following, a cohort effect designates a movement of the entire life–cycle wage profile for a given cohort relative to other cohorts.

Due to the inherent identification problem between age, cohort, and time effects on wages, see Heckman and Robb (1985), wage profiles based on cross–section relationships between age and wages over a sequence of years and movements of life–cycle wage profiles faced by successive cohorts are statistically indistinguishable. I perform the analysis separately for different skill groups. Describing the wage growth experienced by a particular cohort over time or over age (both movements are of course the same), it can be tested whether a uniform time trend operates across different cohorts, apart from the differential age effect. I designate such a uniform time trend as the macroeconomic trend, which conveniently describes wage trends across skill groups representing movements of the entire cross–sectional wage distribution. The framework described in this section was first developed in MaCurdy and Mroz (1995) for the context of wage trends in the United States.[1]

[1] Similar versions of this framework have been applied in Fitzenberger, Hujer, MaCurdy, and Schnabel (1995) for West Germany (based on a shorter time period than considered in this study) and in Gosling et al. (1996) for the UK. The latter study takes a slightly different perspective with respect to the "resolution" of the inherent identification problem. I will come back to this point in section 3.1.3.

3.1.1 Characterization of Wage Profiles

I denote the age of an employee by α and the calendar time by t. A cohort c can be defined by the year of birth. The following identity links the three quantities age, cohort and calendar year:

$$t = c + \alpha \quad . \tag{3.1}$$

Studies of wage trends often investigate movements of "age–earnings-profiles"[2]

$$ln[w(t,\alpha)] = f(t,\alpha) + u \quad . \tag{3.2}$$

The deterministic function f measures the systematic variation in wages and the errors u reflect cyclical or transitory phenomena. For a fixed year t, the function $f(t,\alpha)$ yields the conventional cross–section wage profiles. Movements of f as a function of t describe how cross–section wage profiles shift over time. Recognizing relation (3.1), the cross–sectional relation f as a function of age does not describe "life–cycle" wage growth for any cohort or, put differently, the cross–section relation may very well be the result of "cohort effects". In fact, "cohort–earnings profiles" are statistically indistinguishable from "age–earnings profiles". Wage profiles can also be expressed as a function of cohort and age

$$g(c,\alpha) \equiv g(t-\alpha,\alpha) \equiv f(t,\alpha) \tag{3.3}$$

where the deterministic function g describes how age–earnings-profiles differ across cohorts. Holding age constant, $g(c,\alpha)$ describes the profiles of wages earned by different cohorts over time. Holding the cohort constant yields the profile experienced by a specific cohort over time and age. The latter is often referred to as the "life–cycle profile", because it reflects the wage movements over the life–cycle of a given cohort. During the course of the life–cycle also the economy develops over time. Again this profile reflects two effects such that life–cycle wage growth due to aging and intertemporal shifts in wages are indistinguishable.

The different parameterizations $g(c,\alpha)$ and $f(t,\alpha)$ are equivalent representations of the same wage profile and it is straightforward to translate between the two. Without further assumptions, "pure life–cycle effects" due to aging or "pure cohort effects" cannot be identified. These observations

[2] Alternatively, researchers often describe trends in "experience–earnings-profiles". The identification issue discussed in the following also applies to potential experience being constructed as "age-years of schooling - 6", where both schooling and experience enter the specification of the wage equation, cf. Heckman and Robb (1985). Some examples, among many others, for either the age or the experience approach in the analysis of the wage structure are Blau and Kahn (1996), Buchinsky (1994), Juhn et al. (1993), Steiner and Wagner (1998), and Fitzenberger and Kurz (1997). Since potential experience involves age and schooling information, it seems a much clearer exercise to describe age–earnings profile thereby disentangling the age from the education aspect.

reflect nothing more than the inherent identification problem that prevents one from being able to distinguish among age, period, and cohort effects, cf. Heckman and Robb (1985). Focusing on wage trends for a given cohort, presumably a given set of workers, over time (or equivalently over age), I use the cohort representation of wage profiles as the perspective in the following empirical analysis.

3.1.2 Testing for Uniform Wage Growth

In the following analysis of wage trends, I investigate whether wage trends are uniform across cohorts in the sense that every cohort experiences the same time trend in wages, which is superimposed by age-specific wage growth. The latter can be attributed to labor market experience and may be interpreted as a life–cycle effect. Despite the identification issues discussed above, the existence of a uniform time trend across cohorts is a testable implication in the framework presented here. If such a uniform time trend is found, it is designated as the macroeconomic wage trend for the group of workers considered.[3] However, as will be seen from the empirical results reported in the following, these uniform time trends differ across skill groups.

Taking a cohort perspective, the following two notions of wage growth over time prove useful: First, wage growth for a given cohort in the labor market over time ("Insider Wage Growth"), and second wage growth over time experienced by successive cohorts when entering the labor market ("Entry Wage Growth"). Insider wage growth, i.e. the wage growth of a given cohort c in year t (resp. at age α), is described by the partial derivative of g with respect to t (resp. α):

$$\frac{\partial g}{\partial t}|_c = \frac{\partial g}{\partial \alpha}|_c \equiv g_\alpha(c,\alpha) \equiv g_\alpha \qquad (3.4)$$

comprising the simultaneous change of time and age. Alternatively, holding age constant yields the change of wages earned by different cohorts at specific ages. For the age at labor market entry, α_e, one obtains the growth rate of entry wages

$$\frac{\partial g}{\partial t}|_{\alpha=\alpha_e} = \frac{\partial g}{\partial c}|_{\alpha=\alpha_e} \equiv g_c(c,\alpha_e) = g_c(t-\alpha_e,\alpha_e) \equiv e(t) \quad . \qquad (3.5)$$

Entry wage growth also comprises two effects, namely a change of cohort and time.

[3] If no uniform trend is found, it is of course possible and useful to construct some form of average growth as the macroeconomic trend. However, by construction, such a trend combines age, time, and cohort effects. E.g. aggregating $f(t,\alpha)$ over ages yields an aggregate wage trend for the economy. This may be "contaminated" by cohort effects (like the age composition of the labor force). A decreasing aggregate wage index may very well be compatible with increasing wages for each individual if cohort profiles move downwards over time.

Now, I am at the point to introduce two testable separability conditions implying uniformity of wage trends. If wage growth can be characterized as the sum of a pure aging effect and a pure time effect in the following way:

$$g_\alpha = a(\alpha) + b(t) = a(\alpha) + b(c + \alpha) \tag{3.6}$$

then life–cycle wage growth is independent of the calendar year t. This condition is designated as "uniform insider wage growth hypothesis" which I denote as H_{UI}. It implies that each cohort faces the same wage growth over the life–cycle due to aging. In addition, economy wide shifts are common to all cohorts in the same year but they occur at different points during the life–cycle of each cohort. If the separability condition (3.6) holds, I can construct a "life–cycle wage profile" independently of the calendar year and a macroeconomic time trend independently of age. While condition (3.6) relates to the uniformity of wage growth across cohorts, it leaves the wage level unspecified. The function $a(c+\alpha)$ is designated as the wage growth over the life–cycle and $b(t)$ as the macroeconomic wage growth for the group of workers under investigation. Since $b(t) = b(c + \alpha)$, it can also be viewed as a special kind of cohort effect. Finally, condition (3.6) is violated if interaction terms of α and t enter the specification of g_α.

Integrating back the derivative condition (3.6) with respect to α yields an additive form for the systematic component of the wage function $g(c, \alpha)$:

$$g(c, \alpha) = G + K(c) + A(\alpha) + B(c + \alpha) \tag{3.7}$$

where G is the constant of integration. At a given point in time, the wages of cohorts differ only due to the age–effect, given by $A(\alpha)$, and a cohort–specific level, given by $K(c)$. The "uniform insider wage growth hypothesis" H_{UI} can be tested by investigating whether "interaction terms" $R(\alpha, t)$ enter specification (3.7) which are constructed as integrals of interaction terms of α and t in g_α.

If, in addition to uniform wage growth across cohorts, the growth of entry wages equals the macroeconomic wage growth

$$e(t) = b(t) \tag{3.8}$$

a stronger hypothesis can be formulated which I designate as the "uniform wage growth hypothesis" denoted as H_U. Under this hypothesis, the life–cycle profile of each new labor market cohort is a parallel shift of the profile of the previous cohort corresponding to the uniform time trend $b(t)$ for all cohorts already in the labor market. Again, this is a testable implication. Given specification (3.7), condition (3.8) implies that $K(c)$ is equal to zero for the cohorts entering the labor market during the period of observation.

3.1.3 Empirical Implementation

In order to describe wage profiles and to test the implications of uniform insider and entry wage growth, I specify the wage function $g(c, \alpha)$ by means of a fairly flexible functional form, which nests the uniform wage growth hypotheses as special cases. The specification is estimated for some quantile as a "representative" point of the wage distribution for a given (c, α)–cell. Showing further that, as far as observable, quantile differences above and below this quantile in (c, α)–cells did not change over time, our estimate of $g(c, \alpha)$ provides a parsimonious description of movements in the entire wage distribution.

Turning to the specification of $g(c, \alpha)$, a general regression equation for the wage of individual i in the sample year t can be written as:

$$ln[w_{i,t}] = g(c_i, \alpha_{i,t}) + \overline{u}_t + u_{i,t} \tag{3.9}$$

where $\alpha_{i,t}$ and c_i denote the age of individual i at time t and the cohort of individual i, respectively. I further decompose the error term into a period specific fixed effect $\overline{u}_t$ and a stochastic error term u_{it}. In the empirical analysis, I take the age of 25 years as the entry age into the labor market and I define $\alpha = (\text{age} - 25)/10$. Analogously, since the observation period starts in 1975, I define time $t = (\text{calendar year} - 1975)/10$. Thus, for each cohort, c corresponds to the time t at which α equals zero. For the cohort of age 25 in the year 1975, c equals zero and older cohorts have negative values for c.

As an empirical approximation of the wage profile imposing the hypothesis of uniform insider wage growth, I use polynomials[4] in age, cohort, and time of various degrees:

$$\begin{aligned} A(\alpha) &= A_1\alpha + A_{(2)}(\alpha) = A_1\alpha + A_2\alpha^2 + A_3\alpha^3 \\ B(t) &= B_1 t + B_{(2)}(t) = B_1 t + B_2 t^2 + B_3 t^3 \\ K(c) &= K_1 c + (1-\delta)K_b(c) + \delta K_a(c) \\ \text{with } \delta &= 1 \quad \text{for} \quad c \geq 0 \\ \delta &= 0 \quad \text{else} \end{aligned} \tag{3.10}$$

For older cohorts, entering before the sample period (i.e. before 1975), the cohort term takes the form $K(c) = K_1 c + K_b(c)$ and for younger cohorts, entering during the sample period (i.e. after 1975), the cohort term is $K(c) = K_1 c + K_a(c)$, where:

$$\begin{aligned} K_b(c) &= K_{b2}c^2 + K_{b3}c^3 + \dots \\ K_a(c) &= K_{a2}c^2 + K_{a3}c^3 + \dots \quad . \end{aligned} \tag{3.11}$$

Since c takes the value zero for cohorts of age 25 in 1975, $K(c)$ is zero for this specific cohort and thus, the cohort effects are centered around this cohort. I also include year dummies which are orthogonalized with respect to $B(t)$.

[4]The choice of polynomials is justified since the analysis does not intend to forecast wages outside the observed sample. Using polynomials, it is very clear how I am dealing with the identification issue between age, time, and cohort effects.

Recognizing the problem of identification of the coefficients relating to the linear terms, the wage profile (3.7) takes the form

$$\begin{aligned} g(c,\alpha) &= G + [A_1 - K_1]\alpha + [B_1 + K_1]t + A_{(2)}(\alpha) + B_{(2)}(t) \quad (3.12) \\ &\quad +(1-\delta)K_b(c) + \delta K_a(c) \end{aligned}$$

where G denotes the intercept. In order to estimate period specific fixed effects $\bar{u}_t$, I augment the specification of the estimated wage function by orthogonalized time dummies

$$\tilde{g}(c,\alpha) = g(c,\alpha) + \sum_{i=1975}^{1989-N_b} \kappa_i Y D_i \quad , \qquad (3.13)$$

where N_b is the order of the time polynomial, and the κ_i's are the coefficients of the orthogonalized year dummies YD_i. The coefficients on the time dummies YD_i are orthogonalized against the polynomial in time $B(t) = B_1 t + B_2(t)$ such that $B(t)$ can be interpreted as the trend component and the orthogonalized remaining time effects as the cyclical component.[5] Of course, this decomposition is arbitrary. In the empirical application, I choose a fourth order polynomial in time for $B(t)$ ($N_b = 4$).

The hypothesis of uniform insider wage growth requires equation (3.12) to hold against some more general alternative, whereas the (stronger) uniform wage growth hypothesis additionally requires the coefficients K_a to be zero. Formally, it is also possible to test the hypothesis that the cohort effects K_b are zero. But, since I only observe entry wages for cohorts entering the labor market after 1975, the test of equation (3.8) for older cohorts is not directly based on the entry wages of these cohorts. Instead, it relies on the implications of the hypothesis for the wage profile in later stages of the life-cycle.

In order to formulate a test of the hypothesis of uniform insider wage growth, I consider the following interaction terms of age and time in the derivative g_α:

$$\alpha t, \alpha t^2, \alpha^2 t, \alpha^2 t^2 \quad . \qquad (3.14)$$

[5] Based on the time polynomial $B_1 + B_{(2)}(t)$ of order N_b, the orthogonalized year dummies $YD_{1975}, \ldots, YD_{1989-N_b}$ are constructed as follows: Suppose equation (3.12) is estimated with $\sum_{i=1975}^{N_b+1} \kappa_i \cdot YD_i$ being replaced by $\sum_{i=1}^{16} \kappa_{year(i)} \cdot Dum_{year(i)}$ under the $N_b + 1$ orthogonality restrictions $\sum_{i=1}^{16} i^j \cdot \kappa_{year(i)} = 0$ for $j = 0, 1, \ldots, N_b$, where $Dum_{year(i)}$ represents a dummy for year (i) and $year(i)$ equals 1975, 1976,...,1990 for $i = 1, 2, \ldots, 16$. $YD_{1975}, \ldots, YD_{1989-N_b}$ are derived by solving the restrictions for $\kappa_{year(i)}, i = 16 - N_b, \ldots, 16$, and replacing the resulting expressions in $\sum_{i=1}^{16} \kappa_{year(i)} \cdot Dum_{year(i)}$. Collecting terms for each remaining $\kappa_{year(i)}, i = 1, \ldots, 15 - N_b$, defines $YD_{1975}, \ldots, YD_{1989-N_b}$. Thus, the estimation under the $N_b + 1$ orthogonality restrictions is equivalent to a regression on $YD_{1975}, \ldots, YD_{1989-N_b}$ without restrictions. In a subsequent step, estimates of $\kappa_{year(i)}, i = 16 - N_b, \ldots, 16$, are obtained by means of the orthogonality restrictions.

Assuming that these quantities capture the potential interaction between α and t, the implied non–separable variant of $g(c,\alpha)$ expands (3.12) by incorporating the integrals of (3.14), denoted by $R_1 \dots R_4$. For instance, R_1 is defined as follows:

$$R_1 = \int \alpha(c+\alpha)d\alpha = c\alpha^2/2 + \alpha^3/3 \quad . \tag{3.15}$$

Consequently, as the most general formulation of the wage equation (3.7), I use

$$\begin{aligned}\tilde{g}(c,\alpha) = G &+ [A_1 - K_1]\alpha + (B_1 + K_1]t + A_{(2)}(\alpha) + B_{(2)}(t) \\ &+ (1-\delta)K_b(c) + \delta K_a(c) + \sum_{i=1}^{4}\gamma_i R_i + \sum_{i=1975}^{1989-N_b} \kappa_i YD_i \quad .\end{aligned} \tag{3.16}$$

A formal test of the uniform insider wage growth hypothesis requires all coefficients of the interaction terms $R_1 \dots R_4$ to be jointly zero:

$$\mathbf{H_{UI}}: \quad R_1 - R_4 \quad \text{do not appear in} \quad \tilde{g}(c,\alpha) \tag{3.17}$$

and the test of the stronger hypothesis of uniform wage growth is:

$$\mathbf{H_U}: \quad R_1 - R_4 \quad \text{do not appear in} \quad \tilde{g}(c,\alpha) \quad \text{and} \quad K_a = 0 \quad . \tag{3.18}$$

Only, if the separability condition H_{UI} holds, is it meaningful to construct an index of a life–cycle wage profile as a function of pure aging *and* a macro economic trend index. Otherwise, a different wage profile would apply for each cohort. Provided H_{UI} holds, the life–cycle profile is given by

$$ln[w_L(\alpha)] = k_L + (A_1 - K_1)\alpha + A_{(2)}(\alpha) \tag{3.19}$$

and the macro economic *trend* index is given by

$$ln[w_m(t)] = k_m + (B_1 + K_1)t + B_{(2)}(t) \quad . \tag{3.20}$$

In order to display the cyclical movements of wages, it can be of interest to add the period–specific cyclical effects $\kappa_i YD_i$ to equation (3.20). When interpreting these indices, it is important to recognize that neither the level nor the coefficient on the linear term are identified in a strict econometric sense. In fact, identification relies on the assumption that the coefficient on the linear cohort term is equal to zero. This assumption is motivated by equation (3.6) – provided it is justified in light of the data – which allows to decompose wage growth into a pure age and a pure time effect which are both common to all cohorts in the labor market. In light of this condition, setting the linear cohort term to zero is quite natural. If, for instance, also entry wages grow at the same rate as the time effect $b(t)$ before and during the sample period, the entire cross–section profile $f(\alpha, t)$ exhibits purely parallel shifts over time, a situation, one would not naturally characterize by "cohort effects".[6] In a situation, where uniform insider–wage growth is accepted, a cohort effect describes how the starting point of the common life–cycle profile differs across cohorts. My notion of a cohort effect therefore requires a situation where the differences in starting points do not coincide with the macroeconomic wage growth experienced by the cohorts in the labor market. Thus, I resolve the identification issue with respect to the linear age, cohort, and time terms by setting the coefficient on the linear cohort term equal to zero.

3.1.4 Quantile Regression Approach

So far, I haven't been precise about what wage profiles I am going to estimate and for which I am trying to apply the suggested testing procedure. The literature typically investigates movements in mean log wages based on least squares (or tobit for the case of censoring) estimation procedures. This allows one to measure how the mean of the within wage distribution differs across workers with different socio–economic characteristics and how that mean changes over time. However, it is also of great interest to measure within–group differences and their movement over time. Researchers using mean–based approaches often study whether some measure of within–group wage dispersion (typically the variance of log wages within the group) changes over time, see among others Juhn et al. (1993). Another group of more descriptive studies, see among others OECD (1993, 1996), describes the time trends in quantile differences of wages for some broadly defined groups of workers (like full–time working males or females) in order to analyze trends in wage dispersion on a fairly aggregate level. However, it is rarely analyzed whether within–wage dispersion differs across workers with different characteristics.

Quantile regressions, developed in Koenker and Bassett (1978), provide a very useful tool to study wage differences across and within groups of workers exhibiting different socio–economic characteristics and across time.[7] In this respect, quantile regressions combine the two approaches outlined in the previous paragraph. In addition, quantile regressions exhibit certain robustness properties due to the insensitivity of empirical quantiles to outliers in wages and due the fact that they can be extended to the censored case without losing the robustness properties, see Powell (1986) and Fitzenberger (1997a). Since the data used in this study are topcoded, i.e. wages are censored from

[6] Gosling et al. (1996) take a different perspective. They set the coefficient of the linear time effect to zero in order to describe the life–cycle profile of a given cohort when it ages, i.e. g_α is specified as function of α plus the time dummies which are orthogonalized with respect to the age and the cohort profile.

[7] See Chamberlain (1995), Buchinsky (1994), Fitzenberger, Hujer, MaCurdy, and Schnabel (1995), Fitzenberger and Kurz (1997), and Gosling et al. (1996) taking the quantile regression approach.

above (see data appendix), I now introduce the notation for censored quantile regressions.

For general $\theta \in (0,1)$, I estimate conditional quantiles of wages

$$q_\theta(ln[w_{i,t}]|c,\alpha,\beta^\theta) = \tilde{g}^\theta(c,\alpha,\beta^\theta) \ , \tag{3.21}$$

where $q_{\theta,t}(ln[w_{i,t}]|c,\alpha,\beta^\theta)$ denotes the θ–quantile of the wage in cohort–age–cell (c,α) ($\equiv$ cohort–year–cell (c,t) where $t = c+\alpha$). The vector β^θ comprises the coefficients in equation (3.12) relating to the set of regressors $x_{i,t}$ ($\equiv$ powers of c,α and t; year dummies). In the empirical analysis, I model the following quantiles: $\theta = 0.2, 0.5, 0.8$ (20%–, 50%–, and 80%–quantile).

Quantile regressions are conceptually quite analogous to least squares regressions. In the least squares case, the regression coefficients measure the influence of the regressor variables on the conditional mean of the dependent variable, whereas in the quantile regression case the regression coefficients β^θ represent the influence of the regressor variables on the conditional θ–quantile of the dependent variable. For the median case $\theta = 0.5$, the estimation of the coefficients $\beta^{0.5}$ involves minimization of the sum of the absolute values of the residuals (LAD). The general quantile regression case differs from the LAD case by weighting the residual differently depending on its sign. For general θ, positive residuals enter the distance function with a weight of θ and negative residuals with a weight of $-(1-\theta)$, see Koenker and Bassett (1978). In the presence of censoring, Powell (1986) suggested to censor the response function at the censoring point. This yields a consistent estimator provided that asymptotically a large enough portion of the data is uncensored.

Estimation of the coefficients β^θ by censored quantile regression involves minimization of

$$S_\theta(\beta^\theta) = \sum_{i,t} \rho_\theta \left(ln[w_{i,t}] - min[g^\theta(c,\alpha_t,\beta^\theta), ln(wcens_{i,t})] \right) \ , \tag{3.22}$$

where $ln(wcens_{i,t})$ is the observation specific censoring point (the year specific social security threshold in the context of this study) and the so–called check function is given by

$$\rho_\theta(z) \equiv (\theta - I(z<0))z = sgn_\theta(z) \cdot |z| \quad .$$

The θ–weighted sign function $sgn_\theta(z)$ is defined as

$$sgn_\theta(z) \ \equiv \ \theta I(z>0) \ - \ (1-\theta)I(z<0)$$

and $I(.)$ denotes the indicator function. Thus, the check function takes the absolute value of the residual and weights it differently depending on its sign. The weight is θ if the residual is positive and $(1-\theta)$ if the residual is negative. By variation of θ, different quantiles can be obtained.

Fitzenberger (1998) provides a general treatment of the asymptotic distribution of the linear quantile regression coefficients estimates when heteroskedasticity and autocorrelation of the error term is present in the time series context. Analogous to least squares regression, the basic structure of the asymptotic covariance matrix presented in Fitzenberger (1998) generalizes to the cross–section and time series case. Under standard regularity conditions in the presence of heteroskedasticity and correlation of the error terms, the asymptotic covariance matrix of the quantile regression coefficient estimator $\hat{\beta}^\theta$ minimizing the distance function (3.22) is given by

$$\sqrt{N}\,(\hat{\beta}^\theta - \beta^\theta) \overset{A}{\sim} N(0, L_{\theta,N}^{-1} J_{\theta,N} L_{\theta,N}^{-1}) \tag{3.23}$$

where N denotes the sample size and the matrices $L_{\theta,N}$ and $J_{\theta,N}$ are given by

$$L_{\theta,N} = E\frac{1}{N}\sum_{i,t} f_{\theta,i,t} \cdot I[x'_{i,t}\beta^\theta < ln(wcens_{i,t})] \cdot x_{i,t}x'_{i,t}$$

and

$$J_{\theta,N} = Var\left\{\frac{1}{\sqrt{N}}\sum_{i,t} sgn_\theta(u^\theta_{i,t}) \cdot I[x'_{i,t}\beta^\theta < ln(wcens_{i,t})] \cdot x_{i,t}\right\} .$$

Note, that the $k \times k$ matrix $L_{\theta,N}$ represents the expected value of a sum of squared matrices and the $k \times k$ matrix $J_{\theta,N}$ the variance–covariance matrix of a vector of sums where k is the dimension of the regressor vector $x_{i,t}$.

The above result requires the assumption that the θ–quantile of $u^\theta_{i,t}$ (deviation of wage observation from conditional quantile) conditional on the regressors is equal to zero and that $sgn_\theta(u^\theta_{i,t})$ is uncorrelated with $x_{i,t}$. $f_{\theta,i,t}$ denotes the density of $u^\theta_{i,t}$ at zero conditional on the regressors. The asympotic distribution of the (censored) quantile regression estimator is quite similar to the least squares case, when the error term exhibits heteroskedasticity and autocorrelation. In the well known least squares case, the term $f_{\theta,i,t}$ is missing in the expression for the matrix L_N and the matrix J_N takes account of variances and covariances in $\{u_{i,t} \cdot x_{i,t}\}$ instead of $\{sgn_\theta(u^\theta_{i,t}) \cdot x_{i,t} \cdot I[x'_{i,t}\beta^\theta < ln(wcens_{i,t})]\}$, see Fitzenberger (1997a, 1998).

The coefficient estimates at two different quantiles θ_1 and θ_2 are asymptotically jointly normally distributed, see Powell (1986) and Fitzenberger (1997a), with asymptotic covariance matrix

$$Cov\left\{\sqrt{N}\,(\hat{\beta}^{\theta_1} - \beta^{\theta_1}), \sqrt{N}\,(\hat{\beta}^{\theta_2} - \beta^{\theta_2})\right\} = L_{\theta_1,N}^{-1} J_{\theta_1,\theta_2,N} L_{\theta_2,N}^{-1}$$

where

$$J_{\theta_1,\theta_2,N} = Cov\left\{\frac{1}{\sqrt{N}}\sum_{i,t} h^{\theta_1}_{i,t}, \frac{1}{\sqrt{N}}\sum_{i,t} h^{\theta_2}_{i,t}\right\}$$

and

$$h_{i,t}^{\theta_j} = sgn_{\theta_1}(u_{i,t}^{\theta_j}) \cdot I[x_{i,t}'\beta^{\theta_j} < ln(wcens_{i,t})] \cdot x_{i,t} \quad ,$$

for $j \in \{1,2\}$.

In the context of this study, I assume the error terms to be dependent across individuals within cohort–year–cells and across adjacent cohort–year–cells. The dependence is assumed to take the form of rectangular m–dependence (see appendix) across time and across cohorts such that $J_{\theta,N}$ becomes

$$J_{\theta,N} = \frac{1}{N} \sum_{i_1,t_1,i_2,t_2,|t_1-t_2|\leq m_t,|c_{i_1}-c_{i_2}|\leq m_c} Cov(h_{i_1,t_1}^{\theta}, h_{i_2,t_2}^{\theta}) \quad ,$$

where m_c and m_t are the degrees of m–dependence across cohorts and time, respectively. The middle part of the covariance matrix across quantiles, $J_{\theta_1,\theta_2,N}$, can be rewritten in an analogous way.

A simplified minimum–distance approach[8] can be used for the estimation of quantile regressions when the data on the regressors can be grouped into cells and censoring is not too severe. The approach consists of calculating the respective cell quantiles in a first stage and regressing (by generalized least squares) those empirical quantiles, which are not censored, on the set of regressors in the second stage. For the dataset used in this study, the cell sizes are large enough for making this a fruitful approach (Chamberlain suggests cell sizes of at least 30). However, when censoring is too severe, there is a noticeable efficiency loss involved in such an approach, see the simulation results in Fitzenberger (1997a). Therefore, I use the minimum–distance approach for the two groups of low–skilled and medium–skilled workers, for which censoring is not too severe, but I apply censored quantile regressions directly for the group of high–skilled workers, who exhibit much more censoring. When applying the minimum–distance approach for the first two groups, I use the cell sizes as weights, but I do not attempt to weight the cells efficiently using an estimate of the variance of the empirical quantile. However, my standard error estimates are robust with respect to the weighting procedure (see the next subsection and the appendix).

3.1.5 Block Bootstrap Procedure for Inference

Direct estimation of the asymptotic covariance matrix would involve estimation of the conditional density differing across observations and taking account of the dependency in $sgn_\theta(u_{i,t}^{\theta})$ across observations. Facing these difficulties, researchers have resorted to bootstrap methods as a viable alternative, see Chamberlain (1994), Buchinsky (1994), and Fitzenberger, Hujer,

[8]See Chamberlain (1994), Buchinsky (1994), Fitzenberger, Hujer, MaCurdy, and Schnabel (1995), Gosling et al. (1996), and MaCurdy and Mroz (1995) for studies taking this approach.

MaCurdy, and Schnabel (1995). Fitzenberger (1998) establishes the asymptotic validity of the Moving Blocks Bootstrap method (and therefore the standard bootstrap as a special case) for quantile regressions in the time series context.

In this study, I use a flexible Block Bootstrap approach allowing for standard error estimates which are robust against fairly arbitrary heteroskedasticity and autocorrelation of the error term, see MaCurdy and Mroz (1995) and Fitzenberger, Hujer, MaCurdy, and Schnabel (1995) for such an approach. The appendix provides a detailed description of the Block Bootstrap and establishes its asymptotic validity. The Block Bootstrap approach employed here extends the standard bootstrap procedure in that it draws blocks of observations to form the resamples; for each observation in a block, the entire vector comprising the endogenous variable and the regressors is used, i.e., I do not draw from the estimated residuals. I draw a two–dimensional block of observations of block length four in the cohort and time dimension with replacement, until the resample has become at least as large as the desired resample size. This way standard error estimation takes account of error correlation within a cohort–year–cell (c,t) as well as across cells (c,t) and (c',t')[9] such that $|c-c'| \leq .3$ and $|t-t'| \leq .3$, i.e. I take account of correlation across pairs of cohorts and time periods which are both at most three years apart.

For the weighted least squares estimation based on cell quantiles, I simply draw the blocks of at most 16 cohort–year–cells to form the resample. In addition to the cell quantile and the regressor vector, each cell also has a weight attached (number of workers in that groups) which is used in the weighted least squares regression on the resample. For the censored quantile regressions on individual wage data, drawing a cell implies bringing all individuals in that cell into the resample such that the correlation in the cell ("group effect") is preserved. The censored quantile regression on the resample is then again based on individual data with a weight of unity attached to each observation.

When the design matrix for a resample becomes rank deficient (this happens frequently with dummy specifications) the resample is dismissed. In order to mitigate this problem, the resample size for the highest skill group is chosen to be twice the sample size and the raw bootstrap covariance estimates are rescaled according to the conventional asymptotic rate of convergence, i.e., in this case, the bootstrap covariance estimates are multiplied by a factor of two. Contrasting the results presented in section 3.2 with conventional standard error estimates (the latter are not reported here) indicates that allowing for correlation between the error terms within and across cohort–year–cells, when forming the blocks, changes the estimated standard errors considerably. Thus, it is very likely that such correlation is present and important for inference. However, there is no clear cut decision rule about

[9]Note that c and t are normalized by 10, i.e. they change by .1 for a change of one calendar year.

the choice of blocksize. I experimented somewhat with slightly smaller or larger blocks without changes in the substance of the results.

3.2 Estimation Results

This section applies the framework presented in the previous section to analyze wage trends for full–time working males over time. The goal is to find a parsimonious and comprehensive description of trends in the entire wage distribution for the three skill groups defined in chapter 2. I denote these groups of workers by (U) low–skilled, (M) medium–skilled, and (H) high–skilled and I am going to analyze trends in the 20%–, 50%–, and 80%–quantile ($\theta = 0.2, 0.5, 0.8$) for groups (U) and (M). For skill group (H), I restrict attention to the 20%– and the 50%–quantile ($\theta = 0.2, 0.5$), due to the severe censoring of the wage data for this group, see chapter 2.

The analysis in this section is performed for the entire economy and for Manufacturing (MAN) and Non–Manufacturing (NON–MAN) separately. For the definition of MAN and NON–MAN, I exclude the Government sector, Agriculture, and Non–Profit Organizations from Non–Manufacturing, see tables A.1 and A.2 in the appendix. The separate analysis for MAN and NON–MAN is motivated by various reasons: The descriptive findings in chapters 2 and 4 indicate that wage trends differ between MAN and NON–MAN. Regarding employment trends, the share of NON–MAN in employment increases over time and it is often argued that this part of the economy can possibly absorb unemployed low–skilled workers provided wages are sufficiently flexible there. Also, wage bargaining institutions appear stronger (e.g. in form of higher union density, see Fitzenberger, Haggeney, and Ernst 1998) in MAN compared to NON–MAN. And finally, MAN comprises most of the tradable goods industries, and, thus, it is affected more strongly by international competition compared to NON–MAN.

The analysis for the entire economy is performed both for the group of all employed workers and for the union of employed and unemployed workers in the cohort–year–cells. The latter analysis provides a reference point for the possible selection effects taking place due to changing employment rates over time which might lead to changes in the measured quantiles even though the workers who are continuously employed do not experience a change in their wage. It is likely that the potential wage of workers in a cohort–year–cell, who change their employment status, is not a random draw from the within wage distribution. To obtain an upper bound on the influence of these selection effects on my results, I artificially assign to the group of unemployed workers in a cohort–year–cell the minimum possible wage in the dataset (see also Card et al., 1996, p. 17, for such a strategy).[10] Since the unemployment rate never exceeds 20%, there is no case for which the 20%–quantile for a

[10] I have unemployment rates for males available for five–year intervalls in age and by skill groups over time. For details, see data appendix.

cohort–year–cell in this entire economy with unemployed workers is at this minimum wage.[11] I also contrast the results obtained for employed workers only with the results obtained when unemployed persons are included. This allows me to investigate the robustness of my results to the selection effects induced by changing unemployment rates over time.

The analysis in this section proceeds as follows. Section 3.2.1 presents results on four specifications of the wage equation (3.17) differing in the degree of uniformity in wage growth imposed. Wald test results are presented in section 3.2.2 in order to determine which uniformity restrictions are justified by the data. Finally, section 3.2.3 illustrates the preferred estimates by means of their implied profiles of predicted wages.

3.2.1 Estimated Specifications for Wage Equations

I estimate four specifications of equation (3.13) for the 20%–, 50%–, and 80%–quantile for skill groups (U) and (M) and for the 20%– and the 50%–quantile for (H). The analysis is performed for four different groups of male workers:

1. Entire Economy (full–time working males in the sample)
2. Entire Economy supplemented with unemployed males workers who get assigned the minimum wage in the data
3. Full–time working employees in MAN only
4. Full–time working employees in NON–MAN only

The estimation results for these four settings can be found in tables 3.1 to 3.4, respectively. The standard error estimates are obtained by a block bootstrap procedure using a rectangular block of length four both in the cohort and time dimension. I postpone the discussion of the differences between the four settings until section 3.2.3 where I describe the preferred specifications by means of graphical illustrations.

The most general specification (model 1) is given by (see equation (3.13) – all specifications also include the cyclical year effects YD_i which are orthogonalized with respect to the time trend)

$$\begin{aligned} g(c,\alpha) &= G + a_1\alpha + a_2\alpha^2 + a_3\alpha^3 + b_1 t + b_2 t^2 + b_3 t^3 + b_4 t^4 \quad (3.24) \\ &\quad + \gamma_{b2} c_b^2 + \gamma_{b3} c_b^3 + \gamma_{b4} c_b^4 + \gamma_{a2} c_a^2 + \sum_{j=1}^{4} \rho_j R_j \ , \end{aligned}$$

where $c_b = (1-\delta)c$ and $c_a = \delta c$ are the cohort terms before and after 1975.

[11] In contrast to mean regressions, it is a convenient feature of quantiles, that they are unaffected by the exact assigned wage as long as the assigned wage remains below the estimated quantile.

Models 2 to 4 are restricted versions of model 1:

Model 2: $\rho_j = 0$ for $j = 1, ..., 4$ (H_{UI} imposed),

Model 3: $\rho_j = 0$ for $j = 1, ..., 4$ and $\gamma_{a2} = 0$ (H_U imposed), and

Model 4: $\rho_j = 0$ for $j = 1, ..., 4$, $\gamma_{a2} = 0$ (H_U imposed)
and $\gamma_{b2} = \gamma_{b3} = \gamma_{b4} = 0$.

Due to the severity of censoring for skill group (H), I only estimate versions of model 1 to 4 under the restrictions $a_3 = 0$ and $c_{b4} = 0$ for this group.

The most restricted version, model 4, assumes that wage growth is uniform across cohorts, both during and before the sample, i.e. no "cohort effects" operate for those cohorts entering the labor market before the start of the sample in 1975. Under this scenario, wage growth can be described by a fixed cross–section profile of wages which moves in parallel fashion over time, i.e. the growth along the cross–section profile corresponds to the true life–cycle profile experienced by each cohort. In this situation, I do not consider cohort effects to be operating, which motivates the identifying assumption that the linear cohort effect in models 1 to 4 is arbitrarily set to zero and therefore completely ascribed to the age and time profiles (see discussion at the end of section 3.1.3). However, previewing the results of the next subsection, model 4 is typically not justified by the data.

In contrast, model 3 restricts wage growth to be uniform across all cohorts only during the sample period. Wages of new cohorts entering the labor market grow at the same rate as wages for older cohorts. Nevertheless, it is possible that cross–section age profiles of wages change over time due to "cohort effects" before the start of the sample. Model 2 allows "cohort effects" to operate both for the cohorts entering the labor market before the sample period and during the sample period. However, it still restricts wage growth to be uniform across cohorts after they have entered the labor market.

3.2.2 Testing for Uniformity

Table 3.5 in the appendix of this chapter provides the results on the Wald tests of the wage growth hypotheses H_{UI} and H_U. Starting from model 1, it is tested consecutively whether models 2 to 4 provide a sufficient description of the data. These test results determine the preferred model which are indicated by a "*" in tables 3.1 to 3.4 and which the illustrations of wage profiles in the following subsection are based upon (except for skill group (H) in the cases where uniform wage growth is rejected). Also building on the preferred specifications, table 3.6 provides results on tests investigating uniformity of groups of the preferred coefficient estimates across quantiles. These tests are particularly appropriate since, in almost all cases, the same specification is found across quantiles as the preferred model. The only exception is the case of skill group (H), for which it is unlikely in any case that the age and cohort dimension can be estimated with a lot of precision for the 50%–quantile.

Turning to the results for the uniform wage growth hypotheses (H_{UI} and H_U), i.e. testing the restrictions implied by model 2 and 3 against model 1 and model 3 against model 2. There is a striking uniformity of test results across settings. In all cases both for the skill group (U) and (M), the restrictions implied by model 3 are accepted against model 1 and 2 and the restrictions implied by model 4 against model 3 are decisively rejected by the data (for (U) and (M) the P–values in the first three rows are all above 10% and they are all below 2% in row four and five). The picture is less uniform for skill group (H). For the entire economy (both with and without selection correction for unemployment), uniform insider wage growth is rejected at the 20%–quantile (this finding itself is somewhat surprising, since the individual coefficients for $R_1 - R_4$ in tables 3.1 and 3.2 are all insignificant) and there is strong evidence for cohort effects after 1975, i.e. the new cohorts entering the labor market seem to be different in their life–cycle profile compared to older cohorts. This is consistent with the trend towards higher education which, in particular, affects skill group (H), see also Möller (1996). Thus, it could be the case that the larger young cohorts in (H) differ from their older counterparts with respect to their unobserved ability distribution and one should see the highest impact of this trend in the bottom part of the within distribution (which is the only part, one can observe reliably due to the severity of censoring). For the 50%–quantile, model 4 seems acceptable in light of the data.

Distinguishing between MAN and NON–MAN, the picture changes for (H): While at the 50%–quantile, one obtains model 4 in both parts of the economy for skill group (H), at the 20%–quantile, model 3 seems justified in MAN and model 4 in for NON–MAN. Thus, in contrast to skill groups (U) and (M), there is a difference in the analysis based on the entire economy and when distinguishing between MAN and NON–MAN. Apparently, the estimated separable wage profiles differ in such a way that separability is violated when the entire economy is considered. The difference between the two parts of the economy will become more apparent, when discussing the implied profiles in the next section, providing another ex–post justification for analyzing the two parts separately.

To complete the test results, table 3.6 indicates whether parts of the wage specification differ across quantiles for the preferred specifications. For skill group (U) and the entire economy, there is evidence for the age profiles to be uniform in the upper part of the distribution (80%–50%) but there appear to exist significant differences in the bottom part of the distribution. Researchers often expect increasing dispersion of wages over age (Gosling et al., 1996, p. 6), i.e. the age profile should be steeper at higher quantiles. As will become clearer in the next section, this is not the case both for the bottom and the top part of the wage distribution for (U). In MAN, the age profile does not appear to differ for (U) across quantiles and in NON–MAN it differs significantly only in the lower part of the distribution. For skill group (M), the age profiles differ significantly across quantiles in all settings, whereas for skill group (H) the results are mixed: For the entire economy and in MAN, there is no significant difference across quantiles, but in NON–MAN the age profiles seem to differ. The cohort profiles seem to be quite uniform across quantiles both for (U) and for (H), but they seem to differ for (M), especially in the upper part of the distribution. The cyclical time effects and the time trends differ across quantiles for all skill groups in almost all cases. Relating these findings to the existence of a macroeconomic trend, the data does not seem to support the notion of a uniform shift of the entire distribution within an skill group over time. Thus, one might obtain misleading results where the attention is restricted to a specific point in the distribution (like the median) or to a summary measure like the mean. Finally, the estimated cohort profiles $K_b(.)$ before 1975 appear to be mostly the same across quantiles for (U) and (H), whereas they typically differ significantly for (M), especially between the 80%– and the 50%–quantile.

3.2.3 Graphical Illustrations

This final subsection is concerned with graphical illustrations of the preferred estimated models according to the test results presented in the previous subsection (see figures 3.1 to 3.24 in the appendix of this chapter). These graphical illustrations are the important tools to describe the findings of this study. At the same time they give a clear indication of the deficiencies of the analysis. Since uniform insider wage growth (H_{UI}) is accepted for almost all specifications, it is meaningful to first construct profiles of life–cycle wage growth and of time trends in theses cases. For the entire economy, uniform insider wage growth is not accepted for (H). In these cases, average time trends are constructed in figures 3.9 and 3.12 based on specification 3 acknowledging that this is not the time trend which is experienced uniformly across cohorts. Due to cohort effects being significant in most cases, I then present the predicted cross–sections in two sample year showing how cohort effects were changing cross–section age profiles despite the life–cycle growth being uniform across cohorts.

Life–Cycle Profiles

Figures 3.1 to 3.6 in the appendix depict the predicted life–cycle profiles both for MAN and NON–MAN. The graphs for the entire economy are omitted. The main features for (U) and (M) in the entire economy are also prevalent in the graphs for MAN and NON–MAN (or can be inferred from the difference between the two) and selection effects typically do not seem to be important for the age profiles.[12] The profiles for (H) cannot be constructed for the entire economy since uniform insider wage growth is rejected.

[12]Except for the 20%–quantile where model 3 for the entire economy with selection correction for unemployment predicts an implausibly steep linear age profile, see also the coefficient estimates in table 3.2. Comparing models 3 and 4 for this setting, reveals

Turning to the profiles for (U), life–cycle wage growth in MAN seems to be almost uniform across quantiles and the significant difference between the 50%– and the 20%–quantile is barely noticeable (the profile for 20%–quantile is slightly below the other two). The profile is quite different for NON–MAN, where one finds a significant reduction of the quantile differences with increasing age (quite in contrast to the a priori expectation of increasing dispersion, see Gosling et al., 1996). For (M) both in MAN and NON–MAN, however, on finds increasing wage dispersion with age and the life–cycle profiles are considerably steeper than for (U). The profile at the 80%–quantile in NON–MAN is slightly steeper than its counterpart in MAN and the opposite is true for the 50%–quantile. The profiles for (H) exhibit still steeper wage growth until the age of about 35 to 40 compared to their counterparts for (U) and (M). In NON–MAN, this steep wage growth continues until age 50 exceeding considerably the profiles both for (U) and (M). However, for higher age in MAN, the profile for the 50%–quantile exhibits considerable wage declines. One must note that, for age above 40, the profiles for (H) are notoriously unreliable since almost all empirical 20%– and 50%–quantiles are censored for this age group. This is especially true for MAN where wage levels for (H) are considerably higher than for NON–MAN, see chapter 2. Thus, one must treat the life–cycle profiles for higher ages as out–of–sample predictions for which polynomial specifications are notoriously bad.[13] Hence, the results support the notion that, as far as observable, life–cycle wage growth is steeper for higher skill levels.

Time Trends

Figures 3.7 to 3.18 depict the estimated time trend without cyclical effects from the preferred final specifications (except for skill group (H) in the entire economy). Given acceptance of the uniform wage growth hypothesis, these time trends summarize the shifts in the wage distribution within and between the skill groups over time.

The results for the entire economy in figures 3.7 to 3.9 indicate that inequality within skill groups slightly increased over time. For (U) and (M), wage growth appears quite uniform until the mid 80's, but in the second half of the 80's wage growth was higher at higher quantiles (according to table 3.6, these differences are significant). Wage dispersion within (H) seems to have increased considerably between the 20%– and the 50%–quantile, however, due to the severe censoring, the difference is only close to be significant (P–

that the cohort profile before 1975 seems to capture the quadratic and cubic age effect. This result is somewhat puzzling, however, one should note that the 20%–quantile for this group is often fairly close to the minimum wage with unemployment rates for young workers in (U) being well above 15% in the 80's.

[13] Compared to our analysis in Fitzenberger, Hujer, MaCurdy, and Schnabel (1995), the problem is much more severe here, since the new I_ABS dataset censors all wage observations at the lower of the two possible social security thresholds (see Bender et al., 1996, p. 14) and since I had to correct for the structural break between 1983 and 1984.

Value = .10). Between skill groups, wage growth is uniformly larger for (U) compared to (M), i.e. despite the increase in aggregate wage inequality, the wage differentials between low– and medium–skilled workers tended to become smaller over time. This compression mainly took place during the first half of the sample. For (H), the situation is more complex. Whereas the 20%–quantile experiences an actual fall in real wages, the 50%–quantile exhibits larger growth than its counterpart for (M). At the median, therefore the results are consistent with the U–shaped pattern of wage growth across skill groups based on the purely descriptive analysis in chapter 2 and in Fitzenberger and Franz (1998).

To complete the results on the entire economy, figures 3.10 to 3.12 exhibit the estimated time trends for the entire economy with selection correction for unemployment. These trends are fairly similar to the results discussed so far, except for the 20%–quantile for (U). Here, one finds a strong decline of the relative wage position over time. I take the wage declines both at the 20%–quantile for (U) (with unemployed) and for (H) (in both cases) as evidence that important selection effects are operating here. For (U), those workers at the 20%–quantile remaining employed appear to be different from those workers who are losing their jobs. Note that unemployment is increasing the most for young workers in (U), see Fitzenberger, Hujer, MaCurdy, and Schnabel (1995, appendix 4). This is somewhat consistent with a sorting interpretation, such that the better types in the distribution of unobservable characteristics in (U) are more likely to remain employed over time. For the 20%–quantile in (H), the situation seems to be opposite. Since larger fractions of a cohorts tend to obtain higher education levels, it might be the case that the distribution of unobserved abilities in (H) becomes worse over time. This effect should show up most in the bottom part of the wage distribution, which could explain the difference to the median. Unfortunately, the evidence on this is notoriously plagued by the severity of censoring for (H). Clearly, more research is needed on these selection issues.

Next, the time trends for MAN and NON–MAN in figures 3.13 to 3.18 are to be discussed. MAN exhibits increasing within wage dispersion both for (U) and (M). For (H), the time trends indicate compression of the within group dispersion during the first five years of the sample and increasing dispersion afterwards. At the end of the sample, the trends almost exactly coincide. In stark contrast to the results for the entire economy, wages at the 20%–quantile experienced strong positive growth in real wages over time. Across skill groups, the U–shaped pattern emerges, which is consistent with earlier results. In MAN, wage growth is uniformly higher both for low–skilled and for high–skilled workers relative to the medium skill level.

The findings for NON–MAN are very different. Both for (U) and (H), there is a strong trend towards higher wage dispersion within the skill group and, for both groups, wage growth at the 20%–quantile is particularly low. For (M), there is no clear evidence for increasing wage dispersion within the skill groups. Across skill groups, one finds for the most part an inverse relationship between educational attainment and wage growth. Wage growth for (U) at the 50%– and the 80%–quantile uniformly exceed growth for all quantiles in (M), and wages at the 20%–quantile in (H) exhibit almost no wage growth. At the 50%–quantile for (H), overall wage growth is, however, very similar to (M). The 20%–quantile of (U) experiences slightly less wage growth compared to its counterpart in (M). Finally, overall wage growth in NON–MAN is uniformly smaller than in MAN, which is a puzzle given that the increasing pressures of globalization might have resulted in less wage growth in the tradable–goods industries being mostly MAN industries, see the analysis in chapter 4.

Predicted Cross–Sections $f(\alpha, t)$ for $t = 1976$ and $t = 1988$

Among other things, the international debate on trends in wage inequality points to increasing wage differentials between old (≡ more experienced) and young (≡ less experienced) workers as another dimension of increasing skill differentials, see Juhn et al. (1993) and OECD (1993, 1996). At first glance, considering the results obtained so far, these effects do not seem apparent in West Germany since the uniform wage growth hypothesis is not rejected by the data, thus implying a uniform (and therefore unchanging) life–cycle wage profile across cohorts. However, analogous results were obtained by Gosling et al. (1996) for the UK and by MaCurdy and Mroz (1995) for the U.S., i.e. two countries for which most of the literature states that the age differential has, in fact, increased over time. These apparently contradicting findings can be reconciled, since most of the literature refers to the measured age differential in the cross–section profile $f(\alpha, t)$ whereas my results and the results obtained by MaCurdy and Mroz and by Gosling et al. refer to the age profile $g(c, \alpha)$ for c given. This is just a variant of the standard critique, that an age effect estimated for a cross–section of data could be caused by "cohort effects".

Based on the preferred specification, figures 3.19 to 3.24 depict the predicted cross–section profiles for the years 1976 and 1988 both in MAN and NON–MAN. I have excluded the cyclical time effects (≡ parallel shifts in the profiles relative to each other), which I assume to be of temporary nature. This omission has no effect on the cross–section age differentials. The results for the entire economy are omitted, since they are fairly similar to the results presented here. For skill groups (U) and (M), the figures indicate, that cross–section wage differentials across age have increased uniformly and considerably over time. For (H), this does not seem to be the case, but due to the severity of censoring, one cannot put much confidence in the results for (H) above an age of about 35 to 40. Another striking feature appears to be quite uniform for (U) and (M), namely, cross–section wage profiles increase almost linearly until a certain age and then become almost flat. The increase in cross–section wage differentials across age is triggered by the increase of the age where the profile becomes flat, in fact, reflecting cohort effects before 1975. Older cohorts, who have already entered the labor market before 1975, earn comparatively higher wages and this effect tends to increase the age differential over time. The cohort effect for (U) and (M) seems to grow up to an age of about 35 in 1975 and then to remain at an almost constant level for the cohorts who are older than that. Finally, the results in table 3.6 confirm that, for (U) and (H), these cohort profiles K_b are also quite uniform across quantiles.

3.3 Summary

This chapter provides a comprehensive analysis of wage trends across and within skill groups for full–time working males in West Germany during the time period from 1975 to 1990. Building on a novel empirical framework, the analysis groups the data by skill group, age, and time. Defining cohorts by year of birth, it is investigated whether a parsimonious decomposition of wage growth into age and time effects uniformly describes wage profiles across cohorts. Being able to accept this uniform wage growth hypothesis allows one to construct a uniform life–cycle profile and a uniform time trend in wages for each skill group.

The empirical implementation estimates quantile regressions in order to model the trends in the entire wage distribution. For each skill group, it is tested whether wage trends are uniform across different cohorts and whether these trends imply parallel movements in different quantiles of the wage distribution within skill groups. In order to draw robust inference, block bootstrap covariance estimates are used accounting for dependency of the error term in adjacent cohort–year cells. Acknowledging the possibility of selection effects related to changes in unemployment, a heuristic selection correction is applied. Since Manfacturing and Non–Manufacturing private industries are believed to differ in important aspects, the analysis is also performed separately for the two parts of the economy.

The main findings in this chapter are the following: The results of the uniformity tests indicate that a uniform macroeconomic time trend is present in almost all cases (except for high–skilled workers in the entire economy). However, these trends typically differ slightly across quantiles. For the entire economy, the wage differential between higher and lower skill levels is falling uniformly between low–skilled and medium–skilled workers whereas the situation is mixed between medium–skilled and high–skilled workers. Wages at the 20%–quantile for high–skilled workers grow uniformly less and at the 50%–quantile uniformly more than wages for medium–skilled workers. As a final result for the entire economy, wage inequality within skill groups mostly increased slightly over time. Almost all these results are robust against the heuristic selection correction for unemployment. The exception involves the lower part of the wage distribution for low–skilled workers indicating important selection effects for this group of workers. This finding suggests that the fairly high wage growth in the lower part of the distribution of low–skilled workers has in fact resulted in crowding out of low–ability workers in this group. To substantiate this finding, further research is necessary. However, at this point, the literature has barely started to develop estimators for selection correction in quantile regression problems.

Differentiating between Manufacturing and Non–Manufacturing private industries provides a different perspective to the results for the entire economy. In Manufacturing, wage growth both for low– and high–skilled workers was uniformly higher compared to medium–skilled workers. In Non–Manufacturing, this is also the case for the median, but, just as for the entire economy, all skill differentials were decreasing in the lower part of the within distribution. Also, in Manufacturing wage growth over time tends to be larger than in Non–Manufacturing. Finally, it is also observed for West Germany that wage differentials between young and old workers within a given year tend to rise over time. In the framework of this study, this can be interpreted completely as a cohort effect implying that older cohorts started at higher wage levels compared to younger workers but otherwise experienced the same wage growth due to aging.

Overall, the findings in this chapter mostly confirm the complex patterns found in chapter 2. Despite an increase in overall wage dispersion for full–time working males, skill differentials between low–skilled and medium–skilled workers have narrowed uniformly between 1975 and 1990. One is tempted to interpret this finding as the result of union wage policies striving for lower wage inequality. However, this hypothesis is in confict with the evidence of increasing wage dispersion within the groups of low–skilled and of medium–skilled workers. Especially for low–skilled workers, one would have expected that wages at the lower quantiles should have increased faster. The results, however, also indicate that important selection effects are present here. The trend towards higher within dispersion and the increasing wage differential between medium– and high–skilled workers at the median most likely reflect a skill bias in labor demand. If this is the case, the skill bias operates to a considerable extent via the unobservable ability of the worker. The following chapters will provide more insights on the skill bias of labor demand and on the union wage policy.

3.4 Appendix of Chapter 3

3.4.1 Estimation Results

Table 3.1: Parameter Estimates of Wage Specifications for Entire Economy (Standard Errors in Parentheses - Preferred Final Specification Denoted by *)[a]

Skill Group	(U) Low–Skilled							
Quantile	$\theta = 0.2$				$\theta = 0.5$			
Specificat.	(1)	(2)	(3)*	(4)	(1)	(2)	(3)*	(4)
Inter-cept	4.2349	4.2386	4.2397	4.2016	4.4205	4.4236	4.4254	4.3922
	(.0154)	(.0080)	(.0077)	(.0160)	(.0159)	(.0092)	(.0094)	(.0143)
α	0.2172	0.2123	0.1993	0.2228	0.2133	0.2112	0.1900	0.2067
	(.0272)	(.0207)	(.0137)	(.0234)	(.0281)	(.0228)	(.0168)	(.0193)
α^2	-0.0377	-0.0586	-0.0576	-0.1013	-0.0338	-0.0624	-0.0608	-0.1007
	(.0651)	(.0110)	(.0107)	(.0173)	(.0542)	(.0113)	(.0127)	(.0137)
α^3	0.0014	0.0077	0.0075	0.0141	-0.0006	0.0083	0.0079	0.0146
	(.0138)	(.0022)	(.0022)	(.0037)	(.0114)	(.0022)	(.0025)	(.0029)
t	0.5055	0.5207	0.5329	0.5913	0.5983	0.6115	0.6315	0.6860
	(.0810)	(.0306)	(.0296)	(.0808)	(.0737)	(.0316)	(.0313)	(.0720)
t^2	-1.0427	-1.1056	-1.1077	-1.1122	-1.4190	-1.4756	-1.4790	-1.4885
	(.1744)	(.0830)	(.0838)	(.2029)	(.1659)	(.0851)	(.0875)	(.1772)
t^3	0.8770	0.9279	0.9287	0.9343	1.2745	1.3184	1.3198	1.3280
	(.1315)	(.0857)	(.0868)	(.2077)	(.1288)	(.0875)	(.0885)	(.1794)
t^4	-0.2492	-0.2556	-0.2552	-0.2599	-0.3712	-0.3769	-0.3762	-0.3807
	(.0438)	(.0288)	(.0293)	(.0723)	(.0388)	(.0293)	(.0293)	(.0618)
c_b^2	-0.1066	-0.0944	-0.0749	–	-0.1381	-0.1193	-0.0872	–
	(.0537)	(.0344)	(.0237)		(.0471)	(.0257)	(.0182)	
c_b^3	0.0123	-0.0395	-0.0289	–	-0.0060	-0.0598	-0.0425	–
	(.0903)	(.0260)	(.0201)		(.0765)	(.0161)	(.0130)	
c_b^4	-0.0026	-0.0055	-0.0037	–	-0.0048	-0.0096	-0.0066	–
	(.0099)	(.0060)	(.0049)		(.0077)	(.0033)	(.0028)	
c_a^2	0.0222	0.0141	–	–	0.0270	0.0232	–	–
	(.0311)	(.0237)			(.0349)	(.0286)		
R_1	-0.2283	–	–	–	-0.2525	–	–	–
	(.4111)				(.3442)			
R_2	0.1867	–	–	–	0.1869	–	–	–
	(.2983)				(.2575)			
R_3	0.0823	–	–	–	0.0977	–	–	–
	(.1254)				(.1045)			
R_4	-0.0607	–	–	–	-0.0657	–	–	–
	(.0884)				(.0755)			

a: The estimate of the Covariance Matrix is obtained using a Block Bootstrap Procedure (1000 resamples for skill groups (U) and (M) and 200 resamples for skill group (H)). The blocks allow for dependence across four adjacent time periods and across four adjacent cohorts.

< Table continues on next page >

Table 3.1: < Continued > Parameter Estimates of Wage Specifications for Entire Economy

Skill Group	(U) Low–Skilled				(M) Medium–Skilled			
Quantile	$\theta = 0.8$				$\theta = 0.2$			
Specificat.	(1)	(2)	(3)*	(4)	(1)	(2)	(3)*	(4)
Inter-	4.5845	4.5853	4.5873	4.5551	4.3617	4.3551	4.3551	4.3200
cept	(.0183)	(.0111)	(.0126)	(.0134)	(.0174)	(.0064)	(.0058)	(.0192)
α	0.2140	0.2182	0.1943	0.2087	0.2328	0.2503	0.2499	0.2652
	(.0336)	(.0279)	(.0223)	(.0190)	(.0236)	(.0109)	(.0102)	(.0233)
α^2	0.0127	-0.0691	-0.0673	-0.1058	-0.0551	-0.0923	-0.0922	-0.1162
	(.0649)	(.0148)	(.0175)	(.0147)	(.0501)	(.0081)	(.0085)	(.0172)
α^3	-0.0121	0.0098	0.0094	0.0159	0.0037	0.0140	0.0140	0.0159
	(.0145)	(.0029)	(.0034)	(.0032)	(.0104)	(.0018)	(.0019)	(.0037)
t	0.5979	0.6546	0.6771	0.7317	0.4298	0.4371	0.4374	0.4883
	(.0834)	(.0419)	(.0391)	(.0726)	(.0801)	(.0330)	(.0296)	(.1053)
t^2	-1.4951	-1.6559	-1.6598	-1.6714	-0.9317	-0.9298	-0.9299	-0.9362
	(.1818)	(.0985)	(.1009)	(.1807)	(.1564)	(.0789)	(.0725)	(.2381)
t^3	1.4262	1.5290	1.5307	1.5399	0.7691	0.7515	0.7515	0.7519
	(.1398)	(.1009)	(.0989)	(.1829)	(.1214)	(.0796)	(.0723)	(.2189)
t^4	-0.4356	-0.4473	-0.4464	-0.4510	-0.1966	-0.1943	-0.1943	-0.1954
	(.0414)	(.0346)	(.0325)	(.0632)	(.0372)	(.0274)	(.0244)	(.0700)
c_b^2	-0.1845	-0.1276	-0.0914	–	-0.0726	-0.0430	-0.0425	–
	(.0571)	(.0358)	(.0249)		(.0474)	(.0207)	(.0154)	
c_b^3	0.0601	-0.0665	-0.0470	–	0.0032	-0.0076	-0.0073	–
	(.0810)	(.0232)	(.0197)		(.0517)	(.0163)	(.0125)	
c_b^4	-0.0010	-0.0110	-0.0076	–	0.0066	0.0002	0.0003	–
	(.0091)	(.0048)	(.0046)		(.0069)	(.0038)	(.0029)	
c_a^2	0.0246	0.0261	–	–	-0.0177	0.0003	–	–
	(.0420)	(.0377)			(.0196)	(.0105)		
R_1	-0.6175	–	–	–	-0.1096	–	–	–
	(.3794)				(.2678)			
R_2	0.4244	–	–	–	0.0124	–	–	–
	(.2621)				(.1864)			
R_3	0.2227	–	–	–	0.0575	–	–	–
	(.1245)				(.0807)			
R_4	-0.1432	–	–	–	-0.0195	–	–	–
	(.0842)				(.0547)			

< Table continues on next page >

Table 3.1: < Continued > Parameter Estimates of Wage Specifications for Entire Economy

Skill Group	(M) Medium–Skilled							
Quantile	$\theta = 0.5$				$\theta = 0.8$			
Specificat.	(1)	(2)	(3)*	(4)	(1)	(2)	(3)*	(4)
Inter-cept	4.5225 (.0167)	4.5182 (.0059)	4.5201 (.0064)	4.4765 (.0219)	4.6812 (.0244)	4.6662 (.0087)	4.6690 (.0095)	4.6002 (.0399)
α	0.2947 (.0237)	0.3027 (.0140)	0.2802 (.0107)	0.3008 (.0253)	0.3578 (.0322)	0.3849 (.0197)	0.3530 (.0145)	0.3866 (.0443)
α^2	-0.0369 (.0518)	-0.0967 (.0093)	-0.0929 (.0101)	-0.1239 (.0207)	0.0042 (.0740)	-0.0964 (.0143)	-0.0911 (.0147)	-0.1415 (.0358)
α^3	-0.0010 (.0108)	0.0136 (.0021)	0.0127 (.0023)	0.0153 (.0046)	-0.0099 (.0160)	0.0123 (.0033)	0.0111 (.0034)	0.0149 (.0079)
t	0.4541 (.0753)	0.5016 (.0298)	0.5207 (.0306)	0.5815 (.1235)	0.5056 (.1179)	0.5862 (.0529)	0.6126 (.0587)	0.6797 (.2230)
t^2	-1.1490 (.1451)	-1.2499 (.0765)	-1.2554 (.0800)	-1.2594 (.2819)	-1.4187 (.2315)	-1.5550 (.1395)	-1.5612 (.1506)	-1.4907 (.4982)
t^3	1.0445 (.1144)	1.0970 (.0764)	1.1008 (.0797)	1.0993 (.2632)	1.3952 (.1923)	1.4446 (.1412)	1.4488 (.1501)	1.3802 (.4535)
t^4	-0.3014 (.0400)	-0.3053 (.0252)	-0.3055 (.0266)	-0.3065 (.0852)	-0.4251 (.0667)	-0.4252 (.0479)	-0.4251 (.0508)	-0.4077 (.1431)
c_b^2	-0.1227 (.0530)	-0.0806 (.0319)	-0.0485 (.0253)	–	-0.1924 (.0871)	-0.1251 (.0500)	-0.0793 (.0391)	–
c_b^3	0.0616 (.0568)	-0.0224 (.0274)	-0.0041 (.0243)	–	0.0879 (.0750)	-0.0309 (.0443)	-0.0049 (.0385)	–
c_b^4	0.0060 (.0094)	-0.0016 (.0069)	0.0016 (.0064)	–	0.0112 (.0160)	-0.0015 (.0114)	0.0032 (.0103)	–
c_a^2	0.0155 (.0201)	0.0209 (.0165)	–	–	0.0084 (.0261)	0.0297 (.0220)	–	–
R_1	-0.4057 (.2933)	–	–	–	-0.5735 (.4221)	–	–	–
R_2	0.2711 (.2179)	–	–	–	0.3484 (.3236)	–	–	–
R_3	0.1460 (.0892)	–	–	–	0.2014 (.1295)	–	–	–
R_4	-0.0961 (.0646)	–	–	–	-0.1279 (.0945)	–	–	–

< Table continues on next page >

Table 3.1: < Continued > Parameter Estimates of Wage Specifications for Entire Economy

Skill Group	(H) High–Skilled							
Quantile	$\theta = 0.2$				$\theta = 0.5$			
Specificat.	(1)*	(2)	(3)	(4)	(1)	(2)	(3)	(4)*
Inter-cept	4.5915	4.6175	4.6216	4.6316	4.7731	4.7699	4.7731	4.7656
	(.0679)	(.0470)	(.1355)	(.0769)	(.1096)	(.0700)	(.2841)	(.0894)
α	0.5975	0.4796	0.4270	0.4383	0.4134	0.4259	0.4075	0.4439
	(.0511)	(.0371)	(.0333)	(.0182)	(.1024)	(.0369)	(.0398)	(.0317)
α^2	-0.1794	-0.0777	-0.0847	-0.0839	0.0329	-0.0456	-0.0508	-0.1083
	(.0592)	(.0125)	(.0171)	(.0058)	(.1939)	(.0360)	(.0427)	(.0375)
α^3	–	–	–	–	–	–	–	–
t	0.3212	0.3125	0.3555	0.2934	0.3826	0.3670	0.3719	0.3825
	(.4843)	(.3579)	(.9866)	(.5130)	(.6600)	(.5110)	(2.1371)	(.6018)
t^2	-1.0061	-0.9360	-0.9232	-0.8050	-1.0688	-0.9903	-0.9807	-1.0293
	(1.0658)	(.8361)	(2.2089)	(1.1119)	(1.4023)	(1.1474)	(4.7811)	(1.2891)
t^3	0.8730	0.8289	0.8262	0.7229	1.0699	0.9590	0.9614	1.0318
	(.9079)	(.7410)	(1.9004)	(.9539)	(1.1419)	(.9958)	(4.0975)	(1.0837)
t^4	-0.2377	-0.2316	-0.2318	-0.2011	-0.3230	-0.2827	-0.2848	-0.3116
	(.2636)	(.2210)	(.5531)	(.2803)	(.3210)	(.2918)	(1.1888)	(.3113)
c_b^2	-0.1233	-0.0719	0.0699	–	-0.2933	-0.0861	-0.0078	–
	(.0693)	(.1042)	(.0609)		(.2686)	(.2216)	(.9200)	
c_b^3	-0.1533	-0.0195	0.0327	–	0.0377	-0.0015	0.0215	–
	(.0844)	(.0954)	(.0444)		(.2451)	(.4022)	(4.9800)	
c_b^4	–	–	–	–	–	–	–	–
c_a^2	0.0984	0.0725	–	–	0.0069	0.0207	–	–
	(.0381)	(.0237)			(.0506)	(.0178)		
R_1	0.1871	–	–	–	-0.3940	–	–	–
	(.3466)				(.7405)			
R_2	-0.1496	–	–	–	0.2282	–	–	–
	(.2651)				(.3896)			
R_3	0.1067	–	–	–	0.0584	–	–	–
	(.1027)				(.5664)			
R_4	-0.0420	–	–	–	-0.0840	–	–	–
	(.0989)				(.4221)			

Table 3.2: Parameter Estimates of Wage Specifications for Entire Economy with Selection Correction for Unemployment (Standard Errors in Parentheses - Preferred Final Specification Denoted by *)[a]

Skill Group	(U) Low–Skilled							
Quantile	$\theta = 0.2$				$\theta = 0.5$			
Specificat.	(1)	(2)	(3)*	(4)	(1)	(2)	(3)*	(4)
Inter-cept	4.1918 (.1138)	4.1714 (.0576)	4.1751 (.0464)	4.0410 (.0951)	4.4016 (.0217)	4.3979 (.0092)	4.4004 (.0092)	4.3650 (.0187)
α	0.1794 (.1688)	0.3054 (.1273)	0.2635 (.0972)	0.3493 (.1590)	0.2099 (.0297)	0.2233 (.0214)	0.1942 (.0162)	0.2153 (.0223)
α^2	-0.1218 (.3397)	-0.0041 (.0824)	-0.0002 (.0753)	-0.1237 (.1059)	-0.0153 (.0600)	-0.0637 (.0117)	-0.0610 (.0130)	-0.0985 (.0162)
α^3	-0.0068 (.0805)	0.0012 (.0155)	0.0004 (.0145)	0.0145 (.0212)	-0.0050 (.0122)	0.0090 (.0023)	0.0083 (.0026)	0.0138 (.0034)
t	0.7912 (.6084)	0.2005 (.2392)	0.2401 (.2296)	0.4391 (.4495)	0.6032 (.1081)	0.6151 (.0406)	0.6426 (.0405)	0.6969 (.1014)
t^2	-1.6202 (1.365)	-0.1298 (.9047)	-0.1399 (.8492)	-0.1456 (1.122)	-1.4175 (.2266)	-1.4396 (.1195)	-1.4466 (.1180)	-1.4513 (.2299)
t^3	0.2690 (1.166)	-0.7533 (1.155)	-0.7470 (1.082)	-0.7474 (1.150)	1.1844 (.1894)	1.1857 (.1302)	1.1901 (.1295)	1.1924 (.2138)
t^4	0.3707 (.4079)	0.4762 (.4604)	0.4764 (.4307)	0.4681 (.3967)	-0.3107 (.0638)	-0.3106 (.0467)	-0.3104 (.0470)	-0.3130 (.0683)
c_b^2	-0.0491 (.2699)	-0.2162 (.1348)	-0.1540 (.1044)	–	-0.1402 (.0528)	-0.1076 (.0262)	-0.0643 (.0198)	–
c_b^3	-0.4836 (.5129)	-0.0598 (.0816)	-0.0260 (.0644)	–	-0.0010 (.0785)	-0.0476 (.0170)	-0.0241 (.0146)	–
c_b^4	0.0872 (.0827)	-0.0055 (.0170)	0.0004 (.0128)	–	0.0029 (.0101)	-0.0071 (.0036)	-0.0030 (.0033)	–
c_a^2	-0.1218 (.2231)	0.0445 (.1479)	–	–	0.0153 (.0346)	0.0309 (.0287)	–	–
R_1	2.0772 (2.249)	–	–	–	-0.2502 (.3577)	–	–	–
R_2	-1.9280 (1.819)	–	–	–	0.1238 (.2651)	–	–	–
R_3	-0.2202 (.7003)	–	–	–	0.1123 (.1058)	–	–	–
R_4	0.2634 (.5172)	–	–	–	-0.0601 (.0758)	–	–	–

a: The estimate of the Covariance Matrix is obtained using a Block Bootstrap Procedure (1000 resamples for skill groups (U) and (M) and 200 resamples for skill group (H)). The blocks allow for dependence across four adjacent time periods and across four adjacent cohorts. The selection correction is based on the assumption that unemployed workers would have earned the lowest possible wage, i.e. it is assumed that unemployed workers belong to the lower end of the distribution of unobservables in the wage distribution.

< Table continues on next page >

Table 3.2: < Continued > Parameter Estimates of Wage Specifications for Entire Economy with Selection Correction for Unemployment

Skill Group	(U) Low–Skilled				(M) Medium–Skilled			
Quantile	$\theta = 0.8$				$\theta = 0.2$			
Specificat.	(1)	(2)	(3)*	(4)	(1)	(2)	(3)*	(4)
Inter-	4.5747	4.5740	4.5766	4.5440	4.3350	4.3309	4.3314	4.2956
cept	(.0207)	(.0108)	(.0126)	(.0143)	(.0182)	(.0070)	(.0063)	(.0197)
α	0.2104	0.2197	0.1896	0.2067	0.2471	0.2646	0.2584	0.2724
	(.0363)	(.0271)	(.0228)	(.0203)	(.0243)	(.0146)	(.0119)	(.0263)
α^2	0.0114	-0.0665	-0.0637	-0.0998	-0.0886	-0.0948	-0.0937	-0.1156
	(.0656)	(.0148)	(.0180)	(.0159)	(.0550)	(.0094)	(.0096)	(.0192)
α^3	-0.0124	0.0094	0.0088	0.0145	0.0095	0.0143	0.0141	0.0153
	(.0150)	(.0029)	(.0035)	(.0035)	(.0116)	(.0020)	(.0021)	(.0041)
t	0.6165	0.6542	0.6827	0.7349	0.4887	0.4508	0.4561	0.5089
	(.0865)	(.0368)	(.0360)	(.0769)	(.0836)	(.0337)	(.0299)	(.1071)
t^2	-1.5378	-1.6442	-1.6515	-1.6593	-1.0100	-0.9122	-0.9138	-0.9212
	(.1928)	(.0949)	(.1010)	(.1837)	(.1650)	(.0886)	(.0816)	(.2445)
t^3	1.4058	1.4684	1.4730	1.4773	0.7130	0.6412	0.6423	0.6427
	(.1595)	(.0997)	(.1045)	(.1785)	(.1315)	(.0986)	(.0896)	(.2260)
t^4	-0.4081	-0.4147	-0.4146	-0.4172	-0.1421	-0.1351	-0.1352	-0.1362
	(.0496)	(.0345)	(.0358)	(.0593)	(.0419)	(.0364)	(.0327)	(.0723)
c_b^2	-0.1696	-0.1197	-0.0749	–	-0.0501	-0.0495	-0.0405	–
	(.0556)	(.0355)	(.0257)		(.0549)	(.0226)	(.0164)	
c_b^3	0.0546	-0.0588	-0.0345	–	-0.0436	-0.0113	-0.0063	–
	(.0829)	(.0230)	(.0203)		(.0573)	(.0175)	(.0131)	
c_b^4	0.0042	-0.0094	-0.0052	–	0.0073	-0.0007	0.0003	–
	(.0105)	(.0048)	(.0048)		(.0079)	(.0041)	(.0030)	
c_a^2	0.0239	0.0320	–	–	-0.0130	0.0058	–	–
	(.0454)	(.0376)			(.0201)	(.0139)		
R_1	-0.5443	–	–	–	0.1212	–	–	–
	(.3728)				(.3005)			
R_2	0.3582	–	–	–	-0.1472	–	–	–
	(.2616)				(.2129)			
R_3	0.2144	–	–	–	-0.0006	–	–	–
	(.1277)				(.0922)			
R_4	-0.1354	–	–	–	0.0191	–	–	–
	(.0870)				(.0638)			

< Table continues on next page >

Table 3.2: < Continued > Parameter Estimates of Wage Specifications for Entire Economy with Selection Correction for Unemployment

Skill Group	(M) Medium–Skilled							
Quantile	$\theta = 0.5$				$\theta = 0.8$			
Specificat.	(1)	(2)	(3)*	(4)	(1)	(2)	(3)*	(4)
Inter-cept	4.5119	4.5090	4.5108	4.4698	4.6757	4.6615	4.6644	4.5959
	(.0170)	(.0055)	(.0057)	(.0203)	(.0246)	(.0087)	(.0095)	(.0389)
α	0.2939	0.3015	0.2800	0.2997	0.3611	0.3858	0.3525	0.3857
	(.0238)	(.0132)	(.0099)	(.0252)	(.0328)	(.0203)	(.0149)	(.0434)
α^2	-0.0454	-0.0971	-0.0934	-0.1224	-0.0009	-0.0972	-0.0915	-0.1406
	(.0545)	(.0089)	(.0095)	(.0203)	(.0747)	(.0149)	(.0153)	(.0354)
α^3	-0.0004	0.0134	0.0126	0.0149	-0.0088	0.0123	0.0110	0.0147
	(.0113)	(.0020)	(.0022)	(.0045)	(.0162)	(.0035)	(.0036)	(.0079)
t	0.4863	0.5168	0.5349	0.5910	0.5068	0.5871	0.6145	0.6909
	(.0777)	(.0279)	(.0270)	(.1133)	(.1159)	(.0518)	(.0569)	(.2182)
t^2	-1.1864	-1.2539	-1.2594	-1.2614	-1.4005	-1.5389	-1.5457	-1.5019
	(.1506)	(.0720)	(.0726)	(.2616)	(.2261)	(.1353)	(.1451)	(.4877)
t^3	1.0236	1.0580	1.0619	1.0591	1.3464	1.4000	1.4046	1.3591
	(.1167)	(.0740)	(.0748)	(.2465)	(.1868)	(.1363)	(.1440)	(.4444)
t^4	-0.2791	-0.2815	-0.2817	-0.2823	-0.4020	-0.4030	-0.4030	-0.3922
	(.0403)	(.0249)	(.0256)	(.0804)	(.0646)	(.0459)	(.0485)	(.1405)
c_b^2	-0.1085	-0.0744	-0.0439	–	-0.1878	-0.1237	-0.0762	–
	(.0545)	(.0321)	(.0246)		(.0888)	(.0508)	(.0399)	
c_b^3	0.0539	-0.0194	-0.0021	–	0.0867	-0.0308	-0.0039	–
	(.0614)	(.0276)	(.0237)		(.0756)	(.0452)	(.0394)	
c_b^4	0.0080	-0.0011	0.0020	–	0.0104	-0.0015	0.0033	–
	(.0091)	(.0069)	(.0062)		(.0162)	(.0116)	(.0106)	
c_a^2	0.0143	0.0198	–	–	0.0119	0.0307	–	–
	(.0210)	(.0166)			(.0267)	(.0218)		
R_1	-0.3480	–	–	–	-0.5618	–	–	–
	(.3136)				(.4263)			
R_2	0.2312	–	–	–	0.3480	–	–	–
	(.2317)				(.3284)			
R_3	0.1374	–	–	–	0.1956	–	–	–
	(.0942)				(.1324)			
R_4	-0.0900	–	–	–	-0.1262	–	–	–
	(.0682)				(.0973)			

< Table continues on next page >

Table 3.2: < Continued > Parameter Estimates of Wage Specifications for Entire Economy with Selection Correction for Unemployment

Skill Group	(H) High–Skilled							
Quantile	$\theta = 0.2$				$\theta = 0.5$			
Specificat.	(1)*	(2)	(3)	(4)	(1)	(2)	(3)	(4)*
Inter-cept	4.5492	4.5882	4.5871	4.5446	4.7415	4.7560	4.7592	4.7467
	(.0469)	(.0299)	(.0280)	(.0197)	(.0979)	(.0300)	(.0381)	(.0293)
α	0.6512	0.5586	0.4893	0.4978	0.5985	0.4486	0.4448	0.4446
	(.0450)	(.0305)	(.0218)	(.0174)	(.0748)	(.0298)	(.0364)	(.0275)
α^2	-0.2043	-0.0932	-0.0942	-0.1072	-0.2698	-0.0817	-0.0905	-0.0940
	(.0550)	(.0087)	(.0098)	(.0057)	(.1083)	(.0252)	(.0361)	(.0246)
α^3	–	–	–	–	–	–	–	–
t	0.3846	0.2980	0.3832	0.5256	0.4013	0.3648	0.3830	0.4497
	(.3440)	(.1965)	(.2084)	(.1508)	(.7263)	(.2284)	(.2472)	(.2093)
t^2	-1.2480	-1.0883	-1.1021	-1.3938	-1.1615	-0.9704	-1.0337	-1.1717
	(.7795)	(.4351)	(.5172)	(.3826)	(1.6240)	(.5249)	(.5626)	(.4693)
t^3	1.0887	0.9911	0.9774	1.2702	1.1455	0.9391	1.0137	1.1411
	(.6797)	(.3902)	(.4765)	(.3571)	(1.3945)	(.4639)	(.4972)	(.4037)
t^4	-0.2979	-0.2816	-0.2703	-0.3656	-0.3433	-0.2764	-0.3006	-0.3419
	(.2020)	(.1185)	(.1451)	(.1096)	(.4060)	(.1376)	(.1483)	(.1176)
c_b^2	-0.1128	-0.1640	-0.0054	–	-0.2324	0.0040	0.0669	–
	(.0721)	(.0643)	(.0375)		(.2167)	(.1812)	(.1999)	
c_b^3	-0.1804	-0.0744	0.0005	–	-0.2231	0.0181	0.0368	–
	(.0807)	(.0408)	(.0207)		(.3000)	(1.2814)	(.7814)	
c_b^4	–	–	–	–	–	–	–	–
c_a^2	0.0985	0.0881	–	–	0.0264	0.0135	–	–
	(.0343)	(.0205)			(.0533)	(.0130)		
R_1	0.3216	–	–	–	-0.0940	–	–	–
	(.3333)				(.4881)			
R_2	-0.2634	–	–	–	-0.1755	–	–	–
	(.2437)				(.4863)			
R_3	0.0628	–	–	–	0.4876	–	–	–
	(.0952)				(.6297)			
R_4	0.0053	–	–	–	0.1428	–	–	–
	(.0824)				(.5816)			

Table 3.3: Parameter Estimates of Wage Specifications for Manufacturing (Standard Errors in Parentheses - Preferred Final Specification Denoted by *)[a]

Skill Group	(U) Low–Skilled							
Quantile	$\theta = 0.2$				$\theta = 0.5$			
Specificat.	(1)	(2)	(3)*	(4)	(1)	(2)	(3)*	(4)
Inter-	4.2974	4.2974	4.2995	4.2701	4.4570	4.4613	4.4628	4.4295
cept	(.0217)	(.0093)	(.0096)	(.0147)	(.0173)	(.0101)	(.0104)	(.0138)
α	0.1984	0.1997	0.1749	0.1873	0.1917	0.1861	0.1691	0.1771
	(.0329)	(.0219)	(.0172)	(.0185)	(.0320)	(.0255)	(.0189)	(.0186)
α^2	-0.0394	-0.0640	-0.0621	-0.0927	-0.0342	-0.0585	-0.0572	-0.0905
	(.0694)	(.0122)	(.0136)	(.0139)	(.0614)	(.0133)	(.0147)	(.0136)
α^3	0.0021	0.0090	0.0086	0.0132	0.0005	0.0084	0.0081	0.0133
	(.0147)	(.0025)	(.0028)	(.0030)	(.0126)	(.0026)	(.0029)	(.0029)
t	0.6311	0.6452	0.6688	0.7196	0.6722	0.6857	0.7019	0.7651
	(.1023)	(.0460)	(.0459)	(.0805)	(.0840)	(.0361)	(.0350)	(.0725)
t^2	-1.4818	-1.5198	-1.5246	-1.5365	-1.6413	-1.7025	-1.7058	-1.7268
	(.2071)	(.1150)	(.1183)	(.1949)	(.1839)	(.0930)	(.0967)	(.1822)
t^3	1.3215	1.3420	1.3446	1.3534	1.5006	1.5487	1.5505	1.5641
	(.1540)	(.1130)	(.1151)	(.1906)	(.1412)	(.0947)	(.0973)	(.1863)
t^4	-0.3784	-0.3813	-0.3809	-0.3851	-0.4405	-0.4471	-0.4468	-0.4520
	(.0436)	(.0370)	(.0375)	(.0643)	(.0410)	(.0316)	(.0322)	(.0648)
c_b^2	-0.1427	-0.1104	-0.0728	–	-0.1570	-0.1301	-0.1043	–
	(.0630)	(.0306)	(.0226)		(.0579)	(.0329)	(.0202)	
c_b^3	-0.0506	-0.0569	-0.0365	–	-0.0414	-0.0741	-0.0602	–
	(.0864)	(.0200)	(.0166)		(.0815)	(.0223)	(.0152)	
c_b^4	-0.0100	-0.0096	-0.0061	–	-0.0127	-0.0134	-0.0110	–
	(.0098)	(.0041)	(.0036)		(.0091)	(.0049)	(.0035)	
c_a^2	0.0214	0.0273	–	–	0.0232	0.0187	–	–
	(.0392)	(.0192)			(.0412)	(.0286)		
R_1	-0.1184	–	–	–	-0.2067	–	–	–
	(.3967)				(.3800)			
R_2	0.0387	–	–	–	0.1394	–	–	–
	(.2728)				(.2765)			
R_3	0.0398	–	–	–	0.0737	–	–	–
	(.1248)				(.1138)			
R_4	-0.0077	–	–	–	-0.0410	–	–	–
	(.0851)				(.0814)			

a: The estimate of the Covariance Matrix is obtained using a Block Bootstrap Procedure (1000 resamples for skill groups (U) and (M) and 200 resamples for skill group (H)). The blocks allow for dependence across four adjacent time periods and across four adjacent cohorts.

< Table continues on next page >

Table 3.3: < Continued > Parameter Estimates of Wage Specifications for Manufacturing

Skill Group	(U) Low–Skilled				(M) Medium–Skilled			
Quantile	$\theta = 0.8$				$\theta = 0.2$			
Specificat.	(1)	(2)	(3)*	(4)	(1)	(2)	(3)*	(4)
Inter-cept	4.6008	4.6027	4.6044	4.5740	4.4040	4.4055	4.4062	4.2701
	(.0235)	(.0122)	(.0133)	(.0122)	(.0152)	(.0062)	(.0058)	(.0147)
α	0.2002	0.2009	0.1817	0.1870	0.2385	0.2370	0.2287	0.1873
	(.0424)	(.0310)	(.0240)	(.0197)	(.0194)	(.0103)	(.0086)	(.0185)
α^2	-0.0125	-0.0703	-0.0689	-0.0985	-0.0663	-0.0849	-0.0835	-0.0927
	(.0761)	(.0165)	(.0189)	(.0151)	(.0425)	(.0077)	(.0077)	(.0139)
α^3	-0.0045	0.0112	0.0109	0.0156	0.0077	0.0133	0.0130	0.0132
	(.0157)	(.0032)	(.0037)	(.0033)	(.0086)	(.0016)	(.0016)	(.0030)
t	0.6787	0.7200	0.7382	0.7978	0.4935	0.5032	0.5102	0.7196
	(.1005)	(.0427)	(.0391)	(.0663)	(.0727)	(.0319)	(.0306)	(.0805)
t^2	-1.6997	-1.8237	-1.8274	-1.8491	-1.1506	-1.1830	-1.1849	-1.5365
	(.2195)	(.1082)	(.1113)	(.1720)	(.1402)	(.0817)	(.0794)	(.1949)
t^3	1.6078	1.6903	1.6923	1.7059	1.0001	1.0222	1.0234	1.3534
	(.1633)	(.1120)	(.1128)	(.1778)	(.1099)	(.0823)	(.0793)	(.1906)
t^4	-0.4859	-0.4951	-0.4947	-0.4996	-0.2801	-0.2823	-0.2823	-0.3851
	(.0470)	(.0385)	(.0379)	(.0620)	(.0348)	(.0278)	(.0265)	(.0643)
c_b^2	-0.1711	-0.1306	-0.1015	–	-0.0666	-0.0506	-0.0388	–
	(.0648)	(.0382)	(.0240)		(.0406)	(.0192)	(.0137)	
c_b^3	0.0185	-0.0763	-0.0606	–	0.0178	-0.0107	-0.0040	–
	(.0996)	(.0244)	(.0174)		(.0490)	(.0138)	(.0112)	
c_b^4	-0.0073	-0.0140	-0.0113	–	0.0017	-0.0007	0.0005	–
	(.0107)	(.0050)	(.0038)		(.0068)	(.0031)	(.0026)	
c_a^2	0.0231	0.0211	–	–	0.0090	0.0076	–	–
	(.0526)	(.0406)			(.0202)	(.0115)		
R_1	-0.4602	–	–	–	-0.1500	–	–	–
	(.4593)				(.2321)			
R_2	0.3257	–	–	–	0.1048	–	–	–
	(.3283)				(.1697)			
R_3	0.1648	–	–	–	0.0576	–	–	–
	(.1424)				(.0685)			
R_4	-0.1079	–	–	–	-0.0367	–	–	–
	(.1008)				(.0491)			

< Table continues on next page >

Table 3.3: < Continued > Parameter Estimates of Wage Specifications for Manufacturing

Skill Group	(M) Medium–Skilled							
Quantile	$\theta = 0.5$				$\theta = 0.8$			
Specificat.	(1)	(2)	(3)*	(4)	(1)	(2)	(3)*	(4)
Inter-cept	4.5587 (.0147)	4.5587 (.0057)	4.5598 (.0060)	4.4295 (.0138)	4.6964 (.0261)	4.6884 (.0093)	4.6915 (.0100)	4.5740 (.0122)
α	0.2697 (.0205)	0.2696 (.0112)	0.2570 (.0092)	0.1771 (.0186)	0.3096 (.0335)	0.3322 (.0212)	0.2965 (.0167)	0.1870 (.0197)
α^2	-0.0428 (.0453)	-0.0808 (.0084)	-0.0787 (.0090)	-0.0905 (.0136)	0.0215 (.0821)	-0.0629 (.0157)	-0.0569 (.0164)	-0.0985 (.0151)
α^3	0.0021 (.0098)	0.0118 (.0018)	0.0113 (.0020)	0.0133 (.0029)	-0.0140 (.0178)	0.0070 (.0035)	0.0057 (.0037)	0.0156 (.0033)
t	0.5357 (.0698)	0.5677 (.0273)	0.5782 (.0273)	0.7651 (.0725)	0.6297 (.1396)	0.6611 (.0595)	0.6907 (.0673)	0.7978 (.0663)
t^2	-1.3852 (.1364)	-1.4646 (.0709)	-1.4675 (.0726)	-1.7268 (.1822)	-1.7112 (.2836)	-1.7565 (.1591)	-1.7632 (.1757)	-1.8491 (.1720)
t^3	1.2792 (.1111)	1.3276 (.0712)	1.3295 (.0731)	1.5641 (.1863)	1.6470 (.2364)	1.6426 (.1601)	1.6465 (.1744)	1.7059 (.1778)
t^4	-0.3745 (.0370)	-0.3790 (.0237)	-0.3790 (.0244)	-0.4520 (.0648)	-0.4981 (.0770)	-0.4877 (.0539)	-0.4872 (.0584)	-0.4996 (.0620)
c_b^2	-0.0883 (.0448)	-0.0587 (.0251)	-0.0409 (.0192)	–	-0.1605 (.0940)	-0.1105 (.0468)	-0.0596 (.0372)	–
c_b^3	0.0559 (.0460)	-0.0037 (.0200)	0.0063 (.0173)	–	0.0901 (.0795)	-0.0200 (.0400)	0.0087 (.0360)	–
c_b^4	0.0056 (.0090)	0.0018 (.0048)	0.0036 (.0044)	–	0.0160 (.0166)	0.0001 (.0101)	0.0052 (.0097)	–
c_a^2	0.0127 (.0213)	0.0115 (.0134)	–	–	0.0172 (.0330)	0.0328 (.0196)	–	–
R_1	-0.2953 (.2367)	–	–	–	-0.5020 (.4570)	–	–	–
R_2	0.2086 (.1683)	–	–	–	0.3199 (.3274)	–	–	–
R_3	0.1032 (.0746)	–	–	–	0.2004 (.1424)	–	–	–
R_4	-0.0690 (.0501)	–	–	–	-0.1322 (.0976)	–	–	–

< Table continues on next page >

Table 3.3: < Continued > Parameter Estimates of Wage Specifications for Manufacturing

Skill Group	(H) High–Skilled							
Quantile	$\theta = 0.2$				$\theta = 0.5$			
Specificat.	(1)	(2)	(3)*	(4)	(1)	(2)	(3)	(4)*
Inter-cept	4.6687	4.6649	4.6631	4.6691	4.8171	4.8126	4.8089	4.8071
	(.0695)	(.0830)	(.0870)	(.0652)	(.2132)	(.1096)	(.1833)	(.1232)
α	0.3695	0.4285	0.4219	0.4176	0.3487	0.4096	0.4966	0.4504
	(.0767)	(.0337)	(.0276)	(.0171)	(.1281)	(.0649)	(.0730)	(.0374)
α^2	-0.0364	-0.0893	-0.1025	-0.0908	0.0410	-0.0632	-0.1978	-0.1010
	(.1121)	(.0128)	(.0172)	(.0095)	(.3091)	(.0908)	(.1002)	(.0591)
α^3	–	–	–	–	–	–	–	–
t	0.5129	0.4533	0.3983	0.5060	0.3525	0.2985	0.2530	0.2627
	(.5144)	(.6221)	(.6393)	(.4992)	(1.5986)	(.7899)	(1.3702)	(.9152)
t^2	-1.2597	-1.1440	-0.9002	-1.2182	-0.9155	-0.7592	-0.7540	-0.6821
	(1.1544)	(1.4077)	(1.4350)	(1.1344)	(3.5893)	(1.7476)	(3.0715)	(2.0399)
t^3	1.1909	1.0900	0.8411	1.1161	0.9735	0.7888	0.8665	0.7211
	(1.0015)	(1.2169)	(1.2390)	(.9858)	(3.0746)	(1.4986)	(2.6427)	(1.7501)
t^4	-0.3405	-0.3213	-0.2402	-0.3162	-0.2952	-0.2352	-0.2817	-0.2191
	(.2961)	(.3556)	(.3622)	(.2894)	(.8929)	(.4363)	(.7698)	(.5089)
c_b^2	0.0867	0.0409	0.1822	–	-0.3385	-0.2373	0.3010	–
	(.2483)	(.1261)	(.0728)		(1.1720)	(1.0555)	(.8254)	
c_b^3	0.0535	0.0235	0.0647	–	-0.0487	-0.0733	0.0344	–
	(.2950)	(.1791)	(.0296)		(.3846)	(.3781)	(.3263)	
c_b^4	–	–	–	–	–	–	–	–
c_a^2	-0.0125	0.0242	–	–	-0.0426	-0.0170	–	–
	(.0404)	(.0203)			(.0764)	(.0351)		
R_1	0.0660	–	–	–	-0.1827	–	–	–
	(.7240)				(1.2827)			
R_2	-0.1278	–	–	–	0.0351	–	–	–
	(.4729)				(.7902)			
R_3	-0.1037	–	–	–	0.0246	–	–	–
	(.2756)				(1.0896)			
R_4	0.0690	–	–	–	-0.0618	–	–	–
	(.2217)				(1.2114)			

Table 3.4: Parameter Estimates of Wage Specifications for Non-Manufacturing (Standard Errors in Parentheses – Preferred Final Specification Denoted by *)[a]

Skill Group	(U) Low–Skilled							
Quantile	$\theta = 0.2$				$\theta = 0.5$			
Specificat.	(1)	(2)	(3)*	(4)	(1)	(2)	(3)*	(4)
Inter-cept	4.2008	4.1885	4.1878	4.1224	4.3748	4.3721	4.3729	4.3357
	(.0259)	(.0128)	(.0121)	(.0337)	(.0228)	(.0127)	(.0123)	(.0196)
α	0.1359	0.1561	0.1650	0.2142	0.1940	0.2015	0.1911	0.2257
	(.0464)	(.0324)	(.0230)	(.0475)	(.0369)	(.0312)	(.0207)	(.0292)
α^2	0.0858	-0.0027	-0.0034	-0.0763	0.0555	-0.0464	-0.0456	-0.0941
	(.1136)	(.0204)	(.0201)	(.0351)	(.0847)	(.0165)	(.0169)	(.0226)
α^3	-0.0188	-0.0015	-0.0013	0.0086	-0.0198	0.0047	0.0045	0.0119
	(.0256)	(.0043)	(.0043)	(.0075)	(.0190)	(.0034)	(.0035)	(.0048)
t	0.2306	0.3297	0.3215	0.4138	0.3932	0.4853	0.4949	0.5415
	(.1462)	(.0594)	(.0590)	(.1637)	(.1148)	(.0546)	(.0527)	(.1048)
t^2	-0.2888	-0.4767	-0.4759	-0.4697	-0.7506	-0.9807	-0.9816	-0.9707
	(.3195)	(.1613)	(.1684)	(.3970)	(.2385)	(.1355)	(.1353)	(.2566)
t^3	0.1922	0.2787	0.2790	0.2806	0.6688	0.8114	0.8111	0.8091
	(.2542)	(.1713)	(.1791)	(.3949)	(.1961)	(.1338)	(.1326)	(.2554)
t^4	-0.0449	-0.0511	-0.0518	-0.0596	-0.2065	-0.2217	-0.2210	-0.2252
	(.0787)	(.0603)	(.0629)	(.1348)	(.0689)	(.0438)	(.0433)	(.0867)
c_b^2	-0.1266	-0.0660	-0.0796	–	-0.1162	-0.0553	-0.0394	–
	(.1129)	(.0680)	(.0447)		(.0796)	(.0549)	(.0370)	
c_b^3	0.1062	-0.0024	-0.0098	–	0.1713	-0.0056	0.0031	–
	(.1456)	(.0525)	(.0383)		(.1099)	(.0421)	(.0332)	
c_b^4	0.0084	0.0031	0.0018	–	0.0140	0.0021	0.0036	–
	(.0202)	(.0123)	(.0093)		(.0157)	(.0098)	(.0083)	
c_a^2	-0.0274	-0.0095	–	–	0.0120	0.0112	–	–
	(.0507)	(.0356)			(.0454)	(.0426)		
R_1	-0.5345	–	–	–	-0.7978	–	–	–
	(.7062)				(.5151)			
R_2	0.3279	–	–	–	0.5785	–	–	–
	(.5005)				(.3799)			
R_3	0.1578	–	–	–	0.2725	–	–	–
	(.2329)				(.1647)			
R_4	-0.0978	–	–	–	-0.1904	–	–	–
	(.1613)				(.1158)			

a: The estimate of the Covariance Matrix is obtained using a Block Bootstrap Procedure (1000 resamples for skill groups (U) and (M) and 200 resamples for skill group (H)). The blocks allow for dependence across four adjacent time periods and across four adjacent cohorts.

< Table continues on next page >

Table 3.4: < Continued > Parameter Estimates of Wage Specifications for Non–Manufacturing

Skill Group	(U) Low–Skilled				(M) Medium–Skilled			
Quantile	$\theta = 0.8$				$\theta = 0.2$			
Specificat.	(1)	(2)	(3)*	(4)	(1)	(2)	(3)*	(4)
Inter-	4.5494	4.5546	4.5572	4.5259	4.3306	4.3211	4.3202	4.2822
cept	(.0288)	(.0161)	(.0176)	(.0141)	(.0168)	(.0094)	(.0093)	(.0216)
α	0.2236	0.2196	0.1884	0.2218	0.2061	0.2352	0.2460	0.2605
	(.0486)	(.0367)	(.0278)	(.0278)	(.0275)	(.0166)	(.0143)	(.0278)
α^2	0.0375	-0.0578	-0.0555	-0.0973	-0.0521	-0.0885	-0.0903	-0.1138
	(.1024)	(.0232)	(.0238)	(.0234)	(.0653)	(.0109)	(.0119)	(.0204)
α^3	-0.0197	0.0066	0.0061	0.0123	0.0023	0.0140	0.0144	0.0157
	(.0241)	(.0050)	(.0050)	(.0052)	(.0159)	(.0024)	(.0026)	(.0044)
t	0.5201	0.5893	0.6179	0.6530	0.3531	0.3374	0.3282	0.3857
	(.1406)	(.0771)	(.0746)	(.0848)	(.0773)	(.0461)	(.0452)	(.1111)
t^2	-1.2020	-1.4211	-1.4237	-1.4084	-0.5369	-0.4744	-0.4717	-0.4818
	(.3053)	(.1788)	(.1832)	(.2432)	(.1588)	(.1038)	(.1034)	(.2570)
t^3	1.1367	1.2938	1.2928	1.2878	0.3130	0.2508	0.2489	0.2510
	(.2547)	(.1798)	(.1834)	(.2654)	(.1167)	(.1027)	(.0997)	(.2405)
t^4	-0.3585	-0.3788	-0.3765	-0.3795	-0.0353	-0.0296	-0.0294	-0.0309
	(.0801)	(.0613)	(.0621)	(.0953)	(.0337)	(.0354)	(.0333)	(.0777)
c_b^2	-0.1297	-0.0651	-0.0175	–	-0.0578	-0.0273	-0.0431	–
	(.0925)	(.0631)	(.0498)		(.0604)	(.0270)	(.0193)	
c_b^3	0.1640	-0.0098	0.0161	–	-0.0234	0.0038	-0.0052	–
	(.1236)	(.0489)	(.0450)		(.0682)	(.0202)	(.0150)	
c_b^4	0.0135	0.0015	0.0060	–	0.0110	0.0023	0.0007	–
	(.0207)	(.0114)	(.0113)		(.0093)	(.0046)	(.0034)	
c_a^2	0.0441	0.0335	–	–	-0.0416	-0.0101	–	–
	(.0467)	(.0395)			(.0263)	(.0172)		
R_1	-0.8161	–	–	–	0.0260	–	–	–
	(.5702)				(.3632)			
R_2	0.6028	–	–	–	-0.1335	–	–	–
	(.3992)				(.2458)			
R_3	0.2943	–	–	–	0.0297	–	–	–
	(.1984)				(.1265)			
R_4	-0.2007	–	–	–	0.0161	–	–	–
	(.1362)				(.0815)			

< Table continues on next page >

Table 3.4: < Continued > Parameter Estimates of Wage Specifications for Non–Manufacturing

Skill Group	(M) Medium–Skilled							
Quantile	$\theta = 0.5$				$\theta = 0.8$			
Specificat.	(1)	(2)	(3)*	(4)	(1)	(2)	(3)*	(4)
Inter-cept	4.4986	4.4892	4.4908	4.4545	4.6626	4.6396	4.6413	4.5696
	(.0196)	(.0082)	(.0084)	(.0192)	(.0291)	(.0131)	(.0136)	(.0427)
α	0.3057	0.3223	0.3022	0.3198	0.4237	0.4614	0.4407	0.4815
	(.0321)	(.0169)	(.0128)	(.0204)	(.0421)	(.0241)	(.0183)	(.0451)
α^2	-0.0323	-0.1108	-0.1074	-0.1393	-0.0223	-0.1392	-0.1358	-0.2068
	(.0714)	(.0120)	(.0122)	(.0168)	(.0938)	(.0178)	(.0184)	(.0351)
α^3	-0.0028	0.0153	0.0145	0.0185	-0.0037	0.0188	0.0181	0.0272
	(.0161)	(.0027)	(.0028)	(.0038)	(.0205)	(.0041)	(.0043)	(.0078)
t	0.3825	0.4483	0.4653	0.5183	0.4407	0.5517	0.5686	0.6367
	(.0857)	(.0432)	(.0414)	(.1059)	(.1347)	(.0774)	(.0791)	(.2310)
t^2	-0.8602	-0.9856	-0.9905	-0.9988	-1.2173	-1.3908	-1.3948	-1.3192
	(.1740)	(.1008)	(.1002)	(.2420)	(.2687)	(.1874)	(.1884)	(.5125)
t^3	0.7351	0.7927	0.7963	0.7987	1.2067	1.2633	1.2661	1.1943
	(.1341)	(.0975)	(.0967)	(.2255)	(.2158)	(.1816)	(.1797)	(.4637)
t^4	-0.1989	-0.2032	-0.2034	-0.2050	-0.3665	-0.3660	-0.3659	-0.3473
	(.0451)	(.0314)	(.0315)	(.0728)	(.0752)	(.0598)	(.0588)	(.1455)
c_b^2	-0.1546	-0.0945	-0.0653	–	-0.2432	-0.1622	-0.1320	–
	(.0685)	(.0399)	(.0299)		(.0955)	(.0601)	(.0441)	
c_b^3	0.0482	-0.0388	-0.0220	–	0.0682	-0.0549	-0.0377	–
	(.0761)	(.0339)	(.0287)		(.1091)	(.0513)	(.0418)	
c_b^4	0.0025	-0.0051	-0.0021	–	0.0057	-0.0049	-0.0018	–
	(.0110)	(.0084)	(.0075)		(.0187)	(.0129)	(.0110)	
c_a^2	0.0047	0.0187	–	–	-0.0112	0.0193	–	–
	(.0278)	(.0191)			(.0355)	(.0309)		
R_1	-0.4585	–	–	–	-0.6085	–	–	–
	(.3979)				(.5458)			
R_2	0.2759	–	–	–	0.3467	–	–	–
	(.2770)				(.4120)			
R_3	0.1583	–	–	–	0.1913	–	–	–
	(.1315)				(.1725)			
R_4	-0.0955	–	–	–	-0.1178	–	–	–
	(.0893)				(.1244)			

< Table continues on next page >

Table 3.4: < Continued > Parameter Estimates of Wage Specifications for Non–Manufacturing

Skill Group	(H) High–Skilled							
Quantile	$\theta = 0.2$				$\theta = 0.5$			
Specificat.	(1)	(2)	(3)	(4)*	(1)	(2)	(3)	(4)*
Inter-	4.6052	4.6110	4.6155	4.6174	4.7546	4.7489	4.7561	4.7376
cept	(.0674)	(.0472)	(.0433)	(.0547)	(.0442)	(.2553)	(.0976)	(.0924)
α	0.5742	.6145	0.4873	.4865	.6275	0.7358	0.6116	.5758
	(.0647)	(.0750)	(.0243)	(.0182)	(.0956)	(.1157)	(.0604)	(.0209)
α^2	-0.2220	-.1336	-0.0959	-.0976	.0081	-0.2562	-0.1798	-.1443
	(.0925)	(.0253)	(.0126)	(.0073)	(.2260)	(.0857)	(.0597)	(.0072)
α^3	–	–	–	–	–	–	–	–
t	0.1527	.0566	0.2463	.1282	.2828	0.3370	0.3249	.5774
	(.5255)	(.3808)	(.3232)	(.4144)	(.3094)	(1.8020)	(.6633)	(.6644)
t^2	-0.4807	-.3474	-0.7388	-.3105	-.8549	-1.0610	-0.8797	-1.4472
	(1.1851)	(.8759)	(.7528)	(.9389)	(.6792)	(3.9330)	(1.4301)	(1.4670)
t^3	0.3629	.2967	0.6936	.2324	.8441	0.9975	0.8093	1.2797
	(1.0319)	(.7815)	(.6727)	(.8190)	(.5831)	(3.3384)	(1.2155)	(1.2567)
t^4	-0.0635	-.0747	-0.2023	-.0490	-.2519	-0.2845	-0.2224	-.3541
	(.3031)	(.2334)	(.2021)	(.2418)	(.1682)	(.9641)	(.3534)	(.3659)
c_b^2	0.0278	-.5500	0.0412	–	-.6064	-6.1317	0.1834	–
	(.1658)	(.4468)	(.1178)		(.3390)	(4.6620)	(.5641)	
c_b^3	-0.2260	-.7078	0.0293	–	.0169	-27.114	0.0641	–
	(.1835)	(.6408)	(.1654)		(.5455)	(22.2318)	(.7627)	
c_b^4	–	–	–	–	–	–	–	–
c_a^2	0.0081	.0582	–	–	.0232	0.0385	–	–
	(.0510)	(.0377)			(.0606)	(.0323)		
R_1	0.7276	–	–	–	-1.0335	–	–	–
	(.5634)				(.9333)			
R_2	-0.6395	–	–	–	.5937	–	–	–
	(.4061)				(.5991)			
R_3	-0.0923	–	–	–	.3546	–	–	–
	(.1553)				(.3269)			
R_4	0.1531	–	–	–	-.2678	–	–	–
	(.1401)				(.3043)			

Table 3.5: Tests of Wage Growth Hypothesis – χ^2–Wald–Statistics Obtained Using Block Bootstrap Procedure[a]

Skill Group	(U) Low			(M) Medium			(H) High	
$\theta =$	0.2	0.5	0.8	0.2	0.5	0.8	0.2	0.5
Entire Economy								
$H_{UI} : R_1 - R_4 = 0$ (Spec. 1)	1.16 (.88)	1.84 (.76)	4.70 (.31)	2.20 (.69)	2.85 (.58)	3.29 (.50)	12.05 (.02)	.63 (.96)
$H_U : R_1 - R_4 = 0$, $K_a(c) = 0$ (Spec. 1)	2.86 (.72)	3.65 (.59)	7.16 (.20)	2.30 (.80)	9.45 (.09)	5.82 (.32)	34.04 (.00)	1.69 (.89)
$H_U : K_a(c) = 0$ (Spec. 2)	.35 (.55)	.65 (.41)	.47 (.48)	.001 (.97)	1.61 (.20)	1.82 (.18)	9.37 (.00)	1.36 (.24)
$K_b(c) = 0$, $H_U : K_a(c) = 0$ (Spec. 2)	59.14 (.00)	65.76 (.00)	40.71 (.00)	67.38 (.00)	109.9 (.00)	122.0 (.00)	15.59 (.00)	1.37 (.71)
$K_b(c) = 0$ (Spec. 3)	58.45 (.00)	48.78 (.00)	29.77 (.00)	87.73 (.00)	77.60 (.00)	81.67 (.00)	1.34 (.51)	.00 (1.00)
Entire Economy with Selection Correction for Unemployment								
$H_{UI} : R_1 - R_4 = 0$ (Spec. 1)	2.64 (.61)	2.10 (.71)	3.42 (.48)	2.56 (.63)	2.75 (.59)	2.91 (.57)	34.74 (.00)	7.43 (.11)
$H_U : R_1 - R_4 = 0$, $K_a(c) = 0$ (Spec. 1)	2.77 (.73)	4.10 (.53)	6.01 (.30)	3.38 (.64)	8.27 (.14)	5.58 (.34)	55.11 (.00)	10.49 (.06)
$H_U : K_a(c) = 0$ (Spec. 2)	.09 (.76)	1.16 (.28)	.72 (.39)	.17 (.67)	1.42 (.23)	1.98 (.15)	18.53 (.00)	1.08 (.30)
$K_b(c) = 0$, $H_U : K_a(c) = 0$ (Spec. 2)	16.66 (.00)	66.73 (.00)	38.91 (.00)	57.01 (.00)	94.81 (.00)	116.28 (.00)	22.24 (.00)	1.16 (.76)
$K_b(c) = 0$ (Spec. 3)	19.13 (.00)	38.21 (.00)	22.82 (.00)	62.68 (.00)	72.38 (.00)	75.30 (.00)	.13 (.94)	.11 (.95)
Manufacturing								
$H_{UI} : R_1 - R_4 = 0$ (Spec. 1)	1.59 (.81)	2.68 (.61)	2.54 (.63)	1.21 (.87)	2.26 (.68)	2.63 (.61)	1.71 (.79)	.15 (1.00)
$H_U : R_1 - R_4 = 0$, $K_a(c) = 0$ (Spec. 1)	2.60 (.76)	3.55 (.61)	3.95 (.55)	2.78 (.73)	5.65 (.34)	4.83 (.43)	2.33 (.80)	.58 (.99)
$H_U : K_a(c) = 0$ (Spec. 2)	2.02 (.15)	.42 (.51)	.26 (.60)	.45 (.50)	.74 (.38)	2.80 (.09)	1.43 (.23)	.23 (.63)
$K_b(c) = 0$, $H_U : K_a(c) = 0$ (Spec. 2)	34.03 (.00)	38.88 (.00)	27.62 (.00)	83.47 (.00)	112.0 (.00)	101.1 (.00)	4.34 (.23)	.44 (.93)
$K_b(c) = 0$ (Spec. 3)	24.54 (.00)	38.12 (.00)	22.25 (.00)	99.15 (.00)	101.3 (.00)	59.62 (.00)	6.46 (.04)	1.01 (.60)

< Table continues on next page >

Table 3.5: < Continued > Tests of Wage Growth Hypothesis – χ^2–Wald–Statistics Obtained Using a Block Bootstrap Procedure[a]

Skill Group	(U) Low			(M) Medium			(H) High	
$\theta =$	0.2	0.5	0.8	0.2	0.5	0.8	0.2	0.5
Non–Manufacturing								
$H_{UI}: R_1 - R_4 = 0$ (Spec. 1)	.86 (.92)	2.80 (.59)	3.75 (.44)	4.88 (.29)	1.73 (.78)	3.25 (.51)	5.91 (.21)	2.87 (.58)
$H_U: R_1 - R_4 = 0$, $K_a(c) = 0$ (Spec. 1)	.86 (.97)	4.19 (.52)	7.55 (.18)	7.55 (.18)	5.59 (.34)	4.02 (.54)	7.56 (.18)	8.11 (.15)
$H_U: K_a(c) = 0$ (Spec. 2)	.07 (.78)	.06 (.79)	.71 (.39)	.34 (.55)	.96 (.32)	.39 (.53)	2.37 (.12)	1.42 (.23)
$K_b(c) = 0$, $H_U: K_a(c) = 0$ (Spec. 2)	32.80 (.00)	29.76 (.00)	16.19 (.00)	34.70 (.00)	52.29 (.00)	80.24 (.00)	2.41 (.49)	3.11 (.38)
$K_b(c) = 0$ (Spec. 3)	43.93 (.00)	27.03 (.00)	9.41 (.01)	47.58 (.00)	50.38 (.00)	82.51 (.00)	.33 (.85)	.16 (.93)

a: Test statistics are based on the specifications (Specification number in parenthesis) presented in tables 3.1–3.4. The Block Bootstrap Covariance estimates are obtained as described in these previous tables (P–Values are in Parenthesis).

Table 3.6: Tests of Uniformity of Coefficient Estimates across Quantiles – χ^2–Wald–Statistics Obtained Using a Block Bootstrap Procedure for Final Specification[a]

Skill Group	(U) Low		(M) Medium		(H) High
Hypothesis	50% – 20%	80% – 50%	50% – 20%	80% – 50%	50% – 20%
Entire Economy					
Age Profile	9.03 (.02)	.83 (.84)	38.82 (.00)	600.5 (.00)	3.13 (.21)
Time Trend	60.03 (.00)	30.30 (.00)	68.84 (.00)	49.54 (.00)	7.76 (.10)
Cyclical Time Effect	37.80 (.00)	25.85 (.01)	45.64 (.00)	65.90 (.00)	0.23 (1.00)
K_b Profile	.97 (.61)	.16 (.92)	4.13 (.13)	45.93 (.00)	0.67 (.72)
K_a Profile	–	–	–	–	2.02 (.15)

< Table continues on next page >

Table 3.6: < Continued > Tests of Uniformity of Coefficient Estimates across Quantiles – χ^2–Wald–Statistics Obtained Using a Block Bootstrap Procedure for Final Specification[a]

Skill Group	(U) Low		(M) Medium		(H) High
Hypothesis	50% – 20%	80% – 50%	50% – 20%	80% – 50%	50% – 20%
Entire Economy with Selection Correction for Unemployment					
Age Profile	14.04 (.00)	2.29 (.51)	25.51 (.00)	450.2 (.00)	2.80 (.25)
Time Trend	43.27 (.00)	58.22 (.00)	90.09 (.00)	47.06 (.00)	15.25 (.00)
Cyclical Time Effect	6.94 (.80)	21.34 (.02)	34.31 (.00)	64.16 (.00)	11.59 (.39)
K_b Profile	12.05 (.00)	.89 (.63)	2.77 (.24)	40.97 (.00)	0.30 (.86)
K_a Profile	–	–	–	–	1.27 (.26)
Manufacturing					
Age Profile	1.07 (.78)	2.64 (.44)	118.2 (.00)	139.1 (.00)	0.95 (.62)
Time Trend	15.87 (.00)	15.33 (.00)	104.6 (.00)	17.46 (.00)	9.64 (.05)
Cyclical Time Effect	36.55 (.00)	17.81 (.09)	56.51 (.00)	35.38 (.00)	5.84 (.88)
K_b Profile	2.17 (.34)	.61 (.74)	17.52 (.00)	11.64 (.00)	0.78 (.68)
Non–Manufacturing					
Age Profile	24.15 (.00)	3.71 (.29)	54.27 (.00)	428.3 (.00)	28.72 (.00)
Time Trend	33.04 (.00)	20.92 (.00)	60.92 (.00)	44.63 (.00)	38.90 (.00)
Cyclical Time Effect	22.66 (.02)	14.17 (.22)	65.41 (.00)	42.50 (.00)	9.78 (.55)
K_b Profile	7.31 (.03)	.89 (.64)	1.01 (.60)	57.62 (.00)	–

a: Test statistics are based on the final specifications presented in tables 3.1–3.4, except for (H) at the 50% quantile. In the latter case, the tests always refer to the final specification for the 20% quantile (specification number in parenthesis). The Block Bootstrap Covariance estimates are obtained as described in these previous tables. (P–Values are in Parenthesis.)

3.4.2 Illustration of Estimated Wage Profiles

Figure 3.1: Pure Life–Cycle Wage Profiles for Skill Group (U) at Different Quantiles (Final Specification – Manufacturing)

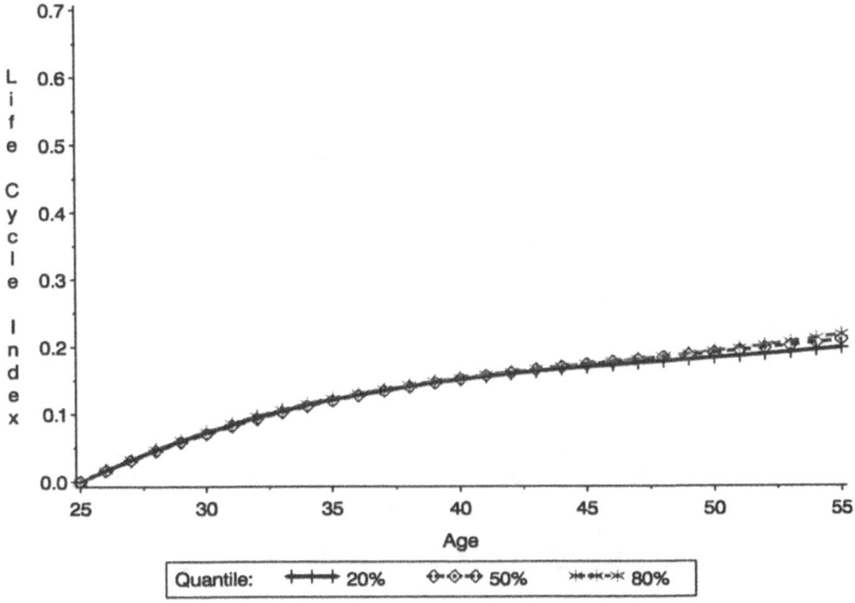

Figure 3.2: Pure Life–Cycle Wage Profiles for Skill Group (M) at Different Quantiles (Final Specification – Manufacturing)

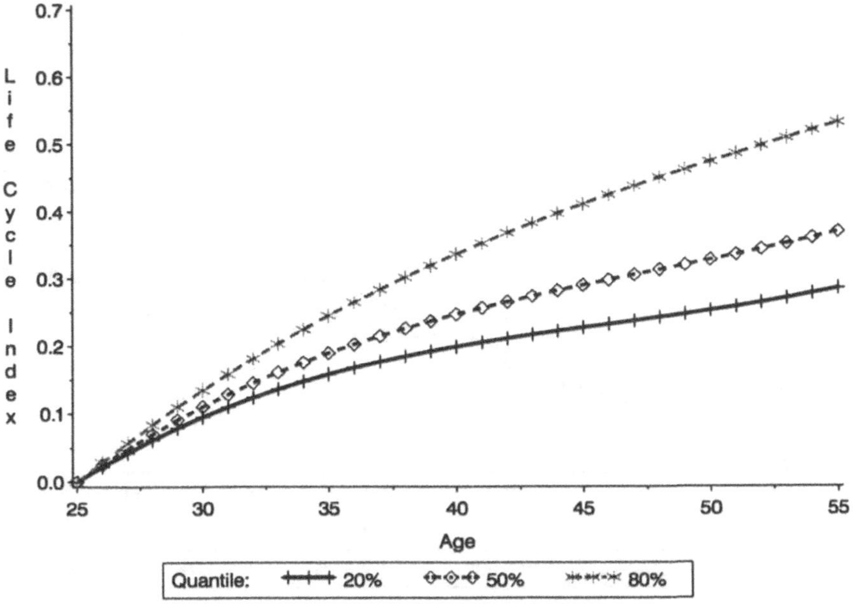

Figure 3.3: Pure Life–Cycle Wage Profiles for Skill Group (H) at Different Quantiles (Final Specification – Manufacturing)

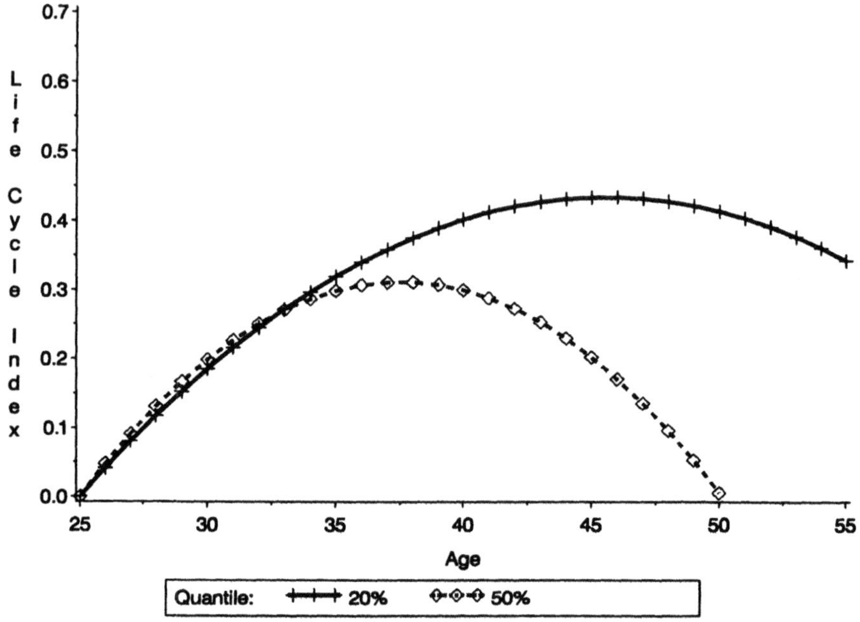

Figure 3.4: Pure Life–Cycle Wage Profiles for Skill Group (U) at Different Quantiles (Final Specification – Non–Manufacturing)

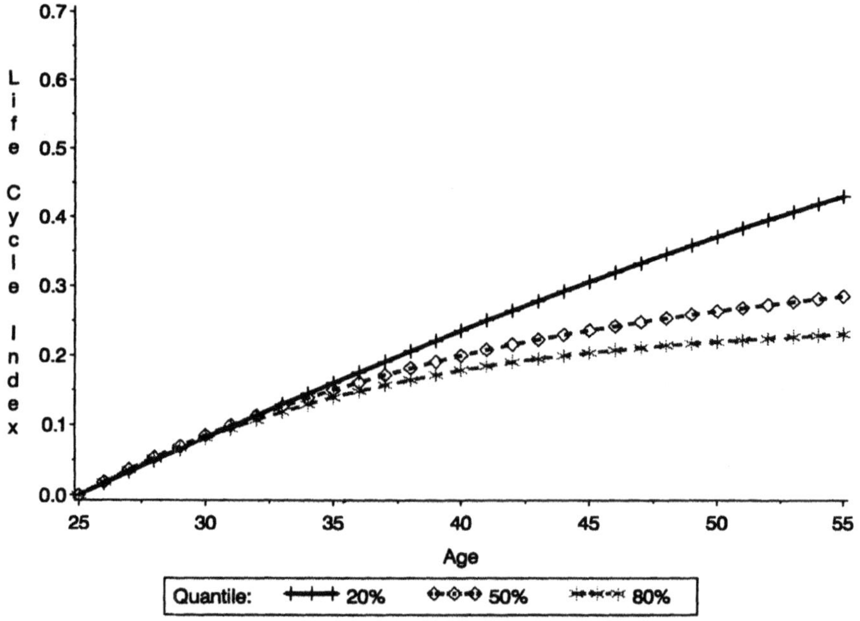

Figure 3.5: Pure Life–Cycle Wage Profiles for Skill Group (M) at Different Quantiles (Final Specification – Non–Manufacturing)

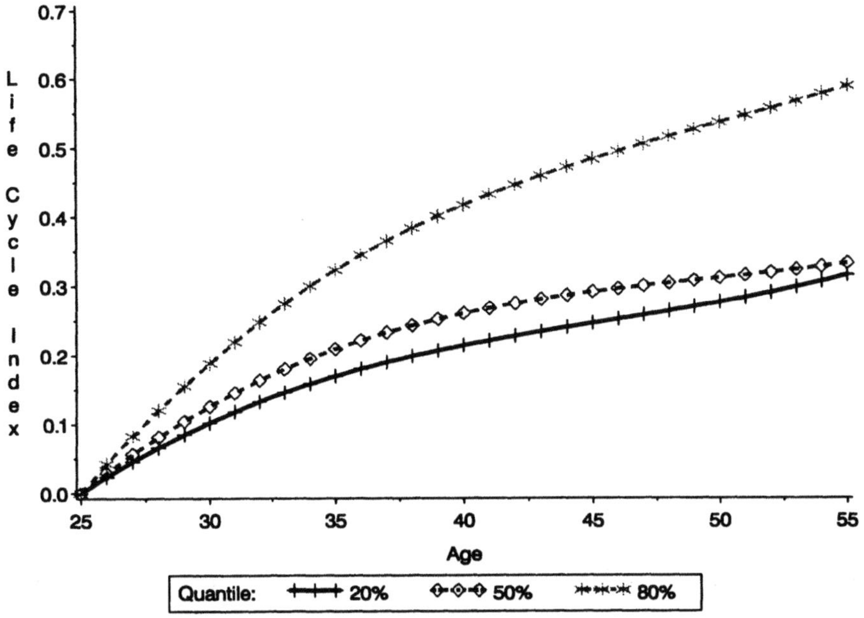

Figure 3.6: Pure Life–Cycle Wage Profiles for Skill Group (H) at Different Quantiles (Final Specification – Non–Manufacturing)

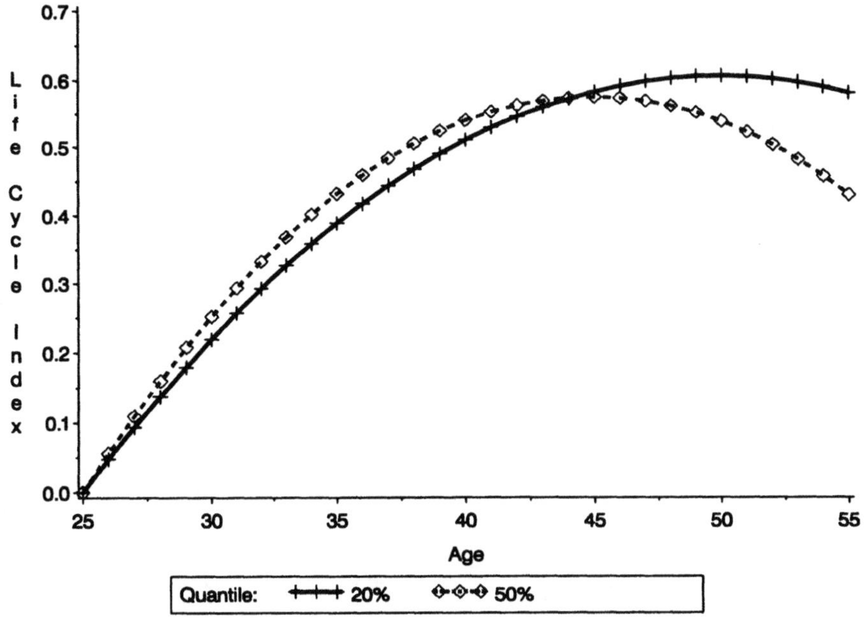

Figure 3.7: Trend–Macro Wage Profiles for Skill Group (U) at Different Quantiles (Final Specification – Entire Economy)

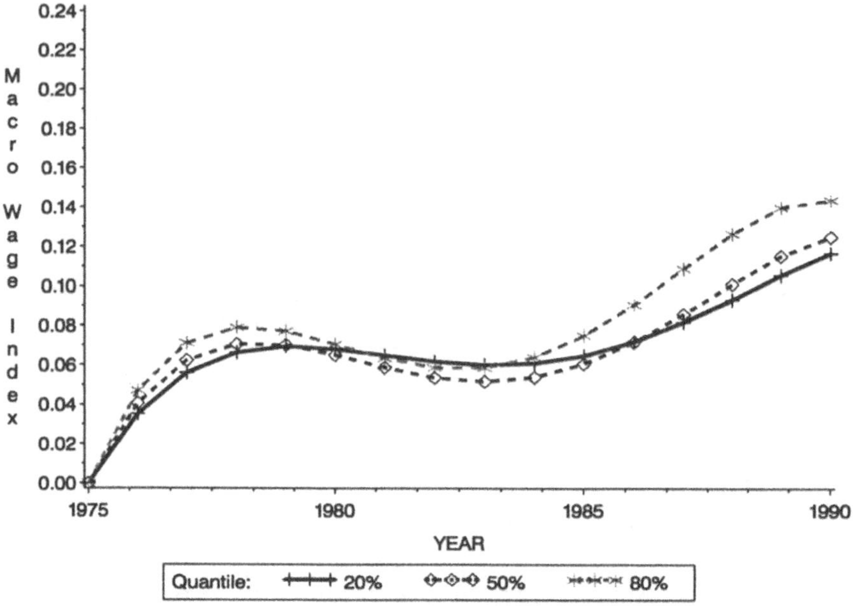

Figure 3.8: Trend–Macro Wage Profiles for Skill Group (M) at Different Quantiles (Final Specification – Entire Economy)

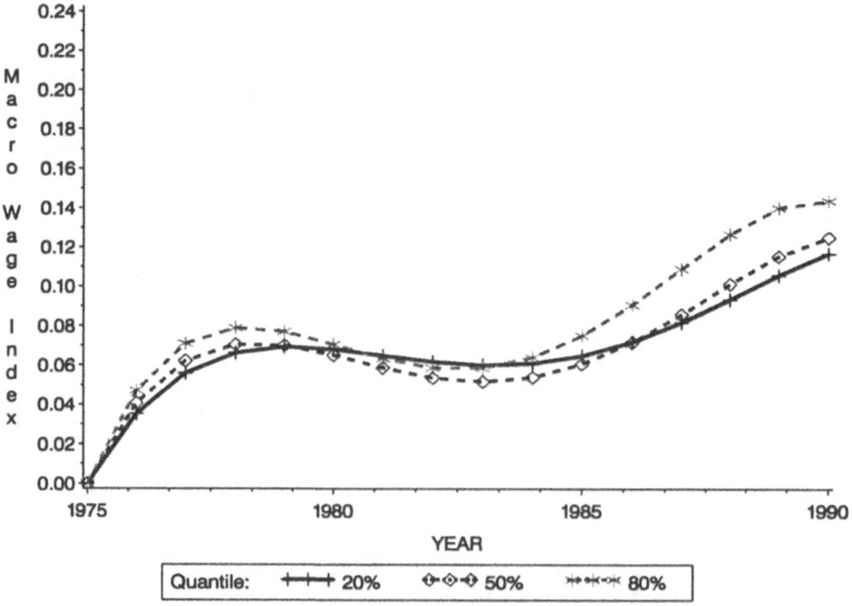

Figure 3.9: Trend–Macro Wage Profiles for Skill Group (H) at Different Quantiles (Specification (3) – Entire Economy)

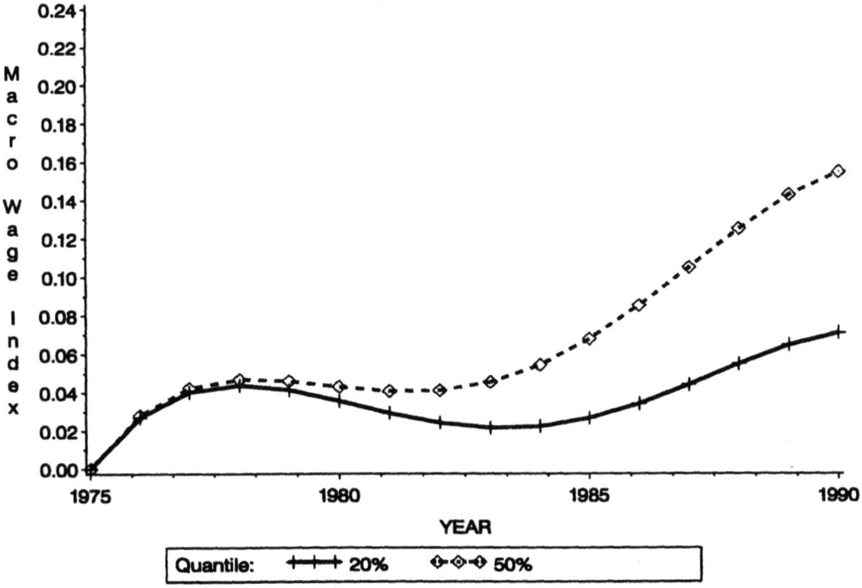

Figure 3.10: Trend–Macro Wage Profiles for Skill Group (U) at Different Quantiles (Final Specification – Entire Economy with Selection Correction for Unemployment)

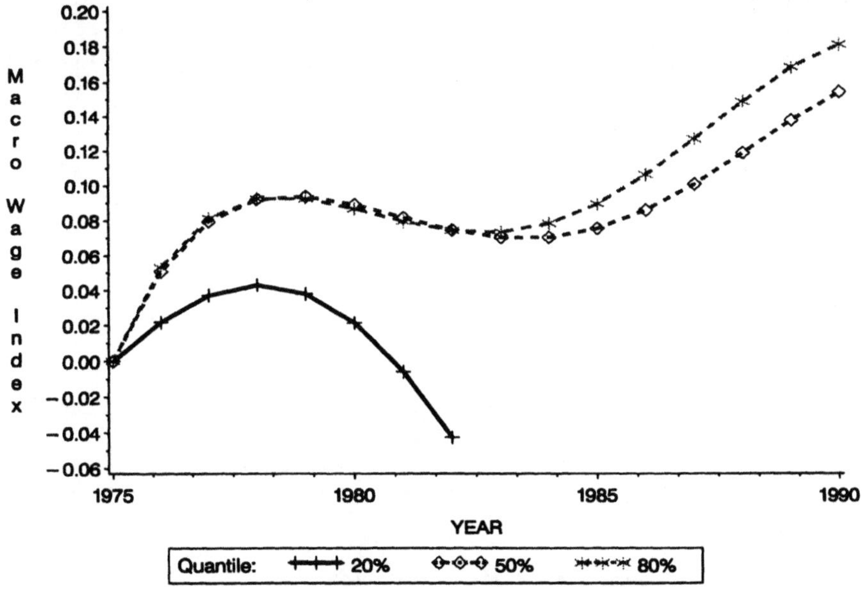

Figure 3.11: Trend–Macro Wage Profiles for Skill Group (M) at Different Quantiles (Final Specification – Entire Economy with Selection Correction for Unemployment)

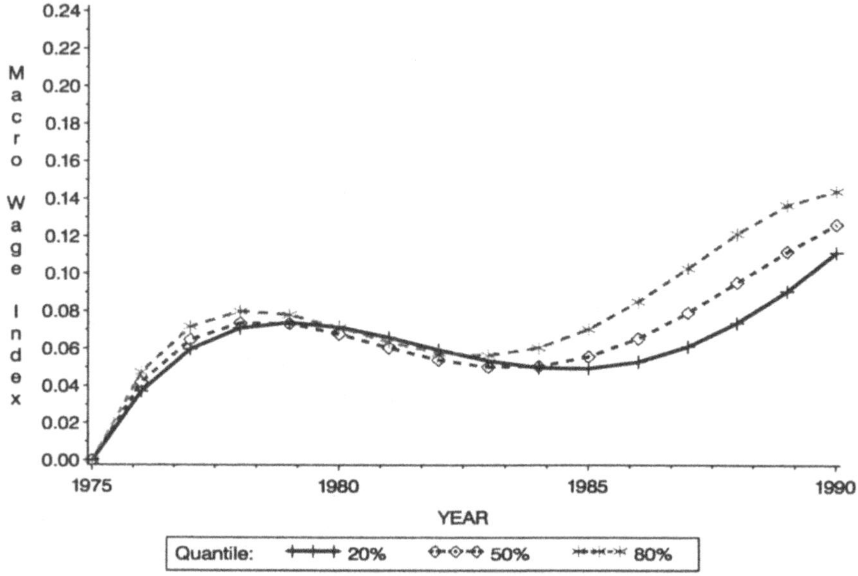

Figure 3.12: Trend–Macro Wage Profiles for Skill Group (H) at Different Quantiles (Specification (3) – Entire Economy with Selection Correction for Unemployment)

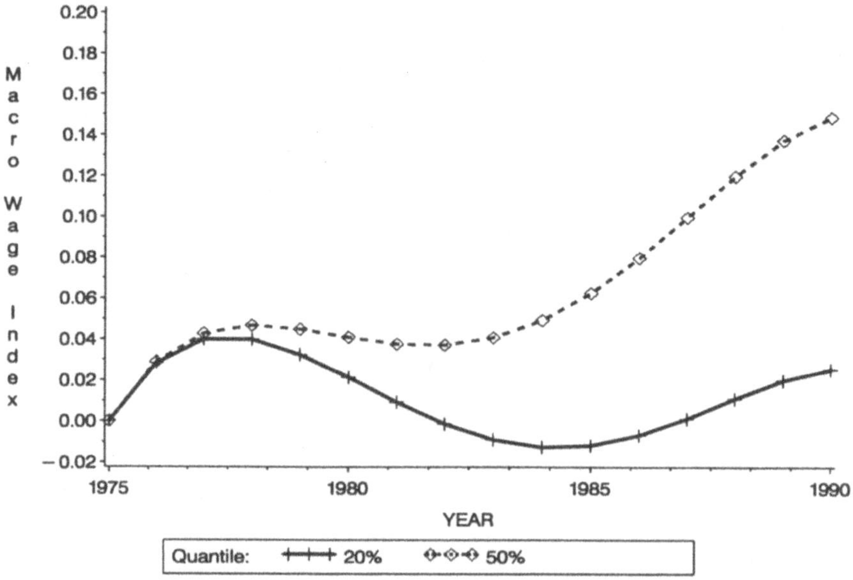

Figure 3.13: Trend–Macro Wage Profiles for Skill Group (U) at Different Quantiles (Final Specification – Manufacturing)

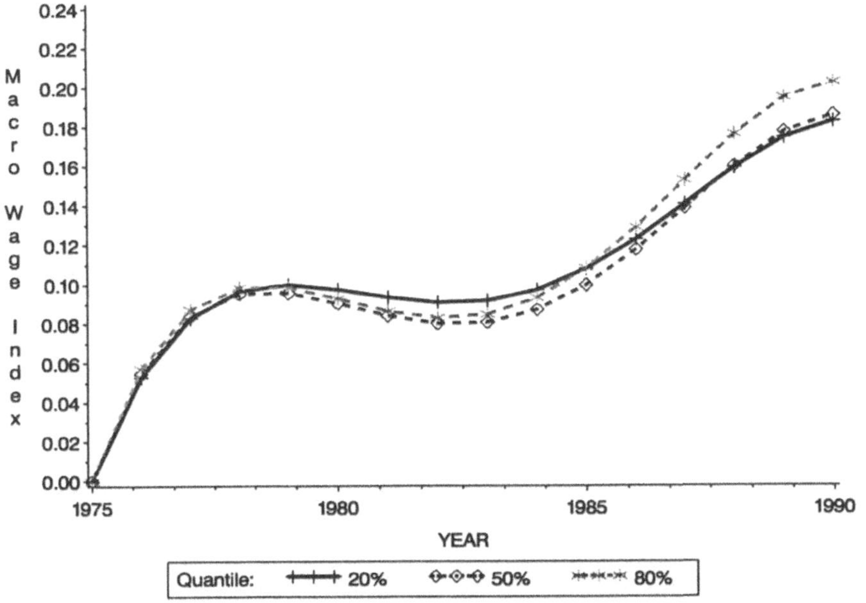

Figure 3.14: Trend–Macro Wage Profiles for Skill Group (M) at Different Quantiles (Final Specification – Manufacturing)

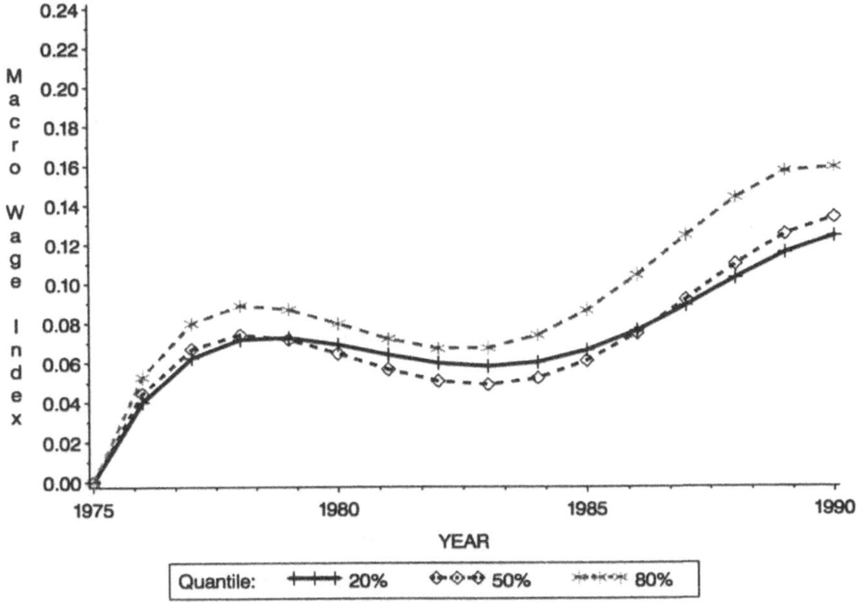

Figure 3.15: Trend–Macro Wage Profiles for Skill Group (H) at Different Quantiles (Final Specification – Manufacturing)

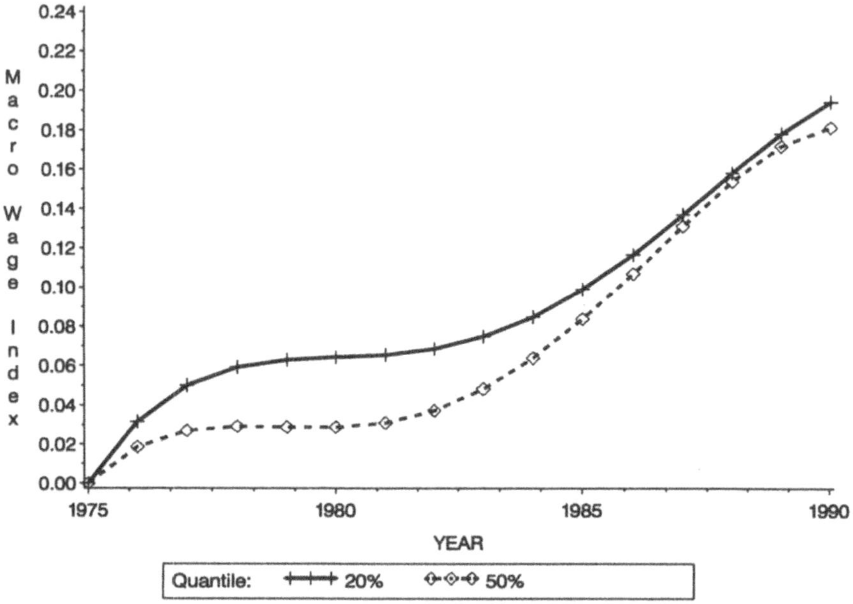

Figure 3.16: Trend–Macro Wage Profiles for Skill Group (U) at Different Quantiles (Final Specification – Non–Manufacturing)

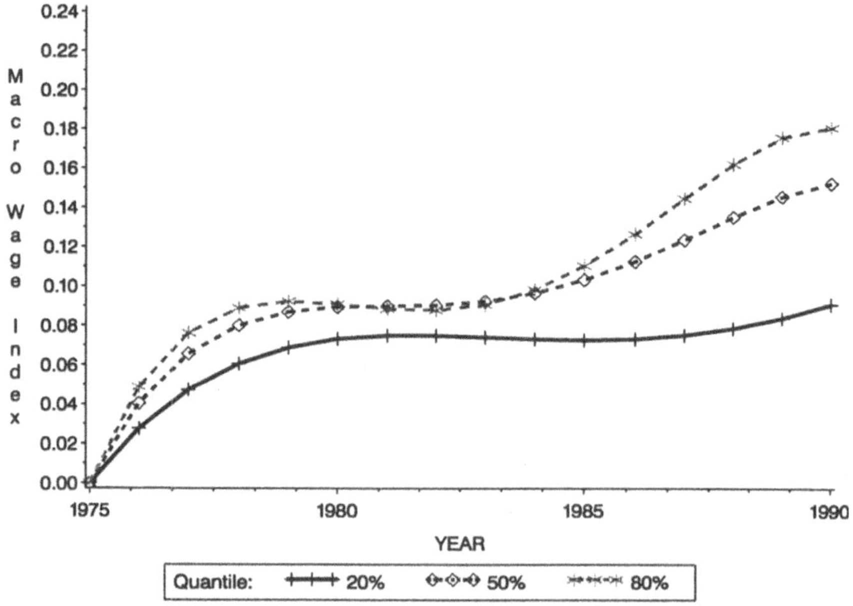

Figure 3.17: Trend–Macro Wage Profiles for Skill Group (M) at Different Quantiles (Final Specification – Non–Manufacturing)

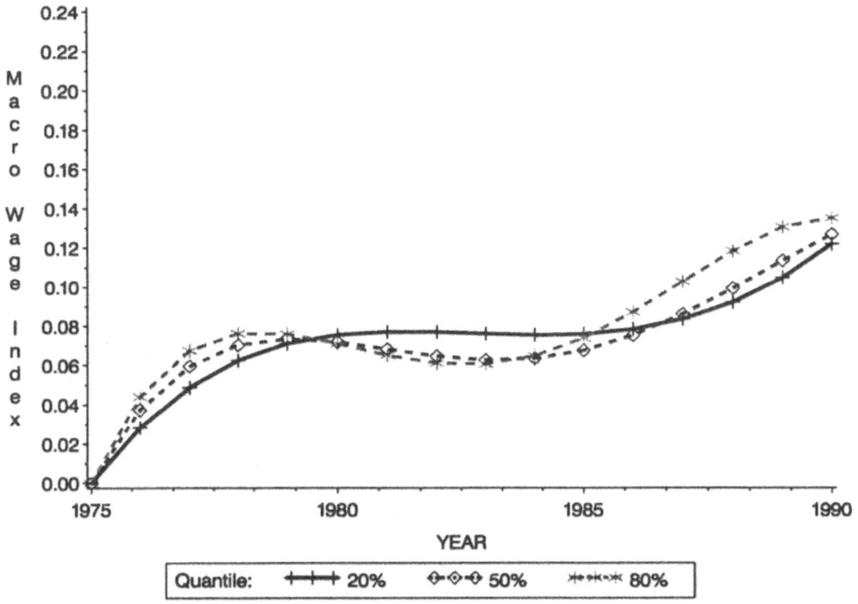

Figure 3.18: Trend–Macro Wage Profiles for Skill Group (H) at Different Quantiles (Final Specification – Non–Manufacturing)

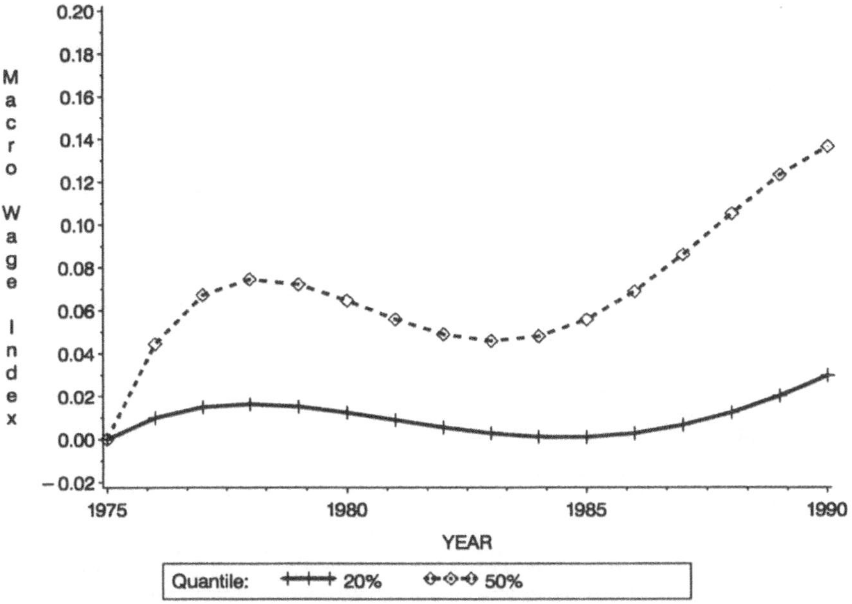

Figure 3.19: Cross–Section of Predicted Wages in 1976 and 1988 for Skill Group (U) at Different Quantiles (Final Specification – Manufacturing)

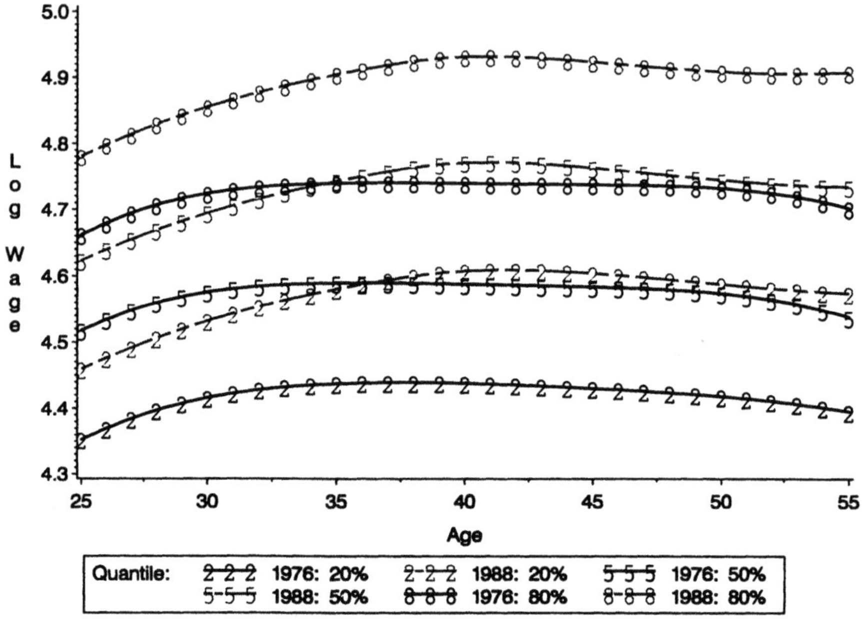

Figure 3.20: Cross–Section of Predicted Wages in 1976 and 1988 for Skill Group (M) at Different Quantiles (Final Specification – Manufacturing)

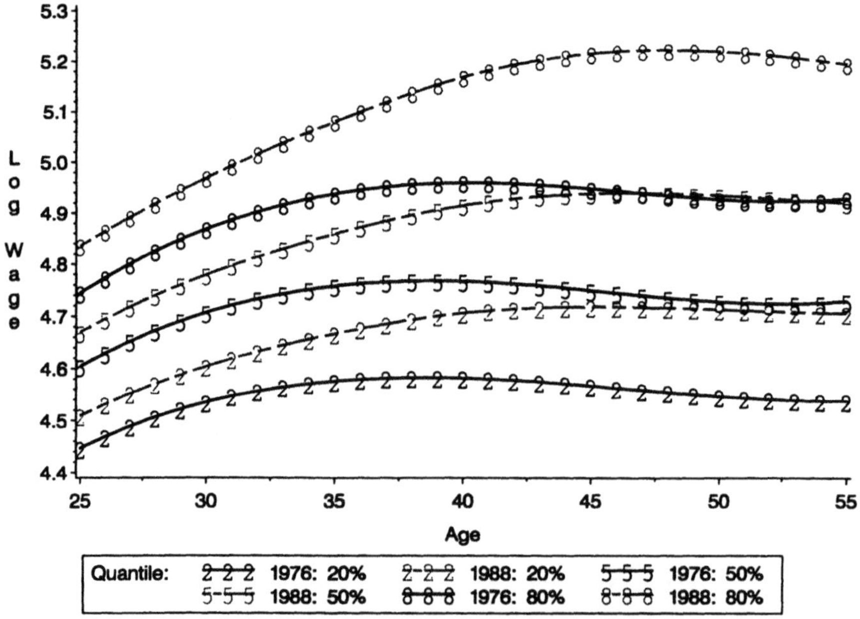

Figure 3.21: Cross–Section of Predicted Wages in 1976 and 1988 for Skill Group (H) at Different Quantiles (Final Specification – Manufacturing)

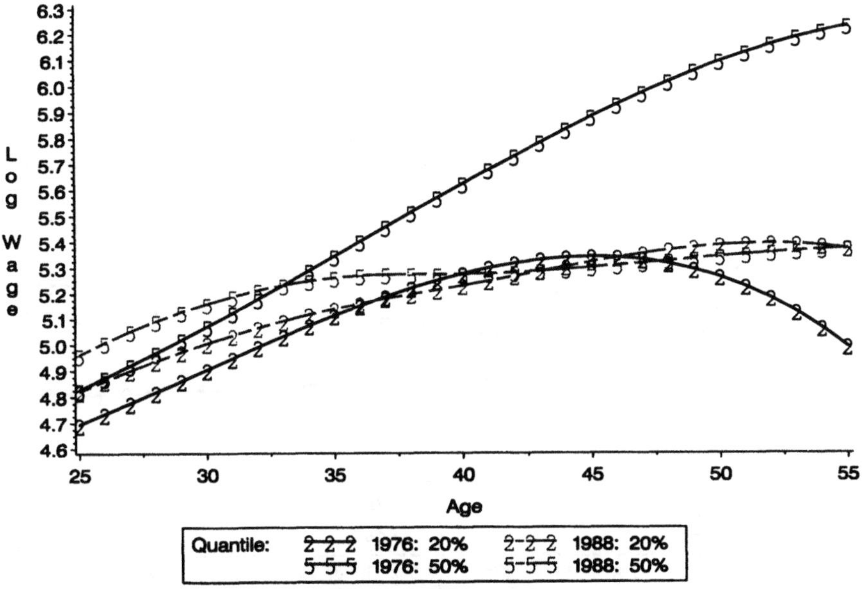

Figure 3.22: Cross–Section of Predicted Wages in 1976 and 1988 for Skill Group (U) at Different Quantiles (Final Specification – Non–Manufacturing)

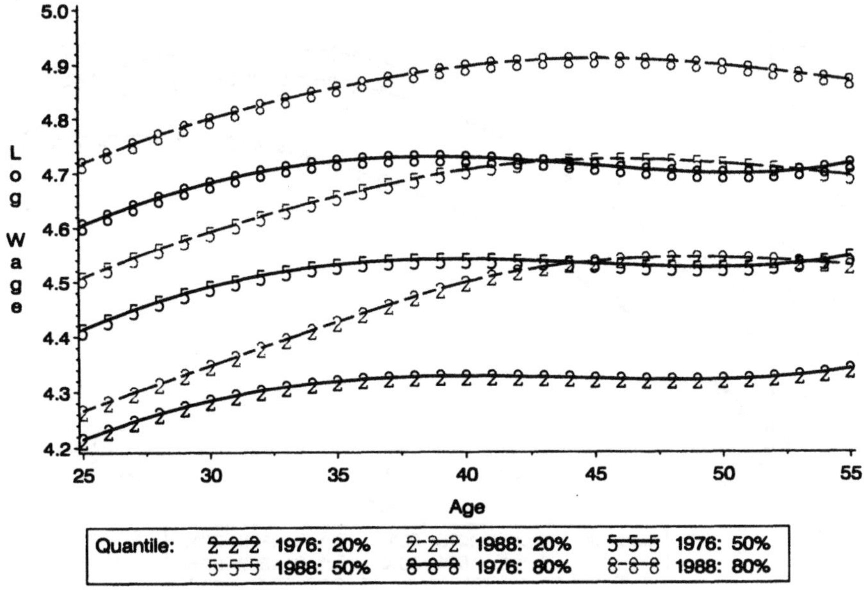

Figure 3.23: Cross–Section of Predicted Wages in 1976 and 1988 for Skill Group (M) at Different Quantiles (Final Specification – Non–Manufacturing)

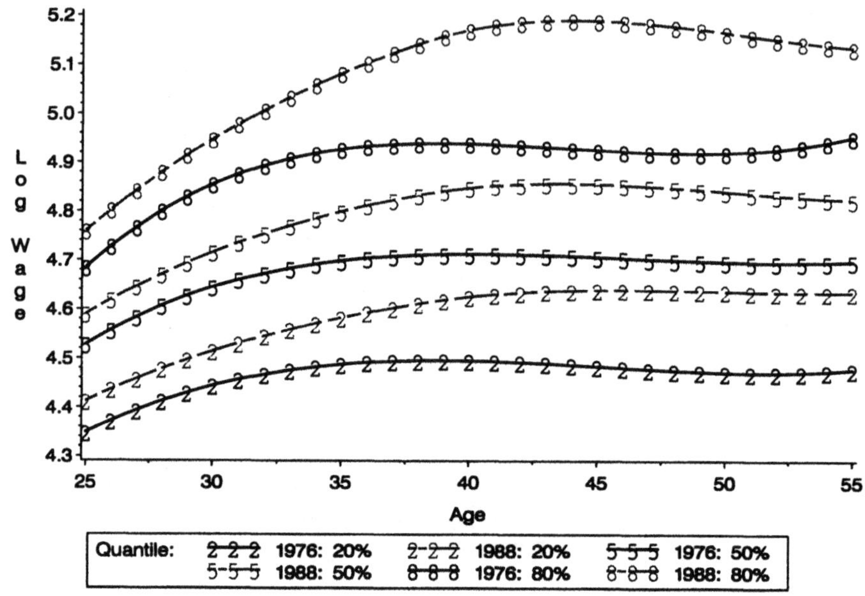

Figure 3.24: Cross–Section of Predicted Wages in 1976 and 1988 for Skill Group (H) at Different Quantiles (Final Specification – Non–Manufacturing)

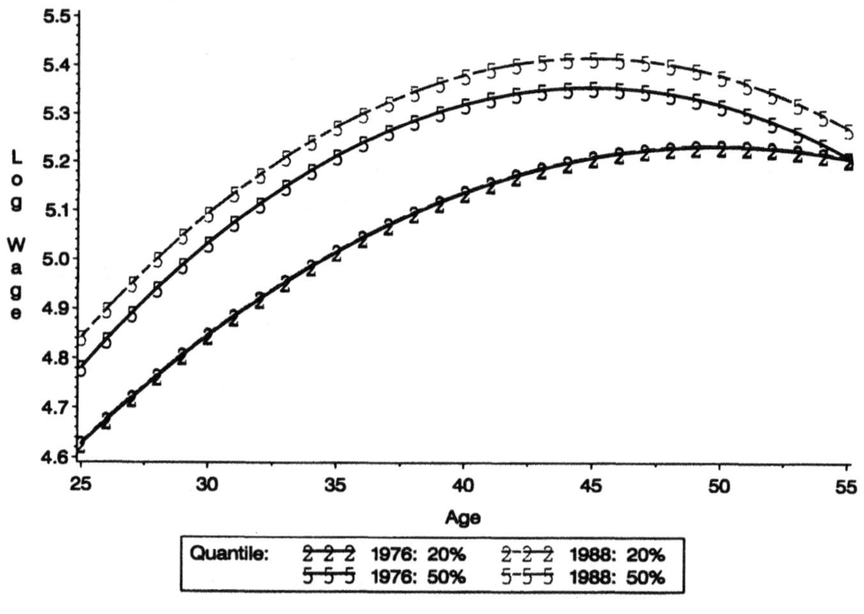

4 Wages, Prices, and International Trade

"Two important mistakes that we make when we analyze data are: (1) taking the theory too seriously, and (2) not taking the theory seriously enough."

Leamer (1996, section 3)

West Germany experienced a considerable trade surplus until 1990 and was viewed as an "export champion" by many commentators. Even though the trade surplus of unified Germany plummetted after 1990, it has been improving continuously since 1991. Nevertheless, the economic policy debate today views gobal competition as one of the great economic challenges for Germany[1] and often considers the German labor market problems (especially concerning unemployment of low–skilled workers) as being aggravated by international competition from low–wage countries resulting in a loss of competitiveness of the German economy. Correspondingly, it is discussed intensively whether the high level of unemployment is due to the general wage level being too high and due to a lack of flexibility in the German wage structure caused by the prevailing wage bargaining system. A considerable increase in earnings inequality since the early 80's has been observed for various industrial countries, the most prominent being the United States, see OECD (1993, 1996). Compared to the United States, the latter study (based on a fairly small set of descriptive statistics) shows that West Germany exhibits an exceptionally stable wage structure since the mid 80's. Trends in international trade differ between West Germany and the United States, with the United States facing a large trade deficit since the early 80's and West Germany a considerable trade surplus. And also trends in wage bargaining institutions differ between West Germany and the United States. The former did not experience the decline in unionism observed for the latter. Thus, West Germany provides a polar case to the developments in the United States in various aspects. The goal of this study is to analyze links between trade developments and the West German labor market and to explore what can be learnt from the differences to the United States, where the latter case is well documented in the literature.

[1] The title of a recent annual report of the German Council of Economic Experts (1995) was "Facing global competition".

The international discussion on trends in wage inequality and employment trends motivated the recent empirical studies on the wage structure in West Germany and its flexibility (see the discussion in chapter 1). Siebert (1995) sees a deficit in empirical research for Germany on the link between international competition and wages. Trying to fill this gap, this chapter is concerned with the effects of international trade on wage and employment trends across skill groups and industries for West Germany during the time period from 1970 until German reunification in 1990. In order to identify possible trade effects on the West German labor market and to disentangle trade from technology effects, this study builds on an augmented version of the classical Heckscher–Ohlin–Samuelson (HOS) framework, which has been used extensively in the recent U.S. literature, see Lawrence and Slaughther (1993), Sachs and Shatz (1994), Leamer (1996), and Baldwin and Cain (1997). In the HOS view, changes in relative product prices are the fundamental intervening variables linking trade developments to labor markets, see Stolper and Samuelson (1941). However, under the experience of large unemployment and a rigid wage structure, the HOS framework has to be augmented along the lines of the "European Model" presented in Krugman (1995).

Empirical results for the United States differ considerably, see the recent survey by Slaughter and Swagel (1997). Building on the HOS view, Lawrence and Slaughter (1993) did not identify trade effects even to operate into the right direction in order to explain the main labor market trends in the United States. On the contrary, Sachs and Shatz (1994), Freeman (1995), Baldwin and Cain (1997), Leamer (1996), or Krugman (1995) arrive at the conclusion that trade effects were operating into the right direction but could only explain a small part of labor market trends. Finally, Wood (1995) concludes that trade effects via import competition from developing countries could, in fact, explain most of the recent labor market trends in the United States.

There exists only a small set of recent studies concerned with empirical research on labor market effects of trade in Germany, see Haisken–DeNew and Zimmermann (1995), FitzRoy and Funke (1996), Lawrence (1994), Neven and Wyplosz (1996), Landmann and Pflüger (1996), Lücke (1997), and the surveys in Hesse (1996) and Paqué (1998). Most studies (see Lawrence or Lücke who base their analysis on a similar framework as used in this study) find little or no trade effects on labor market prospects of different skill groups, while some studies conclude that trade effects have been detrimental to low–skilled workers but, at the same time, the effects have been small (see Hesse and Paqué for the latter conclusion). Lawrence (1994, pp. 18–19) contains a short cross–country comparison where he investigates the correlation between wholesale and import price changes and the ratio between manual and non–manual workers for Germany. He finds a positive relation between price changes and the manual/non–manual employment ratio (significantly so only for wholesale prices) and no decline in the relative price of manual–worker–

intensive products. But, without an analysis of both wage and employment trends, this finding is not conclusive on whether trade effects were operating on the German labor market. Neven and Wyplosz (1996) consider the link between relative price trends and factor intensity again based on the manual/non-manual worker distinction. They find that import prices decline most for skill-intensive industries and therefore reject a simple HOS view for Germany. Estimating a system of wage and employment equations, they find some evidence for import competition hurting the labor market position of low-skilled workers. However, they conclude that a more complicated restructuring process ("defensive innovation") took place involving upgrading of skills and increasing product prices relative to import prices. As a major difference to almost all of the previous studies, this chapter builds upon three skill groups of workers and the relationships found are often non-monotonic across skill levels (see also Hesse, 1996, p. 335).

The remainder of this chapter is organized as follows: Section 4.1 presents the Heckscher-Ohlin-Samuelson (HOS) model as the conceptional basis for this study and discusses necessary extensions and implications for the empirical investigation. Section 4.2 describes the data used in this study. Building on the aforementioned augmented HOS view, section 4.3 develops a series of empirical findings on the relationship between wages, prices, total factor productivity growth, and trade. The section finishes with an interpretation of the evidence found for West Germany and compares it with the U.S. experience reported in the literature. Section 4.4 builds on a slightly more structural approach in order to estimate the impact of trade and technology trends on factor remuneration rates. Section 4.5 concludes and the final appendix of this chapter provides a list of variable definitions, tables containing empirical results, and graphical illustrations.

4.1 Augmenting the HOS Framework

As the conceptional basis for the empirical analysis, this study takes the view of a classic Heckscher-Ohlin-Samuelson (HOS) model. In the HOS view, changes in product prices form the fundamental link between trade and labor markets, and it is mainly this link which is explored by the empirical analysis in this study. If trade competition hurts the labor market position of low-skilled workers, the HOS line of argument is as follows: due to an increase in the abundance of low-skilled workers abroad the relative supply of those products, whose production makes intensive use of low-skilled workers, increases abroad. In general equilibrium, this increase results in a reduction of the relative price of low-skilled-worker-intensive products. According to the Stolper-Samuelson theorem, relative factor prices are linked to relative output prices such that the relative wage position of low-skilled labor deteriorates in general equilibrium.

There are two further implications which have been discussed intensively in the literature, see Lawrence and Slaughter (1993), under the heading of differential between– and within–industry employment effects. First, production adjusts such that the domestic production of the low–skilled–worker–intensive products decreases and of the high–skilled–worker–intensive products increases, i.e. between industries skill upgrading occurs in the sense that the importance of the high–skilled–worker-intensive industries increase. Second, within industries the decline in the relative wage of low–skilled workers implies a substitution towards low–skilled workers along the industries' isoquants. In fact, the combination of the first and second effect is necessary to guarantee full employment of all production factors in general equilibrium.

Of course, the HOS model requires a bulk of highly unrealistic assumptions, but the argument that, for trade to have an impact on factor prices, prices of traded goods have to change accordingly proves quite robust in trade theory, see Lawrence and Slaughter (1993, pp. 188–189), Richardson (1995), and Leamer (1996, section 1).[2] It is this focus on relative prices as transmission channel that characterizes the approach favored by the majority of trade theorists and that differentiates this approach from quantitiy based approaches (factor content studies) favored by some trade and labor economists, see Wood (1995) and Freeman (1995). I decided to use a HOS based approach since my goal was to obtain a first appraisal of trade effects on labor markets in West Germany without having to specify the "rest of the world" and since it allows for a closer link between theoretical concepts and empirical work.

Factor content studies amount to analyze the labor market effects of trade by estimating the labor content of imports and adding this to the domestic labor supply. The impact on factor prices is then determined as a standard reaction to factor supply increases in (partial) labor market equilibrium, see Wood (1995) and Freeman (1995). Trade theorists have criticized quantity based approaches on theoretical grounds, see Lawrence and Slaughter (1993) and Richardson (1995). On the one hand, in the case of a small open economy, relative product prices are given by the world market and, given production technology, relative factor prices are only determined by relative product prices, irrespective of the volume of imports. On the other hand, (net) trade depends on tastes as well as on supplies. E.g. with inelastic demand and increasing import competition, price changes with corresponding changes of factor prices can occur with almost no change in net trade. Section 4.3.2 will continue the critical assessment of the factor content approach in light of some empirical findings.

For the purpose of this study, the classic HOS view has to be modified to gain empirical relevance regarding the following two issues. First, when relative factor prices are rigid, i.e. not sufficiently responsive to the effects of product price changes on factor demand, the HOS view can be modified

[2] A counter example is the case of (incomplete) specialization of countries to the production of different goods or when there are industry specific input factors, see Jones (1995) and Leamer (1996, section 1). Then some of the conclusions of HOS theory change.

such that factor price rigidities result in unemployment of the factor which is used intensively in the industry whose relative product price declines. This is taken as a working assumption in this study which appears to be quite common in the economic policy debate on trade effects in Europe. Factor price rigidities in trade models have been considered in the literature, see Krugman (1995). Krugman's treatment under the heading of a "European" model involves relative factor price rigidities.[3] As such, his approach appears broadly consistent with my working assumption. However, it remains an open question what determines relative goods and factor prices. A rigorous general (dis)equilibrium formulation of such a model is lacking which should take account of the stylized features of the West German wage bargaining system, see Franz (1996, chapters 7 and 8).

Second, standard HOS theory assumes factor prices to be equal across industries. Empirically, wages differ systematically within and across industries among workers with the same observable characteristics. Nevertheless, with a fixed relative inter-industry factor price structure in the long run, see Krueger and Summers (1988) and Fitzenberger and Kurz (1997), trade effects are still likely to operate via relative product prices in an analogous way as in the standard model provided one takes account appropriately of between-industry employment shifts. An analogous defence holds with respect to the unobserved within industry distribution being fairly stable. However, the empirical analysis in this study could be severely affected by unobservable shifts in the composition of the factor inputs across industries over time or by changes in industry specific rents, see Borjas and Ramey (1995) and Hesse (1996, section 4.4). Such changes could very well be due to trade effects.

Technical Progress

Analogous to the impact of trade, a controversial discussion has evolved around the effects of technology on the wage structure. Most of the literature emphasizes the importance of skill biased technological change saving low-skilled labor as a major driving force for changes in factor prices or employment, see Berman et al. (1994) for the United States and Möller (1996) for Germany. Trade economists, see among others Richardson (1995, p. 41), are inclined to argue that only an industry bias in technological change has an impact on the wage structure in a HOS view, which is, however, only a first order result in general equilibrium, see Leamer (1996, section 3) and Krugman (1995). As an empirical note on this, industry bias and factor bias of technological change are observationally equivalent when technology trends are identified by total factor productivity growth based on a log-linear

[3]Building on Krugman (1995), Landmann and Pflüger (1996) provide a theoretical and empirical appraisal both of trade and technology effects on labor markets in OECD countries.

specification (Cobb–Douglas) of the production technology.

Assessing the Augmented HOS Framework for West Germany

The goal of this study is to identify possible trade effects on the West German labor market and to disentangle trade from technology effects in the light of HOS theory. The fundamental working hypothesis is that changes in relative industry product prices encompass the effects of globalization, and therefore, that the price effects reflect the respective Stolper–Samuelson effects on factor prices – or, alternatively, leading to unemployment of the factor whose relative factor price is prevented from falling. Concretely, the empirical analysis in this study addresses the following questions:

- How do relative factor intensities across industries relate to export and import performance and to changes in relative product prices?
- Can relative factor price trends be related to relative factor intensities across industries and respective changes in relative product prices?
- Are there differential shifts in factor intensities between and within industries as a result of Stolper–Samuelson effects on factor prices?
- If relative factor price trends are not in accordance with Stolper–Samuelson effects, do factor employment trends correspond to the rigidity–in–relative–factor–prices hypothesis?
- Can a bias in technological trends explain differential factor price and employment trends across input factors?
- Do industries which are not exposed to international trade experience different labor market trends?

To address these questions, this study uses a dataset which combines national accounts data for industries with a micro dataset providing wage and employment information for different skill groups of labor across industries. The analysis consists of descriptive evidence on each of the aforementioned questions.

4.2 Description of the Data

To study the relationship between wages, prices, and international trade, it is natural to use detailed industry data comprising wage and employment figures for different skill levels of labor. For the United States such data are available and widely used, see among others Berman, Bound, and Griliches (1994), Lawrence and Slaughter (1993), or Leamer (1996). For West Germany, I had to construct such a dataset building on national account data and on the I_ABS dataset ("IAB–Beschäftigtenstichprobe"), a 1% random sample from German Social Security Accounts. Additional information was merged with these two main data sources. The analysis in this study is restricted to the pre–unification situation for West Germany up to 1990. This section describes the most important features of the data used. Further details can be found in the appendix.

The national accounts provide data from 1970 to 1990 for former West Germany at the 2– and 3–digit industry level (58 industries in total). These data comprise information on value added, production (shipment) value, net capital stock, total employment, wage bill, exports, imports, and the respective price deflators. After 1990 export and import data are only available for unified Germany. I decided to work with the 49 industries given by the industry classification in the appendix and I consider 36 industries to produce tradable goods, i.e. industries whose final products are tradable. Tables A.1 and A.2 in the appendix comprise the industry classification and provide information which industries are traded–goods industries and which industries are subject to strong government market regulations ("regulated industries"). For my definition of a "regulated industry", I only consider types of government regulations, where market access is strictly controlled or where subsidies are crucial for the industry to survive. The traded–goods industries are mainly Manufacturing industries. Their share in total employment decreased from 48.7% in 1970, to 41.8% in 1980, and to 38.8% in 1990 corresponding to the well known trends for manufacturing.

Trade flow data in the national accounts are based on production (shipment) values of goods and services, i.e. export and import figures comprise value added as well as material inputs of the respective industry. Therefore, the trade data do not correspond directly to production (value added) of the industry and the impact of trade is not restricted to industries classified as traded–goods industries.[4] The focus here is on the primary effects within the industry adding the final value to a product. However, for consistency, I define measures of trade exposure relative to the production value of the respective industry, e.g. the export share of industry i is defined as $EXP_{i,t}/PV_{i,t}$.

The second dataset, the I_ABS, is merged with the industry data from the national accounts since the latter only provide limited information on different skill types of labor.[5] Based on the I_ABS data, I distinguish three

[4] For a complete analysis of the impact of trade, an input–output approach is warranted. This is, however, beyond the scope of this study. A more comprehensive analysis would be plagued by various data problems. E.g. input–output tables are not available for every year.

[5] Mainly for Manufacturing industries, separate data for manual (blue collar, "Arbeiter") and non–manual (white collar, "Angestellte") employees is available after 1977. I decided to use the I_ABS instead, since it allows for a clearer definition of skill types by formal education and offers the potential for a more detailed analysis in further research. Even though "Angestellte" generally exhibit a higher skill level compared to "Arbeiter", this distinction is problematic when the analysis is not restricted to Manufacturing. In particular, in some service–industries many jobs requiring only low skills are performed

skill groups of workers, as defined in chapter 2 and in the data appendix, which I label as low-skilled (U), medium-skilled (M), and high-skilled (H) workers. For each skill group, I calculate median wages and employment shares in each industry and year. In 1975, the estimated employment shares (see appendix for details) were 32.2% for (U), 64.2% for (M), and 3.7% for (H). For 1990, these shares changed to 15.7% for (U), 76.6% for (M), and 7.7% for (H).

4.3 Descriptive Evidence

As the basic conception to analyze the data, I take a classic Heckscher–Ohlin–Samuelson (HOS) approach as described in Lawrence and Slaughter (1993, pp. 188–189) or Leamer (1996, section 1). However, this view has to be complemented by the existence of (involuntary) unemployment, see Krugman (1995) and Landmann and Pflüger (1996). The working hypothesis used here is that, when a shock (trade, technology) causes relative wages to decline in equilibrium, keeping up the relative wage of one type of labor at a higher level results in unemployment of this type of labor.

The focus of this study is to identify links between trade and labor market trends in West Germany as opposed to other driving forces of labor market developments, such as technical progress. As the main part of the empirical analysis in this study, this section identifies a series of empirical regularities concerning comovements between different variables which would be considered as endogenous within a complete structural model. As described in the first section of this chapter, a HOS view has certain implications on comovements between endogenous variables in the face of certain shocks. Without estimating a complete structural model, the empirical analysis in the subsequent section 4.4 builds on a tighter link between theoretical arguments and the empirical specification.

To describe the general picture, section 4.3.1 presents economy-wide trends. Section 4.3.2 contains the main part of the analysis which is concerned with trends across industries. A first summary and interpretation of the descriptive evidence in this section is given in section 4.3.3. The results discussed in this section mainly refer to the tables and figures presented in the appendix of this chapter. This appendix also contains a list of variable definitions.

4.3.1 Aggregate Trends

This section presents aggregate trends in trade exposure, prices, wages, and employment. Figure 4.1 depicts trends in trade exposure for West Germany from 1970 to 1990. Aggregate trade exposure (exports plus imports relative

by "Angestellte" who most likely would be "Arbeiter" if they were (still) working in Manufacturing.

to aggregate value added) increases steadily from 39% in 1970 to 60% in 1985 and then swings back to 55% in 1990. West Germany always experienced a trade surplus which, however, exhibits a considerable cyclical behavior. From about 2.5% of aggregate value added in 1970 the trade surplus increases to about 6% in 1974, then decreases to 1% in 1980, and then increases again to about 6% in 1986. Afterwards, the trade surplus remains at this level until 1990.

Figure 4.2 exhibits export and import deflators relative to the aggregate producer price index (PPI – deflator of aggregate value added) as well as trends in the terms of trade based on the ratio of the export and import deflators. Import Prices exhibit an upward trend relative to export prices and to the PPI until about 1985. After 1985 export and import prices decrease relative to the aggregate PPI.[6] Terms of trade deteriorate until 1981, remain constant until 1985, and then improve again. Despite the trade surplus, the considerable decline of import prices in the late 80's and early 90's corresponds to the common perception of greater import competition. Export prices appear to follow import prices suggesting that West German products are sold abroad for cheaper than in Germany. The changes in the trend behavior of the trade surplus in 1980 and 1986 is conspiciously associated with opposite changes in the terms of trade and might be related to the US–dollar cycle. This is not the case for the change around 1975.

Turning to wages and employment across skill groups, figure 4.3 depicts aggregate real wages for all employees from 1970 to 1990 and for the three skill groups from 1975 to 1990. Employees in Germany experienced considerable wage growth from 1970 until 1980 and then from 1985 onwards. During the period from 1980 to 1985 real wages appear to be stagnating. After 1985, real wages deflated by the consumer price index were increasing more strongly than real wages deflated by the aggregate product price index. This difference corresponds to the considerable fall in import prices. Wage trends across skill groups exhibit a U-shaped behavior. Wages for both low–skilled (U) and high–skilled labor (H) improved relative to medium–skilled labor (M).

Figures A.2 and A.1 in the appendix show the (un)employment side of the labor market trends. Aggregate unemployment was increasing around 1975 and from 1980 to 1983, and did not decrease considerably after these recessions (persistence) even though aggregate employment was increasing steadily. The aggregate trends hide considerable differences across skill groups. Relative unemployment rates of (U) was increasing considerably after 1975 until 1984, whereas unemployment of (M) and (H) remains lower than the aggregate figure with the relative unemployment experience of (H) improving slightly during the course of the 80's. Employment trends differ even more. Employment of (H) almost doubled from 1975 to 1990 whereas

[6]It could be suspected that import price trends are mainly driven by the prices for raw materials. However, it will be seen later that on average these findings hold up for the traded–goods industries.

employment of (U) decreased by almost 50%. Again trends for (M) are in between.

These labor market trends are consistent with a skill bias in labor demand in addition to wage bargaining between unions and employers' associations providing mostly binding floors for wages for (U). These wage floors were preventing (U)'s relative wage to fall, thus resulting in the severe increase of unemployment and reduction of employment in this group in the face of a considerable reduction of the labor supply of (U), see also Möller (1996) on this interpretation. Conventional accounts of wage trends across skill types in West Germany, see Abraham and Houseman (1995) and OECD (1993, 1996), do not find the trends reported here. According to the two–sides–of–the–same–coin hypothesis discussed in the introduction, relative unemployment trends in Germany are the result of the rigid wage structure translating the skill bias in labor demand into high unemployment of low–skilled labor instead of a decline in relative wages, as it is the stylized picture for the United States, see Freeman (1995), Krugman (1995), and Landmann and Pflüger (1996).

The two popular candidates in the literature explaining the skill bias in labor demand trends are (skill) biased trends in technical progress, see Bound and Johnson (1993) for the United States and Möller (1996) for Germany, and effects from international trade (globalization). However, based on aggregate numbers for West Germany from 1975 to 1990, for an argument emphasizing the impact of trade to be convincing, this would have to be reconciled with the observations that, in general, West Germany experienced a considerable trade surplus and that, in particular, labor market prospects for low–skilled workers deteriorated most strongly during the period from 1975 to 1985, i.e. both at a time when the trade surplus was deteriorating and at a time when it was improving.

4.3.2 Trends Across Industries

The following section presents the major empirical trends across industries. The subsequent section then provides a comprehensive interpretation of these findings.

Trade Exposure and Factor Intensity

In order to determine the comparative advantages of West Germany and their trends, it is explored how exports and imports differ across industries by their relative use of different factors. A simple measure for qualitative differences in relative factor usage can be obtained by calculating weighted averages of export shares, import shares, trade exposure, and trade surplus across traded–goods industries using the different factor inputs as weights. Such a weighted average is higher if and only if the respective trade measure exhibits on average higher values in industries using the respective factor intensively.[7]

Table 4.1 provides weighted statistics for the two years 1970 and 1990. For instance, in 1970 the weighted average of export shares was 0.144 based on capital input as weights and 0.230 based on employment of high–skilled labor (H) as weights. Thus, capital–intensive industries exhibit lower export shares compared to (H)–intensive industries. Trade exposure (exports plus imports relative to shipments) increases from 29%–37% (depending on the weights) in 1970 to 50%–58% in 1990. Among the three skill groups, the trade exposure exhibits a U–shaped pattern whereas the trade surplus increases monotonically with the skill level. Thus, West Germany exhibits a comparative advantage in human capital intensive production. Trade exposure and the differences in trade surplus across skill groups of labor increase over time. Nevertheless West Germany exhibits a considerable trade surplus even when weighting is based on (U). Therefore, it seems unlikely that a factor content of trade interpretation could possibly imply any negative trade effects on the demand for (U) (such as the findings by Sachs and Shatz (1994) or Wood (1995) for the United States). However, changes (or the lack thereof) in trade volumes are not necessary linked to trade effects on factor prices. Trade volumes can change due to differences in domestic demand even though relative product prices remain the same, see Krugman (1995), Leamer (1996), and Baldwin and Cain (1997), and thus, factor prices do not change either in a HOS world. In addition, changes in the trade surplus have to be analyzed differently compared to changes in exports and imports under a situation of balanced trade, see Baldwin and Cain (1997, p. 7), since, for instance, increased imports of goods intensive in (U) need not be detrimental to the labor market position of this group of workers, if these imports are not matched by a reduction in domestic production of such goods (in order to generate the necessary production of export goods). To sum up, despite the existence of a considerable trade surplus for West Germany until 1990 (which is in stark contrast to the U.S. experience, see Sachs and Shatz, 1994, p. 5), it could very well be the case that the labor market position of low–skilled workers (U) was in fact hurt by trade effects.

Product, Export, and Import Prices

We now turn to the fundamental transmission channel in the HOS view. If a production factor is hurt by trade effects this should coincide with a decline in the relative price of the goods whose production uses this factor intensively. Since industry exports and imports are not measured in value added terms and since exports and imports are not the same kind of goods (intra–industry trade), table 4.2 and figures 4.5 to 4.7 present separate product, export and

[7] To give a simple example, take an economy with two industries and let $g_{i,j}$ be the share of factor $j \in \{L, K\}$ (labor and capital) employed in industry $i = 1, 2$ with $g_{1,j} + g_{2,j} = 1$. If x_i is the industry characteristic of interest, then $g_{1,L} \cdot x_1 + g_{2,L} \cdot x_2 > g_{1,K} \cdot x_1 + g_{2,K} \cdot x_2$ implies that x_i is larger in the labor–intensive industry.

import price trends for the traded–goods industries relative to the aggregate PPI (deflator of aggregate value added).

Between 1970 and 1980, and after 1985, all three price indices were decreasing relative to the aggregate. Especially after 1985, export and import prices were strongly decreasing relative to industry product prices with the relative decline being about twice as large for import prices compared to export prices. The relative price declines apparently occurred almost entirely within industries, with only little indication that between industries the employment share was increasing for those industries who were experiencing a comparatively small or large price decline.[8] The observed decline in the relative price of traded goods has been observed for the United States as well, see Lawrence and Slaughter (1993) and Sachs and Shatz (1994). This is often explained by the demand for manufacturing goods being fairly inelastic such that comparatively high productivity growth results in a decline in the share of manufacturing employment and, at the same time, in lower prices.

Figures 4.5 to 4.7 depict average trends in product, export, and import price changes between 1970 and 1990, respectively, (before 1975 weighting across industries uses the 1975 skill distribution within industries) based on different factor inputs. The graphs respresent the estimated dummy coefficients from a weighted least squares regressions of a relative price index (normalized to zero in 1970), $py_{i,t}, px_{i,t}$, and $pm_{i,t}$, on year dummies for 1970 to 1990 without an intercept where the different factor inputs across industries i and years t are used as weights.

Contrasting figures 4.5 to 4.7, product prices decreased on average less than export or import prices irrespective of which input factor is used intensively. Export and import price trends appear more volatile than product price changes. Relating price changes to factor input intensities across industries, price changes were relatively unfavorable for capital–intensive industries. Among the different skill types of labor, both (U)– and (H)–intensive industries experienced stronger relative price declines compared to (M)–intensive industries.[9] A separate regression exercise where relative prices were estimated as a function of time dummies and interaction terms involving relative factor inputs and a linear time trend proves that the larger declines for capital relative to total labor and the U–shape across skill levels are both highly significant (results are available upon request). The HOS implications of these price trends would be that wages both for (U) and (H) should have

[8]Here and in the following, such a statement is based on the estimated trends not being sensitive to whether industry dummies are included. In fact, the estimate with industry dummies suggests about a 1% larger decline for product prices (-0.169 versus -0.158) and a 1% smaller decline for import prices (-0.310 versus -0.303) for the period from 1970 to 1990.

[9]This result provides a new interpretation of the results in Lawrence (1994) for Germany who finds that wholesale and import price changes were positively related to the ratio between manual and non–manual workers. Since manual workers are typically either of skill type (U) or (M) and non–manual worker are either of skill type (M) or (H), the dominance of the (H) effect appears to drive Lawrence's result.

declined relative to (M) and that average wages should have increased relative to returns to capital.

With import prices decreasing the most, there is some indication that West German producers could isolate themselves to some extent from increasing import competition, e.g. by product differentiation, price differentiation between domestic and foreign markets, or quality upgrading, see FitzRoy and Funke (1996) and Neven and Wyplosz (1996) for arguments along these lines. Thus, in stark contrast to the United States, see Sachs and Shatz (1994), the price pressures were not associated with a deterioration of the trade surplus.

Wages

In a HOS world without frictions, there exists an integrated aggregate market for factor inputs. Since in reality wages for workers of the same observable characteristics differ across industries, one has to consider interindustry differences (among others), see table 4.3 for wage trends across traded–goods industries. Average real wage growth was higher in the 70's than in the 80's and accelerated slightly in the second half of the 80's. With respect to the three skill types, the U–shaped behavior found above for the aggregate numbers is even more noticeable here. Relative wage increases from 1975 to 1990 were highest for (H), +30%, followed by (U), +25%, and by (M) experiencing the smallest wage increases, +20%. These relative wage effects are in opposite direction to the HOS general equilibrium effects predicting an inverse U–shape. At this point, it is important to recognize that wage bargaining might have pushed up wages at the bottom of the distribution, i.e. in particular for (U) corresponding to the increase in its relative unemployment rate. The analysis will return to this point when discussing employment trends.

Contrasting average wage growth to within industry changes indicates that high–wage industries for (U) and (M) were slightly increasing their employment share. From 1975 to 1990, the growth of wages averaged across skill groups was considerably higher than wage growth within all skill groups, reflecting the shift towards higher skill levels in employment. In light of the decline of product prices for the traded–goods industries, the growth of product wages (relative to the industry product prices) was considerably higher than with respect to the deflator of the aggregate value added. This effect is more pronounced in West Germany compared to the United States, see Lawrence and Slaughter (1993), where a decline in the relative price of manufacturing goods appears to explain partly the finding of stagnating real consumption wages and increasing product wages.

Employment and Factor Shares

For the traded–goods industries, table 4.4 presents trends in factor input ratios.[10] The capital–labor ratio is found to increase over time which appears to occur entirely within industries. Trends in capital intensities across skill groups differ considerably. Whereas the ratio between capital and (U) increases, the ratio stagnates for (M), and actually declines for (H). The results on aggregate trends for the employment ratios between the three skill groups reported above are confirmed for the traded–goods industries. From 1975 to 1990, the ratio of (M) relative to (U) increases by 2.9 and the ratio of (H) relative to (M) by 0.035 (note that (M) is the largest group). Almost all of the changes occur within industries but there is some indication that industries with a more highly skilled labor force increase in importance over time.[11] This is particularly true for industries using (U) intensively. Thus, in accordance with a vast bulk of evidence for the United States, see Lawrence and Slaughter (1993), Berman et al. (1994), and Slaughter and Swagel (1997), there is strong evidence of skill upgrading within industries and to a smaller extent between industries. This violates the prediction of differential between–and–within industry movements in relative employment following from a HOS general equilibrium model, but the finding can be integrated into an augmented HOS view.

Considering employment and wage trends together, one finds a skill bias in labor demand for (H) both versus (M) and (U), since relative employment of (H) increased despite an improvement of its relative wage position. The situation is less clear for the pair (M) versus (U), since relative employment of (U) declined despite its improving wage position. Therefore, table 4.3 provides trends in factor shares across industries. As long as the elasticity of substitution between factors is above one, changes in the factor shares provide a better measure of a potential bias in factor demand trends compared to raw factor input measures, see Berman et al. (1994, p. 371) and Hamermesh (1993). The elasticity of substitution between different types of skilled labor is likely to be above one, see Möller (1996) and chapter 5.[12] Since the share for (U) declines considerably (–16.3 percentage points between 1975 and 1990), the overall findings suggest a strong skill bias in labor demand trends. There is some evidence of between industry effects such that industries with a high share of (U) in the total wage bill experienced a decline of their employment share.

Turning to capital–labor substitution, I do not pursue the difficult and often frustrating task to obtain a measure for the user costs of capital.[13] The elasticity of substitution between capital and total labor input is likely to be

[10]The following interpretion assumes that the utilization rate of capital and of employed labor is constant over time.

[11]Such a conclusion is based on the observation that the estimated change is slightly larger, when the regression function does not include industry dummies.

[12]Also based on the $I_A BS$ data, Möller estimates substitution elasticities between the skill groups (U), (M), and (H) which are greater than unity.

[13]Various studies actually assume that capital is a quasi–fixed production factor, see among others Berman et al. (1994) and Machin et al. (1996), avoiding the need to obtain a measure for the price of capital.

below one, see Hamermesh (1993) and Deutsche Bundesbank (1995).[14] The results in table 4.3 show that labor's share was increasing until 1980 and then declining during the 80's. In 1990, labor's share was still on average around 6% percentage points higher than in 1970. Again, there is some evidence of between industry effects such that industries with a high total labor share experienced a decline of their employment share.

Overall, in the augmented HOS view allowing for rigidities in relative factor prices, the interpretation of a skill bias in labor demand is consistent with trade effects operating against (U) relative to (M) and (H), but it is at odds with the relative trends between (M) and (H). The findings for capital versus labor remain ambiguous with respect to the direction of shocks to relative factor demand.

Technical Progress

The observation of skill upgrading within industries in light of increasing skill premia is often considered as prima facie evidence of a skill bias in technical progress. As mentioned in the introduction, an intensive debate has evolved about discriminating between trade versus technology effects on labor market. Following e.g. Leamer (1996, p. 23) or Baldwin and Cain (1997), I obtain total factor productivity (TFP) trends for each industry as the so-called Solow-residual (logarithmic change)[15] calculated as

$$\Delta tfp_i = \Delta y_i - \theta_K \Delta k_i - \theta_L \Delta l_i$$

when referring to total labor and as

$$\Delta tfp_i = \Delta y_i - \theta_K \Delta k_i - \theta_U \Delta l(u)_i - \theta_M \Delta l(m)_i - \theta_H \Delta l(h)_i$$

when labor is disaggregated into three skill groups. TFP growth is assumed to be restricted to value added in the industry, see Leamer (1996) for a discussion involving material inputs. The θ's represent the factor remuneration shares in value added.

Table 4.5 and figure 4.4 present some empirical findings. The qualitative nature of the results reported here was robust with respect to which year the choice of factor shares was based upon despite considerable differences in the actual numbers. TFP grows fairly steadily from 1970 to 1990 and basically all estimated growth occurs within industries in the sense that trends in total employment shares were not systematically related to TFP growth, see table 4.5. Turning to trends in figure 4.4, obtained when weighting by different factor inputs,[16] TFP growth on average was higher in capital-intensive

[14] Deutsche Bundesbank (1995) estimates an aggregate CES production function for Germany using capital and total hours as inputs for which the estimated elasticity of substitution between capital and labor amounts to 0.8.

[15] Alternatively, one could use more direct measures on technology trends such as R&D expenditures, patents or computer usage, see Machin et al. (1996).

[16] As for figures 1–3, the weights for the three skill groups before 1975 are based on 1975 employment shares.

industries compared to industries using (M) intensively. Since (M) represents the largest groups of worker, this finding is also true relative to total labor (not reported here). Among the three skill types, one finds again a U-shaped pattern. Overall, from 1970 to 1990, both (U)- (+34%) and (H)-intensive (+41%) industries were experiencing consistently higher TFP growth compared to (M)-intensive industries (+39%). Compared to other production factors, TFP growth was considerably higher in (H)-intensive industries. When pursuing a formal regression exercise, where TFP growth was estimated as a function of time dummies and interaction terms involving relative factor inputs and a linear time trend, the differences in figure 4.4 were found to be highly significant (results are available upon request).

The empirical evidence suggests that technical progress was favoring the wage position of (H) relative to both (M) and (U) and also the wage position of (U) relative to (M), which is consistent with the findings on wage trends. However, the evidence on the bias in labor demand being monotonic in the skill level is at odds with the trends for (U), unless the demand for (U)-intensive products is fairly inelastic. Related but conflicting results were obtained by Lawrence and Slaughter (1993, p. 199), Sachs and Shatz (1994, p. 41), and Baldwin and Cain (1997, p. 28). Both the first and the third study find TFP growth increasing monotonically in the skill intensity. However, this finding is rejected by Sachs and Shatz who omit the computer industry. When omitting the industry 27 (see table A.1 in the appendix) for West Germany, the results in this section remain virtually unchanged. Thus, compared to the United States, the findings obtained for West Germany appear to be much more robust.

Non–Traded–Goods Industries and Regulated Industries

Non–traded–goods industries are not directly (or to a lesser extent) exposed to foreign competition compared to traded–goods industries, see Freeman (1995).[17] Considering wage bargaining, it appears likely that wage–setters in non–traded–goods industries face less of a restraint in setting higher wages. Also price setters should feel less of a restraint to increase prices in the non–traded–goods industries.

Contrasting the wage effects in table 4.6 with trends for traded–goods industries in table 4.3 reveals that until 1975 wage growth was similar on average, but after 1975 wage growth was actually considerably smaller in the non–traded goods industries for all skill groups. The wage results are actually quite similar for regulated industries only, see table 4.7. In contrast to traded–goods industries, one finds an increasing dispersion of wages across skill groups over time, both for the non–traded–goods and the regulated industries. Also in contrast to the traded–goods industries, there is a slight

[17] The validity of this claim depends upon to what extent non–traded goods are used as inputs for the production of traded goods, factor markets for traded and non–traded goods are integrated, and income effects of trade result in demand shifts.

between-industry-shift away from industries with high wages. The trends in factor input ratios for the three skill types are similar to the traded-goods industries with within-industry employment trends being positively related to the skill level (these results are available upon request). Regarding product wages the differences would even be larger since product prices in non-traded goods industries grew considerably relative to traded-goods industries (see the above discussion on relative price trends). Thus, prices rather than wages appear consistent with the aforementioned shielding hypothesis.

4.3.3 Interpretation

The following interpretation of the empirical findings in this section contrasts the evidence obtained for West Germany with the well known findings for the United States in the literature. The findings presented in this section are consistent with a skill bias in labor demand in addition to wage bargaining between unions and employers' associations providing wage floors, which are mostly binding for (U). These wage floors were preventing (U)'s relative wage to fall, thus resulting in the reduction of employment for this group. Despite a considerable reduction of the labor supply of (U), relative unemployment trends in Germany appear to be associated to the rigid wage structure effectively translating the skill bias in labor demand into higher unemployment of (U) instead of an increasing dispersion of relative wages. The latter is the stylized picture for the United States, see Freeman (1995) and Krugman (1995).

The two popular candidates in the literature explaining the skill bias in labor demand trends are effects from international trade (globalization) and from (skill) biased trends in technical progress. Taking the first candidate, import competition (decline of import prices) was increasing – especially after 1985 – and export prices and product prices in the traded-goods industries were apparently following with a time lag but did not decrease by the same amount. Price trends were in favor of (M), thus, according to a HOS general equilibrium view, they should be associated with a decline of the relative wage position of both (U) and (H). The corresponding results for the United States are highly disputed, with Lawrence and Slaughter (1993) and Baldwin and Cain (1997) finding price changes favoring low-skilled labor and Sachs and Shatz (1994) and Leamer (1996) finding the opposite results (in Leamer's case only for the 70's). Overall for the United States, most of the literature agrees that trade effects were small or nonexisting.

Real wages were rising steadily in West Germany, which is consistent with price declines being comparatively larger for capital-intensive industries[18] resulting in overall capital intensity to increase over time. The U-shaped trend in skills is inconsistent with price declines being larger for industries using (U)

[18] Capital user costs are notoriously difficult to measure, thus, the argument relies on the trend of the deflator of aggregate value added being a proxy for the trend in user costs of capital.

or (H) intensively. However, taking the augmented HOS view and allowing for wage floors, that prevent (U)'s relative wage to fall, then, trends for (U) – but not for (H) – relative to (M) are consistent with trade effects. (U)–intensive industries were experiencing disproportionate price declines and (U)'s relative wage was increasing, thus, the employment share of these industries as well as the within industry usage of (U) was decreasing. Wage trends in West Germany differ from the United States experience of stagnating real wages and monotonically increasing skill premia.

Turning to technical progress, the results on total factor productivity growth are somewhat supportive for the existence of biased trends in technological progress. (H)–intensive industries were experiencing the largest growth in total factor productivity. The ranking with respect to technical progress puts capital after (H) as second, (U) third, and (M) last. Technical progress induced a U–shaped bias in labor demand across skills and was favorable to capital relative to total labor. Therefore, the technological trends are consistent with the observed relative wage and employment trends between (M) and (H) (assuming an elasticity of substitution above one). Such a technology effect could only apply to (U) relative to the other two skill groups and to capital relative to total labor, if the respective elasticity of substitution is below one. This is likely to be the case for capital relative to total labor but not for low–skilled labor relative to other skill types. Thus, technology trends are consistent with a decrease in the capital factor income share, which is the long–term development in the traded–goods industries. For the United States, most of the evidence suggests that technical progress is faster in more skill intensive industries (only disputed by Sachs and Shatz, 1994), such that the skill bias in technological trends is the dominant driving force for labor market trends.

Compared to traded–goods industries, wages were growing to a lesser extent in non–traded–goods industries and in regulated industries, which is not in accordance with these industries being shielded from intensified import competition. In addition, one also finds increasing wage dispersion and pervasive skill upgrading. Overall, the experience in the non–traded–goods industries is much more similar to the United States experience and it is an open question how the wage bargaining system could have increased relative wages in the traded–goods industries when import competition in these industries was presumably increasing. An answer to this question is most likely related to industry specific rents, which arise in the presence of a large trade surplus, see Borjas and Ramey (1995).

4.4 Somewhat More Structural Evidence

This section turns to a somewhat more structural estimation approach trying to disentangle the effects of relative output price changes from the effects of technical progress. As emphasized by Leamer (1996), there exists a trade off between a tight structural specification of the relationship between prices, wages, and trade and a data analysis with a "light" touch of HOS theory. A tight specification allows for the precise investigation of the relevance of some hypothesis. However, the chosen model could be incorrectly specified and it might not capture the various facets of the problem. This section attempts a slightly more structural analysis compared to the descriptive evidence presented in section 4.3.

4.4.1 Structural Estimation Approach

I follow Leamer's (1996, section 3) approach in estimating "mandated" factor price changes resulting from technical change and from changes in relative industry output prices. Leamer's analysis is based on a long–run HOS view, where a set of zero profit conditions, $p = A'w$, describes the relationship between output prices and factor remuneration rates and where p is the vector of product prices, w the vector of factor remuneration rates, and A the matrix of factor input intensities. With more industries than input factors, this set of equations $p = A'w$ can be used within a regression framework to estimate what Leamer calls "mandated" changes in factor remuneration rates by regressing output price changes across industries i on the respective factor shares, i.e.

$$\Delta py_i = \theta_{K,i}\widehat{\Delta r_k} + \theta_{L,i}\widehat{\Delta w}$$

when considering only capital and labor and

$$\Delta py_i = \theta_{K,i}\widehat{\Delta r_k} + \theta_{U,i}\widehat{\Delta w(U)} + \theta_{M,i}\widehat{\Delta w(M)} + \theta_{H,i}\widehat{\Delta w(H)}$$

when considering capital and three skill types of labor. The estimated coefficients ($\widehat{\Delta r_k}$, $\widehat{\Delta w(.)}$) on each factor share $\theta_{.,i}$ represent the estimated change in the factor remuneration rate resulting from a change in output prices which are warranted in light of long–run zero profit conditions. This is the Stolper–Samuelson (1941) transmission channel. However, one has to take account of the fact that output prices do not only change for trade related reasons.

Leamer's analysis attempts to identify trade ("globalization") versus technology effects on remuneration ratios. He emphasizes, however, that such a decomposition is plagued by a fundamental identification problem relating to the "pass–through" of TFP growth. On the one hand, TFP growth within industry could result in decreasing relative output prices ("complete pass–through"), on the other hand it could increase factor remuneration rates without changing output prices ("no pass–through"). In his analysis, Leamer assumes a constant "pass–through" rate across industries and studies the sensitivity of "mandated" factor remuneration changes with respect to this rate.[19] The component of TFP growth across industries which is not absorbed by output price changes together with the zero profit conditions de-

[19] Lawrence and Slaughter (1993, p.203) calculate effective output prices as the sum of actual output price changes and TFP growth. Their discussion implicitly assumes a

fine the factor remuneration rate changes "mandated" by technology. With a constant "pass–through" rate across industries, the sign of the changes of remuneration rates is independent of the "pass–through" rate and can be estimated by regressing TFP growth rates across industries i on the respective factor shares as follows

$$\Delta tfp_i = \theta_{K,i}\widehat{\Delta r_k} + \theta_{L,i}\widehat{\Delta w}$$

when considering only capital and labor and

$$\Delta tfp_i = \theta_{K,i}\widehat{\Delta r_k} + \theta_{U,i}\widehat{\Delta w(U)} + \theta_{M,i}\widehat{\Delta w(M)} + \theta_{H,i}\widehat{\Delta w(H)}$$

when considering capital and the three skill types of labor. The estimated coefficients ($\widehat{\Delta r_k}$, $\widehat{\Delta w(.)}$) on each factor share $\theta_{.,i}$ represent the estimated change in the factor remuneration rate resulting from technological progress assuming "no pass–through". Thus, assuming zero profit conditions across industries the differential qualitative impacts of technology and trade can to some extent be evaluated by regressing price changes, TFP changes, and the sum of both on the respective factor shares.

One may wonder whether this analysis is still meaningful in the presence of unemployment. I would argue that this is the case because "mandated" factor price changes define an equilibrium–benchmark. If wages of some type of labor increase by more than this benchmark, this is consistent with increasing unemployment of this factor.

4.4.2 Estimation Results

Table 4.8 in the appendix provides the regression results both for total labor and capital referring to the changes from 1970 to 1990 and for the three skill types of labor and capital referring to the changes from 1975 to 1990. The estimation results were obtained for output price changes relative to the deflator of aggregate value added, thus the estimated factor remuneration changes are also relative to this aggregate deflator. TFP growth by itself from 1970 to 1990 "mandates" remuneration increases both for capital and labor whereby the effect for capital is slightly larger. Overall effects as well as the difference between capital and labor are larger when 1990 shares are used compared to 1970 shares. Differentiating between three skill types of labor, TFP growth by itself from 1975 to 1990 "mandates" remuneration increases for capital, low–skilled, and high–skilled labor but a decline for medium–skilled labor. The exact size of the effects differs depending on the year for which shares are used but the qualitative results are the same. However, the estimated coefficients for high–skilled labor are obviously too large in absolute

zero "pass–through" such that the effective price changes drive factor remuneration. Their analysis is consistent with assuming that output prices are given by the world market and therefore the impact of technological change is fully absorbed by factor remuneration rates.

values (log differences!), hence, my discussion only relies on the qualitative results.

Price changes are affected by TFP growth as well as by trade. Assuming a constant "pass-through" of TFP growth across industries, the trade induced changes are a linear combination of the estimates referring to the sum of TFP growth and price changes and the estimates referring to price changes alone. Thus, in most cases, the qualitative nature of trade effects can be determined. This is due to the fact that most estimated coefficients in the TFP and price regressions are found to be of opposite sign. Thus, the results in table 4.8 can be interpreted in the following way. Industry output price changes were favoring total labor relative to capital. When differentiating between three different skill types of labor, trade effects were unfavorable for capital. Trade effects on real earnings from 1975 to 1990 were positive for medium-skilled labor (M) and negative for high-skilled labor (H). Only for low-skilled labor (U), the sign of the trade effects is unclear since the coefficient estimates are of opposite sign in the two cases. Also the ranking between (U) and (M) changes since the sum of TFP growth and price changes favors (U) relative to (M) whereas price changes by themselves strongly favor (M).

4.4.3 Summary

The results in this section can be summarized as follows. Technological change was favorable to capital relative to total labor and both to low- and to high-skilled labor relative to medium-skilled labor. Technological change actually appears to "mandate" lower real wages of medium-skilled labor. On the other hand, trade effects (identified by changes in industry output prices) were favorable for medium-skilled labor and unfavorable both for high-skilled labor and for capital. The effect is ambiguous for low-skilled workers. Overall, one might conclude that this is bad news for a mere trade based explanation of relative wage changes across skill groups. However, it could, in fact, mean that trade effects were mitigating changes in the wage structure, in particular, such that medium-skilled labor did not lose relative to high-skilled labor to the same order of magnitude as, for instance, in the United States. Also, according to these calculations technological change did not "mandate" wage declines for low-skilled labor relative to medium-skilled labor or capital but only relative to high-skilled labor. This is something of a puzzle for a technology explanation of wage and employment trends for low-skilled labor, thus, this analysis could only explain the fact that employment of (U) was declining so strongly by referring to increased import competition in (U)-intensive industries. As a cautionary note, the absolute size of some coefficient estimates in this section, in particular for (H), prohibits anything more than a qualitative interpretation.

4.5 Conclusions

For the time period from 1970 to 1990, this chapter investigates links between trends in industry output prices, wages, and trade in West Germany by establishing a series of empirical regularities and then by using a slightly more structural approach to discriminate between trade and technology effects on wages. The main findings are that despite a considerable trade surplus, import competition for the traded–goods industries was increasing and disproportionately so after 1985. The relative wages of both low– and high–skilled labor were increasing (the changes being small in international comparison) but at the same time import competition was increasing disproportionately for the industries using these factors intensively. Employment of high–skilled labor was increasing whereas employment and the factor income share of low–skilled labor were decreasing. This suggests a skill bias in labor demand trends favoring more skilled labor. Thus, together with the wage bargaining system setting "too high wages" and the disproportionate increase in unemployment for low–skilled labor, the results suggest that trade might have partly explained labor market trends for low–skilled labor, namely, a negative trend in demand for low–skilled labor resulting in higher unemployment of this group since its relative wage did not fall. Total factor productivity growth was favoring both low– and high–skilled labor, i.e. technological change augmenting high–skilled labor is consistent with labor market trends for this group. Medium–skilled labor appears to have experienced unfavorable total factor productivity changes but favorable trade effects. Overall, employment of medium–skilled labor was increasing but wages were growing slower compared to low–skilled and high–skilled labor. High wage growth for low–skilled labor is most likely due to the wage bargaining system where downward pressure on wages of low–skilled labor was low in trade surplus industries and these wages were copied in the remaining traded–goods industries ("pattern bargaining"). Somewhat surprisingly, wage growth was uniformly higher in the traded–goods industries compared to the non–traded–goods industries and compared to the industries which are subject to government regulation, even though the latter industries presumably are shielded from increasing import competition. I conclude this chapter by pointing out that, in order to move beyond the mainly descriptive analysis pursued here, the next two chapters analyze in more detail the skill bias in labor demand and the outcome of wage bargaining.

4.6 Appendix of Chapter 4

4.6.1 Variable Definitions

Abbreviation	Definition
V.A./V.A.$_i$	Gross value added obtained from the national accounts, current prices
PY/PY$_i$	Deflator of gross value added obtained from the national accounts
PC	Consumer price index (deflator of aggregate private consumption)
Y/Y$_i$	Gross value added obtained from the national accounts, in constant prices
PV/PV$_i$	Gross production (shipment) value obtained from the national accounts, current prices
EXP	Aggregate exports in current prices
IMP	Aggregate imports in current prices
EXP$_i$	Exports of goods produced in industry i in current prices
IMP$_i$	Imports of the type of goods produced in current prices
Skill Group (U)	Skill group of workers without vocational training degree and without post secondary degree ("ohne abgeschlossene Berufsausbildung und ohne FH/Universitätsabschluß")
Skill Group (M)	Skill group of workers with vocational training degree and without post secondary degree ("mit abgeschlossener Berufsausbildung und ohne FH/Universitätsabschluß")
Skill Group (H)	Skill group of workers with post secondary degree ("FH/Universitätsabschluß")
W/W$_i$	Average annual earnings per worker obtained by dividing total labor costs by the number of employees from the national accounts, in current prices
W(J)/W(J)$_i$	Median of annual average daily earnings for skill group J (J=U,M,H) obtained from social security accounts ("I$_A$BS"), not including employers' contribution to social insurances, in current prices
L/L$_i$	Employees obtained from the national accounts
L(J)/L(J)$_i$	Employees of skill group J (J=U,M,H) obtained from social security accounts ("I$_A$BS")
K/K$_i$	Net capital stock (equipment and plants) obtained from the national accounts, in constant prices

- A variable with index i refers to industry i. The same variable without index refers to the aggregate economy. Lowercase letters indicate logarithms.
- All variables are for West Germany only ("Bundesrepublik Deutschland" before October 3, 1990).

4.6.2 Tables of Results

Table 4.1: Weighted[a] Averages of Exports, Imports, Trade Exposure, and Trade Surplus Across Traded–Goods Industries Relative to Industry Production Values

	Variables			
	$\frac{EXP_{i,t}}{PV_{i,t}}$	$\frac{IMP_{i,t}}{PV_{i,t}}$	$\frac{(EXP_{i,t}+IMP_{i,t})}{PV_{i,t}}$	$\frac{(EXP_{i,t}-IMP_{i,t})}{PV_{i,t}}$
Weights	Year = 1970			
$K_{i,t}$	0.144	0.167	0.311	-0.023
$L_{i,t}$	0.179	0.121	0.302	0.058
$L(U)_{i,t}$	0.175	0.132	0.307	0.043
$L(M)_{i,t}$	0.179	0.113	0.293	0.066
$L(H)_{i,t}$	0.230	0.141	0.370	0.089
Weights	Year = 1990			
$K_{i,t}$	0.242	0.260	0.502	-0.018
$L_{i,t}$	0.292	0.236	0.528	0.056
$L(U)_{i,t}$	0.299	0.270	0.568	0.029
$L(M)_{i,t}$	0.285	0.214	0.499	0.071
$L(H)_{i,t}$	0.334	0.241	0.575	0.093

a: Industry weights are the average factor inputs in 1975 and 1990 for each industry.

Table 4.2: Time Trends in Product, Export, and Import Prices Across Traded–Goods Industries[a,d]

Price Index[d]	Relative to Deflator of Aggregate Value Added							
	Without Industry Dummies				With Industry Dummies			
	1975	1980	1985	1990	1975	1980	1985	1990
$py_{i,t} - py_t$[b]	-0.084	-0.127	-0.134	-0.158	-0.091	-0.141	-0.146	-0.169
$px_{i,t} - py_t$[b]	-0.067	-0.125	-0.127	-0.229	-0.065	-0.128	-0.128	-0.227
$pm_{i,t} - py_t$[b]	-0.161	-0.209	-0.168	-0.310	-0.159	-0.210	-0.166	-0.303

a: The numbers reported in the table are coefficient estimates from a regression in each industry on a set of year dummies, where the dummy variable for the first year (1970 or 1975) is omitted. Whithout industry dummies the estimated coefficients on the year dummies capture the overall trends, whereas with industry dummies included they comprise the average within industry trend. All estimations are weighted least squares regressions where each industry observation is weighted by total employment in that industry.

b: Change relative to 1970.

c: Change relative to 1975.

d: Price changes are estimated as logarithmic differences. Relative prices are normalized to zero in 1970.

Table 4.3: Time Trends in Wages and Factor Shares Across Traded–Goods Industries[a]

	Without Industry Dummies				With Industry Dummies			
	1975	1980	1985	1990	1975	1980	1985	1990
Wage Index[d]	Relative to Deflator of Aggregate Value Added							
$w_{i,t} - py_t^b$	0.160	0.334	0.401	0.486	0.148	0.324	0.382	0.463
$w(u)_{i,t} - py_t^c$	–	0.132	0.188	0.253	–	0.130	0.181	0.243
$w(m)_{i,t} - py_t^c$	–	0.104	0.137	0.196	–	0.104	0.131	0.185
$w(h)_{i,t} - py_t^c$	–	0.203	0.257	0.303	–	0.204	0.257	0.302

	Without Industry Dummies				With Industry Dummies			
	1975	1980	1985	1990	1975	1980	1985	1990
Factor	Ratio Wage Bill to Industry Value Added[e]							
$L_{i,t}^b$	0.037	0.087	0.050	0.059	0.039	0.092	0.058	0.066
Factor	Ratio Wage Bill to Total Industry Wage Bill							
$L(U)_{i,t}^c$	–	-0.068	-0.126	-0.163	–	-0.065	-0.118	-0.153
$L(M)_{i,t}^c$	–	0.051	0.091	0.111	–	0.047	0.085	0.103
$L(H)_{i,t}^c$	–	0.017	0.035	0.052	–	0.017	0.034	0.050

a,b,c: See table 4.2.

d: Wage changes are estimated as logarithmic changes.

e: The factor shares of total labor is the ratio between total wage bill and total value added. The shares of the three skill groups are relative to the total industry wage bill. The capital share is omitted, since I assume it amounts to one minus total labor's share.

Table 4.4: Time Trends in Factor Input Ratios Across Traded–Goods Industries Estimated as Absolute Changes of the Ratios[a]

Factor Ratio	Without Industry Dummies				With Industry Dummies			
	1975	1980	1985	1990	1975	1980	1985	1990
$K_{i,t}/L_{i,t}^b$	0.022	0.025	0.034	0.035	0.022	0.026	0.035	0.039
$L(M)_{i,t}/L(U)_{i,t}^c$	–	0.775	1.801	2.928	–	0.723	1.685	2.777
$L(H)_{i,t}/L(M)_{i,t}^c$	–	0.007	0.020	0.035	–	0.008	0.018	0.033
$K_{i,t}/L(U)_{i,t}^c$	–	0.100	0.276	0.441	–	0.099	0.264	0.439
$K_{i,t}/L(M)_{i,t}^c$	–	-0.020	-0.020	-0.026	–	-0.017	-0.019	-0.018
$K_{i,t}/L(H)_{i,t}^c$	–	-2.243	-3.603	-4.385	–	-2.202	-3.481	-4.011

a,b,c: See table 4.2.

Table 4.5: Time Trends in Total Factor Productivity Across Traded–Goods Industries[a]

Factor Shares	Total Factor Productivity Referring to Capital and Total Labor[b,d]							
	Without Industry Dummies				With Industry Dummies			
	1975	1980	1985	1990	1975	1980	1985	1990
1970	0.044	0.162	0.237	0.317	0.044	0.165	0.238	0.315
1990	0.061	0.180	0.260	0.342	0.061	0.184	0.262	0.342
Factor Shares	Total Factor Productivity Referring to Capital and three Skill Groups of Labor[c,d]							
1975	–	0.118	0.207	0.306	–	0.119	0.206	0.301
1990	–	0.076	0.129	0.196	–	0.078	0.128	0.193

a,b,c: See table 4.2.

d: Changes in total factor productivity are estimated as logarithmic changes.

Table 4.6: Time Trends in Wages Across Non-Traded–Goods Industries[a]

	Without Industry Dummies				With Industry Dummies			
	1975	1980	1985	1990	1975	1980	1985	1990
Wage Index[d]	Relative to Deflator of Aggregate Value Added							
$w_{i,t} - py_t$ [b]	0.165	0.262	0.264	0.305	0.166	0.271	0.277	0.330
$w(u)_{i,t} - py_t$ [c]	–	0.072	0.071	0.104	–	0.080	0.086	0.128
$w(m)_{i,t} - py_t$ [c]	–	0.079	0.085	0.121	–	0.081	0.089	0.127
$w(h)_{i,t} - py_t$ [c]	–	0.105	0.148	0.163	–	0.107	0.153	0.167

Table 4.7: Time Trends in Wages Across Regulated Industries[a]

	Without Industry Dummies				With Industry Dummies			
	1975	1980	1985	1990	1975	1980	1985	1990
Wage Index[d]	Relative to Deflator of Aggregate Value Added							
$w_{i,t} - py_t$ [b]	0.168	0.237	0.232	0.270	0.173	0.249	0.248	0.291
$w(u)_{i,t} - py_t$ [c]	–	0.073	0.058	0.077	–	0.078	0.065	0.085
$w(m)_{i,t} - py_t$ [c]	–	0.065	0.064	0.101	–	0.068	0.069	0.106
$w(h)_{i,t} - py_t$ [c]	–	0.099	0.134	0.142	–	0.102	0.137	0.145

a,b,c: See table 4.2.

d: Wage changes are estimated as logarithmic changes.

Table 4.8: Weighted Regression Results of Relative Output Price Changes[d], Total Factor Productivity Growth, and the Sum of Both on Factor Income Shares[a]

	TFP–Growth		TFP–Growth plus Output Price Change[d]		Output Price Change[d]	
Factor	Total Factor Productivity Referring to Capital and Total Labor Using 1970 Factor Shares[b]					
	Coeff.	t-stat	Coeff.	t-stat	Coeff.	t-stat
K	0.328	1.5	-0.450	2.0	-0.778	2.1
L	0.316	2.3	0.491	3.7	0.175	0.8
Factor	Total Factor Productivity Referring to Capital and Total Labor Using 1990 Factor Shares[b]					
K	0.367	1.7	-0.171	0.8	-0.538	1.4
L	0.332	1.0	0.341	1.0	0.010	1.0
Factor	Total Factor Productivity Referring to Capital and Three Skill Groups of Labor Using 1975 Factor Shares[c]					
	Coeff.	t-stat	Coeff.	t-stat	Coeff.	t-stat
K	0.437	2.8	-0.211	1.6	-0.648	3.1
$L(U)$	0.919	2.9	0.711	2.7	-0.208	0.5
$L(M)$	-0.357	1.7	0.514	2.9	0.871	3.1
$L(H)$	3.488	2.7	-2.544	2.4	-6.032	3.6
Factor	Total Factor Productivity Referring to Capital and Three Skill Groups of Labor Using 1990 Factor Shares[c]					
K	0.489	4.1	-0.124	0.8	-0.613	3.0
$L(U)$	1.171	2.9	0.446	0.7	-0.725	1.1
$L(M)$	-0.520	3.5	0.374	2.3	0.894	3.5
$L(H)$	2.525	4.9	-1.167	2.0	-3.692	4.1

a: The left hand side variables in the regressions are logarithmic changes. Industry weights are the employment shares of the year for which factor shares are used to calculate TFP growth.

b: Change relative to 1970.

c: Change relative to 1975.

d: Output price changes are relative to deflator of aggregate value added.

4.6.3 Figures

Figure 4.1: Aggregate Trade Exposure (Relative to Total Value Added)

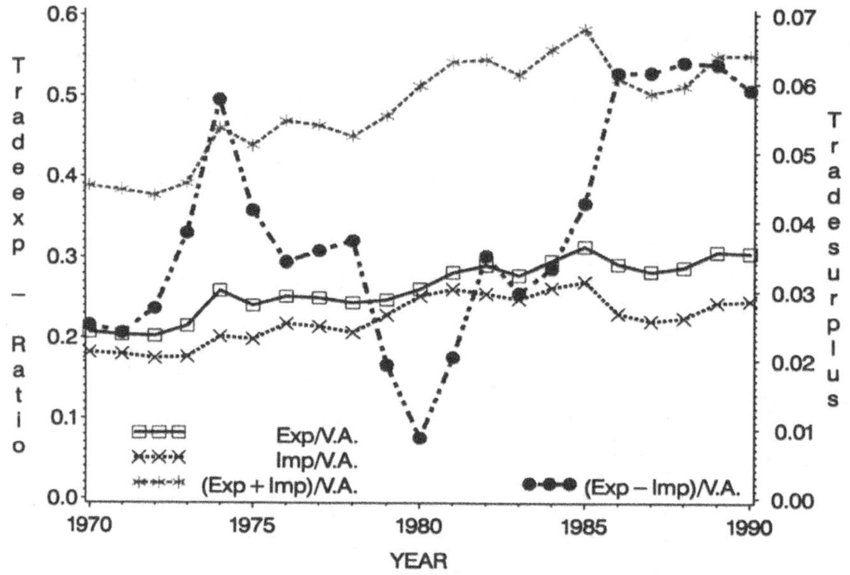

Figure 4.2: Export and Import Prices Relative to Aggregate PPI

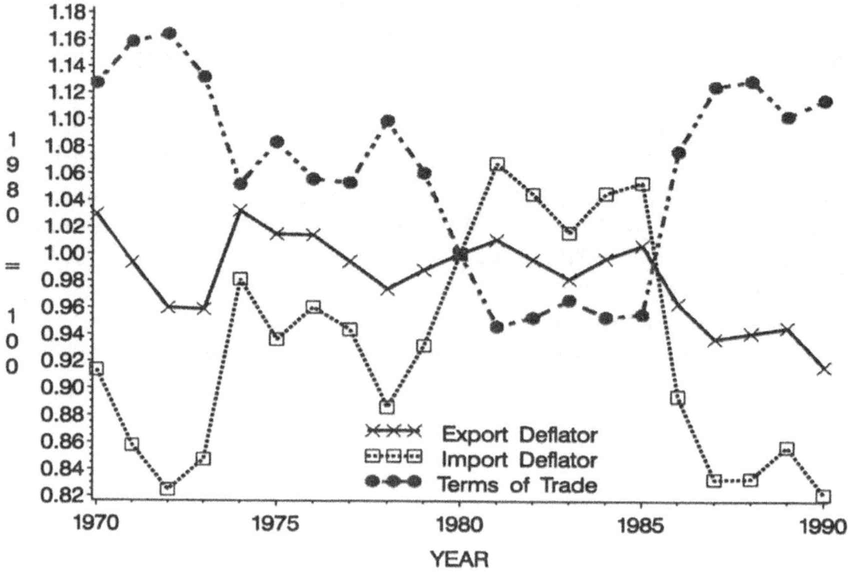

Figure 4.3: Aggregate Real Wages 1980=100 Medians (CPI adj.)

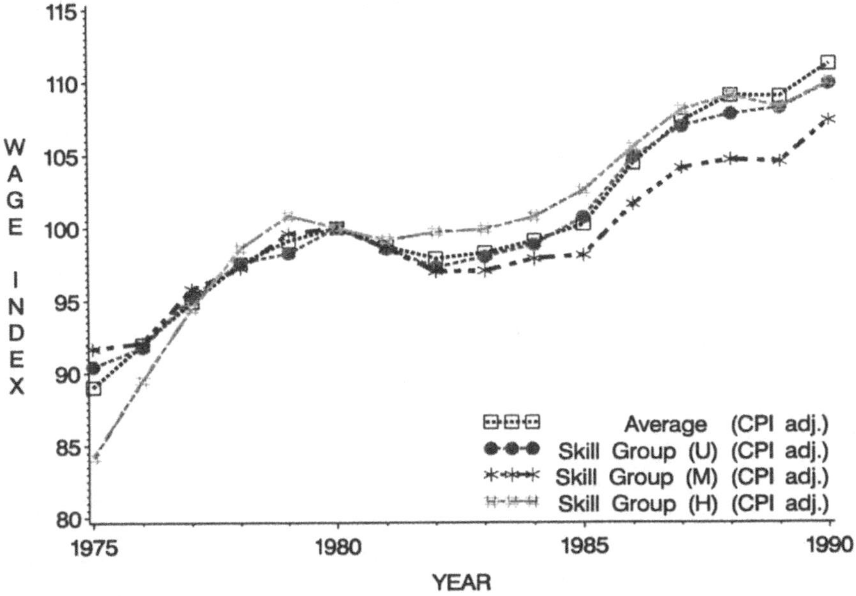

Figure 4.4: Average Time Trends in Total Factor Productivity (Based on Capital and Labor) Across Traded-Goods Industries – Logarithmic Changes (Weighted by Annual Factor Inputs)

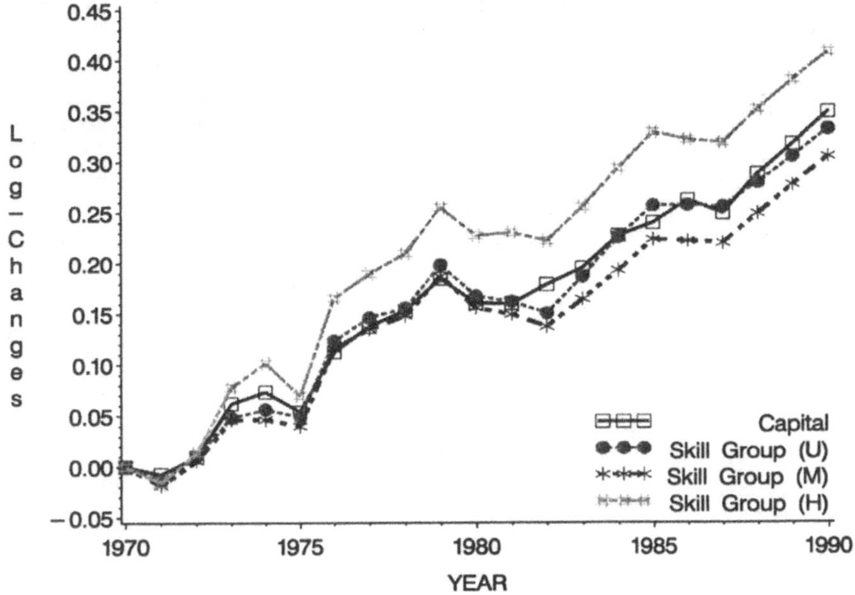

Figure 4.5: Average Time Trends in Product Prices Across Trade-Goods Industries (Weighted by Annual Factor Inputs) – Changes Relative to Deflator of Aggregate Value Added

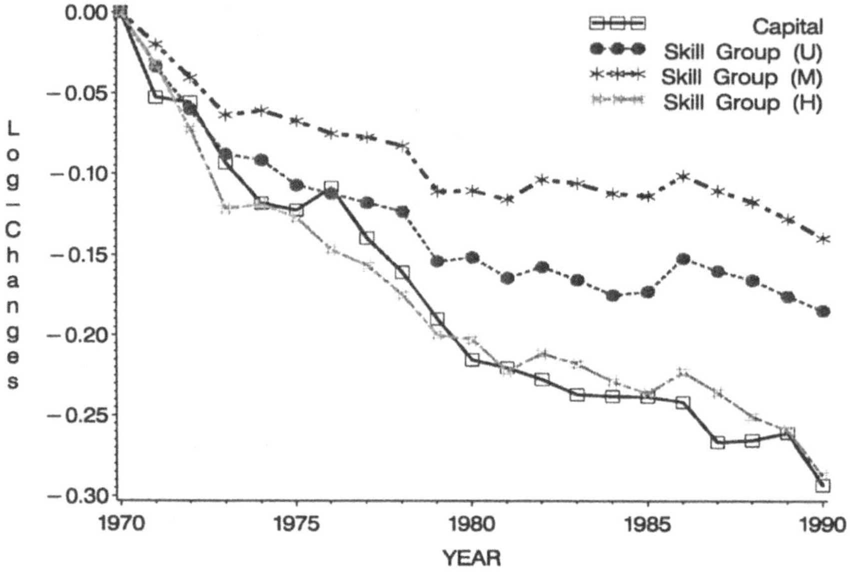

Figure 4.6: Average Time Trends in Export Prices Across Traded-Goods Industries (Weighted by Annual Factor Inputs) – Changes Relative to Deflator of Aggregate Value Added

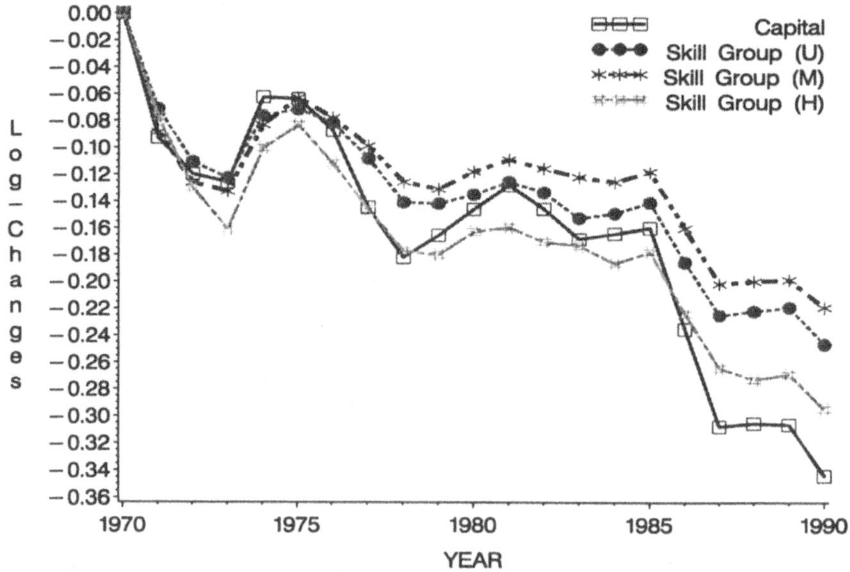

Figure 4.7: Average Time Trends in Import Prices Across Traded-Goods Industries (Weighted by Annual Factor Inputs) – Changes Relative to Deflator of Aggregate Value Added

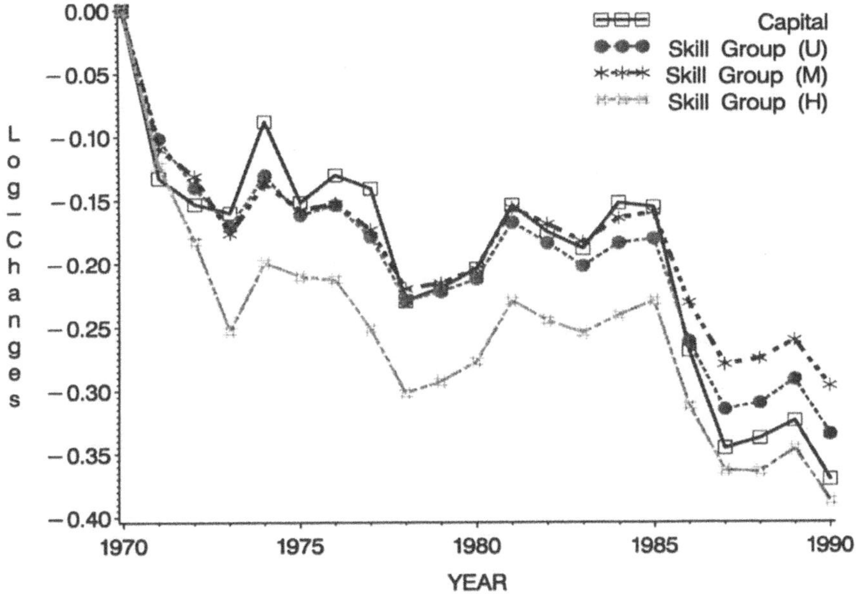

5 The Skill Structure of Labor Demand

The combination of intensified competition in a global economy and of labor–saving technical progress requires flexibility in wages, ...
Siebert (1997, p. 53)

In a simple demand and supply framework, the pervasive reduction in employment ratios between unskilled and skilled labor seems to offer only two alternative outcomes. In Krugman's (1994, 1995) or Freeman's (1995) characterization, either the US scenario of increasing wage dispersion in order to mitigate the adverse employment effects for the low–skilled or the European scenario of a rigid wage structure and ever increasing unemployment. This chapter provides a theoretical and empirical analysis of the determinants of the structure of labor demand across skill groups in West Germany for the time period from 1975 to 1990. The analysis has two goals: First, to determine the driving forces behind the "unfavorable" labor market trends for low–skilled workers. And second, to investigate whether and to what extent the structure of labor demand reacts to changes in the wage structure. This allows to analyze whether increased wage flexibility could also mitigate the unequal distribution of unemployment in West Germany following the stylized view of the US labor market mentioned above.

Analyzing the effects of wage flexibility, it is very important to distinguish two aspects. The first aspect concerns the impact of a general wage reduction on labor demand for all skill groups without a change in the dispersion of wages both across and within skill groups. And the second aspect concerns the impact of greater wage dispersion on the risk of unemployment across skill groups for a given employment level (or for a given output level). This chapter focuses on the second aspect without questioning the importance of the first. Changes in the wage structure clearly affect relative factor demand whereas uniform changes in the wage level could even be approximately neutral with respect to relative factor demand.

Referring to the stylized facts on wage growth in chapter 2, average wage growth for low–skilled workers was slightly higher from 1975 onwards compared to medium– and high–skilled workers. However, wage trends are not necessarily negatively related to the skill level. In particular in Manufacturing, one finds a U–shaped pattern with average wage growth for medium–

skilled workers lying below the trend both for low–skilled and high–skilled workers. These results are confirmed in chapter 3 based on estimated time trends for full–time working males controlling for the age of workers. Simply taking the raw trends in wages could be affected by composition changes in the labor force which are unrelated to changes in the price per efficiency unit of labor. Also this chapter uses estimated wage trends for the empirical analysis controlling for the age distribution of the workers.

There exists a small but growing German literature, which analyzes empirically the determinants of the skill bias in labor demand, see among others Beißinger and Möller (1998), Falk and Koebel (1997), Falk and Pfeiffer (1997), Fitzenberger and Franz (1998), Möller (1996), Pischke (1998), and Steiner and Wagner (1997). The stylized facts of employment trends across skill groups are presented in the chapters 2 and 4. Employment of low–skilled workers declines by about 50% over the time period from 1975 to 1990 whereas employment of high–skilled workers almost doubles. Using a shift–share analysis, skill upgrading occurs mostly within and not between industries. Most studies emphasize the importance of skill–biased technological change as the driving force. According to this hypothesis, new technologies make more highly skilled workers disproportionately more productive resulting in a skill bias of labor demand. The technological explanation is substantiated by the fact that skill upgrading basically occurs in the entire industrialized world rendering explanations based on national driving forces less credible. However, there are (at least) two alternative hypotheses for the skill bias in labor demand. First, the effects of globalization due to increased international trade with countries abundant in low–skilled labor, and second, the complementarity between capital and skilled labor. In addition, the economic policy debate often argues that wage compression resulted in an even stronger skill bias for employment trends in West Germany.

This chapter analyzes the determinants of the skill structure of labor demand. Even if the skill bias in labor demand is not mainly caused by changes in the wage structure, it is then investigated whether increased wage flexibility can help to reduce the adverse effects for low–skilled workers. The empirical analysis uses the conventional approach of a translog cost function and associated share equations. Compared to most of the literature, this study exhibits the following dinstinguishing features: First, in addition to the impact of average wage differences across skill groups, I also analyze the relevance of wage dispersion within skill groups on labor demand. Second, I estimate both static models of factor demand assuming cost minimizing behavior on average and partial adjustment models for factor demand allowing for short–run deviations from cost minimizing behavior. Third, the factor demand models are estimated using instrumental variable techniques in order to accommodate the likely endogeneity of wages and output. Fourth, in order to approximate the wage distribution per efficiency unit of labor, I use estimated trends in various quantiles of the wage distribution for full–time working males within a skill group controlling for age. These estimated indices are used as the relevant factor price measures. Fifth, standard error estimates are obtained using a block bootstrap procedure being robust against fairly arbitrary forms of heteroskedasticity and autocorrelation. Sixth, instead of proxying technological progress by a time trend, I use various technology indicators as determinants of labor demand. And seventh, I allow the impact of capital to differ between equipment and structures.

As a final introductory remark, it has to be kept in mind that the causality between the wage structure and employment is not as simple as often referred to in the economic policy debate and as it might appear in this chapter. The subsequent chapter 6 tries to model simultaneously the skill structure of wages and employment. Focusing on relative employment of workers without formal occupational degree (low–skilled), one finds that employment of this group decreased from 1976 to 1989 by 3.1 Million persons in West Germany whereas employment of workers with occupational degree (medium– and high–skilled) increased by around 5.1 Million persons (see German Council of Economic Experts, 1994, p. 257). The main question of this chapter is whether this adverse trend against low–skilled workers could have been mitigated by a more flexible wage structure while average wages remain at the same level. As discussed in chapter 1 and 2, Nickell and Bell (1996) raise some doubts about this possibility by pointing out that during the 1980's wages of low–skilled workers in West Germany were about twice as large as in the United States whereas the unemployment rates were about the same.

The remainder of this chapter is structured as follows: Section 5.1 presents the theoretical model of factor demand. The conventional approach of a translog cost function and associated share equations is extended to encompass the effects of wage dispersion within skill groups and to allow for short–run deviations from optimal behavior in the long run. Section 5.2 describes the database for the empirical analysis. Section 5.3 presents how the theoretical model developed in section 5.1 is implemented empirically and discusses the estimation results. Complementing the discussion of the empirical results, section 5.4 comprises the results of three simulation experiments. Section 5.5 summarizes the main findings obtained in this study. The appendix of this chapter contains detailed estimation results.

5.1 A Translog Approach

This section presents the empirical model used to estimate the skill structure of labor demand. The model consists of a conventional translog cost function and share equations resulting from cost minimizing behavior. The purpose is to analyze the determinants of relative labor demand for three skill groups: low–skilled (U), medium–skilled (M) and high–skilled (H) workers. Specifically, I attempt to quantify the impact of different factors on relative labor demand. Among these factors, the structure of wages plays a prominent role.[1] In comparison to factor demand systems, the estimation of a translog cost function and share equations represents a more general approach and requires less assumptions on the separability of factor inputs in the production process.[2]

The approach developed here extends upon standard translog cost functions in two respects. First, in addition to average prices for homogenous factor inputs also quantile differences in wages within the three skill groups are considered in a heuristic way.[3] Second, in addition to the static model also a dynamic version is developed which allows heuristically for factor adjustment costs. Following Nissim (1984) and Lindquist (1995), who suggest the estimation of the share equations as a multivariate error–correction model (see also Anderson and Blundell, 1982, and Ronning, 1986) this approach is augmented here by the estimation of the cost function taking account of the fact that factor inputs are not necessarily at their long–run optimal level.

The remainder of this section consists of two parts: The first subsection presents the conventional static translog cost function approach in the presence of quasi–fixed factors. The second subsection introduces the specific extensions introduced in this study.

5.1.1 Translog Cost Function and Share Equations

The basis of the empirical analysis in this study consists of the following specification of variable costs in an industry given output and given the usage of quasi–fixed input factors. The latter comprises equipment and structures (plants), the R&D–intensity, the share of firms reporting product or process innovations (only in MAN=Manufacturing), and the input intensity in final products of the electrical industry and of the computer industry (only in NON–MAN=Non–Manufacturing). The estimated specification differs by whether only the demand for the three types of labor or whether, in addition to labor, also the demand for material inputs (V) is considered, i.e. whether the cost function comprises only the cost of labor or, in addition, also the cost of material inputs. Since the first case ("without material inputs") is nested in the second ("with material inputs"), the following presentation considers the latter more general case and, when necessary, points to the differences. Hence, the translog cost function for industry i is given by (see Hamermesh, 1993, chapter 2):

---

[1] See e.g. Schulte zur Surlage (1985), Kugler et al. (1989), and Entorf (1996, section 6) for research using average factor prices at the aggregate level and Falk and Koebel (1997), Falk and Pfeiffer (1997), and Steiner and Wagner (1997) at the sectoral level.

[2] See Hamermesh (1993, chapter 2) for a general treatment and Steiner and Wagner (1997) for a direct estimation of the elasticity of substitution between two skill types of workers.

[3] See also the related study Fitzenberger and Franz (1998).

$$ln(C_{i,t}) = \alpha_i + \alpha_y\, ln(Y_{i,t}) + \frac{1}{2}\alpha_{yy}\, ln(Y_{i,t})^2 + \alpha_{ka}\, ln(KA_{i,t}) + \tag{5.1}$$

$$\frac{1}{2}\alpha_{kaka}\, ln(KA_{i,t})^2 + \alpha_{kb}\, ln(KB_{i,t}) + \frac{1}{2}\alpha_{kbkb}\, ln(KB_{i,t})^2 + \alpha_{rd}\, RD_{i,t} +$$

$$\frac{1}{2}\alpha_{rdrd}\, RD_{i,t}^2 + \alpha_{pd}\, PD_{i,t} + \frac{1}{2}\alpha_{pdpd}\, PD_{i,t}^2 + \alpha_{pz}\, PZ_{i,t} + \frac{1}{2}\alpha_{pzpz}\, PZ_{i,t}^2 +$$

$$\alpha_{el}\, EL_{i,t} + \frac{1}{2}\alpha_{elel}\, EL_{i,t}^2 + \alpha_{co}\, CO_{i,t} + \frac{1}{2}\alpha_{coco}\, CO_{i,t}^2 +$$

$$\sum_{j\in\{U,M,H,V\}} \alpha_{i,j}\, ln(w_{j,i,t}) + \frac{1}{2}\sum_{j,j'\in\{U,M,H,V\}} \beta_{j,j'}\, ln(w_{j,i,t})\, ln(w_{j',i,t})$$

$$+ \sum_{j'\in\{Y,KA,KB\}} \sum_{j\in\{U,M,H,V\}} \gamma_{j',j}\, ln(j'_{i,t})\, ln(w_{j,i,t})$$

$$+ \sum_{\substack{j'\in\{RD,PD,\\ PZ,EL,CO\}}} \sum_{j\in\{U,M,H,V\}} \gamma_{j',j}\, j'_{i,t}\, ln(w_{j,i,t}) \ ,$$

where $C_{i,t}$: variable costs ($\equiv$ real wage bill and costs of material inputs)
$Y_{i,t}$: real output (=value added without material inputs and total shipments with material inputs)
$KA_{i,t}$: real level of net capital stock in form of equipment
$KB_{i,t}$: real level of net capital stock in form of structures (plants)
$RD_{i,t}$: research and development expenditure (R&D) as share of total shipments
$PD_{i,t}$: share of firms reporting product innovations (only available for MAN industries)
$PZ_{i,t}$: share of firms reporting process innovations (only available for MAN industries)
$EL_{i,t}$: ratio of material inputs from electrical goods industry (31)[a] to total shipments (only used for NON–MAN industries)
$CO_{i,t}$: ratio of material inputs from computer industry (27)[a] to total shipments (only used for NON–MAN industries)
$w_{j,i,t}$: real average wage of skill group $j \in \{U, M, H\}$ and real price of material inputs $j = V$ (i.e. $w_{V,i,t} \equiv p_{V,i,t}$ and $L_{V,i,t} \equiv V_{i,t}$)
$\alpha_., \beta_., \gamma_.$: parameters of the cost function
i : industry i
t : time period (year) t
($C_{i,t}$ and $w_{j,i,t}$ are deflated by the consumer price index, $Y_{i,t}$, $KA_{i,t}$, and $KB_{i,t}$, as well as the numerators in $EL_{i,t}$, and $CO_{i,t}$ by their respective deflators.)

a: see tables A.1 and A.2 in the appendix for the industry classification

Here and in the following, it is understood that the terms involving PD

and PZ only apply for MAN and the terms involving EL and CO only for NON–MAN.

The translog cost function in (5.1) serves as a second–order Taylor–approximation to a general cost function. This study of factor demand is restrictive, since it models the demand for labor and for material inputs taking capital and technology as given. Hence, it should be viewed as being concerned with short– or medium–run behavior in factor demand. The use of capital as a quasi–fixed input factor allows to investigate directly whether a higher level of capital enhances the relative demand for more highly skilled labor (capital–skill complementarity). Obviously, when endogenizing capital demand, one could uncover substitutive and complementary relationships among factor inputs via the estimated cross–price elasticities of factor demand. However, the larger the estimated model, the more difficult it becomes to obtain a reliable and consistent picture of factor demand. In addition, it is difficult to estimate reliable user costs of capital, which hopefully should vary sufficiently across industries and which at the same time should not be correlated too closely with other regressors. Since for the U.S., Krusell et al. (1997) find that in an analysis of the causes for the rise in the wage differential across skills, one had to distinguish between equipment ($KA_{i,t}$) and structures ($KB_{i,t}$), this distinction is also made in this study. They argue convincingly that mainly the equipment component of the capital stock is responsible for the capital–skill complementarity.

With regard to technology, the variables $RD_{i,t}$, $PD_{i,t}$, and $PZ_{i,t}$ in MAN and $RD_{i,t}$, $EL_{i,t}$, and $CO_{i,t}$ in NON–MAN are used as proxy variables for technological progress in the production process for industry i. These measures avoid the unsatisfactory use of time trends as proxies for technological progress as, for instance, in Fitzenberger and Franz (1998).[4] R&D–intensity has been suggested among others in Machin et al. (1996). $PD_{i,t}$ and $PZ_{i,t}$ are a similar measure except that the focus is on realizations instead of expenditure. Since R&D–intensity in NON–MAN is only available at a very aggregated level and since $PD_{i,t}$ and $PZ_{i,t}$ are only available for MAN, I follow the suggestion by Papaconstantinou et al. (1996) and use the input coefficients from the electrical goods industry ($EL_{i,t}$) and from the computer industy ($CO_{i,t}$) as proxies for embodied technology diffusion. The idea here is, that recently the use of new technologies has mostly been associated with purchases from these high–tech industries. All technology variables considered here are measured in flows, whereas the production technology would rather require stocks. However, stocks of R&D capital or of other technology measures would have to be estimated themselves involving intricate assumptions about depreciation rates, see Nadiri and Prucha (1996). As a justification for the approach taken here, it can be argued that given depre-

[4]Traditionally, studies of the non–neutrality (factor bias) of technological progress have analyzed whether, given all other considered determinants, demand for some factor has moved autonomously over time, see among others Bergström and Panas (1992), Betts (1997), Falk and Pfeiffer (1997), or Falk and Koebel (1997).

ciation rates a higher technology flow variable is associated in the long run with a higher stock of the respective technology variable (see also Machin et al. 1996, 1997, and Neven and Wyplosz, 1996).

Cost minimizing behavior implies linear homogeneity of the cost function in factor prices. This results in the following restrictions:

$$\sum_{j\in\{U,M,H,V\}} \alpha_{i,j} = 1, \quad \sum_{j\in\{U,M,H,V\}} \beta_{j,j'} = \sum_{j'\in\{U,M,H,V\}} \beta_{j,j'} = 0$$

$$\text{and} \quad \sum_{j\in\{U,M,H,V\}} \gamma_{j',j} = 0 \quad \text{for all } j' \in \{y, ka, kb, rd, pd, pz, el, co\} \quad ;$$

these restrictions are imposed upon the estimated models in this chapter. It is not assumed that the implied partial production function is linear homogenous in the three types of labor and material inputs, since capital is assumed as quasi–fixed.

Shepard's Lemma for factor demand arising from cost minimization implies that the elasticities of the cost function with respect to one factor price correspond to the share of this factor in total (variable) costs. Therefore, the share for factor $j \in \{U, M, H, V\}$ in industry i in given by:

$$S_{j,i,t} \equiv \frac{w_{j,i,t} \cdot L_{j,i,t}}{C_{i,t}} = \frac{\partial ln(C_{i,t})}{\partial ln(w_{j,i,t})} \quad .$$

Differentiation of the specification in equation (5.1) results in the following linear share equations:

$$\begin{aligned} S_{j,i,t} \quad = \quad & \alpha_{i,j} + \beta_{j,U}\, ln(w_{U,i,t}) + \beta_{j,M}\, ln(w_{M,i,t}) + \beta_{j,H}\, ln(w_{H,i,t}) \\ & + \beta_{j,V}\, ln(p_{V,i,t}) + \gamma_{y,j}\, ln(Y_{i,t}) + \gamma_{ka,j}\, ln(KA_{i,t}) \\ & + \gamma_{kb,j}\, ln(KB_{i,t}) + \gamma_{rd,j}\, ln(RD_{i,t}) + \gamma_{pd,j}\, ln(PD_{i,t}) \\ & + \gamma_{PZ,j}\, ln(PZ_{i,t}) + \gamma_{el,j}\, ln(EL_{i,t}) + \gamma_{co,j}\, ln(CO_{i,t}) \, , \end{aligned} \qquad (5.2)$$

where symmetry in the cross–partial derivatives of the cost function implies

$$\beta_{j,j'} = \beta_{j',j} \quad \text{for all } j, j' \in \{U, M, H, V\} \, .$$

The empirical analysis involves the simultaneous estimation of equations (5.1) and (5.2). Based on the parameter estimates, the output–, capital–, and technology–constant factor price elasticities of the demand for the three types of labor and for material inputs can be determined as:

$$\eta_{j,j',i,t} = \begin{cases} \frac{\beta_{j,j}}{S_{j,i,t}} + S_{j,i,t} - 1 & \text{for} \quad j = j' \\ \frac{\beta_{j,j'}}{S_{j,i,t}} + S_{j',i,t} & \qquad\quad j \neq j' \; , \end{cases} \qquad (5.3)$$

where

$$\eta_{j,j',i,t} \equiv \begin{cases} \frac{\partial ln(L_{j,i,t})}{\partial ln(w_{j',i,t})} & \text{for} \quad j \in \{U, M, H\} \\ \frac{\partial ln(V_{i,t})}{\partial ln(w_{j',i,t})} & \text{for} \quad j = V \end{cases} \quad \text{and} \quad j' \in \{U, M, H, V\} \, .$$

Whereas the above estimates could be obtained by estimating solely the share equations, also estimation of the cost function is necessary to evaluate the reaction of factor demand with respect to changes in other variables. Considering changes in $X \in \{ln(Y), ln(KA), ln(KB), RD, PD, PZ, EL, CO\}$, it follows from equation (5.2) that

$$\frac{\partial S_{j,i,t}}{\partial X_{i,t}} = \begin{cases} S_{j,i,t} \cdot \frac{\partial ln(L_{j,i,t})}{\partial X_{i,t}} - S_{j,i,t} \cdot \frac{\partial ln(C_{i,t})}{\partial X_{i,t}} & \text{for} \quad j \in \{U, M, H\} \\ S_{j,i,t} \cdot \frac{\partial ln(V_{i,t})}{\partial X_{i,t}} - S_{j,i,t} \cdot \frac{\partial ln(C_{i,t})}{\partial X_{i,t}} & \text{for} \quad j = V \ . \end{cases}$$

Then, the reaction of factor demand with respect to changes in $X_{i,t}$ is given by

$$\frac{\partial ln(V_{i,t})}{\partial X_{i,t}} = S_{j,i,t}^{-1} \frac{\partial S_{j,i,t}}{\partial X_{i,t}} + \frac{\partial ln(C_{i,t})}{\partial X_{i,t}} \tag{5.4}$$

$$\equiv S_{V,i,t}^{-1} \gamma_{x,V} + \frac{\partial ln(C_{i,t})}{\partial X_{i,t}} \quad \text{for } j = V$$

and

$$\frac{\partial ln(L_{j,i,t})}{\partial X_{i,t}} = S_{j,i,t}^{-1} \frac{\partial S_{j,i,t}}{\partial X_{i,t}} + \frac{\partial ln(C_{i,t})}{\partial X_{i,t}}$$

$$\equiv S_{j,i,t}^{-1} \gamma_{x,j} + \frac{\partial ln(C_{i,t})}{\partial X_{i,t}} \quad \text{for } j \in \{U, M, H\} \ .$$

These estimates allow to determine whether and to what extent changes in X are non–neutral in their effect on the demand for the different factor inputs. Following the literature (see Bergström and Panas, 1992, and Betts, 1997), I define an increase in X as j–using (complementary to j), j–neutral, or j–saving (substitutive to j) if $\gamma_{x,j}$ is greater than, equal to, or less than zero. Then, the hypothesis of skill–biased technological change implies that $\gamma_{x,H} > \gamma_{x,M} > \gamma_{x,U}$ and, presumably, $\gamma_{x,H} > 0$ and $\gamma_{x,U} < 0$, i.e. if X is one of the technology measures (RD, PD, PZ, EL, CO), an exogenous increase in X should raise the relative demand for workers with higher skill levels. In addition to the $\gamma_{x,.}$ coefficients, the coefficients α_x and α_{xx} measure Hicks–neutral technical progress proxied by the technology indicator X, which does not exhibit an influence on relative factor demand.

Analogous to the technology variables, one can classify the impact of capital and output. Capital of type KA or KB (output) and the demand for factor j are in a complementary/neutral/substitutive relationship, if $\gamma_{ka,j}$, $\gamma_{kb,j}$ (or $\gamma_{y,j}$) $>/=/< 0$. In light of equation (5.4), one should keep in mind, that different signs of $\gamma_{x,j}$ and $\gamma_{x,j'}$ for $j \neq j'$ imply an increase in the relative demand for the complementary factor in reaction to an increase in $X_{i,t}$. In contrast, with equal signs, one cannot deduce directly the change in relative factor demand from the difference between $\gamma_{x,j}$ and $\gamma_{x,j'}$ since $\gamma_{x,j}$ is weighted by $S_{j,i,t}^{-1}$ in equation (5.4).

5.1.2 Extensions

This subsection introduces the specific extensions in this study to the conventional translog cost function approach presented in the previous subsection.

Quantile Differences in Wages

The translog cost function in equation (5.1) is extended by the effects of wage dispersion within the three skill groups. This way, it is attempted to take account heuristically of the fact that, even after controlling for age, sex, employment status and industry affiliation, the three skill groups are far from representing a group of homogenous workers, who are equally paid according to the simple model outlined above. Therefore, an analysis of factor demand and wage inequality has to take account both of wage differences between and within different groups of workers. Obviously, it would be most satisfactory to develop a complete theory of wage differences between and within groups and their impact on labor demand. However, this issue is not even mentioned in the comprehensive text book by Hamermesh (1993) on labor demand and I am not aware of any other study (apart from the related study Fitzenberger and Franz, 1998) suggesting an estimable model for this problem. In the approach suggested here, the estimated impact of the within–group wage dispersion does not necessarily reflect the cost minimizing behavior of firms. On the one hand, they can result from changes in workers' incentives when wage dispersion is reduced or increased for a given type of workers. And, on the other hand, a change can reflect differences in the unobserved ability distribution within the skill groups. For instance, this is likely to happen, if, assuming a fixed a priori ability distribution, younger cohorts of workers tend to have higher educational attainments. Then, the ability distribution for low–skilled workers becomes narrower over time and, for high–skilled workers, it increases over time. Both effects can have an impact on the estimated relative labor demand.

Turning to the suggested heuristic extension in this study, the translog cost function in equation (5.1) as an approximation of the true cost function is augmented by linear terms involving the relative differences between the 80%–quantile and the median and between the median and the 20%–quantile as well as by their interaction terms with average wages. Denoting the quantile differences for workers of type j in industry i and time period t by $dq8050_{j,i,t} = ln(w_{j,i,t}^{80\%}) - ln(w_{j,i,t}^{50\%})$ for $j \in \{U, M\}$ (due to the severe censoring of wages in group (H), the 80%–quantile is not considered here) and $dq5020_{j,i,t} = ln(w_{j,i,t}^{50\%}) - ln(w_{j,i,t}^{20\%})$ for $j \in \{U, M, H\}$, then the extended translog cost function is given by

$$ln(\tilde{C}_{i,t}) = ln(C_{i,t}) + \sum_{j \in \{U,M\}} \alpha_j^{8050}\, dq8050_{j,i,t} \qquad (5.5)$$

$$+ \sum_{j \in \{U,M,H\}} \alpha_j^{5020} \, dq5020_{j,i,t}$$

$$+ \sum_{j \in \{U,M,H,V\}} \sum_{j' \in \{U,M\}} \gamma_{j,j'}^{8050} \, ln(w_{j,i,t}) \, dq8050_{j',i,t}$$

$$+ \sum_{j \in \{U,M,H,V\}} \sum_{j' \in \{U,M,H\}} \gamma_{j,j'}^{5020} \, ln(w_{j,i,t}) \, dq5020_{j',i,t} \quad .$$

The extended share equations become

$$\tilde{S}_{j,i,t} = S_{j,i,t} + \sum_{j' \in \{U,M\}} \gamma_{j,j'}^{8050} \, dq8050_{j',i,t} \qquad (5.6)$$

$$+ \sum_{j' \in \{U,M,H\}} \gamma_{j,j'}^{5020} \, dq5020_{j',i,t} \, .$$

Estimation proceeds under the additional restrictions

$$\sum_{j \in \{U,M,H,V\}} \gamma_{j,j'}^{8050} = \sum_{j \in \{U,M,H,V\}} \gamma_{j,j'}^{5020} = 0$$

in order to keep linear homogeneity in average factor prices. These functional form assumptions imply a reaction of the cost function and of the share equations with respect to changes in within–group wage dispersion given the level of average wages. For the estimation without quantile differences, the empirical analysis in this chapter takes median wages as the representative average wage. However, when quantile differences are involved, the average wage is approximated by the average of the 20%–quantile, the median, and the 80%–quantile for group (U) and (M) and by the average of the 20%–quantile and the median for group (H). This allows to distinguish changes in wage dispersion for a given level of average wages ("average–preserving–spreads") from changes in the level of average wages representing parallel shifts of the entire wage distribution.[5] The reaction of demand for factor j with respect to changes in the quantile differences can be determined analogous to equation (5.4).

Dynamics in Factor Adjustment

A standard problem in the conventional estimation of static cost functions and share equations lies in the neglect of the dynamics in factor adjustment,

[5]The approach taken here differs from our earlier study, Fitzenberger and Franz (1998), where, in both cases, we approximated average wages by median wages. There, variation in a dispersion measure involves a change in the 20%– or 80%–quantile for a given level of the median, i.e. an increase in the 80%–50%–difference at the same time corresponds to a situation with higher wages and an increase in the 50%–20%–difference to a situation with lower wages in parts of the wage distribution.

see Franz (1993, section 4.3) and Hamermesh (1993, chapter 6). Typically, adjustment of the amount of factor inputs involves costs by itself (e.g. hiring or firing costs for labor), thus preventing firms from an instantaneous adjustment to the long–run optimal level. If the latter is described by a static model as formulated above, conventional estimates are plagued by autocorrelation in the error term of the estimated static cost functions and share equations.

Following Anderson and Blundell (1982), it is possible to estimate systems of share equations as a multivariate linear error–correction model even though this system is singular because the shares always add up to unity. Whereas the earlier literature (see also the critical appraisal of the literature in Ronning 1986, 1992), which is cited in Anderson and Blundell's paper, had focussed on highly restrictive and implausible formulations of the dynamics, the crucial insight of Anderson and Blundell is that, for each lag and for each difference term, it is necessary to introduce all but one share into the specification. Then, the authors show that it is possible to identify both the long–run and the short–run parameters determining factor demand even though there exists an identification problem with respect to the adjustment parameters (coefficients of the error–correction terms). In order to avoid the involved notation in their paper, this issue is discussed in the following for the special case of the partial adjustment model estimated in this study.

To my knowledge, Nissim (1984) and Lindquist (1995) represent the only empirical studies of dynamic factor demand using the approach suggested by Anderson and Blundell. A drawback of this approach has been so far that it does not integrate the estimation of the cost function itself. As pointed out above, simultaneous estimation of the cost function and the share equations is necessary if one is interested in the reaction of factor demand with respect to changes in variables other than factor prices (see equation 5.4). As a heuristic solution to this problem, I suggest in the following a simple modification of the translog cost function in the spirit of it being a second–order approximation. The cost function should describe the long–run cost minimizing behavior of the firm, i.e. it corresponds to the stable long–run solution of the dynamic model for the share equations. At the same time, actual observed costs involve higher costs due to deviations from the long–run optimal behavior. Accordingly, the long–run cost function is augmented by a quadratic form in the short–run deviations from long–run optimal shares.

In this study, I restrict attention to the partial adjustment model as a dynamic alternative to static estimation. Empirical estimates of more involved dynamic error–correction models did not yield satisfactory models (the results are not reported here). In addition, one should keep in mind that autocorrelation of the error term in the static model can also be dealt with by using autocorrelation–consistent standard errors if one is only interested in long–run relationships. Therefore, the dynamic model considered here is given by the following partial adjustment model for the share equations, which are rewritten in error–correction form,

$$\Delta S_{j,i,t} = \sum_{j' \in \{U,M,H,V\}} \tilde{d}_{j,j'} \cdot (S_{j',i,t-1} - \bar{S}_{j',i,t}) \quad \text{for} \quad j \in \{U,M,H,V\} \tag{5.7}$$

and by the following cost function

$$ln(\hat{C}_{i,t}) = ln(C_{i,t}) + \sum_{j,j' \in \{U,M,H,V\}} sc_{j,j'} \cdot (S_{j,i,t} - \bar{S}_{j,i,t}) \cdot (S_{j',i,t} - \bar{S}_{j',i,t}) \tag{5.8}$$

where $C_{i,t}$: long–run cost function
$\hat{C}_{i,t}$: actual observed level of costs in period t
$\bar{S}_{j,i,t}$: long–run optimal share according to equation (5.2) or (5.6) as a function of the parameters of the long–run cost function $C_{i,t}$ (or $\tilde{C}_{i,t}$, respectively) and the variables in time period t
$S_{j,i,t}$: actual observed share in period t
$\tilde{d}_{j,j'}$: adjustment parameters in share equations
$sc_{j,j'}$: parameters describing excess costs due to deviation of actual shares from their long–run optimal level

The above model assumes that the long–run optimal shares $\bar{S}_{j,i,t}$ are consistent with minimization of the long–run cost function $C_{i,t}$, while, in the short run, shares can differ from their long–run optimal level and it takes time for them to adjust. During the adjustment process, actual costs are higher than their long–run optimal level, which is modelled heuristically by a quadratic form in the deviations of the actual shares from their long–run optimal level. Thus, positive definiteness of the matrix formed by the coefficients $sc_{j,j'}$ is an empirically testable implication for the consistency of the approximation.

When estimating the above system, the parameters of the long–run cost function and the parameters $sc_{j,j'}$ are identified. Anderson and Blundell (1982) show that this is not the case for the adjustment parameters $\tilde{d}_{j,j'}$ due to the adding–up condition for the shares, see also Ronning (1986). Analogous to the static case, estimation of a system of dynamic share equations proceeds by omitting one equation completely and, in addition, one lagged share as a regressor in the remaining equations (see also Nissim, 1984, and Lindquist, 1995). Let V be the omitted share, then the estimated model for the shares becomes

$$\Delta S_{j,i,t} = \sum_{j' \in \{U,M,H\}} d_{j,j'} \cdot (S_{j',i,t-1} - \bar{S}_{j',i,t}) \quad \text{for} \quad j \in \{U,M,H\} \tag{5.9}$$

and only nine parameters $d_{j,j'}$ can be estimated. While the adding–up condition provides three further conditions to identify adjustment parameters of the omitted share equation for factor V (d_{VU},d_{VM},d_{VH}), it is not possible to recover the $\tilde{d}_{j,j'}$ in any of the four equations. This is the case because the estimated parameters can be linked to the model parameters in equations (5.7) only by the following three conditions for each of the equations $j \in \{U, M, H\}$

$$d_{j,U} = \tilde{d}_{j,U} - \tilde{d}_{j,V} \;, \quad d_{j,M} = \tilde{d}_{j,M} - \tilde{d}_{j,V} \;, \quad \text{and} \quad d_{j,H} = \tilde{d}_{j,H} - \tilde{d}_{j,V} \;.$$

However, for the purpose of this study, the above identification problem is of no concern, since the focus here is on the estimation of the long–run factor demand equations.

5.2 Data

To study the relationship between average wages, wage dispersion, and employment, it is natural to use industry data comprising wage and employment figures for different skill levels of labor. For this study, I had to construct such a dataset by merging national account data with the IAB–Beschäftigtenstichprobe ($\mathrm{I_A BS}$) dataset, a 1% random sample from German Social Security Accounts. In addition, the following data from various sources are merged with the basic dataset:

- Skill specific unemployment rates from Microcensus data
- Data on R&D expenditure (taken from the ANBERD database of the OECD, 1997)
- Shares of firms in Manufacturing Industries reporting Product (PD) or Process (PZ) Innovations (taken from the ifo Firm Panel described in Schneeweis and Smolny, 1996)
- Real material inputs from the computer industry and the electrical goods industry (see table A.1 for the industry classification) to the industries in NON–Manufacturing (taken from the Input–Output tables of the Federal Statistical Office)
- Gross union densities and predicted net union densities (taken from Fitzenberger, Haggeney, and Ernst, 1998)
- Indices for bargained wages (taken from the Federal Statistical Office)

The analysis is restricted to the pre–unification situation for West Germany up to 1990. This section describes the most important features of the data used while the appendix A.3 provides further details and the detailed industry classification.

The national accounts provide data from 1970 to 1990 for former West Germany at the 2– and 3–digit industry level (58 industries in total). These data comprise information on value added, production (shipment) value, net capital stock, total employment, wage bill, material inputs, and the respective price deflators. I decided to work with the 49 industries given by the industry classification in the appendix (tables A.1 and A.2). Price deflators for material inputs and shipment are only available at a more aggregated level compared to the classification used here. This is not a big problem for Non–Manufacturing where prices and real values are available for a number of industries. The situation is more serious for Manufacturing. Here, I use production price indices (taken from the commodities' statistics of the Federal Statistical Office) as the price deflator for shipments. This allows to construct real shipments, real material inputs, and a price deflator for material inputs.

The second dataset (I_ABS) is merged with the national accounts data since the latter only provide limited information on different skill types of labor. Based on the I_ABS data, I distinguish three skill groups of workers, as defined in chapter 2 and in the data appendix, which I label as low–skilled (U), medium–skilled (M), and high–skilled (H) workers. For each skill group, I calculate wage quantiles and employment shares in each industry and year. In 1975, the estimated employment shares were 32.2% for (U), 64.2% for (M), and 3.7% for (H). For 1990, these shares changed to 15.7% for (U), 76.6% for (M), and 7.7% for (H).

Unfortunately, the I_ABS does not include any information on hours worked. However, one can distinguish between full–time and part–time employment. While using employment figures for all workers (male and female, part–time and full–time), this study only considers wage trends for full–time working males in order to minimize the impact of participation changes and composition bias. It is assumed that wages for this group provide a better picture of trends in the price per efficiency unit of labor. Though somewhat questionable, the underlying assumption is that wages for different types of labor reflect their relative productivities. Put differently, it seems very difficult (and beyond the scope of this study) to implement empirically the model presented in section 5.1 when distinguishing workers by gender and by whether they work part–time or full–time.

5.3 Empirical Analysis

This section describes how the theoretical model developed in section 5.1 is implemented empirically and presents the estimation results.

5.3.1 Implementation

The empirical analysis of the translog model presented in section 5.1 involves the simultaneous estimation of the cost function and the share equations. Estimation proceeds separately for Manufacturing (MAN) and for Non–Manufacturing (NON–MAN) in West Germany during the time period

1975 to 1990, see tables A.1 and A.2 in the appendix for the industry classification. The analysis omits the sectors agriculture, government, and private households and non–profit organizations. Union membership differs considerably between MAN and NON–MAN (see Fitzenberger, Haggeney, and Ernst, 1998) and collective bargaining appears somewhat more important in MAN compared to NON–MAN. Also employment trends differ considerably, with the employment share of MAN declining continuously, and wage growth appears slightly larger in MAN.

The estimated models differ in three aspects: First, the analysis is either restricted to the demand for the three types of labor (without material inputs) or it also involves the demand for material inputs. Second, the model is estimated either without or with quantile differences of the wage distribution within skill groups as determinants of factor demand. And third, either the static model or the model allowing for partial adjustment in factor demand is considered. The first two aspects define models 1 to 4 as described in the following table:

Table 5.1: Definition of Models 1 to 4

Model 1 :	Without Material Inputs and Without Quantile Differences
Model 2 :	With Material Inputs and Without Quantile Differences
Model 3 :	Without Material Inputs and With Quantile Differences
Model 4 :	With Material Inputs and With Quantile Differences

The empirical analysis of the translog cost function and the share equations uses the total wage bill (without material inputs) or the sum of the wage bill and nominal material inputs as costs and defines the shares accordingly. Due to the censoring of wages, the shares for the three skill groups are approximated based on the median of the marginal wage distribution within the group (using data for males and females as well as for full–time and part–time workers). However, the wage arguments in the specification of the cost function and the share equations represent wage indices for full–time working males in order to obtain a measure of wage trends per efficiency unit of labor, which is unaffected by composition changes in the labor force (i.e. unaffected by changes in the share of part–time or of female workers and by the age structure of employees). The wage indices used are the result of censored quantile regressions, which are estimated separately for each of the 46 industries in MAN and NON–MAN and for each of the skill groups at the 20%–, 50%– and 80%–quantile (for (H) only at the 20%– and 50%–quantile). The estimation of the censored quantile regressions consider only full–time working males and the set of regressors consists of a second order age polynomial and of dummies for the years 1976 to 1990. The coefficient estimates for the time dummies are used as the wage indices for the different quantiles. The time trend at the median represents the average wage $w_{j,i,t}$ in the models without quantile differences (1 and 2). In the model with quantile differences, the average wage is approximated by the average of the three quantile indices for (U) and (M) and by the average of the two quantile indices for (H). The quantile differences themselves are given by the differences of the respective time trends at the different quantiles. The estimated models are pooled across MAN (32 industries) and across NON–MAN (14 industries). The results confirm that the models differ sufficiently between the two parts of the economy justifying the estimation of speparate relationships. Due to the log–linear structure of the estimated models and due to the presence of industry dummies in all equations, the use of wage indices is innocuous for the estimates.[6]

For the estimation pursued here, output and wages are likely to be endogenous variables. As shown in the next chapter, realized output is likely to depend on the marginal costs of production (in the presence of a downward slopping output demand curve) and, when setting wages, wage bargaining takes account of the demand function for each type of labor. In fact, Berman et al. (1994) and Machin et al. (1996, 1997) avoid the estimation of the impact of wages on factor demand because of this endogeneity problem (among other reasons). In contrast to most of the work for Germany (including section 3.2 in our earlier study Fitzenberger and Franz, 1998), the estimated model in this study does not treat output and wages as exogenous variables. Instead, instrumental variable (IV) estimation techniques are applied to overcome the likely endogeneity problem. Of course, the validity of this approach depends critically on the availability of good instruments. In fact, it is not easy to find a sufficient number of good and economically meaningful instruments. Thus, it proves necessary to use industry dummies and time dummies to control for common unobservable effects (over time for a given industry and across industries in a given time period) which reasonably can be assumed as being exogenous to an individual observation. In addition, the set of instruments comprises the levels of the quasi–fixed input factors, which are likely to be predetermined in the short run, import prices, which are determined on the world market, gross and net union density, as proxies for the bargaining power of unions in wage setting, and indices for bargained wage, which can be assumed as being predetermined at the firm level. In addition to net union density, I use gross union density as an additional instrument, since it involves the union members who are not employed in the industry. Thus, on the one hand, it is a proxy for the number of unemployed union members and, on the other hand, for the union's capacity to raise public support (and understanding during a strike) for its demands. The use of bargained wages as instruments is somewhat problematic. As outcomes of wage bargaining, they are likely to depend upon labor demand. However, since they are predetermined at the firm level and since actual wages can be higher than

[6]This would not be the case for alternative approaches to the estimation of factor demand, e.g. via a generalized McFadden cost function as implemented in Falk and Koebel (1997).

bargained wages, the use of these instruments seems nevertheless justified.

Summing up, the set of instruments is given by the following list:

- Industry Dummies
- Time Dummies
- Level of quasi–fixed input factors
- Import Prices
- Gross and Net Union Density
- Indices for Bargained Wages (differing by sex and by the blue–collar/white–collar "Arbeiter/Angestellte" distinction) and their interaction with net and gross union density

Since the dynamic partial adjustment model involves lagged endogenous variables in the share equations, I estimate the model in first differences using an IV version of the estimation procedure for panel data suggested by Anderson and Hsiao (1981) and Arrellano and Bond (1991). First differencing of the cost function still involves industry dummies due to the interaction terms with factor prices. I take the exact first difference of the cost function such that the level intercepts of the share equations are estimated via the cost function. Since the cost function does not involve lagged endogenous variables and since first differencing of the share equations eliminates the industry dummies, this procedure still yields consistent estimates. For comparability, I also estimate the static equation in first differences. This way, estimation only takes account of the short–run determinants of labor demand, which seems consistent with the use of the quasi–fixed input factors as regressors and instruments. Since the models are estimated in first differences, all instruments are also used in first differences. For those exogenous variables in the cost function involving squares also the differences of the squared variables is used as instrument. When estimating the partial adjustment model by the Arrellano–Bond procedure, I use the second and the third lag of the shares as additional instruments.

The cost functions in equations (5.1), (5.5), and (5.8), and the share equations (5.2), (5.6), and (5.7), respectively, are estimated using IV techniques as a simultaneous system of seemingly unrelated regressions ("SUR"). Since the shares sum up to unity ($\sum_{j\in\{U,M,H(,V)\}} S_{j,i,t} = 1$), I omit the equation for $S_{H,i,t}$ for the models without material inputs and the equation for $S_{V,i,t}$ for the models with material inputs. In order to avoid that the estimates depend upon which share equation is omitted, the cross–equation restrictions (equality of certain coefficients) are imposed in the second step but not in the first step of the SUR–estimation (see Berndt, 1991, p. 474, and Bergström and Panas, 1992). Estimation proceeds as weighted IV–SUR estimation where total employment is used as weight for an industry.

The estimation of a translog cost function involves a well known methodological problem: It is not guaranteed that the estimated cost function is everywhere concave in factor prices (as required by microeconomic theory). This problem occurred, for instance, in our earlier study Fitzenberger and Franz (1998), where we estimated a positive own–price elasticity for factor demand of (H) in NON–MAN. However, imposing concavity on the translog specification would typically result in substitution effects which are close to the Cobb–Douglas case, since the latter represents the first–order approximation and always satisfies the concavity restriction. Alternatively, one could choose a flexible functional form in the original data (not in logarithms) and impose concavity directly on the estimated specification without loosing flexibility to the same extent as for the translog specification (see Falk and Koebel, 1997, for an application). However, an implementation of this approach requires information on the levels of factor prices, whereas the approach taken here uses estimated wage trends controlling for the age composition of the skill groups. As shown by the results presented in the following section, the strategy chosen here is successful in the sense that it does not lead to the inconsistency of positive own–price elasticities.

I conclude this subsection with some remarks on the estimation of the standard errors. First differencing introduces an MA(1) process into the error term of the estimated models. In addition, as pointed out above, the static model might be plagued by autocorrelation of the error term in the level equation due to adjustment costs for factor demand. Such autocorrelation introduces further complicated autocorrelation patterns into the first differenced equations. Also, it is unclear whether the partial adjustment model completely takes account of the autocorrelation in the level equation. Therefore, in order to draw robust inference, standard errors are estimated by a block bootstrap procedure based on 1000 resamples, where resamples are formed by drawing blocks of observations with replacement from the sample (see appendix for details on the block bootstrap procedure). The standard errors estimated by the block bootstrap procedure are robust against heteroskedasticity and autocorrelation of fairly general form. In addition, basing the two steps of the SUR–estimation procedure on the same resample automatically takes account of the sampling error in the first step parameter estimates, which are predetermined in the second step. In the empirical implementation in this study, the blocks consist of five adjacent observations over time for a given industry (experimenting for some specifications with a larger block length did not seem to change standard errors in an important way). This allows to accommodate autocorrelation of the error term in each equation and non–constant correlation (not taken account of by the SUR approach) of error terms across equations. The resample size in this study is chosen to be twice as large as the sample size in order to mitigate problems with singular samples, i.e. samples for which not all dummy coefficients are identified. This way, in fact, not a single singular resample was drawn in my application. According to the asymptotic rate involved, the bootstrap variance–covariance matrix had to be multiplied by two.

5.3.2 Estimation Results

The estimated parameters of the (extended) translog cost function (with the exception of the industry effects) are given in tables 5.4 and 5.5 for the static model and in tables 5.6 and 5.7 for the partial adjustment model. As an illustration, the implied factor price elasticities are calculated both for three industries in MAN (industries 4, 16, and 17) and for three industries in NON–MAN (industries 36, 37, and 43) in table 5.8. This subsection gives an overview of the estimation results in two parts. First, the coefficient estimates are discussed. Second, the estimated factor price reactions are evaluated through the implied elasticities of factor demand. A further evaluation of the estimated static models is provided by the simulation results in section 5.4.

Starting with the static models in tables 5.4 and 5.5, an increase in output both in MAN and NON–MAN seems to reduce the relative demand for low-skilled labor (U) ($\gamma_{yU} < 0$) and to benefit the demand for material inputs ($\gamma_{yV} > 0$).[7] The results for (M) and (H) depend upon whether material inputs are considered. Without material inputs, output growth benefits the demand for (M) both in MAN and NON–MAN and for (H) in MAN. With material inputs output growth reduces the relative demand for (M) both in MAN and NON–MAN and for (H) in MAN. A further evaluation of the total output effects on factor demand is given by the simulation experiment in section 5.4. According to equation 5.4 the total effects involve further coefficients from the cost function.

Turning to the effects of an increase in the capital stock, the findings typically show opposite signs for equipment (KA) and for plants (KB). Since both components of capital are likely to be correlated, this might be indicative of multicollinearity. However, such differencies are to be expected from the findings in Krusell et al. (1997) for the United States and the coefficients prove mostly significant. The results obtained here are fairly robust across specifications but they differ between MAN and NON–MAN. In MAN, an increase in KA benefits the demand for (M) and (H) ($\gamma_{kaM}, \gamma_{kaH} > 0$) whereas an increase in KB benefits solely the demand for (U) ($\gamma_{kbU} > 0$). In NON–MAN, the impact of an increase in KA seems to exhibit a U–shaped pattern with regard to the skill level benefitting both (U) and (H). In addition, it tends to reduce the relative demand for material inputs (V). The situation for KB is almost opposite since an increase only reduces the demand for (U). Overall, the evidence for the classical hypothesis of a capital–skill comple-

[7] To simplify the exposition, I infer here and in the following the direction of the change in relative factor demand from the sign of $\gamma_{\cdot}$, e.g. the demand for (U) relative to (M) and (H). However, it should be kept in mind, that with equal signs one cannot infer the direction of change from the difference of the $\gamma_{\cdot}$ coefficients. This refers to the discussion above concerning equation (5.4).

mentarity is mixed. Typically, this hypothesis relates to KA and not to KB. Therefore, the capital–skill complementarity is confirmed for (H) and (M) in MAN and only for (H) in NON–MAN. However, the complex patterns do not allow for the conclusion that capital–skill complementarity has been a major factor explaining the skill bias in labor demand trends. Overall, the findings here show that it is not justified to pool the two forms of capital (as done in our earlier study Fitzenberger and Franz, 1998). There, we found a U–shaped pattern in MAN and a confirmation of the capital–skill complementarity in NON–MAN. And, as a final remark relating to the next point, it should be mentioned that an increase of the capital stock often embodies new technology making it hard to distinguish the two effects.

Instead of modelling technological progress as a residual time trend, the estimated models in this study consider three measures of technological progress both for MAN and NON–MAN. Starting with the results in MAN, only R&D–intensity (RD) seems to show a robust and significant influence on the structure of factor demand. An increase in RD increases monotonically the demand for more highly skilled workers confirming the notion of skill–biased technological change. Interestingly, an increase in RD also seems to reduce the relative demand for material inputs. There exists weak evidence for an influence of the share of product innovators PD slightly reducing the demand for (M) and (H) and increasing the demand for material inputs. In NON–MAN, the findings are less clear–cut: Only in the models without material inputs, RD shows a significantly positive influence on the relative demand for (H). In all models, the alternative technology indicators EL exhibits a significantly negative influence on the relative demand for (H) and in the models with material inputs also CO exhibits a significantly negative influence on (H) and EL on (M). The demand for material inputs appears positively related to the two alternative indicators. However, this result should be treated with great caution since these indicators, in fact, measure the input coefficients for a subset of material inputs. Relying mainly on the results without material inputs, the evidence for skill–biased technological change in NON–MAN is much weaker although the high absolute value of γ_{rdH} is likely to dominate the negative effect of EL. Note that RD is very imprecisely estimated for NON–MAN (see data appendix) which is reflected in the high estimated standard errors. The mere size of the coefficient estimates γ_{rdU}, γ_{rdM}, and γ_{rdH} indicates a very strong technology effect in NON–MAN.

Turning to average factor prices, their impact on the shares in MAN is mostly insignificant whereas one finds significant effects in NON–MAN. In NON–MAN, the share of almost all factors (especially for the model without material inputs) is negatively affected by an increase in the own factor prices. Thus, for the share to decline, an increase of the factor price results in a large decline in the demand for the respective factor such that the share for this factor decreases. From these findings, it follows that factor demand tends to be more elastic in NON–MAN compared to MAN. The detailed analysis of the reaction to factor prices is facilitated when evaluating the implied elasticities given in table 5.8.

Considering the factor demand elasticities with respect to changes in average factor prices, table 5.8 presents the estimates implied by the static models for selected industries in MAN (industries 14,26,27) and in NON–MAN (industries 46,50,61). The presented elasticities are calculated from the coefficient estimates according to equation 5.3 based on the average shares during the sample period. Some robust findings emerge: First, both for MAN and NON–MAN, own–price elasticities of factor demand are significantly negative in all cases, except one. The exception involves material inputs in the trade sector. Therefore, in contrast to some findings in Fitzenberger and Franz (1998), the estimated models basically satisfy a necessary condition for concavity of the cost function. Second, the estimated own–price elasticities exhibit an inverse U–shaped pattern across skill groups. Both for (U) and (H), labor demand is more elastic compared to (M) ($|\eta_{U,U,i,.}| > |\eta_{M,M,i,.}|$ and $|\eta_{H,H,i,.}| > |\eta_{M,M,i,.}|$). And, again in contrast to the findings in Fitzenberger and Franz (1998), this is the case both for MAN and NON–MAN. Compared to the demand for the three skill types of labor, the own–price elasticity for material inputs is considerably smaller in absolute value (in the trade sector, it is not even significantly different from zero). Third, the own–price elasticity for (U) is considerably larger and for (H) slightly larger in NON–MAN compared to MAN. There is no clear pattern for (M). Fourth, basically all factors are substitutes since the estimated cross–price elasticities are mostly significantly positive. Substitutability is particularly large between (U) and (M) both in MAN and NON–MAN and between (H) and (M) in MAN. The cross–price elasticities involving material inputs and (U) are also fairly large and mostly significantly positive. In NON–MAN, one finds some significant negative values regarding material inputs and (M) or (H), respectively. Overall, the results for the average factor prices consistently show an inverse U–shaped behavior of own–price elasticities and fairly large substitution effects between the three types of labor. These findings are in rough accordance with Fitzroy and Funke (1994). Based on aggregate data for two skill groups, these authors show that the own–price elasticity for less skilled workers is larger in absolute value than for more skilled workers. Similar to the results in our earlier study Fitzenberger and Franz (1998) for MAN, this study shows a somewhat more complex picture.

To conclude the presentation of the static models, I will discuss the effects of wage dispersion within the three skill groups implemented by the difference between the 80%– and the 50%–quantile of the within wage distribution (for U and M) and the difference between the 50%– and the 20%–quantile (for U,M, and H). Turning to the coefficient estimates in tables 5.4 and 5.5, it is, at first, difficult to evaluate the results. In the models without material inputs, only a small number of coefficients proves significant. The number is somewhat larger in the model with material inputs. In addition, different coefficients are significant in MAN and NON–MAN and their signs often differ as well. Thus, it is useful to move to the discussion of the implied factor demand elasticities. But, before doing so, two important coefficient estimates will be discussed. Since it is often argued that wage flexibility for low–skilled workers is reduced due to wage floors set by the wage bargaining system, the coefficients relating to $dq5020_{U,i,t}$ are of particular interest. The coefficients in the share equations γ_{UU}^{5020} and γ_{MU}^{5020} prove insignificant both in MAN and NON–MAN. However, the linear impact coefficient α_U^{5020} is significantly positive in MAN and significantly negative in NON–MAN (the latter only in the model without material inputs). Taken literally, the result for MAN (NON–MAN) shows that variable costs increase (decrease) significantly with a rise in wage dispersion for (U) below the median. Given that average factor prices remain the same, this implies that, according to equation 5.4, demand for all variable inputs increases (decreases) significantly in MAN (NON–MAN). This conclusion is not rejected by the elasticity estimates in table 5.8 even though some of the elasticities are not significant (standard errors also comprise the sampling variability from the insignificant coefficients in the share equations).

Turning to the estimated factor demand elasticities with respect to quantile differences in table 5.8, the interpretation becomes more simple. In MAN, the above finding is basically confirmed that employment of all inputs increases with an increase of wage dispersion for (U) below the median. There is slight evidence for the model with material inputs that an increase of the wage dispersion for (M) below the median reduces demand for (U) and raises the demand for all other variable factors. But this result is not present in the model without material inputs. Increasing the wage dispersion for (M) above the median tends to raise significantly the demand for (M) and (H) and to reduce the demand for (U). There are no robust significant results like this for the other quantile differences in MAN. Considering NON–MAN, one even finds a smaller number of significant effects. Dispersion below the median for (H) tends to increase significantly the demand for all labor types but this finding only shows up in the model without material inputs. As discussed in the previous paragraph, the demand for all labor inputs in the model without material inputs tends to decrease with an increase of wage dispersion for (U) below the median. However, no such significant effect is present in the model with material inputs. Here, an increase in wage dispersion for (M) above the median tends to increase strongly the demand for (U) and to decrease strongly the demand for (H). In addition, it tends to raise the demand for (M) and for material inputs but the latter coefficients are not always significant. This time, no significant effects of a change in wage dispersion for (M) above the median can be found in the model without material inputs. No further significant effects of wage dispersion can be found for the industries in NON–MAN. Overall, since the significant effects found for NON–MAN are not robust to whether material inputs are included in the specification, one can conclude that there is some evidence for an impact of wage dispersion on labor demand in MAN and close to no such evidence for NON–MAN. However, since the modelling of the impact of wage dispersion in this study is fairly heuristic, further research on this topic is needed.

This section concludes with the presentation of the results for the partial adjustment model. The estimated coefficients are given in tables 5.6 and 5.7. Even though the error–correction adjustment parameters $d_{j,j'}$ (see equation 5.7) are mostly significant, the estimated dynamics often prove unsatisfactory. In MAN model 1, d_{MM} is not negative, i.e. the model does not guarantee adjustment to the long–run optimal level in factor demand. And in model 3, d_{UU} is not significantly negative whereas d_{MM} becomes significantly negative. For NON–MAN with and without material input and for MAN with material inputs, the $d_{j,j'}$ coefficients are more robust across specifications and the signs of the coefficients on the lagged own share prove significantly negative in each equation. Turning to the additional coefficients $sc_{j,j'}$ in the cost function indicating the additional costs due to short–run deviations in factor demand from its long–run optimal level, the results show that none of the estimated coefficients is significant and for MAN some of the diagonal effects ($j = j'$) are even negative. Thus, the correction for short–run deviations from long–run optimal behavior do not manifest themselves in the expected way. This indicates that the heuristic approach suggested here for the correction of the cost function is not successful in the empirical implementation. In addition, compared to the static models, the partial adjustment model shows close to no significant estimates for the long–run parameters. Therefore, the results for the partial adjustment model are somewhat unsatisfactory and I decided to evaluate the estimated factor demand elasticities presented above and the simulation results in the next section based on the estimated static models. Possibly, the implementation of the Arrellano–Bond procedure while accounting for the endogeneity of factor prices and output does not leave enough information to estimate precisely both the dynamics of factor adjustment and the long–run determinants of factor demand.

5.4 Simulation Results

This subsection is concerned with the implications of the estimation results presented in the previous section. I restrict the attention to the static models since, as argued in the previous section, the estimated dynamic models did not perform satisfactorily. From a policy point of view, it is of interest to quantify the reaction of the skill structure of labor demand with respect to changes in the wage structure in order to evaluate the extent by which wage changes could have mitigated the trend against lower skilled workers. It is also possible to quantify the impact of output changes on labor demand for the three types of labor. Thus, for an evaluation of the magnitudes, I use the estimation results here to perform the following simulation experiments:

1. What are the necessary changes in relative average wages between the three skill groups to equalize the unemployment rates of the three skill groups in 1990?

2. What are the necessary changes in wages dispersion within the skill groups to equalize the unemployment rates of the three skill groups in 1990?

3. What is the impact on labor demand and on unemployment rates of a 10% increase of output in MAN? What in NON–MAN?

Before turning to the details, some general remarks about the design of these experiments are in order. The first two simulation experiments are concerned with output–constant effects of changes in the wage structure. The wage elasticities obtained in table 5.8 describe the reaction of labor demand for a given output involving the pure substitution effect along a given isoquant. Thus, the first two experiments are only concerned with the distribution of employment (and therefore unemployment) among the three skill types of labor. For the models with material inputs, this notion has to be made more precise. Put differently, only the wage ratios (and the ratio to the price for material inputs) matters for the factor input given output and it is not possible to increase the input of all factors by changing the factor price structure. Therefore, in the model without material inputs, it is not possible to raise simultaneously employment for all three skill groups. In order to analyze the level of total employment, one would have to endogenize the output effects with respect to changes in factor prices. This is not attempted in this chapter. It is to be expected (see the next chapter) that concomitant reductions (increases) in the wage level are associated with employment gains (reductions) due to a likely increase (reduction) in output.

The third experiment is concerned with the effect of an exogenous increase in output. This might be the result of an expansionary fiscal policy or of an autonomous shift in output demand (e.g. due to exchange rate changes, due to taste shifts, or due to wealth effects). Hereby, it is possible to quantify whether and to what extent mere output growth can alleviate the unemployment problem for the different skill groups. For instance, if it is the case that output growth benefits mostly the group with the lowest unemployment rate then it seems very unlikely that general unemployment can be considerably reduced this way (see also the simulation experiment in Falk and Koebel (1997) showing – this argument is my interpretation of their simulation results – that output growth has to be so large to eliminate the unemployment problem for low–skilled workers such that very soon demand for all other skill groups would exceed the supply). At given factor prices, possible output growth is limited by the fixed supply of the three types of labor. A further problem of this experiment lies in the fact, that with material inputs the total effect on labor demand remains unclear since, in this study, I do not model the complete input–output structure of the economy. Therefore, it is unclear to what extent changes in the factor demand for material inputs translates into labor demand changes in those industries producing the material inputs.

Next, the description of the details of the three simulation experiments follows:

1. The goal is to determine the necessary changes in relative average wages across skill groups in order to equalize unemployment rates across skill groups. Actual unemployment rates in 1990 are given later in this section in table 5.3. The goal of equal unemployment rates can be formulated by means of the following equations

$$\frac{L_H^*}{L_U^*} = \frac{\sum_i L_{H,i}^*}{\sum_i L_{U,i}^*} = \frac{LS_H}{LS_U} \quad \text{and} \quad \frac{L_M^*}{L_U^*} = \frac{\sum_i L_{M,i}^*}{\sum_i L_{U,i}^*} = \frac{LS_M}{LS_U}\,, \tag{5.10}$$

where LS_j : labor supply of skill group $j \in \{U, M, H\}$ in 1990 (derived by the definition of the skill specific unemployment rate $ur_j = 1 - L_j/LS_j$)

L_j : actual total employment of skill group $j \in \{U, M, H\}$ in 1990 ($L_j = \sum_i L_{j,i}$ equals the sum of employment of group j across industries i)

$L_{j(,i)}^*$: hypothetical employment level in situation with equal unemployment rates

The hypothetical employment levels in the situation with equal unemployment rates can be expressed as a first–order Taylor series expansion around actual employment levels. After rearranging terms, this yields

$$L_j^* = \sum_i L_{j,i}^* = \sum_i \left\{ L_{j,i} + L_{j,i}\, \eta_{j,H,i} \left[ln\left(\frac{w_{H,i}^*}{w_{U,i}^*}\right) - ln\left(\frac{w_{H,i}}{w_{U,i}}\right)\right]\right.$$

$$+ L_{j,i}\, \eta_{j,M,i} \left[ln\left(\frac{w_{M,i}^*}{w_{U,i}^*}\right) - ln\left(\frac{w_{M,i}}{w_{U,i}}\right)\right]$$

$$\left. + L_{j,i}\, \eta_{j,V,i} \left[ln\left(\frac{p_{V,i}^*}{w_{U,i}^*}\right) - ln\left(\frac{p_{V,i}}{w_{U,i}}\right)\right]\right\}$$

$$= L_j + \Delta_{HU} \sum_i L_{j,i}\eta_{j,H,i} + \Delta_{MU} \sum_i L_{j,i}\eta_{j,M,i} + \Delta_{VU} \sum_i L_{j,i}\eta_{j,V,i}$$

where $w^*_{j,i}$: hypothetical average wage level for skill group $j \in \{U, M, H\}$ in situation with equal unemployment rates (year 1990 for industry i)

$p^*_{V,i}$: hypothetical price of material inputs in situation with equal unemployment rates (year 1990 for industry i)

$\Delta_{j,U}$: necessary change (assumed to be common across industries i) in logarithmic differences of average factor prices between factor $j \in \{M, H, V\}$ and skill group (U) in order to achieve a situation with equal unemployment rates

In order to obtain a unique solution, the necessary changes $\Delta_{j,U}$ are assumed to be the same across industries i irrespective of the differences in wage levels. Also, from a practical point of view, it seems more likely that equal relative changes across all industries could be implemented compared to changes of the interindustry wage structure. Using the two conditions (5.10), one obtains the following two linear equations in $\Delta_{j,U}$

$$LS_U \left[L_H + \Delta_{HU} \sum_i L_{H,i}\eta_{H,H,i} + \Delta_{MU} \sum_i L_{H,i}\eta_{H,M,i} \right. \tag{5.11}$$

$$\left. + \Delta_{VU} \sum_i L_{H,i}\eta_{H,V,i} \right] - LS_H \left[L_U + \Delta_{HU} \sum_i L_{U,i}\eta_{U,H,i} \right.$$

$$\left. + \Delta_{MU} \sum_i L_{U,i}\eta_{U,M,i} + \Delta_{VU} \sum_i L_{U,i}\eta_{U,V,i} \right] = 0$$

$$LS_U \left[L_M + \Delta_{HU} \sum_i L_{M,i}\eta_{M,H,i} + \Delta_{MU} \sum_i L_{M,i}\eta_{M,M,i} \right.$$

$$\left. + \Delta_{VU} \sum_i L_{M,i}\eta_{M,V,i} \right] - LS_M \left[L_U + \Delta_{HU} \sum_i L_{U,i}\eta_{U,H,i} \right.$$

$$\left. + \Delta_{MU} \sum_i L_{U,i}\eta_{U,M,i} + \Delta_{VU} \sum_i L_{U,i}\eta_{U,V,i} \right] = 0$$

For the model without material inputs, equation system (5.11) can be solved exactly for the necessary changes $\Delta_{H,U}$ and $\Delta_{M,U}$ (formally, the solution is obtained assuming $\Delta_{V,U} = 0$). With material inputs as production factor, one needs a further equation to obtain a solution for the necessary changes. Since the interest lies here in the impact of changes in the wage structure (as opposed to changes in the wage level) on the distribution of unemployment, I use the additional condition that total employment remains unchanged.

Table 5.2: Estimated Changes in Wage Structure to Equalize Unemployment Rates in 1990

Necessary Changes in Ratios of Average Wages Across Skill Groups according to equation system (5.11) and (5.12)

Wage Ratio	Model 1[a]	Model 2[b]	Model 3[c]	Model 4[d]
$ln(w_H) - ln(w_U)$ [$\equiv \Delta_{HU}$]	0.109	0.067	0.131	0.076
$ln(w_M) - ln(w_U)$ [$\equiv \Delta_{MU}$]	0.062	0.050	0.066	0.065

Necessary Changes in Wage Dispersion below Median Within Skill Groups according to equation system (5.13)

Wage Ratio	Model 3[c]	Model 4[d]
$dq5020_M$ [$\equiv \Delta_{M,5020}$]	-0.067	0.042
$dq5020_U$ [$\equiv \Delta_{U,5020}$]	0.419	0.305

a: Static Model Without Material Inputs and Without Quantile Differences in table 5.4.
b: Static Model With Material Inputs and Without Quantile Differences in table 5.5.
c: Static Model Without Material Inputs and With Quantile Differences in table 5.4.
d: Static Model With Material Inputs and With Quantile Differences in table 5.5.

Based on the same approximation as above, one obtains the following equation

$$
\begin{aligned}
(L_H^* + L_M^* + L_U^*) \; - \; (L_H + L_M + L_U) \; &= \qquad (5.12) \\
\Delta_{HU} \sum_i \{L_{H,i}\eta_{H,H,i} + L_{M,i}\eta_{M,H,i} + L_{U,i}\eta_{U,H,i}\} &+ \\
\Delta_{MU} \sum_i \{L_{H,i}\eta_{H,M,i} + L_{M,i}\eta_{M,M,i} + L_{U,i}\eta_{U,M,i}\} &+ \\
\Delta_{VU} \sum_i \{L_{H,i}\eta_{H,V,i} + L_{M,i}\eta_{M,V,i} + L_{U,i}\eta_{U,V,i}\} &= 0 \,.
\end{aligned}
$$

The equation system (5.11) and (5.12) can be solved exactly for the necessary changes $\Delta_{H,U}$, $\Delta_{M,U}$, and $\Delta_{V,U}$ according to the model with material inputs.

Table 5.2 contains the solutions for $\Delta_{H,U}$ and $\Delta_{M,U}$ for the four estimated static models. While the necessary change of average wages between skill group (M) and (U) proves fairly robust across models, this is not the case for the wage ratio between skill groups (H) and (U). Equalization of unemployment requires an additional spread of around 5 to 6.6 percent in average wages between workers of type (M) and of type (U). The necessary increase in the wage ratio between (H) and (U) differs between 6.7 and 13.1 percent depending upon the estimated model. The estimated changes are smaller (especially between (H) and (U)) when material inputs are considered (models 2 and 4). As discussed in the previous section, material inputs interact significantly with the input of different types of labor such that the smaller changes appear more reliable.

The results reported here are considerably smaller than those obtained for the same simulation experiment in Fitzenberger and Franz (1998, section 4) corresponding to model 1 here. In addition to the differences in the estimated models (as discussed before), also the calculation of the necessary changes differs here from that earlier study. There, we had regressed the differences of the actual employment ratio in industry i and the aggregate supply of labor types $(L_{j,i}/L_{j',i} - LS_j/LS_{j'})$ on the elasticity differences across industries. The estimated coefficients were interpreted as the necessary logarithmic changes in average wage ratios. This procedure assumes that, on average, hypothetical employment ratios should equal the supply ratio using the fact that the regression function would estimate the average difference as a function of the changes in the wage ratios. Due to the nonlinearity in the division operation, this procedure guarantees equalization of employment ratios only on average and only approximately in the aggregate, whereas the approach taken here is exact. Therefore, the results obtained here seem more reliable.[8]

2. In the policy debate, it is often argued that wage flexibility in West Germany is reduced in the lower part of the distribution due to wage floors set by the prevailing wage bargaining system (see Blau and Kahn, 1996, for an international perspective). Therefore, the second simulation experiment is concerned with the necessary changes in the wage dispersion below the median for the two lower skill groups (U) and (M). Based on the same approximation as above, one obtains the following equations in $dq5020_{M,i}$ and $dq5020_{U,i}$ for $j \in \{U, M, H\}$

$$L_j^* = \sum_i L_{j,i}^* = L_j + \Delta_{M,5020} \sum_i L_{j,i}\eta_{j,M5020,i} + \Delta_{U,5020} \sum_i L_{j,i}\eta_{j,U5020,i}$$

where $\Delta_{j,5020}$: necessary change (assumed to be common across industries i) in logarithmic differences between 50%– and 20%–quantile of wages within skill group $j \in \{M, H\}$ in order to achieve a situation with equal unemployment rates.

[8] Applying the procedure suggested here to the estimation results in Fitzenberger and Franz (1998) also reduces the necessary changes between (H) and (U) from above 0.4 to $\Delta_{HU} = 0.206$. However, the necessary change between (M) and (U) is $\Delta_{MU} = 0.146$ which is about the same value as obtained in the earlier study. Nevertheless, the changes still remain larger than those obtained for the models estimated here, which could be due to the inconsistent (non–negative) own–price elasticities for labor of type (H) in NON–MAN obtained in the earlier study.

Again, in order to obtain a unique solution, the necessary changes $\Delta_{j,5020}$ are assumed to be the same across industries i irrespective of the differences in wage dispersion. Using the two conditions (5.10), one obtains the following two linear equations in $\Delta_{j,5020}$

$$LS_U \left[L_H + \Delta_{M,5020} \sum_i L_{H,i}\eta_{H,M5020,i} + \Delta_{U,5020} \sum_i L_{H,i}\eta_{H,U5020,i} \right] - \quad (5.13)$$

$$LS_H \left[L_U + \Delta_{M,5020} \sum_i L_{U,i}\eta_{U,M5020,i} + \Delta_{U,5020} \sum_i L_{U,i}\eta_{U,U5020,i} \right] = 0$$

$$LS_U \left[L_M + \Delta_{M,5020} \sum_i L_{M,i}\eta_{M,M5020,i} + \Delta_{U,5020} \sum_i L_{M,i}\eta_{M,U5020,i} \right] -$$

$$LS_M \left[L_U + \Delta_{M,5020} \sum_i L_{U,i}\eta_{U,M5020,i} + \Delta_{U,5020} \sum_i L_{U,i}\eta_{U,U5020,i} \right] = 0 .$$

These equations can be solved exactly for the necessary changes in the within dispersion.

The results can be found in table 5.2. Whereas the exact number differ considerably between model 3 and 4, the qualitative pattern is robust. Equalization of unemployment rates would require a large increase of 30 to 42 percent in the within dispersion for low–skilled workers (U) below the median. Since the labor demand elasticities with respect to changes in the wage dispersion are estimated for given average wages, this increase for (U) involves a considerable reduction of wages in the lower part of the distribution. Compared to this number, within dispersion for medium–skilled workers (M) should only change little and it remains unclear whether it should increase or decrease.

3. Finally, I consider the impact of a 10% increase in output on labor demand in MAN and in NON–MAN for the year 1990. The calculation proceeds as follows. First, I determine for each industry the elasticity of demand for labor of type $j \in \{U, M, H\}$ with respect to changes in output according to equation (5.4). Second, the predicted changes in employment of labor type j are then determined for each industry i by

$$\Delta L^*_{j,i} = L_{j,i} \cdot (e^{\eta_{j,Y}\, 0.1} - 1) \ .$$

Third, summing across all industries in MAN and NON–MAN yields the total employment effect for each skill group. I also calculate the implied impact on the aggregate unemployment rates.

Table 5.3 contains the estimated changes in labor demand in reaction to a 10% increase of output in each industry for MAN and NON–MAN, respectively. The results for models 1 and 3 (without material inputs) imply that most of the employment effects benefit medium– and high–skilled labor

Table 5.3: Actual Unemployment Rates in 1990 and Estimated Changes in Skill Specific Labor Demand and Unemployment Rates in Reaction to a 10% Increase in Output[e]

Skill Specific Unemployment Rates in 1990 (in percent)

ur_U	ur_M	ur_H
11.4	5.6	4.4

Estimated Changes in MAN

Variable	Model 1[a]	Model 2[b]	Model 3[c]	Model 4[d]
$\frac{\Delta L^*_{U,MAN}}{L_{U,MAN}}$ [f]	-0.23	-0.08	0.36	-0.01
Δur_U [g]	0.21	0.07	-0.32	0.01
$\frac{\Delta L^*_{M,MAN}}{L_{M,MAN}}$ [f]	2.51	-0.66	1.80	-1.04
Δur_M [g]	-2.37	0.62	-1.70	0.98
$\frac{\Delta L^*_{H,MAN}}{L_{H,MAN}}$ [f]	2.28	-0.52	1.64	-0.87
Δur_H [g]	-2.18	0.50	-1.56	0.83

Estimated Changes in NON–MAN

Variable	Model 1[a]	Model 2[b]	Model 3[c]	Model 4[d]
$\frac{\Delta L^*_{U,NON-MAN}}{L_{U,NON-MAN}}$ [f]	0.03	0.36	0.88	-0.44
Δur_U [g]	-0.03	-0.32	-0.78	0.39
$\frac{\Delta L^*_{M,NON-MAN}}{L_{M,NON-MAN}}$ [f]	2.43	-8.02	2.74	-7.51
Δur_M [g]	-2.29	7.57	-2.58	7.09
$\frac{\Delta L^*_{H,NON-MAN}}{L_{H,NON-MAN}}$ [f]	2.02	-4.82	2.25	-4.51
Δur_H [g]	-1.93	4.60	-2.16	4.32

a,b,c,d: See table 5.2.

e: Output refers to value added in model 1 and 3 (without material inputs) and to total shipments in model 2 and 4 (with material inputs).

f: Relative change of employment in MAN and NON–MAN, respectively, in percent.

g: Change in aggregate unemployment rate (in percentage points) due to change in employment in MAN or NON–MAN, respectively.

whereas grows in employment of low–skilled labor is fairly small or even negative.[9] The results for models 2 and 4 (with material inputs) prove fairly unsatisfactory. In all cases, except for one, an increase in output implies a reduction in employment. As mentioned above, these numbers are, however, misleading, since they do not encompass the indirect employment effects due to increases in material inputs. To obtain the total employment effects, it would be necessary to take account of the entire input–output effects. The results for the models with material inputs might reflect a growing tendency for outsourcing which is possibly correlated with output trends.

Overall, one can conclude that according to the estimated models presented in this chapter higher output growth cannot mitigate the skill bias in labor demand, i.e., in particular, higher output growth does not provide a panacea for the higher unemployment rates of low–skilled workers. This conclusion corresponds in spirit to the simulation results in Falk and Koebel (1997).

5.5 Conclusions

This chapter is concerned with the influence of the wage structure across three skill groups on the structure of labor demand. It is this link which is at the heart of the economic policy debate discussing the lack of wage flexibility being an important reason for the persistence of unemployment. Modelling the cost minimizing behavior of firms for given output, this analysis focuses on estimating the impact of changes in the wage structure (as opposed to changes in the wage level) on the distribution of unemployment. In addition, the analysis considers to what extent factor demand can be explained by different technology measures and by the level of the capital stock. The empirical investigation is performed separately for Manufacturing and Non–Manufacturing. A translog cost function and the associated share equations are estimated to quantify the impact of the wage structure on factor demand.

The empirical results are as follows: First, the partial adjustment models prove less satisfactory than the static models. Therefore, the following results refer to the latter. Second, the empirical models confirm the relevance of differences in average wages across skill groups for the structure of labor demand. The models typically provide estimates consistent with microeconomic theory. Third, the elasticities of labor demand with respect to wage changes exhibit a U–shaped pattern across skill groups with both the demand for low–skilled and for high–skilled workers being more elastic with respect to changes in the average wage compared to medium–skilled workers. The elasticities of labor demand are somewhat higher in Non–Manufacturing compared to Manufacturing (especially so for low–skilled workers). Also, low–skilled and medium–skilled workers are close substitutes in Non–Manufacturing. Fourth,

[9] This result for NON–MAN is in contrast to Fitzenberger and Franz (1998) where output growth in NON–MAN tended to benefit both (U) and (H) relative to (M).

there is some evidence for an impact of wage dispersion on labor demand in MAN and close to no such evidence for NON–MAN. Interestingly, the evidence in MAN implies that increasing the wage dispersion of low–skilled workers below the median would raise the demand for all types of workers. Fifth, some of the technology measures prove significant confirming the hypothesis of skill–biased technological change without having to measure technological progress by a mere time trend. In contrast, the evidence for the capital–skill complementarity hypothesis is only mixed.

In order to evaluate further the empirical results, three simulation results are obtained based on the estimated models. The goal of the first two experiments is to equalize the unemployment rates of the three skill groups in 1990 by changes in the wage structure, given output and given all other determinants of factor demand. The results show first that the average wage gap between low–skilled and medium–skilled workers would have to increase by around 5 to 6 percent and between low–skilled and high–skilled workers by between 7 and 13 percent. Second, the same goal can be reached when the wage dispersion below the median for low–skilled is increased by between 30 and 40 percent. For medium–skilled workers, the direction of change remains unclear. The third experiment concerns the impact of a 10% increase in output on labor demand and on unemployment rates. The results indicate that the increase in labor demand is fairly small and concentrated among medium– and high–skilled workers. Thus, while changes in the wage structure can mitigate the negative trend against low–skilled workers, the beneficial effects of further output growth for this group seem very limited. As a final caveat, it has to be emphasized that a higher dispersion of wages in the lower part of the wage distribution can create serious incentive problems, since labor income might be close to transfer payments and the marginal tax rates (benefit reduction ratio) can be very high. However, there are possibilities to avoid the problem of "working poor" as it occurs in the United States without having to reduce the level of transfer payments. For instance, one could raise the threshold levels defining the maximum income without any reduction of transfer payments (see Jerger and Spermann, 1997, on how to implement such incentive schemes).

5.6 Appendix of Chapter 5: Estimation Results

Table 5.4: Estimation Results for Static Model Without Material Inputs (Translog Cost Function and Share Equations)[a]

Para-meter	Manufacturing[b] Model 1[c] Without QD[d] Coeff. (s.e.)	Model 3[c] With QD[d] Coeff. (s.e.)
β_{UU}	-0.005 (0.083)	-0.023 (0.105)
β_{UM}	-0.003 (0.081)	0.010 (0.101)
β_{MM}	0.010 (0.080)	-0.006 (0.098)
γ_{yU}	-0.104 (0.047)	-0.060 (0.034)
γ_{kaU}	-0.127 (0.026)	-0.109 (0.021)
γ_{kbU}	0.252 (0.041)	0.200 (0.040)
γ_{pdU}	0.010 (0.022)	0.022 (0.021)
γ_{pzU}	0.009 (0.014)	-0.002 (0.016)
γ_{rdU}	-0.670 (0.225)	-0.384 (0.153)
γ_{yM}	0.077 (0.040)	0.043 (0.029)
γ_{kaM}	0.065 (0.025)	0.054 (0.022)
γ_{kbM}	-0.186 (0.034)	-0.148 (0.034)
γ_{pdM}	-0.008 (0.017)	-0.018 (0.016)
γ_{pzM}	-0.008 (0.012)	-0.000 (0.013)
γ_{rdM}	0.308 (0.237)	0.094 (0.193)
α_{y}	0.183 (0.498)	0.100 (0.154)
α_{yy}	0.059 (0.160)	0.070 (0.051)
α_{ka}	0.419 (0.844)	0.275 (0.213)
α_{kaka}	-0.099 (0.240)	-0.041 (0.069)
α_{kb}	0.041 (1.105)	0.164 (0.256)
α_{kbkb}	0.131 (0.462)	0.036 (0.118)
α_{rd}	1.000 (6.633)	1.578 (1.460)
α_{rdrd}	-2.848 (35.05)	-5.783 (5.552)
α_{pd}	0.011 (0.406)	-0.019 (0.161)
α_{pdpd}	-0.120 (0.864)	-0.015 (0.377)
α_{pz}	0.244 (0.578)	-0.088 (0.232)
α_{pzpz}	-0.363 (1.263)	0.353 (0.497)
α_{U}^{8050}	– –	0.060 (0.300)
α_{M}^{8050}	– –	-0.146 (0.269)
α_{U}^{5020}	– –	0.475 (0.255)

Table 5.4: < Continued > Estimation Results

Parameter	Manufacturing[b] Model 1[c] Without QD[d] Coeff.	(s.e.)	Model 3[c] With QD[d] Coeff.	(s.e.)
α_{M}^{5020}	–	–	-0.146	(0.272)
α_{H}^{5020}	–	–	0.037	(0.036)
γ_{UU}^{8050}	–	–	0.006	(0.073)
γ_{UM}^{8050}	–	–	-0.487	(0.089)
γ_{UU}^{5020}	–	–	0.002	(0.071)
γ_{UM}^{5020}	–	–	-0.141	(0.097)
γ_{UH}^{5020}	–	–	0.002	(0.003)
γ_{MU}^{8050}	–	–	0.023	(0.072)
γ_{MM}^{8050}	–	–	0.374	(0.069)
γ_{MU}^{5020}	–	–	0.011	(0.063)
γ_{MM}^{5020}	–	–	0.097	(0.081)
γ_{MH}^{5020}	–	–	-0.003	(0.003)
Parameters Estimated Implicitly[e]				
β_{UH}	0.008	(0.004)	0.013	(0.019)
β_{MH}	-0.007	(0.003)	-0.004	(0.015)
β_{HH}	-0.001	(0.001)	-0.009	(0.010)
γ_{yH}	0.027	(0.010)	0.017	(0.008)
γ_{kaH}	0.062	(0.010)	0.055	(0.007)
γ_{kbH}	-0.066	(0.016)	-0.051	(0.016)
γ_{pdH}	-0.002	(0.007)	-0.004	(0.007)
γ_{pzH}	-0.001	(0.006)	0.002	(0.007)
γ_{rdH}	0.362	(0.077)	0.290	(0.106)

a: Specifications comprise Sector Dummies in the Cost Function, equations (5.1), (5.5), and (5.8), and in Share Equations, equations (5.2), (5.6), and (5.7), respectively. The coefficients relating to these dummy variables are omitted here.

b: Sectors 4 to 35 in Table A.1.

c: See model definitions in table 5.1.

d: Specifications without [Equations (5.1) and (5.2)] or [Equations (5.5) and (5.6)] with Quantile Differences (QD) within the skill groups.

e: Parameters resulting from the explicitely estimated parameters due to the restrictions imposed on the specification.

Table 5.4: < Continued > Estimation Results

Para– meter	Non–Manufacturing[b]			
	Model 1[c] Without QD[d]		Model 3[c] With QD[d]	
	Coeff.	(s.e.)	Coeff.	(s.e.)
β_{UU}	-0.208	(0.045)	-0.072	(0.047)
β_{UM}	0.176	(0.045)	0.029	(0.045)
β_{MM}	-0.155	(0.048)	0.006	(0.049)
γ_{yU}	-0.035	(0.016)	-0.013	(0.016)
γ_{kaU}	0.054	(0.008)	0.057	(0.008)
γ_{kbU}	-0.207	(0.027)	-0.236	(0.021)
γ_{rdU}	-1.703	(3.129)	-0.697	(2.860)
γ_{elU}	0.577	(0.633)	0.279	(0.557)
γ_{coU}	-2.441	(3.538)	-1.580	(3.643)
γ_{yM}	0.024	(0.014)	0.020	(0.017)
γ_{kaM}	-0.060	(0.010)	-0.064	(0.006)
γ_{kbM}	0.129	(0.032)	0.146	(0.024)
γ_{rdM}	-3.564	(4.293)	-4.052	(3.876)
γ_{elM}	0.004	(0.640)	0.198	(0.554)
γ_{coM}	2.818	(3.831)	3.012	(4.356)
α_{y}	-1.103	(0.812)	-0.961	(0.285)
α_{yy}	0.315	(0.194)	0.304	(0.072)
α_{ka}	0.015	(0.476)	0.189	(0.154)
α_{kaka}	0.043	(0.125)	-0.005	(0.045)
α_{kb}	0.379	(1.950)	1.548	(0.605)
α_{kbkb}	-0.080	(0.396)	-0.331	(0.135)
α_{rd}	-187.312	(149.3)	-50.005	(86.54)
$\alpha_{rdrd}/100$	1007.382	(816.9)	262.806	(444.5)
α_{el}	0.147	(13.39)	-3.370	(9.670)
α_{elel}	80.265	(857.5)	303.721	(540.2)
α_{co}	3.769	(56.43)	-28.111	(56.71)
$\alpha_{coco}/100$	64.950	(406.8)	92.350	(391.5)
α_{U}^{8050}	–	–	0.072	(0.199)
α_{M}^{8050}	–	–	-0.126	(0.284)
α_{U}^{5020}	–	–	-0.340	(0.135)

Table 5.4: < Continued > Estimation Results

Para–meter	Non–Manufacturing[b]			
	Model 1[c] Without QD[d]		Model 3[c] With QD[d]	
	Coeff.	(s.e.)	Coeff.	(s.e.)
α_M^{5020}	–	–	0.252	(0.355)
α_H^{5020}	–	–	0.210	(0.052)
γ_{UU}^{8050}	–	–	0.067	(0.050)
γ_{UM}^{8050}	–	–	0.000	(0.052)
γ_{UU}^{5020}	–	–	0.003	(0.029)
γ_{UM}^{5020}	–	–	0.034	(0.071)
γ_{UH}^{5020}	–	–	0.007	(0.005)
γ_{MU}^{8050}	–	–	-0.085	(0.045)
γ_{MM}^{8050}	–	–	-0.008	(0.048)
γ_{MU}^{5020}	–	–	-0.019	(0.026)
γ_{MM}^{5020}	–	–	-0.094	(0.061)
γ_{MH}^{5020}	–	–	-0.002	(0.005)
Parameters Estimated Implicitly[e]				
β_{UH}	0.032	(0.013)	0.043	(0.018)
β_{MH}	-0.021	(0.012)	-0.035	(0.019)
β_{HH}	-0.011	(0.004)	-0.009	(0.008)
γ_{yH}	0.012	(0.009)	-0.006	(0.008)
γ_{kaH}	0.006	(0.008)	0.007	(0.008)
γ_{kbH}	0.078	(0.014)	0.090	(0.013)
γ_{rdH}	5.267	(2.040)	4.750	(2.329)
γ_{elH}	-0.581	(0.328)	-0.476	(0.302)
γ_{coH}	-0.376	(1.366)	-1.432	(1.624)

a: Specifications comprise Sector Dummies in the Cost Function, equations (5.1), (5.5), and (5.8), and in Share Equations, equations (5.2), (5.6), and (5.7), respectively. The coefficients relating to these dummy variables are omitted here.

b: Sectors 2, 3, 36 to 47 in Table A.1.

c: See model definitions in table 5.1.

d: Specifications without [Equations (5.1) and (5.2)] or [Equations (5.5) and (5.6)] with Quantile Differences (QD) within the skill groups.

e: Parameters resulting from the explicitely estimated parameters due to the restrictions imposed on the specification.

Table 5.5: Estimation Results for Static Model with Material Inputs (Translog Cost Function and Share Equations)[a]

Para-meter	Manufacturing[b] Model 2[c] Without QD[d] Coeff. (s.e.)	Manufacturing[b] Model 4[c] With QD[d] Coeff. (s.e.)
β_{UU}	-0.002 (0.018)	-0.000 (0.029)
β_{UM}	0.022 (0.021)	0.025 (0.031)
β_{UH}	0.003 (0.001)	0.002 (0.002)
β_{MM}	0.070 (0.022)	0.065 (0.033)
β_{MH}	0.005 (0.002)	0.010 (0.002)
β_{HH}	0.000 (0.000)	0.001 (0.000)
γ_{yU}	-0.048 (0.011)	-0.041 (0.009)
γ_{kaU}	-0.048 (0.011)	-0.042 (0.011)
γ_{kbU}	0.097 (0.020)	0.084 (0.018)
γ_{pdU}	0.001 (0.006)	0.005 (0.006)
γ_{pzU}	0.003 (0.005)	-0.001 (0.006)
γ_{rdU}	-0.098 (0.073)	-0.048 (0.071)
γ_{yM}	-0.054 (0.013)	-0.056 (0.009)
γ_{kaM}	0.022 (0.011)	0.016 (0.010)
γ_{kbM}	-0.022 (0.031)	-0.013 (0.025)
γ_{pdM}	-0.012 (0.009)	-0.016 (0.007)
γ_{pzM}	0.005 (0.006)	0.005 (0.005)
γ_{rdM}	0.393 (0.126)	0.330 (0.107)
γ_{yH}	-0.000 (0.003)	-0.003 (0.002)
γ_{kaH}	0.024 (0.005)	0.020 (0.004)
γ_{kbH}	-0.023 (0.007)	-0.017 (0.006)
γ_{pdH}	-0.002 (0.002)	-0.003 (0.002)
γ_{pzH}	0.001 (0.002)	0.002 (0.002)
γ_{rdH}	0.222 (0.050)	0.195 (0.051)
α_{y}	0.707 (0.241)	0.705 (0.244)
α_{yy}	-0.010 (0.071)	-0.035 (0.072)
α_{ka}	0.084 (0.305)	0.154 (0.295)
α_{kaka}	0.040 (0.097)	0.033 (0.090)
α_{kb}	0.112 (0.345)	0.118 (0.379)
α_{kbkb}	-0.050 (0.128)	-0.075 (0.145)
α_{rd}	-1.794 (1.751)	-1.591 (2.053)
α_{rdrd}	5.046 (6.837)	4.728 (7.836)
α_{pd}	-0.024 (0.089)	-0.074 (0.091)
α_{pdpd}	0.056 (0.207)	0.205 (0.209)
α_{pz}	-0.201 (0.196)	-0.252 (0.188)
α_{pzpz}	0.601 (0.405)	0.717 (0.381)

Table 5.5: < Continued > Estimation Results

Para-meter	Manufacturing[b]			
	Model 2[c] Without QD[d]		Model 4[c] With QD[d]	
	Coeff.	(s.e.)	Coeff.	(s.e.)
α_U^{8050}	–	–	-0.188	(0.330)
α_M^{8050}	–	–	-0.266	(0.246)
α_U^{5020}	–	–	0.642	(0.205)
α_M^{5020}	–	–	0.587	(0.280)
α_H^{5020}	–	–	0.056	(0.047)
γ_{UU}^{8050}	–	–	0.027	(0.035)
γ_{UM}^{8050}	–	–	-0.146	(0.040)
γ_{UU}^{5020}	–	–	0.002	(0.023)
γ_{UM}^{5020}	–	–	-0.074	(0.034)
γ_{UH}^{5020}	–	–	-0.001	(0.001)
γ_{MU}^{8050}	–	–	0.092	(0.044)
γ_{MM}^{8050}	–	–	0.122	(0.032)
γ_{MU}^{5020}	–	–	-0.030	(0.030)
γ_{MM}^{5020}	–	–	-0.058	(0.038)
γ_{MH}^{5020}	–	–	-0.005	(0.001)
γ_{HU}^{8050}	–	–	0.004	(0.013)
γ_{HM}^{8050}	–	–	0.042	(0.011)
γ_{HU}^{5020}	–	–	-0.010	(0.007)
γ_{HM}^{5020}	–	–	0.010	(0.009)
γ_{HH}^{5020}	–	–	-0.000	(0.000)
Parameters Estimated Implicitly[e]				
β_{UV}	-0.023	(0.009)	-0.028	(0.007)
β_{MV}	-0.097	(0.007)	-0.100	(0.007)
β_{HV}	-0.009	(0.003)	-0.013	(0.003)
β_{VV}	0.120	(0.012)	0.127	(0.009)
γ_{yV}	0.102	(0.015)	0.100	(0.009)
γ_{kaV}	0.002	(0.023)	0.006	(0.021)
γ_{kbV}	-0.052	(0.047)	-0.054	(0.040)
γ_{pdV}	0.012	(0.008)	0.014	(0.008)
γ_{pzV}	-0.008	(0.009)	-0.006	(0.008)
γ_{rdV}	-0.516	(0.179)	-0.476	(0.165)
γ_{VU}^{8050}	–	–	-0.123	(0.074)
γ_{VM}^{8050}	–	–	-0.018	(0.063)
γ_{VU}^{5020}	–	–	0.038	(0.036)
γ_{VM}^{5020}	–	–	0.122	(0.055)
γ_{VH}^{5020}	–	–	0.005	(0.002)

a,b,c,d,e: See table 5.4.

Table 5.5: < Continued > Estimation Results

Para- meter	Non–Manufacturing[b] Model 2[c] Without QD[d] Coeff. (s.e.)	Model 4[c] With QD[d] Coeff. (s.e.)
β_{UU}	-0.034 (0.019)	-0.018 (0.021)
β_{UM}	0.029 (0.017)	0.010 (0.020)
β_{UH}	0.006 (0.006)	0.007 (0.006)
β_{MM}	0.047 (0.017)	0.073 (0.023)
β_{MH}	0.006 (0.005)	0.005 (0.006)
β_{HH}	-0.001 (0.001)	-0.000 (0.001)
γ_{yU}	-0.015 (0.008)	-0.020 (0.009)
γ_{kaU}	0.016 (0.005)	0.018 (0.005)
γ_{kbU}	-0.074 (0.010)	-0.078 (0.009)
γ_{rdU}	-0.956 (2.008)	-0.952 (1.854)
γ_{elU}	0.215 (0.395)	0.180 (0.393)
γ_{coU}	-1.950 (2.242)	-1.927 (2.128)
γ_{yM}	-0.065 (0.020)	-0.059 (0.021)
γ_{kaM}	-0.001 (0.011)	0.000 (0.010)
γ_{kbM}	0.011 (0.020)	0.003 (0.021)
γ_{rdM}	-0.017 (2.839)	0.361 (2.898)
γ_{elM}	-0.857 (0.511)	-0.950 (0.581)
γ_{coM}	-1.593 (3.555)	-1.060 (3.756)
γ_{yH}	-0.011 (0.004)	-0.010 (0.004)
γ_{kaH}	0.009 (0.003)	0.008 (0.003)
γ_{kbH}	0.018 (0.005)	0.019 (0.005)
γ_{rdH}	0.218 (0.533)	0.475 (0.661)
γ_{elH}	-0.317 (0.102)	-0.323 (0.122)
γ_{coH}	-0.764 (0.722)	-1.013 (0.724)
α_{y}	-0.738 (0.259)	-0.564 (0.317)
α_{yy}	0.329 (0.059)	0.273 (0.073)
α_{ka}	0.278 (0.117)	0.120 (0.132)
α_{kaka}	-0.040 (0.029)	0.009 (0.037)
α_{kb}	0.466 (0.473)	0.839 (0.434)
α_{kbkb}	-0.095 (0.099)	-0.178 (0.093)
α_{rd}	-16.890 (52.92)	-14.943 (74.72)
$\alpha_{rdrd}/100$	76.163 (314.3)	12.506 (488.4)
α_{el}	-1.212 (4.902)	1.965 (6.114)
α_{elel}	334.168 (282.6)	195.700 (349.1)
α_{co}	-53.524 (22.12)	-44.735 (23.87)
$\alpha_{coco}/100$	293.269 (170.8)	253.246 (172.9)

Table 5.5: < Continued > Estimation Results

Para-meter	Non-Manufacturing[b]			
	Model 2[c] Without QD[d]		Model 4[c] With QD[d]	
	Coeff.	(s.e.)	Coeff.	(s.e.)
α_U^{8050}	–	–	0.170	(0.298)
α_M^{8050}	–	–	0.560	(0.295)
α_U^{5020}	–	–	0.002	(0.143)
α_M^{5020}	–	–	0.088	(0.398)
α_H^{5020}	–	–	0.009	(0.043)
γ_{UU}^{8050}	–	–	0.014	(0.017)
γ_{UM}^{8050}	–	–	0.051	(0.019)
γ_{UU}^{5020}	–	–	0.004	(0.015)
γ_{UM}^{5020}	–	–	0.042	(0.034)
γ_{UH}^{5020}	–	–	0.001	(0.006)
γ_{MU}^{8050}	–	–	-0.089	(0.041)
γ_{MM}^{8050}	–	–	-0.031	(0.046)
γ_{MU}^{5020}	–	–	-0.008	(0.024)
γ_{MM}^{5020}	–	–	0.062	(0.065)
γ_{MH}^{5020}	–	–	0.002	(0.005)
γ_{HU}^{8050}	–	–	-0.010	(0.010)
γ_{HM}^{8050}	–	–	-0.031	(0.011)
γ_{HU}^{5020}	–	–	-0.001	(0.006)
γ_{HM}^{5020}	–	–	0.020	(0.016)
γ_{HH}^{5020}	–	–	-0.001	(0.001)
Parameters Estimated Implicitly[e]				
β_{UV}	-0.001	(0.006)	0.001	(0.006)
β_{MV}	-0.082	(0.012)	-0.087	(0.013)
β_{HV}	-0.012	(0.003)	-0.012	(0.003)
β_{VV}	0.083	(0.015)	0.087	(0.015)
γ_{yV}	0.092	(0.020)	0.089	(0.024)
γ_{kaV}	-0.024	(0.014)	-0.027	(0.014)
γ_{kbV}	0.045	(0.025)	0.056	(0.029)
γ_{rdV}	0.755	(2.950)	0.116	(2.924)
γ_{elV}	0.960	(0.636)	1.093	(0.641)
γ_{coV}	4.306	(2.573)	4.001	(2.965)
γ_{VU}^{8050}	–	–	0.086	(0.041)
γ_{VM}^{8050}	–	–	0.011	(0.052)
γ_{VU}^{5020}	–	–	0.005	(0.030)
γ_{VM}^{5020}	–	–	-0.124	(0.084)
γ_{VH}^{5020}	–	–	-0.002	(0.009)

a,b,c,d,e: See table 5.4.

Table 5.6: Estimation Results for Partial Adjustment Model Without Material Inputs (Translog Cost Function and Share Equations)[a]

Parameter	Manufacturing[b] Model 1[c] Without QD[d] Coeff. (s.e.)	Manufacturing[b] Model 3[c] With QD[d] Coeff. (s.e.)
d_{UU}	-0.456 (0.187)	-0.155 (0.170)
d_{UM}	-0.505 (0.324)	0.249 (0.301)
d_{MU}	0.149 (0.161)	-0.245 (0.082)
d_{MM}	0.079 (0.286)	-0.730 (0.194)
sc_{UM}	-217.674 (133.6)	33.211 (89.88)
sc_{UU}	-98.125 (84.10)	-14.523 (63.10)
sc_{MM}	-110.567 (80.39)	65.670 (63.79)
β_{UU}	-0.739 (0.733)	0.175 (0.111)
β_{UM}	0.709 (0.633)	-0.166 (0.120)
β_{MM}	-0.684 (0.566)	0.166 (0.129)
γ_{yU}	0.046 (0.196)	-0.023 (0.054)
γ_{kaU}	-0.268 (0.255)	-0.089 (0.057)
γ_{kbU}	0.439 (0.340)	0.167 (0.081)
γ_{pdU}	0.253 (0.274)	0.057 (0.041)
γ_{pzU}	-0.179 (0.230)	-0.016 (0.031)
γ_{rdU}	3.293 (3.245)	-0.041 (0.423)
γ_{yM}	-0.035 (0.158)	0.025 (0.039)
γ_{kaM}	0.195 (0.199)	0.057 (0.041)
γ_{kbM}	-0.358 (0.253)	-0.153 (0.057)
γ_{pdM}	-0.184 (0.208)	-0.041 (0.033)
γ_{pzM}	0.134 (0.174)	0.010 (0.026)
γ_{rdM}	-2.666 (2.552)	-0.209 (0.449)
α_{y}	0.054 (0.410)	0.126 (0.234)
α_{yy}	0.071 (0.109)	0.045 (0.067)
α_{ka}	0.565 (0.305)	0.379 (0.153)
α_{kaka}	-0.124 (0.102)	-0.055 (0.059)
α_{kb}	-0.075 (0.374)	0.145 (0.231)
α_{kbkb}	0.148 (0.185)	0.025 (0.120)
α_{rd}	-1.450 (2.609)	-0.020 (1.815)
α_{rdrd}	14.732 (12.52)	2.741 (7.655)
α_{pd}	0.117 (0.292)	-0.051 (0.150)

Table 5.6: < Continued > Estimation Results

Para-meter	Manufacturing[b] Model 1[c] Without QD[d] Coeff.	(s.e.)	Manufacturing[b] Model 3[c] With QD[d] Coeff.	(s.e.)
α_{pdpd}	-0.315	(0.625)	0.068	(0.325)
α_{pz}	0.083	(0.510)	-0.150	(0.280)
α_{pzpz}	-0.006	(1.135)	0.516	(0.606)
α_{U}^{8050}	–	–	0.044	(0.257)
α_{M}^{8050}	–	–	-0.212	(0.305)
α_{U}^{5020}	–	–	0.143	(0.202)
α_{M}^{5020}	–	–	0.131	(0.228)
α_{H}^{5020}	–	–	-0.045	(0.018)
γ_{UU}^{8050}	–	–	-0.051	(0.177)
γ_{UM}^{8050}	–	–	-0.641	(0.223)
γ_{UU}^{5020}	–	–	-0.075	(0.141)
γ_{UM}^{5020}	–	–	0.099	(0.263)
γ_{UH}^{5020}	–	–	0.011	(0.015)
γ_{MU}^{8050}	–	–	0.081	(0.132)
γ_{MM}^{8050}	–	–	0.354	(0.145)
γ_{MU}^{5020}	–	–	0.084	(0.128)
γ_{MM}^{5020}	–	–	-0.092	(0.196)
γ_{MH}^{5020}	–	–	-0.007	(0.011)
Parameters Estimated Implicitly[e]				
β_{UH}	0.030	(0.126)	-0.009	(0.018)
β_{MH}	-0.025	(0.092)	-0.000	(0.016)
β_{HH}	-0.005	(0.034)	0.009	(0.005)
γ_{yH}	-0.011	(0.049)	-0.002	(0.024)
γ_{kaH}	0.073	(0.064)	0.032	(0.024)
γ_{kbH}	-0.080	(0.095)	-0.014	(0.035)
γ_{pdH}	-0.069	(0.068)	-0.016	(0.012)
γ_{pzH}	0.045	(0.058)	0.006	(0.011)
γ_{rdH}	-0.627	(0.776)	0.250	(0.210)

a,b,c,d,e: See table 5.4.

Table 5.6: < Continued > Estimation Results

Parameter	Non–Manufacturing[b] Model 1[c] Without QD[d] Coeff. (s.e.)	Model 3[c] With QD[d] Coeff. (s.e.)
d_{UU}	-0.583 (0.206)	-0.578 (0.205)
d_{UM}	-0.300 (0.183)	-0.247 (0.202)
d_{MU}	0.075 (0.172)	-0.087 (0.121)
d_{MM}	-0.231 (0.156)	-0.498 (0.145)
sc_{UM}	254.437 (324.2)	333.783 (467.0)
sc_{UU}	76.280 (160.1)	120.861 (206.8)
sc_{MM}	119.821 (206.6)	130.402 (295.5)
β_{UU}	-0.100 (0.229)	-0.111 (0.247)
β_{UM}	0.148 (0.201)	0.132 (0.270)
β_{MM}	-0.214 (0.191)	-0.154 (0.322)
γ_{yU}	0.102 (0.071)	0.056 (0.079)
γ_{kaU}	-0.003 (0.048)	0.001 (0.034)
γ_{kbU}	-0.219 (0.083)	-0.170 (0.161)
γ_{rdU}	3.814 (12.57)	0.536 (13.69)
γ_{elU}	-2.901 (2.548)	-2.203 (3.382)
γ_{coU}	4.191 (14.41)	0.301 (17.09)
γ_{yM}	-0.083 (0.070)	-0.033 (0.103)
γ_{kaM}	-0.011 (0.050)	-0.016 (0.051)
γ_{kbM}	0.135 (0.089)	0.089 (0.311)
γ_{rdM}	-10.592 (13.37)	-6.740 (24.86)
γ_{elM}	2.432 (2.536)	1.710 (6.176)
γ_{coM}	-3.341 (12.61)	2.319 (21.49)
α_y	-1.242 (0.484)	-0.783 (1.410)
α_{yy}	0.348 (0.104)	0.240 (0.301)
α_{ka}	-0.020 (0.259)	0.016 (0.374)
α_{kaka}	0.036 (0.071)	0.042 (0.099)
α_{kb}	2.486 (1.024)	2.157 (3.619)
α_{kbkb}	-0.499 (0.214)	-0.463 (0.655)
α_{rd}	-171.503 (135.1)	-71.252 (157.2)
$\alpha_{rdrd}/100$	881.630 (840.2)	359.900 (1088)

Table 5.6: < Continued > Estimation Results

Parameter	Non–Manufacturing[b] Model 1[c] Without QD[d] Coeff.	(s.e.)	Model 3[c] With QD[d] Coeff.	(s.e.)
α_{el}	-8.107	(11.22)	-13.781	(38.20)
α_{elel}	502.628	(597.6)	800.080	(1462)
α_{co}	14.614	(41.74)	43.375	(128.7)
$\alpha_{coco}/100$	-69.784	(296.8)	-215.304	(462.4)
α_U^{8050}	–	–	0.048	(1.241)
α_M^{8050}	–	–	0.747	(1.737)
α_U^{5020}	–	–	0.081	(0.214)
α_M^{5020}	–	–	0.452	(0.559)
α_H^{5020}	–	–	0.009	(0.502)
γ_{UU}^{8050}	–	–	0.022	(0.171)
γ_{UM}^{8050}	–	–	-0.280	(0.299)
γ_{UU}^{5020}	–	–	0.051	(0.141)
γ_{UM}^{5020}	–	–	0.124	(0.342)
γ_{UH}^{5020}	–	–	0.014	(0.027)
γ_{MU}^{8050}	–	–	-0.061	(0.289)
γ_{MM}^{8050}	–	–	0.243	(0.495)
γ_{MU}^{5020}	–	–	-0.033	(0.160)
γ_{MM}^{5020}	–	–	-0.216	(0.647)
γ_{MH}^{5020}	–	–	-0.007	(0.038)
Parameters Estimated Implicitly[e]				
β_{UH}	-0.047	(0.061)	-0.022	(0.064)
β_{MH}	0.067	(0.051)	0.021	(0.082)
β_{HH}	-0.020	(0.025)	0.000	(0.040)
γ_{yH}	-0.019	(0.020)	-0.023	(0.033)
γ_{kaH}	0.014	(0.017)	0.015	(0.026)
γ_{kbH}	0.084	(0.024)	0.081	(0.196)
γ_{rdH}	6.779	(4.174)	6.204	(16.54)
γ_{elH}	0.469	(0.613)	0.493	(3.913)
γ_{coH}	-0.850	(3.492)	-2.620	(6.099)

a,b,c,d,e: See table 5.4.

Table 5.7: Estimation Results for Partial Adjustment Model with Material Inputs (Translog Cost Function and Share Equations)[a]

	Manufacturing[b]	
	Model 2[c]	Model 4[c]
Para-	Without QD[d]	With QD[d]
meter	Coeff. (s.e.)	Coeff. (s.e.)
d_{UU}	-0.384 (0.148)	-0.434 (0.141)
d_{UM}	-0.121 (0.063)	-0.114 (0.057)
d_{UH}	-0.572 (0.278)	-0.539 (0.236)
d_{MU}	-0.231 (0.129)	-0.241 (0.108)
d_{MM}	-0.930 (0.080)	-0.937 (0.076)
d_{MH}	-0.637 (0.411)	-0.491 (0.338)
d_{HU}	-0.086 (0.039)	-0.052 (0.030)
d_{HM}	-0.010 (0.024)	-0.013 (0.021)
d_{HH}	-0.516 (0.125)	-0.525 (0.102)
sc_{UM}	-37.947 (88.81)	16.765 (92.16)
sc_{UU}	124.522 (134.7)	172.305 (151.2)
sc_{MM}	31.841 (66.31)	19.780 (76.79)
sc_{UH}	515.789 (534.5)	305.514 (403.3)
sc_{MH}	-579.157 (305.2)	-402.523 (264.1)
sc_{HH}	531.212 (448.8)	349.586 (323.5)
β_{UU}	0.070 (0.030)	0.097 (0.042)
β_{UM}	-0.024 (0.033)	-0.070 (0.039)
β_{UH}	0.007 (0.006)	0.007 (0.005)
β_{MM}	0.119 (0.034)	0.158 (0.040)
β_{MH}	0.000 (0.002)	0.005 (0.004)
β_{HH}	-0.001 (0.002)	0.002 (0.002)
γ_{yU}	-0.021 (0.026)	-0.014 (0.017)
γ_{kaU}	-0.044 (0.030)	-0.040 (0.021)
γ_{kbU}	0.091 (0.039)	0.075 (0.036)
γ_{pdU}	0.021 (0.016)	0.018 (0.012)
γ_{pzU}	-0.010 (0.019)	-0.009 (0.015)
γ_{rdU}	-0.288 (0.289)	-0.148 (0.174)
γ_{yM}	-0.043 (0.012)	-0.038 (0.009)
γ_{kaM}	0.018 (0.011)	0.013 (0.011)
γ_{kbM}	-0.019 (0.018)	-0.016 (0.019)
γ_{pdM}	-0.016 (0.006)	-0.017 (0.006)
γ_{pzM}	0.008 (0.007)	0.007 (0.007)
γ_{rdM}	0.303 (0.162)	0.304 (0.163)
γ_{yH}	-0.007 (0.010)	-0.009 (0.007)
γ_{kaH}	0.018 (0.011)	0.013 (0.007)

Table 5.7: < Continued > Estimation Results

Para–meter	Manufacturing[b]			
	Model 2[c] Without QD[d]		Model 4[c] With QD[d]	
	Coeff.	(s.e.)	Coeff.	(s.e.)
γ_{kbH}	-0.014	(0.011)	-0.006	(0.008)
γ_{pdH}	-0.006	(0.004)	-0.005	(0.002)
γ_{pzH}	0.003	(0.005)	0.003	(0.003)
γ_{rdH}	0.351	(0.090)	0.291	(0.089)
α_y	0.554	(0.147)	0.681	(0.152)
α_{yy}	0.009	(0.049)	-0.053	(0.050)
α_{ka}	0.187	(0.224)	0.166	(0.189)
α_{kaka}	0.034	(0.083)	0.057	(0.072)
α_{kb}	0.026	(0.247)	-0.036	(0.268)
α_{kbkb}	-0.035	(0.126)	-0.006	(0.135)
α_{rd}	-1.431	(3.002)	-1.483	(2.112)
α_{rdrd}	11.159	(14.35)	10.236	(11.07)
α_{pd}	0.206	(0.154)	0.140	(0.174)
α_{pdpd}	-0.426	(0.340)	-0.295	(0.390)
α_{pz}	-0.168	(0.263)	-0.245	(0.243)
α_{pzpz}	0.520	(0.587)	0.685	(0.546)
α_U^{8050}	–	–	-0.032	(0.241)
α_M^{8050}	–	–	-0.276	(0.228)
α_U^{5020}	–	–	0.729	(0.238)
α_M^{5020}	–	–	0.529	(0.273)
α_H^{5020}	–	–	0.001	(0.009)
γ_{UU}^{8050}	–	–	-0.007	(0.080)
γ_{UM}^{8050}	–	–	-0.172	(0.078)
γ_{UU}^{5020}	–	–	-0.017	(0.049)
γ_{UM}^{5020}	–	–	-0.040	(0.074)
γ_{UH}^{5020}	–	–	-0.000	(0.004)
γ_{MU}^{8050}	–	–	0.076	(0.046)
γ_{MM}^{8050}	–	–	0.037	(0.065)
γ_{MU}^{5020}	–	–	-0.055	(0.042)
γ_{MM}^{5020}	–	–	-0.076	(0.062)
γ_{MH}^{5020}	–	–	-0.005	(0.003)
γ_{HU}^{8050}	–	–	0.015	(0.024)
γ_{HM}^{8050}	–	–	0.075	(0.028)
γ_{HU}^{5020}	–	–	-0.026	(0.015)
γ_{HM}^{5020}	–	–	0.019	(0.030)

Table 5.7: < Continued > Estimation Results

Para–meter	Manufacturing[b]			
	Model 2[c] Without QD[d]		Model 4[c] With QD[d]	
	Coeff.	(s.e.)	Coeff.	(s.e.)
γ_{HH}^{5020}	–	–	-0.001	(0.001)
Parameters Estimated Implicitly[e]				
β_{UV}	-0.052	(0.012)	-0.035	(0.013)
β_{MV}	-0.094	(0.009)	-0.093	(0.008)
β_{HV}	-0.006	(0.005)	-0.014	(0.006)
β_{VV}	0.147	(0.015)	0.128	(0.013)
γ_{yV}	0.072	(0.018)	0.061	(0.014)
γ_{kaV}	0.008	(0.028)	0.014	(0.023)
γ_{kbV}	-0.058	(0.035)	-0.054	(0.033)
γ_{pdV}	0.000	(0.016)	0.005	(0.013)
γ_{pzV}	-0.000	(0.019)	-0.001	(0.016)
γ_{rdV}	-0.366	(0.320)	-0.447	(0.235)

a,b,c,d,e: See table 5.4.

Para–meter	Non–Manufacturing[b]			
	Model 2[c] Without QD[d]		Model 4[c] With QD[d]	
	Coeff.	(s.e.)	Coeff.	(s.e.)
d_{UU}	-0.284	(0.094)	-0.290	(0.096)
d_{UM}	-0.139	(0.050)	-0.120	(0.049)
d_{UH}	0.112	(0.139)	0.022	(0.129)
d_{MU}	-0.130	(0.170)	-0.113	(0.187)
d_{MM}	-0.673	(0.103)	-0.681	(0.116)
d_{MH}	-0.681	(0.567)	-0.651	(0.546)
d_{HU}	-0.076	(0.041)	-0.086	(0.044)
d_{HM}	0.026	(0.032)	0.022	(0.032)
d_{HH}	-0.784	(0.148)	-0.783	(0.143)
sc_{UM}	95.292	(94.87)	131.166	(102.2)
sc_{UU}	-97.343	(87.33)	-181.575	(88.73)
sc_{MM}	-7.271	(38.02)	-4.354	(44.70)
sc_{UH}	-22.758	(623.2)	-324.446	(516.6)
sc_{MH}	-139.726	(356.1)	115.093	(342.9)
sc_{HH}	491.613	(646.6)	150.451	(837.2)

Table 5.7: < Continued > Estimation Results

Para-meter	Non-Manufacturing[b] Model 2[c] Without QD[d] Coeff. (s.e.)	Model 4[c] With QD[d] Coeff. (s.e.)
β_{UU}	-0.036 (0.069)	-0.007 (0.088)
β_{UM}	0.079 (0.059)	0.045 (0.078)
β_{UH}	-0.010 (0.016)	-0.009 (0.019)
β_{MM}	-0.016 (0.058)	0.028 (0.073)
β_{MH}	0.021 (0.011)	0.020 (0.013)
β_{HH}	-0.001 (0.004)	-0.002 (0.004)
γ_{yU}	0.006 (0.033)	0.016 (0.034)
γ_{kaU}	-0.011 (0.014)	-0.010 (0.016)
γ_{kbU}	-0.052 (0.028)	-0.050 (0.038)
γ_{rdU}	-6.349 (6.436)	-6.482 (6.027)
γ_{elU}	-1.742 (0.889)	-1.721 (0.873)
γ_{coU}	-0.010 (5.952)	-0.634 (5.936)
γ_{yM}	-0.108 (0.029)	-0.107 (0.034)
γ_{kaM}	0.017 (0.020)	0.017 (0.021)
γ_{kbM}	0.012 (0.039)	0.008 (0.044)
γ_{rdM}	1.433 (7.054)	1.261 (6.375)
γ_{elM}	-0.672 (0.958)	-0.738 (0.920)
γ_{coM}	-0.863 (4.511)	-0.291 (4.679)
γ_{yH}	-0.021 (0.007)	-0.023 (0.008)
γ_{kaH}	0.014 (0.006)	0.015 (0.006)
γ_{kbH}	0.014 (0.009)	0.012 (0.011)
γ_{rdH}	1.139 (2.162)	1.218 (2.079)
γ_{elH}	0.154 (0.254)	0.151 (0.285)
γ_{coH}	-1.006 (0.997)	-0.868 (1.183)
α_{y}	-1.056 (0.245)	-0.966 (0.237)
α_{yy}	0.424 (0.057)	0.396 (0.056)
α_{ka}	0.124 (0.114)	0.052 (0.120)
α_{kaka}	-0.029 (0.030)	-0.005 (0.030)
α_{kb}	1.499 (0.288)	1.706 (0.313)
α_{kbkb}	-0.292 (0.061)	-0.344 (0.068)
α_{rd}	-37.924 (74.85)	-1.112 (81.89)
$\alpha_{rdrd}/100$	129.673 (464.8)	-65.553 (507.1)
α_{el}	1.678 (4.678)	-1.733 (4.959)
α_{elel}	151.690 (259.3)	305.210 (283.7)

Table 5.7: < Continued > Estimation Results

Parameter	Non–Manufacturing[b]			
	Model 2[c] Without QD[d]		Model 4[c] With QD[d]	
	Coeff.	(s.e.)	Coeff.	(s.e.)
α_{co}	-27.915	(27.29)	-19.746	(30.66)
$\alpha_{coco}/100$	153.312	(173.4)	82.663	(185.8)
α_U^{8050}	–	–	0.089	(0.168)
α_M^{8050}	–	–	0.229	(0.176)
α_U^{5020}	–	–	0.071	(0.105)
α_M^{5020}	–	–	0.252	(0.241)
α_H^{5020}	–	–	0.022	(0.031)
γ_{UU}^{8050}	–	–	-0.024	(0.051)
γ_{UM}^{8050}	–	–	-0.092	(0.126)
γ_{UU}^{5020}	–	–	0.014	(0.052)
γ_{UM}^{5020}	–	–	-0.016	(0.126)
γ_{UH}^{5020}	–	–	0.008	(0.014)
γ_{MU}^{8050}	–	–	-0.053	(0.070)
γ_{MM}^{8050}	–	–	0.029	(0.109)
γ_{MU}^{5020}	–	–	0.034	(0.051)
γ_{MM}^{5020}	–	–	-0.013	(0.099)
γ_{MH}^{5020}	–	–	0.009	(0.010)
γ_{HU}^{8050}	–	–	0.004	(0.019)
γ_{HM}^{8050}	–	–	0.007	(0.034)
γ_{HU}^{5020}	–	–	-0.015	(0.014)
γ_{HM}^{5020}	–	–	0.029	(0.041)
γ_{HH}^{5020}	–	–	-0.001	(0.003)
Parameters Estimated Implicitly[e]				
β_{UV}	-0.033	(0.026)	-0.029	(0.026)
β_{MV}	-0.085	(0.034)	-0.093	(0.032)
β_{HV}	-0.010	(0.009)	-0.009	(0.009)
β_{VV}	0.118	(0.029)	0.122	(0.028)
γ_{yV}	0.123	(0.035)	0.115	(0.037)
γ_{kaV}	-0.021	(0.020)	-0.021	(0.019)
γ_{kbV}	0.027	(0.035)	0.030	(0.040)
γ_{rdV}	3.777	(5.521)	4.003	(5.472)
γ_{elV}	2.260	(0.897)	2.308	(0.880)
γ_{coV}	1.878	(3.587)	1.794	(3.684)

a,b,c,d,e: See table 5.4.

Table 5.8: Estimated Labor Demand Elasticities for Selected Sectors[a] (Estimated Standard Errors in Parentheses)

Static Model Without Material Inputs and Without Quantile Differences in Table 5.4 (Model 1)			
	Sector[b] **14** Chem. Prod.	Sector[b] **26** Machinery	Sector[b] **27** Off./D. Proc.
$\eta_{U,U,i,\cdot}$	-0.797 (0.371)	-0.878 (0.547)	-0.874 (0.534)
$\eta_{U,M,i,\cdot}$	0.639 (0.366)	0.742 (0.538)	0.598 (0.526)
$\eta_{U,H,i,\cdot}$	0.157 (0.017)	0.136 (0.025)	0.276 (0.024)
$\eta_{M,M,i,\cdot}$	-0.330 (0.123)	-0.222 (0.105)	-0.364 (0.130)
$\eta_{M,U,i,\cdot}$	0.218 (0.125)	0.147 (0.107)	0.150 (0.132)
$\eta_{M,H,i,\cdot}$	0.112 (0.005)	0.075 (0.004)	0.214 (0.005)
$\eta_{H,H,i,\cdot}$	-0.885 (0.008)	-0.926 (0.011)	-0.778 (0.004)
$\eta_{H,U,i,\cdot}$	0.287 (0.031)	0.245 (0.045)	0.190 (0.017)
$\eta_{H,M,i,\cdot}$	0.597 (0.026)	0.681 (0.037)	0.588 (0.014)
	Sector[b] **46** Construction	Sector[b] **50** Trade	Sector[b] **61** Insurance
$\eta_{U,U,i,\cdot}$	-2.421 (0.323)	-2.794 (0.395)	-2.698 (0.377)
$\eta_{U,M,i,\cdot}$	2.137 (0.319)	2.447 (0.390)	2.345 (0.372)
$\eta_{U,H,i,\cdot}$	0.285 (0.098)	0.347 (0.120)	0.353 (0.115)
$\eta_{M,M,i,\cdot}$	-0.366 (0.056)	-0.347 (0.054)	-0.378 (0.056)
$\eta_{M,U,i,\cdot}$	0.348 (0.052)	0.319 (0.051)	0.331 (0.052)
$\eta_{M,H,i,\cdot}$	0.019 (0.014)	0.028 (0.014)	0.047 (0.014)
$\eta_{H,H,i,\cdot}$	-1.201 (0.098)	-1.152 (0.082)	-1.077 (0.060)
$\eta_{H,U,i,\cdot}$	0.858 (0.297)	0.714 (0.248)	0.557 (0.181)
$\eta_{H,M,i,\cdot}$	0.343 (0.260)	0.438 (0.217)	0.520 (0.158)

Table 5.8: < Continued > Estimated Labor Demand Elasticities

Static Model with Material Inputs and Without Quantile Differences in Table 5.5 (Model 2)			
	Sector[b] **14** Chem. Prod.	Sector[b] **26** Machinery	Sector[b] **27** Off./D. Proc.
$\eta_{U,U,i,.}$	-0.974 (0.282)	-0.976 (0.287)	-0.976 (0.287)
$\eta_{U,M,i,.}$	0.547 (0.340)	0.669 (0.347)	0.601 (0.346)
$\eta_{U,H,i,.}$	0.082 (0.024)	0.082 (0.024)	0.128 (0.024)
$\eta_{U,V,i,.}$	0.346 (0.144)	0.225 (0.147)	0.247 (0.147)
$\eta_{M,M,i,.}$	-0.419 (0.117)	-0.469 (0.070)	-0.460 (0.092)
$\eta_{M,U,i,.}$	0.185 (0.115)	0.133 (0.069)	0.156 (0.090)
$\eta_{M,H,i,.}$	0.063 (0.014)	0.050 (0.008)	0.102 (0.011)
$\eta_{M,V,i,.}$	0.171 (0.043)	0.286 (0.026)	0.202 (0.034)
$\eta_{H,H,i,.}$	-0.953 (0.008)	-0.954 (0.008)	-0.916 (0.003)
$\eta_{H,U,i,.}$	0.147 (0.043)	0.148 (0.044)	0.094 (0.018)
$\eta_{H,M,i,.}$	0.335 (0.075)	0.453 (0.077)	0.286 (0.031)
$\eta_{H,V,i,.}$	0.471 (0.109)	0.353 (0.111)	0.537 (0.045)
$\eta_{V,V,i,.}$	-0.088 (0.016)	-0.169 (0.018)	-0.155 (0.018)
$\eta_{V,U,i,.}$	0.027 (0.011)	0.020 (0.013)	0.022 (0.013)
$\eta_{V,M,i,.}$	0.039 (0.010)	0.131 (0.012)	0.068 (0.011)
$\eta_{V,H,i,.}$	0.020 (0.005)	0.018 (0.006)	0.065 (0.005)
	Sector[b] **46** Construction	Sector[b] **50** Trade	Sector[b] **61** Insurance
$\eta_{U,U,i,.}$	-1.569 (0.369)	-4.673 (2.177)	-1.684 (0.432)
$\eta_{U,M,i,.}$	0.860 (0.341)	3.172 (2.014)	0.938 (0.400)
$\eta_{U,H,i,.}$	0.129 (0.112)	0.657 (0.662)	0.158 (0.131)
$\eta_{U,V,i,.}$	0.580 (0.108)	0.843 (0.638)	0.588 (0.127)
$\eta_{M,M,i,.}$	-0.525 (0.057)	-0.277 (0.264)	-0.532 (0.059)
$\eta_{M,U,i,.}$	0.141 (0.056)	0.409 (0.260)	0.136 (0.058)
$\eta_{M,H,i,.}$	0.037 (0.017)	0.094 (0.079)	0.048 (0.018)
$\eta_{M,V,i,.}$	0.347 (0.037)	-0.225 (0.170)	0.347 (0.038)
$\eta_{H,H,i,.}$	-1.022 (0.068)	-1.149 (0.263)	-0.997 (0.043)
$\eta_{H,U,i,.}$	0.391 (0.341)	1.319 (1.328)	0.262 (0.218)
$\eta_{H,M,i,.}$	0.692 (0.316)	1.462 (1.229)	0.551 (0.202)
$\eta_{H,V,i,.}$	-0.062 (0.148)	-1.631 (0.576)	0.185 (0.095)
$\eta_{V,V,i,.}$	-0.247 (0.029)	0.018 (0.018)	-0.239 (0.028)
$\eta_{V,U,i,.}$	0.054 (0.010)	0.009 (0.006)	0.046 (0.010)
$\eta_{V,M,i,.}$	0.196 (0.021)	-0.018 (0.013)	0.186 (0.020)
$\eta_{V,H,i,.}$	-0.002 (0.005)	-0.008 (0.003)	0.009 (0.004)

Table 5.8: < Continued > Estimated Labor Demand Elasticities

Static Model Without Material Inputs and with Quantile Differences in Table 5.4 (Model 3)						
	Sector[b] **14** Chem. Prod.		Sector[b] **26** Machinery		Sector[b] **27** Off./D. Proc.	
$\eta_{U,U,i,.}$	-0.881	(0.414)	-1.002	(0.609)	-0.995	(0.595)
$\eta_{U,M,i,.}$	0.700	(0.395)	0.831	(0.581)	0.685	(0.568)
$\eta_{U,H,i,.}$	0.181	(0.096)	0.171	(0.141)	0.310	(0.138)
$\eta_{M,M,i,.}$	-0.355	(0.130)	-0.244	(0.112)	-0.391	(0.138)
$\eta_{M,U,i,.}$	0.239	(0.135)	0.165	(0.115)	0.172	(0.142)
$\eta_{M,H,i,.}$	0.116	(0.026)	0.079	(0.022)	0.219	(0.027)
$\eta_{H,H,i,.}$	-0.953	(0.082)	-1.025	(0.119)	-0.816	(0.045)
$\eta_{H,U,i,.}$	0.331	(0.175)	0.308	(0.254)	0.214	(0.095)
$\eta_{H,M,i,.}$	0.622	(0.137)	0.717	(0.199)	0.602	(0.074)
$\eta_{U,U5020,i,.}$	0.485	(0.512)	0.489	(0.651)	0.490	(0.643)
$\eta_{M,U5020,i,.}$	0.493	(0.248)	0.490	(0.247)	0.494	(0.248)
$\eta_{H,U5020,i,.}$	0.369	(0.224)	0.320	(0.255)	0.418	(0.224)
$\eta_{U,U8050,i,.}$	0.089	(0.407)	0.100	(0.536)	0.102	(0.528)
$\eta_{M,U8050,i,.}$	0.098	(0.303)	0.092	(0.296)	0.101	(0.306)
$\eta_{H,U8050,i,.}$	-0.178	(0.402)	-0.288	(0.510)	-0.067	(0.315)
$\eta_{U,M5020,i,.}$	-0.783	(0.537)	-1.077	(0.749)	-1.061	(0.736)
$\eta_{M,M5020,i,.}$	-0.003	(0.311)	-0.021	(0.301)	0.005	(0.316)
$\eta_{H,M5020,i,.}$	0.214	(0.386)	0.383	(0.487)	0.047	(0.305)
$\eta_{U,M8050,i,.}$	-2.341	(0.683)	-3.359	(0.932)	-3.297	(0.917)
$\eta_{M,M8050,i,.}$	0.412	(0.247)	0.341	(0.241)	0.445	(0.250)
$\eta_{H,M8050,i,.}$	0.767	(0.337)	1.197	(0.467)	0.344	(0.243)
$\eta_{U,H5020,i,.}$	0.047	(0.053)	0.052	(0.056)	0.052	(0.056)
$\eta_{M,H5020,i,.}$	0.032	(0.048)	0.032	(0.048)	0.031	(0.048)
$\eta_{H,H5020,i,.}$	0.044	(0.049)	0.047	(0.051)	0.040	(0.048)

Table 5.8: < Continued > Estimated Labor Demand Elasticities

Static Model Without Material Inputs and with Quantile Differences in Table 5.4 (Model 3)			
	Sector[b] **46** Construction	Sector[b] **50** Trade	Sector[b] **61** Insurance
$\eta_{U,U,i,.}$	-1.403 (0.365)	-1.547 (0.447)	-1.511 (0.426)
$\eta_{U,M,i,.}$	1.036 (0.341)	1.100 (0.418)	1.062 (0.398)
$\eta_{U,H,i,.}$	0.367 (0.151)	0.447 (0.184)	0.448 (0.176)
$\eta_{M,M,i,.}$	-0.171 (0.060)	-0.156 (0.059)	-0.180 (0.061)
$\eta_{M,U,i,.}$	0.169 (0.056)	0.144 (0.054)	0.150 (0.056)
$\eta_{M,H,i,.}$	0.002 (0.025)	0.012 (0.025)	0.030 (0.025)
$\eta_{H,H,i,.}$	-1.148 (0.219)	-1.108 (0.183)	-1.045 (0.134)
$\eta_{H,U,i,.}$	1.104 (0.454)	0.920 (0.379)	0.707 (0.277)
$\eta_{H,M,i,.}$	0.044 (0.466)	0.188 (0.389)	0.338 (0.285)
$\eta_{U,U5020,i,.}$	-0.321 (0.242)	-0.317 (0.288)	-0.318 (0.275)
$\eta_{M,U5020,i,.}$	-0.364 (0.131)	-0.364 (0.132)	-0.364 (0.132)
$\eta_{H,U5020,i,.}$	0.018 (0.429)	-0.042 (0.373)	-0.122 (0.297)
$\eta_{U,U8050,i,.}$	0.575 (0.307)	0.685 (0.377)	0.656 (0.358)
$\eta_{M,U8050,i,.}$	-0.031 (0.197)	-0.032 (0.198)	-0.034 (0.199)
$\eta_{H,U8050,i,.}$	0.464 (0.541)	0.397 (0.474)	0.309 (0.382)
$\eta_{U,M5020,i,.}$	0.497 (0.769)	0.553 (0.885)	0.538 (0.854)
$\eta_{M,M5020,i,.}$	0.132 (0.396)	0.133 (0.396)	0.130 (0.396)
$\eta_{H,M5020,i,.}$	1.612 (1.022)	1.385 (0.884)	1.079 (0.705)
$\eta_{U,M8050,i,.}$	-0.127 (0.553)	-0.127 (0.619)	-0.127 (0.601)
$\eta_{M,M8050,i,.}$	-0.136 (0.344)	-0.136 (0.344)	-0.136 (0.344)
$\eta_{H,M8050,i,.}$	0.045 (0.670)	0.016 (0.571)	-0.022 (0.448)
$\eta_{U,H5020,i,.}$	0.266 (0.077)	0.278 (0.084)	0.275 (0.082)
$\eta_{M,H5020,i,.}$	0.208 (0.054)	0.207 (0.054)	0.207 (0.054)
$\eta_{H,H5020,i,.}$	0.093 (0.097)	0.112 (0.088)	0.139 (0.078)

Table 5.8: < Continued > Estimated Labor Demand Elasticities

Static Model with Material Inputs and with Quantile Differences in Table 5.5 (Model 4)			
	Sector[b] **14** Chem. Prod.	Sector[b] **26** Machinery	Sector[b] **27** Off./D. Proc.
$\eta_{U,U,i,.}$	-0.945 (0.468)	-0.946 (0.478)	-0.946 (0.477)
$\eta_{U,M,i,.}$	0.609 (0.500)	0.732 (0.510)	0.664 (0.509)
$\eta_{U,H,i,.}$	0.075 (0.032)	0.075 (0.032)	0.121 (0.032)
$\eta_{U,V,i,.}$	0.262 (0.129)	0.139 (0.132)	0.161 (0.131)
$\eta_{M,M,i,.}$	-0.451 (0.177)	-0.488 (0.106)	-0.485 (0.138)
$\eta_{M,U,i,.}$	0.206 (0.169)	0.145 (0.101)	0.173 (0.133)
$\eta_{M,H,i,.}$	0.089 (0.015)	0.065 (0.009)	0.122 (0.012)
$\eta_{M,V,i,.}$	0.156 (0.038)	0.277 (0.023)	0.190 (0.030)
$\eta_{H,H,i,.}$	-0.951 (0.015)	-0.951 (0.016)	-0.915 (0.006)
$\eta_{H,U,i,.}$	0.135 (0.057)	0.135 (0.058)	0.088 (0.023)
$\eta_{H,M,i,.}$	0.472 (0.079)	0.592 (0.081)	0.342 (0.033)
$\eta_{H,V,i,.}$	0.345 (0.090)	0.224 (0.092)	0.484 (0.037)
$\eta_{V,V,i,.}$	-0.072 (0.013)	-0.151 (0.015)	-0.137 (0.015)
$\eta_{V,U,i,.}$	0.020 (0.010)	0.013 (0.012)	0.014 (0.012)
$\eta_{V,M,i,.}$	0.036 (0.009)	0.127 (0.010)	0.064 (0.010)
$\eta_{V,H,i,.}$	0.015 (0.004)	0.011 (0.005)	0.058 (0.004)
$\eta_{U,U5020,i,.}$	0.685 (0.461)	0.678 (0.471)	0.685 (0.468)
$\eta_{M,U5020,i,.}$	0.468 (0.282)	0.531 (0.243)	0.506 (0.258)
$\eta_{H,U5020,i,.}$	0.334 (0.304)	0.320 (0.309)	0.516 (0.224)
$\eta_{V,U5020,i,.}$	0.694 (0.225)	0.695 (0.226)	0.701 (0.227)
$\eta_{U,U8050,i,.}$	0.280 (0.588)	0.314 (0.607)	0.290 (0.598)
$\eta_{M,U8050,i,.}$	0.345 (0.319)	0.154 (0.276)	0.230 (0.292)
$\eta_{H,U8050,i,.}$	-0.054 (0.398)	-0.026 (0.409)	-0.133 (0.268)
$\eta_{V,U8050,i,.}$	-0.358 (0.315)	-0.363 (0.316)	-0.380 (0.323)
$\eta_{U,M5020,i,.}$	-0.698 (0.624)	-0.747 (0.641)	-0.722 (0.635)
$\eta_{M,M5020,i,.}$	0.250 (0.351)	0.363 (0.300)	0.322 (0.321)
$\eta_{H,M5020,i,.}$	0.898 (0.394)	0.881 (0.402)	0.715 (0.274)
$\eta_{V,M5020,i,.}$	0.755 (0.279)	0.761 (0.280)	0.777 (0.283)
$\eta_{U,M8050,i,.}$	-2.789 (0.825)	-2.831 (0.852)	-2.833 (0.840)
$\eta_{M,M8050,i,.}$	0.441 (0.262)	0.162 (0.222)	0.286 (0.236)
$\eta_{H,M8050,i,.}$	1.043 (0.398)	1.075 (0.400)	0.271 (0.269)
$\eta_{V,M8050,i,.}$	-0.295 (0.283)	-0.292 (0.285)	-0.299 (0.292)
$\eta_{U,H5020,i,.}$	0.046 (0.065)	0.045 (0.066)	0.046 (0.065)
$\eta_{M,H5020,i,.}$	0.029 (0.055)	0.039 (0.055)	0.035 (0.055)
$\eta_{H,H5020,i,.}$	0.054 (0.056)	0.053 (0.056)	0.055 (0.055)
$\eta_{V,H5020,i,.}$	0.064 (0.055)	0.064 (0.055)	0.065 (0.055)

a: Elasticities are based on estimated coefficients in tables 5.4 and 5.5. The calculation follows equations (5.3) and (5.4), respectively, for the mean of the factor share $S_{j,i,.}$ during the time period from 1975 to 1990.

Table 5.8: < Continued > Estimated Labor Demand Elasticities

Static Model with Material Inputs and with Quantile Differences in Table 5.5 (Model 4)			
	Sector[b] **46** Construction	Sector[b] **50** Trade	Sector[b] **61** Insurance
$\eta_{U,U,i,.}$	-1.265 (0.396)	-2.878 (2.337)	-1.328 (0.464)
$\eta_{U,M,i,.}$	0.510 (0.360)	1.105 (2.126)	0.527 (0.422)
$\eta_{U,H,i,.}$	0.148 (0.120)	0.772 (0.708)	0.181 (0.141)
$\eta_{U,V,i,.}$	0.607 (0.101)	1.001 (0.594)	0.620 (0.118)
$\eta_{M,M,i,.}$	-0.447 (0.065)	0.084 (0.301)	-0.451 (0.067)
$\eta_{M,U,i,.}$	0.084 (0.059)	0.142 (0.274)	0.077 (0.061)
$\eta_{M,H,i,.}$	0.032 (0.019)	0.069 (0.089)	0.043 (0.020)
$\eta_{M,V,i,.}$	0.331 (0.039)	-0.296 (0.181)	0.332 (0.040)
$\eta_{H,H,i,.}$	-0.983 (0.097)	-1.001 (0.379)	-0.973 (0.062)
$\eta_{H,U,i,.}$	0.450 (0.365)	1.549 (1.421)	0.300 (0.233)
$\eta_{H,M,i,.}$	0.592 (0.355)	1.073 (1.382)	0.487 (0.227)
$\eta_{H,V,i,.}$	-0.059 (0.182)	-1.621 (0.709)	0.186 (0.116)
$\eta_{V,V,i,.}$	-0.242 (0.029)	0.021 (0.019)	-0.235 (0.029)
$\eta_{V,U,i,.}$	0.056 (0.009)	0.010 (0.006)	0.048 (0.009)
$\eta_{V,M,i,.}$	0.187 (0.022)	-0.023 (0.014)	0.178 (0.022)
$\eta_{V,H,i,.}$	-0.002 (0.006)	-0.008 (0.004)	0.009 (0.005)
$\eta_{U,U5020,i,.}$	0.080 (0.294)	0.469 (1.614)	0.094 (0.334)
$\eta_{M,U5020,i,.}$	-0.024 (0.176)	-0.113 (0.392)	-0.024 (0.176)
$\eta_{H,U5020,i,.}$	-0.056 (0.411)	-0.220 (1.395)	-0.035 (0.295)
$\eta_{V,U5020,i,.}$	0.010 (0.142)	0.007 (0.141)	0.010 (0.143)
$\eta_{U,U8050,i,.}$	0.408 (0.312)	1.649 (1.754)	0.460 (0.345)
$\eta_{M,U8050,i,.}$	-0.109 (0.349)	-1.066 (0.700)	-0.110 (0.350)
$\eta_{H,U8050,i,.}$	-0.405 (0.766)	-2.020 (2.379)	-0.193 (0.575)
$\eta_{V,U8050,i,.}$	0.303 (0.294)	0.265 (0.294)	0.309 (0.295)
$\eta_{U,M5020,i,.}$	0.871 (0.818)	4.596 (3.745)	0.987 (0.908)
$\eta_{M,M5020,i,.}$	0.291 (0.421)	0.942 (0.922)	0.284 (0.419)
$\eta_{H,M5020,i,.}$	1.221 (0.892)	4.424 (3.359)	0.804 (0.619)
$\eta_{V,M5020,i,.}$	-0.102 (0.425)	-0.049 (0.413)	-0.113 (0.427)
$\eta_{U,M8050,i,.}$	1.494 (0.450)	6.054 (2.074)	1.652 (0.496)
$\eta_{M,M8050,i,.}$	0.472 (0.316)	0.136 (0.677)	0.467 (0.316)
$\eta_{H,M8050,i,.}$	-1.137 (0.647)	-6.057 (2.309)	-0.523 (0.464)
$\eta_{V,M8050,i,.}$	0.582 (0.315)	0.575 (0.307)	0.580 (0.316)
$\eta_{U,H5020,i,.}$	0.032 (0.141)	0.144 (0.699)	0.036 (0.159)
$\eta_{M,H5020,i,.}$	0.014 (0.047)	0.030 (0.085)	0.014 (0.047)
$\eta_{H,H5020,i,.}$	-0.051 (0.093)	-0.224 (0.284)	-0.029 (0.071)
$\eta_{V,H5020,i,.}$	0.006 (0.040)	0.007 (0.040)	0.006 (0.040)

b: See classification in table A.1.

c: $\eta_{j,j'\,pd,i,.} = \partial ln(L_{j,i,.})/\partial dq\,pd_{j',i,.}$ for $j, j' \in \{U, M, H\}$ and $pd \in \{8050, 5020\}$ according to equation (5.4).

6 Heterogeneous Labor in a Model of Wage Bargaining

Economists have tended to handicap themselves unduly by their reluctance to examine the empirical implications of particular solution concepts ...

Pencavel (1991, p. 129)

Despite its alleged importance for skill specific labor market trends in West Germany, explicit empirical modelling of union wage bargaining has rarely taken place (the comprehensive recent survey on unions and unemployment from a German perspective in Jaeger, 1996, does not even mention this issue). In the Phillips–Curve or the Wage–Curve tradition, there have been some attempts to proxy the outcome of wage bargaining by postulating separate wage setting relations for the different skill types of labor depending upon group specific unemployment rates (see Nickell and Bell, 1995, and Beißinger and Möller, 1998). This chapter tries to go further in the empirical modelling of wage bargaining by developing an empirically operational structural model of wage bargaining and employment determination in West Germany which can be put directly to the data. Wage bargaining is assumed to set average wages and wage dispersion for each of the two different skill groups (U = low–skilled "unskilled") and (M = medium–skilled). Management at the firm level has free discretion to decide on employment. This "right–to–manage" assumption corresponds to the prima facie view of wage setting in West Germany: Wage bargaining occurs at the sectoral level between trade unions and employers' associations such that it appears impossible to implement efficient contracts imposing wages and employment at the firm level (see Franz, 1996, chapter 8, and Jaeger, 1996).

However, the above view has two major problems. First, one can observe that effective wages paid at the firm level are often higher than negotiated wages (see Schnabel, 1994).[1] Despite this wage gap, there exists considerable

[1] However, Schnabel argues that part of the gap between effective and bargained wages measured at the aggregate level is due to measurement problems. This is the case because wage negotiations at the sectoral level do not only set baseline wages, which effective wages can be compared with, but they also establish rules for additional payments due to overtime, shift work, and bonuses. Therefore, it is very difficult to construct

evidence that trends in effective wages closely follow negotiated wages except for cyclical variations (see Franz, 1996, section 8.2, Gärtner, 1989, and Möller, 1990, section 5.4). This corresponds to the notion of pattern bargaining, which implies that annual wage growth is first negotiated for one leading industry and then the rest of the economy copies this increase in percent with only slight modification (in the 70's and 80's, the leading industry used to be the metal industry in the region of Nordwürttemberg–Nordbaden, see Meyer, 1995) accommodating the specific situation in the respective industry and firm. Thus, summing up, it appears safe to assume in this study that wage bargaining determines the trend behavior of effective wages.

A second problem with the "right–to–manage" model lies in the possibility that unions and employers' associations agree to measures which influence employment given the wages set in the agreement (e.g. work rules, reduction in overtime). The goal could be to move firms away from the labor demand curve in order to achieve an efficient bargaining outcome (see Franz, 1996, section 8.2.2.2, and Pencavel, 1991, chapter 4). However, the recent attempts in Germany under the label "coalition–for–work" ("Bündnis für Arbeit") have so far not been successful precisely because the employers' association cannot commit to an employment target which is then implemented at the firm level. Since firms would have to employ more workers than optimal given the current wage, they have an incentive to go back to the labor demand curve.[2] Hall and Lilien (1979) emphasize the monitoring problems for unions since management is better informed about the state of the firm and therefore always has an incentive to misrepresent the firm's economic situation in order to reduce employment. Thus, it seems unlikely that efficient bargaining occurs under the West German wage setting institutions. As a final note it should be mentioned that Layard et al. (1991, section 2.3) challenge conventional thinking about efficient bargaining over wages and employment. Based on an insider–outsider model, they argue that, in general equilibrium, it is not necessarily the case that employment under efficient bargaining is actually higher than under the right–to–manage model.

Even though, one can resonably argue, that sectoral bargaining cannot reach binding agreements on employment levels, it has to be mentioned as

---

the relevant negotiated wage for each worker. Nevertheless, Schnabel can establish the existence of a gap between 7–12% in the 1990's using unpublished detailed data from one particular employers' association.

[2]Building on suggestions in public finance on how to prevent free–rider behavior, Winker (1998) suggests the introduction of marketable certificates to implement efficient wage and employment contracts. The idea is that firms can trade certificates, which require them to increase employment by a certain amount, such that the employment target is implemented in a cost efficient way. Despite its theoretical appeal, this idea is unlikely to be practical. First, it is difficult to determine the initial allocation of the certificates, since in a dynamic economy employment changes all the time, firms die and new firms are founded. Thus, the introduction of marketable certificates could have an enormous distributional effect across firms. Second, firms can leave the employers' association. Third, the certificates require a control system ensuring that firms actually meet the employment target.

a caveat that, in West Germany, bargaining between unions and employers also covers many other aspects in addition to wages. It involves, for instance, standard hours of work (very important during the 80's!), sickness pay, or overtime premia. Modelling these aspects is, however, beyond the scope of this study. As a justification for restricting the attention to wages, it can be pointed out that, in contrast to wages, these aspects are not a bargaining issue in every year.

Having considered some objections to the right–to–manage approach, I now turn to the specification of the bargaining outcome itself. According to the bilateral monopoly relationship between trade union and employers' association, it would be natural to assume that the bargaining outcome can be described by the maximization of the following Nash product

$$\max_{\{w\}} \; (\Gamma[w,L]-\bar{\Gamma})^{up}\,(\Pi[w,L]-\bar{\Pi})^{1-up}$$

with respect to wages w subject to labor demand being determined by management at the firm level for given wages as $L(w)$. Here, the following notation is used:

w	: wages for different skill groups
L	: vector of employment of different skill groups
$\Gamma[w,L]$	: union utility level depending on wages and employment
$\bar{\Gamma}$	: union reference level
$\Pi[w,L]$	: profit level for the set of firms represented by the employers' association
$\bar{\Pi}$	: reference level of employers' association
up	: relative weight (= bargaining power) of union in bargaining process

Provided suitable functional form assumptions are made for Γ, Π, and $L(w)$ and appropriate instruments are available, the structural parameters of this model can be estimated. However, tractability dictates a more modest approach at this point. I follow Pencavel and Holmlund (1988) and assume that wage bargaining is the outcome of a monopoly union model, where union utility $\Gamma[w,L]$ is maximized at the sectoral level with respect to wages subject to labor demand $L(w)$ being determined unilaterally by management at the firm level. When interpreting the structural estimates, I do acknowledge that the estimated $\Gamma[w,L]$ is an approximation of the Nash product presented above. Disregarding efficiency wage considerations, it is clear that a positive weight of wages in the utility function ($\Gamma_w > 0$) represents the union's positive evaluation of higher wages. This is the case since employment is a "sufficient" measure for wages in the profit function due to the constrained optimization subject to the system of labor demand equations. Therefore, the weight of employment in Γ combines the positive evaluation of higher employment both by firms and the union. Hence, employment can ceteris paribus be viewed as a proxy for profits. The approach taken in this study is not informative about the different weights attributed to wages and employment by the union alone. It is only possible to estimate the evaluation by the combined bargaining process whereby the weight given to wages is attributed to the union. Put differently, it is observationally equivalent whether the union puts a high weight to wages and has a low bargaining power or whether wages have only a low weight in the union's utility and it has a high bargaining power.

So far, the empirical implementation of structural wage bargaining models has been very rare (see De la Croix et al. 1995, as a recent exception, and the surveys in Pencavel, 1991, and Jaeger, 1996) and, to my knowledge, it has been restricted to modelling homogeneous labor. This study represents the first attempt to estimate a structural model of wage bargaining for heterogeneous labor taking account both of wage differences across and within two skill groups. It is motivated by the emphasis of the policy debate on the lack of wage flexibility being the outcome of wage bargaining.

The model developed here takes a static perspective on the wage bargaining process: A monopoly union maximizes its one–period utility subject to static labor demand functions for the two types of labor. Labor demand is assumed to depend upon average wages and wage dispersion. Static modelling can be justified as a long–run view neglecting the dynamics involved, e.g. due to adjustment costs when changing factor inputs.[3] To address this problem, some of the estimates presented in the following take account of possible habit formation in the union utility function and inference will take account of autocorrelation in the error terms being the result of delayed adjustment to the estimated long–run relationships.

The remainder of this chapter is organized as follows. Section 6.1 introduces the structural model of wage bargaining and the specification of labor demand. Section 6.2 describes the data used. Section 6.3 develops the estimation approach and presents the estimation results. Section 6.4 concludes. A final appendix contains further information on the data sets used and tables with estimation results.

6.1 A Structural Model of Wage Bargaining

This section develops an empirically operational monopoly union model in the context of two types of labor (U = low–skilled workers) and (M = medium–skilled workers). In the most general version, the union not only cares about average wages for the two types of labor (and implicitly about the wage ratio between the two) but also about wage dispersion within the two groups of workers. As described in the introduction and without repeating this each

[3]De la Croix et al. (1995) estimate a dynamic bargaining model for homogeneous labor based on aggregate data allowing for habit formation in the union utility function and adjustment costs for factor inputs. Given the difficulties involved, when obtaining the estimates presented in this study, it seems unlikely that a dynamic model for heterogeneous labor can be estimated satisfactorily.

time, the maximization exercise of the union is assumed to represent the outcome of wage bargaining at the sectoral level between a trade union and an employers' association.

6.1.1 Union Objective Function

The theoretical foundation of a union's utility function has generated a lively debate in the literature (see the contributions by Oswald (1985) and Pencavel (1985) in a famous issue of the Scandinavian Journal of Economics and the treatment in Pencavel's (1991) textbook). The international discussion focuses on the following problems:

- First, is it possible to aggregate the preferences of individual union members such that the aggregate preferences only depend on average wages and employment?
- Second, does union leadership represent the aggregate preferences of the members ("principal-agent-problem")?
- And third, do unemployed union members exert the same influence on union action compared to employed members ("Insider-Outsider-Problem")?

In addition, the specific wage bargaining institutions in West Germany raise a fourth problem:

- Since wage bargaining takes place at the sectoral level and its outcome typically extends to employees, who are not union members, does the union only care about wages and employment among its members?

In this study, the trade union's utility function is assumed to be an extension of the Stone–Geary objective function, as suggested in Pencavel and Holmlund (1989), with the novel features that unions care both about average wages for the two groups of labor as well as about within-group wage dispersion.[4] Hence, the functional form of trade union utility is given by

$$\Gamma(w_U, w_M, d_U, d_M, L) = \{ln(w_U) - ln(\bar{w}_U)\}^{\alpha_U} \cdot \{ln(w_M) - ln(\bar{w}_M)\}^{\alpha_M} \quad (6.1)$$

$$\cdot\{\bar{d}_U - d_U\}^{\alpha_{dU}} \cdot \{\bar{d}_M - d_M\}^{\alpha_{dM}} \cdot \{ln(L) - ln(\bar{L})\}^{\alpha_L}$$

[4]This idea on how to incorporate within group dispersion was, in fact, mentioned in a footnote by Pencavel (1985, p. 218). However, to my knowledge, this study represents the first empirical implementation.

where	w_j	: average wage of workers of type j with $j \in \{U, M\}$
	d_j	: measure of within-group wage disperson of workers of type j with $j \in \{U, M\}$
	$L = L_U + L_M$	: total employment as sum of employment of workers of type (U) and of workers of type (M)
	α_U, α_M, α_{dU}, α_{dM}, α_L	: weighting factors in union utility
	$ln(\bar{w}_U)$, $ln(\bar{w}_U)$, $\bar{d}_U$, $\bar{d}_U$, $ln(\bar{L})$	: reference levels for different arguments of union utility function

In the following, I first discuss some specific aspects of the functional form in equation (6.1). Afterwards, I address more generally the four issues raised above in order to provide a justification of the Stone–Geary utility function chosen here.

Since preferences are invariant to positive monotonic transformations of the entire utility function, it is assumed without loss of generality that the weighting factors sum up to unity. Unions are expected to care about employment and about average wages such that α_U, α_M, and α_L are non-negative. In addition, unions tend to favor a more egalitarian wage distribution implying that also α_{dU} and α_{dM} are non-negative. For consistency, the Stone–Geary formulation requires each difference in braces to be positive, i.e. average wages and employment have to be larger and the dispersion measures have to be smaller than their respective reference level.[5] For the empirical specification chosen in this study, as will become clear later, the consistency condition is not empirically testable.

For the purpose of the theoretical model developed in this section, it suffices to treat the reference levels for the different arguments in the utility function as exogenous constants. However, the reference levels can depend upon various variables influencing the outcome of wage bargaining for one industry at a point of time. Therefore, the empirical analysis specifies the reference levels themselves as functions of various factors. For instance, the reference level for average wages in one industry is likely to depend upon the alternative income when a worker in this industry becomes unemployed. The alternative income itself is a function of the wages in other parts of the economy and of the likelihood to find a new job. The former might depend upon general productivity growth in the economy and the latter upon

[5]It might be viewed as a weakness of the Stone–Geary utility function, that the marginal utility for one argument is infinite when the respective term in braces becomes zero and that, at the same time, the marginal utility for all other arguments is zero (if they are larger than their reference level). In further research, it might prove useful to use a specification allowing for larger substitutability of the arguments such as a CES– or an addilog function, see Pencavel (1991, p. 90). However, in my view, this would complicate the empirical implementation without changing the main qualitative implications of the theoretical model.

the unemployment rate. Also, the reference level for wage dispersion can depend upon the unemployment rate such that the union accommodates its distributional goals in the presence of high unemployment. And finally, habit persistence can be introduced by letting the reference levels for current wages or employment to depend upon their past levels.

The specification in equation (6.1) assumes that the union cares only about total employment irrespective of the distribution between (U) and (M).[6] This assumption seems a reasonable approximation since union membership consists of both groups and it does not prevent the model to take account of differences in the labor market situation for the two groups. For instance, the reference levels for the wages of the two groups can depend negatively upon the unemployment rates for the two groups. If this is the case, a negative shock to labor demand for one group without affecting the other group results in wage moderation for the first group even though the union only cares about total employment.

Turning to the justification of the utility function (6.1) in light of the four issues raised at the beginning of this subsection: As advocated by Pencavel (1985, 1991), the Stone–Geary function provides a flexible and an empirically tractable approximation of union utility with respect to problem 1 and 2. Exact aggregation is typically infeasible with heterogeneous members, i.e. a "microfoundation" of the union utility such as the requirement that it should represent a utilitarian specification is by no means less ad hoc than the Stone–Geary specification. In addition, if union leaders pursue their own self interests subject to their reelection prospects, which depend on the members' preferences, exact aggregation becomes even more doubtful and the best one can hope for is a suitable approximation of union preferences rationalizing its actions. The third problem, the existence of Insider–Outsider–effects implies that unions care mostly (exclusively in an extreme version) about the interests of its employed members. In the presence of a positive shock to employment, the union is then rather willing to exchange it for a wage increase, whereas when a negative shock occurs, the union puts more weight on employment and is willing to decrease substitute lower wages for a stabilization of employment. These considerations can possibly be integrated into the Stone–Geary formulation: For instance, by letting the employment reference level depend upon past employment levels or by letting the reference level for wages only depend upon changes in unemployment rates but not upon the level of unemployment rates themselves.

Despite the fact, that the majority of employees is not member of a union (average union density among employees lies between 30% and 35% during

[6] As an alternative in the spirit of the Sone–Geary specification, one could have two separate arguments $\{ln(L_U) - ln(\bar{L_U})\}$ and $\{ln(L_M) - ln(\bar{L_M})\}$ in the utility function with specific weighting factors. Unfortunately, the first–order conditions of the optimization problem in this case would result in an empirical model which would be considerably more difficult to estimate. Also, due to the nonlinearity of the specification, the two models are not formally nested rendering a test between the two more difficult.

the time period 1975 to 1990), the outcome of wage bargaining typically also applies to non-union members as the labor contract for the individual worker often simply refers to the union wage agreement. This occurs because of three reasons:

- First, the employer is member of the employers' association, for which the contract is binding.
- Second, the contract is extended by the government to non-union members ("Allgemeinverbindlicherklärung").
- Third, the employer does not want to provide an incentive for union membership.

In addition, it has to be pointed out that German law does not allow collective agreements to discriminate explicitly between union and non–union members. Thus, it is plausible that unions care about employment and wages of all workers as a proxy for these variables for union membership. This assumption corresponds to the self assessment of German unions who claim to act in the interest of all workers and, thereby, hope to induce them to become union members.

6.1.2 The Optimality Conditions and the Constraints

Having discussed the union objective function in the previous subsection, I turn next to the optimality conditions arising from the first–order conditions of the optimization problem. The union maximizes utility with respect to the level of average wages and with respect to wage dispersion subject to a system of labor demand functions. The reaction of labor demand to wage setting must take account both of substitution effects (as considered in the previous chapter) and of output effects due to changing labor costs in the industry. Endogenizing the output effects is rarely done by the recent literature on the skill structure of wages and labor demand.

Maximization of the union utility with respect to average wages and measures of wage dispersion yields the following set of first–order conditions

$$\frac{\partial \Gamma}{\partial X'} = \frac{\alpha_X \cdot \Gamma}{\{X' - \bar{X}'\}} + \frac{\alpha_L \cdot \Gamma \cdot \eta_{LX}}{\{ln(L) - ln(\bar{L})\}} = 0$$

for $X' \in \{ln(w_U),\ ln(w_M),\ d_U,\ d_M\}$, $\bar{X}'$ being the corresponding reference levels, and, for notational simplicity, $X \in \{U, M, dU, dM\}$ being the corresponding abbreviations in subscripts. Since the union utility function assumes that the union cares in the same way about employment of the two types of workers, it is necessary to derive the elasticities of total employment with respect to the determinants of labor demand. The parameter η_{LX} represents the elasticity of total employment L with respect to changes in X'

combining both the reaction of L_U and of L_M as given by

$$\eta_{LX} = \frac{\partial ln(L)}{\partial X'} = \frac{\partial ln(L)}{\partial ln(L_U)} \cdot \frac{\partial ln(L_U)}{\partial X'} + \frac{\partial ln(L)}{\partial ln(L_M)} \cdot \frac{\partial ln(L_M)}{\partial X'} \quad (6.2)$$
$$= \bar{s}_U \eta'_{UX} + \bar{s}_M \eta'_{MX}$$

where $\bar{s}_U = L_U/L$, $\bar{s}_M = L_M/L$, and η'_{UX}, η'_{MX} denote the total elasticities of demand for L_U and L_M, respectively, with respect to changes in X' taking account of output reactions.

After rearranging terms, the four first-order conditions for maximum union utility can be written in the following form:

$$\alpha_U \cdot \{ln(L) - ln(\bar{L})\} + \alpha_L \cdot \{\bar{s}_U \eta'_{UU} + \bar{s}_M \eta'_{MU}\} \cdot \{ln(w_U) - ln(\bar{w}_U)\} = 0 \quad (6.3)$$
$$\alpha_M \cdot \{ln(L) - ln(\bar{L})\} + \alpha_L \cdot \{\bar{s}_U \eta'_{UM} + \bar{s}_M \eta'_{MM}\} \cdot \{ln(w_M) - ln(\bar{w}_M)\} = 0$$
$$\alpha_{dU} \cdot \{ln(L) - ln(\bar{L})\} + \alpha_L \cdot \bar{s}_U \cdot \eta'_{UdU} \cdot \{d_U - \bar{d}_U\} = 0$$
$$\alpha_{dM} \cdot \{ln(L) - ln(\bar{L})\} + \alpha_L \cdot \bar{s}_M \cdot \eta'_{MdM} \cdot \{d_M - \bar{d}_M\} = 0$$

In order to make the first-order conditions operational, I need to derive expressions for the elasticity of total employment (L) with respect to changes in the decision variables of the union. The reaction of labor demand must take account both of substitution effects along the isoquant and of output effects due to changing labor costs in the industry. To endogenize output, I suggest a simple two step procedure where output demand and labor demand at given level of output are treated separately. Output demand at the industry level is given by the following iso–elastic specification

$$ln(Y^D) = ln(D) + \eta \cdot [ln(P_Y) - ln(\bar{P}_Y)] \quad (6.4)$$

where Y^D : real output demand in industry
D : demand shifter
η : demand elasticity
P_Y : output price in industry
$\bar{P}_Y$: aggregate price level.

In addition to the factor input of low–skilled labor (U) and of medium–skilled labor (M), it is assumed that firms minimize costs with respect to material inputs. Analogous to the previous chapter, capital input and technology indicators are taken as quasi-fixed in the short run. Therefore, the variable cost function (and the conditional production function) only involve factor input decision for given capital and technology. Arising from cost minimizing behavior of the firm, the union faces the following three factor demand functions at given output, capital, and technology,

$$ln(L_U^D) = ln(L_{U,0}^D) + \eta_{UU} ln(w_U) + \eta_{UM} ln(w_M) + \eta_{UV} ln(p_V) \quad (6.5)$$
$$+\eta_{UdU} d_U + \eta_{UY} ln(Y)$$

$$\begin{aligned} ln(L_M^D) &= ln(L_{M,O}^D) + \eta_{MU} ln(w_U) + \eta_{MM} ln(w_M) + \eta_{MV} ln(p_V) \\ &\quad + \eta_{MdM} d_M + \eta_{MY} ln(Y) \\ ln(V) &= ln(V_O^D) + \eta_{VU} ln(w_U) + \eta_{VM} ln(w_M) + \eta_{VV} ln(p_V) + \eta_{VY} ln(Y) \end{aligned}$$

where (in addition to previously defined symbols)

$L_{U,O}^D, L_{M,O}^D, V_O^D$	: autonomous levels of factor demand in industry
$\eta_{i,j}$	: elasticity of factor demand i with respect to changes in variable j
V	: level of material inputs in industry
p_V	: price level of material inputs

Changes in capital and technology are treated as exogenous in this model and they result in changes of the above autonomous levels of factor demand. A novelty (as in the previous chapter) of my approach is that it explicitly considers wage dispersion within the two groups of labor. If within group wage dispersion decreases (as it is often stated in the policy debate in Germany) then demand for this type of labor should fall implying positive coefficients η_{UdU} and η_{MdM}. The factor demand functions at the industry level should be perceived as a heuristic aggregation of firm specific demand functions for heterogeneous labor and material inputs depending among other things upon an exogenous distribution of wages.

The elasticity of total employment L with respect to changes in the decision variables of the union (η_{LX}) as given in equation (6.2) combines the elasticities of labor demand for the two types of labor (U,M) modelled in equation (6.5) and the output reaction with respect to changes in factor prices. The total elasticity for each type of labor is given by

$$\eta'_{jX} = \eta_{jX} + \eta_{jY} \cdot \eta_{YX}$$

where $j \in \{U, M\}$ and η_{YX} represents the elasticity of output with respect to changes in X'. The latter elasticity influences the demand for L_U and L_M via the output elasticity of labor demand.

To complete the derivation of the model in this section, it remains to analyze the output reaction with respect to changes in average wages and the level of wage dispersion. Turning to the output reaction parameters η_{YX} with $X \in \{U, M, dU, dM\}$, it is assumed that firms maximize profits

$$P_Y(Y) \cdot Y - C(Y)$$

under monopolistic competition where $P_Y(Y)$ represents the inverse of the output demand function given by equation (6.4). As an approximation, I treat the entire industry as a monopoly. Substitution across industries is reflected by the autonomous demand level D and the aggregate price level $\bar{P}_Y$ in equation (6.4). Output demand at the firm level is likely to be more elastic due to monopolistic competition within the industry.

The first–order condition of profit maximization at the industry level implies that

$$\frac{dln(Y)}{dln(mc)} = \eta$$

for marginal costs $mc = dC(Y)/dY$.[7] Wages influence output via their effect on marginal costs. Assuming that marginal costs do not depend upon output, it follows that

$$\eta_{YX} = \frac{dln(Y)}{dX'} = \frac{dln(Y)}{dln(mc)} \cdot \frac{dln(mc)}{dX'} = \eta \frac{dln(mc)}{dX'}$$

and it suffices to evaluate $dln(mc)/dX'$ for X' being any argument of the cost function (and not an argument of the output demand function). Since the firm is assumed to maximize profits taking factor prices as given, marginal costs can be written as

$$mc = w_U \cdot \frac{\partial L_U}{\partial Y} + w_M \cdot \frac{\partial L_M}{\partial Y} + p_V \cdot \frac{\partial V}{\partial Y}$$

where the reactions of factor inputs with respect to changes in output result from the cost minimization problem. In order to derive a closed–form solution for the derivatives in the first–order condition of the union's optimization problem, it is assumed that the elasticities

$$\frac{\partial ln(L_U)}{\partial ln(Y)} = \eta_{UY}, \frac{\partial ln(L_M)}{\partial ln(Y)} = \eta_{MY}, \text{ and } \frac{\partial ln(V)}{\partial ln(Y)} = \eta_{VY}$$

are all constant but do not necessarily take the same value. In light of the empirical results in this study, it is not justified to assume homotheticity (or even constant returns to scale) of the production function conditional on capital and technology (i.e. that these output elasticities are the same or even equal to unity, respectively, see the discussion of equation (6.5) above). Now, marginal costs can be rewritten as

$$mc = \frac{w_U L_U}{Y} \cdot \eta_{UY} + \frac{w_M L_M}{Y} \cdot \eta_{MY} + \frac{p_V V}{Y} \cdot \eta_{VY} = s'_U \cdot \eta_{UY} + s'_M \cdot \eta_{MY} + s'_V \cdot \eta_{VY}$$

where s'_U, s'_M, and s'_V are defined accordingly. Differentiating mc under the assumption of constant elasticities with respect to changes in output and rearranging terms yields[8]

$$\frac{\partial ln(mc)}{\partial ln(w_U)} = \frac{1}{mc} \cdot \{s'_U \cdot \eta_{UY} \cdot (1 + \eta_{UU}) + s'_M \cdot \eta_{MY} \cdot \eta_{MU} + s'_V \cdot \eta_{VY} \cdot \eta_{VU}\},$$

[7] This follows since the first–order condition states that $(1 + 1/\eta)P_0 Y^{1/\eta} = mc$ with $P_0 = \bar{P}_Y D^{-1/\eta}$.

[8] Treating average wage levels as the price for two types of homogeneous labor (homogeneous within each skill group), Shepard's Lemma (as applied in the previous chapter) would imply a simpler and less restrictive expression for the elasticity of marginal costs with respect to changes in w_U and w_M. Differentiating $dC/dw_j = L_j(w_U, w_M, p_V, Y)$ for

$$\frac{\partial ln(mc)}{\partial ln(w_M)} = \frac{1}{mc} \cdot \{s'_U \cdot \eta_{UY} \cdot \eta_{UM} + s'_M \cdot \eta_{MY} \cdot (1+\eta_{MM}) + s'_V \cdot \eta_{VY} \cdot \eta_{VM}\},$$

$$\frac{\partial ln(mc)}{\partial d_U} = \frac{1}{mc} \cdot \{s'_U \cdot \eta_{UY} \cdot \eta_{UdU}\}, \text{ and } \frac{\partial ln(mc)}{\partial d_M} = \frac{1}{mc} \cdot \{s'_M \cdot \eta_{MY} \cdot \eta_{MdM}\}$$

Then, it is possible to obtain a closed–form solution for the total elasticities of demand for L_U and L_M as

$$\eta'_{jX} = \eta_{jX} + \eta_{jY} \cdot \eta \cdot \frac{\partial ln(mc)}{\partial X'}$$

where $j \in \{U, M\}$ and $X \in \{U, M, dU, dM\}$. The derivation of this result concludes the theoretical considerations required to allow for the estimation of the first–order conditions of the wage bargaining problem (provided suitable estimates of the output demand and factor demand elasticities are available).

6.1.3 Comparative Statics of the Wage Bargaining Model

The comparative statics of the wage bargaining model allow to evaluate how the reaction of the endogenous observable variables to certain shocks depends upon certain parameter values, in particular, upon those of the unobservable union objective function. This will facilitate the interpretation of the empirical results obtained in this study. However, it proves less practical to determine the total reaction of the endogenous variables with output being endogenous. Only at the cost of further highly restrictive conditions, it would be possible to derive an analytic reduced form with endogenous output. Also because of this reason, the empirical analysis in the remainder of this study does not follow the strategy used in Pencavel (1985) and Pencavel and Holmlund (1989) where a system of analytic reduced form equations is estimated with the parameter restrictions arising from the structural model being imposed on the estimates.

As a simple alternative to the complete comparative statics of the model, I derive instead the system of reduced form solutions, when output is constant, yielding a simple and well known structure. From this result, it is possible to evaluate the total reactions in a simple way. Using the four first–order conditions, the set of labor demand equations allows for an explicit analytic solution for labor input, average wages and the level of wage dispersion.

$j \in \{U, M\}$ with respect to Y and rearranging terms yields

$$\frac{\partial ln(mc)}{\partial ln(w_U)} = \frac{s'_U \cdot \eta_{UY}}{mc} \quad \text{and} \quad \frac{\partial ln(mc)}{\partial ln(w_M)} = \frac{s'_M \cdot \eta_{MY}}{mc}.$$

These expressions coincide with the derivation suggested in the main text only under the assumption of constant elasticities of factor demand with respect to changes in output. There, I avoid the use of Shepard's Lemma in order to derive in the same way the elasticities both with respect to average wages and with respect to wage dispersion.

Assuming a log–linear approximation for total employment, the system of reduced form equations at given level of output can be written as

$$\begin{aligned} ln(L) &= ln(\bar{L}) + \alpha_L \cdot \{ln(\tilde{L}) - ln(\bar{L})\} \\ ln(w_U) &= ln(\bar{w}_U) - \frac{\alpha_U}{\eta_{LU}} \cdot \{ln(\tilde{L}) - ln(\bar{L})\} \\ ln(w_M) &= ln(\bar{w}_M) - \frac{\alpha_M}{\eta_{LM}} \cdot \{ln(\tilde{L}) - ln(\bar{L})\} \\ ln(d_U) &= \bar{d}_U - \frac{\alpha_{dU}}{\eta_{LdU}} \cdot \{ln(\tilde{L}) - ln(\bar{L})\} \\ ln(d_M) &= \bar{d}_M - \frac{\alpha_{dM}}{\eta_{LdM}} \cdot \{ln(\tilde{L}) - ln(\bar{L})\} \end{aligned} \tag{6.6}$$

where

$$ln(\tilde{L}) = ln(L_0) + \eta_{LU} ln(\bar{w}_U) + \eta_{LM} ln(\bar{w}_M) + \eta_{LdU}\bar{d}_U + \eta_{LdM}\bar{d}_U$$

denotes the maximum possible level of employment when the union is forced to accept just the reference levels for average wages and wage dispersion. Note that $ln(L_0)$, as defined implicitly above, also comprises the output effects on total labor demand.

According to the above equations (6.6), the difference between this maximum $ln(\tilde{L})$ and its reference level for employment $ln(\bar{L})$ (so to speak the union's internal "employment margin") is distributed among the various arguments in the union's utility function according to the weights α_X and to the elasticities η_{LX} $(X \in \{U, M, dU, dM\})$. The higher the weight the larger the union chooses the differences between the respective variable and its reference level. At the same time, the allocation of the internal "employment margin" to each argument depends upon its relative price in employment units (the elasticities in the denominator): the higher the respective elasticity in absolute terms the smaller becomes the difference to the reference level.

To conclude, three types of shocks to this system are discussed also illustrating the comparative statics with endogenous output. I consider an increase in

1. one of the reference levels for average wages,

2. the autonomous component of output demand, and

3. the relative demand for medium–skilled versus low–skilled labor.

In the first scenario, $ln(\tilde{L})$ decreases since the employment elasticities η_{LM} and η_{LU} are typically negative. Without loss of generality, let it be $\bar{w}_U$ which is increased. Then, the differences between all arguments and their reference levels decrease in absolute values. Thus, total employment and the wage for medium–skilled workers falls absolutely, since their reference levels ($\bar{L}$,$\bar{w}_M$) remain the same. In contrast, the wage of low–skilled workers increases by $(1 - \alpha_U)$ times the increase of its reference level. Assuming that wage dispersion exhibits a positive influence on labor demand, the dispersion measures d_U and d_M increase. And finally, the output effect is likely to be negative since total employment falls.

The second scenario concerns an increase of the autonomous component of output demand. This results in an increase of $ln(L_0)$ (refer to the definition after equation system (6.6)) and thus increases the internal "employment margin" of the union. All differences to the respective reference levels, which themselves remain fixed, become larger: Employment and average wage levels increase and wage dispersion decreases. At the same time, output grows.

The final third scenario involves the relative demand between medium–skilled and low–skilled labor. Assuming that total labor demand is unaffected by this change, i.e. $ln(L_0)$ remains unchanged, the model does not exhibit any impact on its endogenous variables (at least up to the first–order log–linear approximation chosen here – when larger than infinitesimal changes are involved, all total labor demand elasticities change due to different weighting between L_U and L_M). This result is a direct outcome of the assumption that the union cares about total employment, irrespective of the division between low–skilled and medium–skilled workers. However, in the empirical part of this study, I allow for the possibility that the reference levels for wages depend upon the unemployment rate of the respective group of workers. If unemployment has a negative influence on the reference level for average wages then the change in relative unemployment resulting from the change in relative labor demand leads to a decrease of the reference level for low–skilled workers and to an increase for medium–skilled workers. Based on the first scenario, this implies a lower wage for low–skilled workers and a higher wage for medium–skilled workers thus mitigating the relative employment. This last scenario shows that the likely consequences of a skill bias in labor demand can be tested within the framework developed here. If unions only care about total employment and the wage reference levels are not affected by group specific unemployment, then such a bias in labor demand trends will result in an ever decreasing share of low–skilled employees. This corresponds to the prima facie evidence for West Germany. The following empirical part will address this point in more detail.

6.2 Data

To study the relationship between average wages, wage dispersion, and employment, it is natural to use industry data comprising wage and employment figures for different skill levels of labor since wage bargaining in West Germany typically occurs at the industry level. For this study, I had to construct such a dataset by merging national account data with the IAB–Beschäftigtenstichprobe (I$_A$BS) dataset, a 1% random sample from German

Social Security Accounts. In addition, skill specific unemployment rates from Microcensus data, predicted sectoral union densities (taken from Fitzenberger, Haggeney, and Ernst, 1998), and data on R&D expenditure (taken from the ANBERD database of the OECD, 1997) are merged with the basic data set. The analysis is restricted to the pre–unification situation for West Germany up to 1990. This section describes the most important features of the data used while the appendix provides further details and the detailed industry classification.

The national accounts provide data from 1970 to 1990 for former West Germany at the 2– and 3–digit industry level (58 industries in total). These data comprise information on value added, production (shipment) value, net capital stock, total employment, wage bill, material inputs, and the respective price deflators. I decided to work with the 49 industries given by the industry classification in the appendix (table A.1). Price deflators for material inputs and shipment are only available at a more aggregated level compared to the classification used here. While this is not a big problem for Non–Manufacturing (here prices and real values are available for a number of industries), the situation is more serious for Manufacturing. Here, I use production price indices (taken from the commodities' statistics of the Federal Statistical Office) as the price deflator for shipments. This allows to construct real shipments, real material inputs, and a price deflator for material inputs.

The second data set ($I_A BS$) is merged with the national account data since the latter only provide limited information on different skill types of labor. The $I_A BS$ is based on the reporting requirements of the German social security system. It is a 1% random sample of all individual social security accounts during the years 1975 to 1990. The earnings data and other relevant information of each person paying contributions to the social security system are recorded over the entire life-cycle in order to calculate the individual pensions. About 80 percent of the German employees are covered by this mandatory pension system.

Based on the $I_A BS$ data, I distinguish three skill groups of workers, as defined in chapter 2 and in the data appendix, which I label as low–skilled (U), medium–skilled (M), and high–skilled (H) workers. For each skill group, I calculate wage quantiles and employment shares in each industry and year. In 1975, the estimated employment shares were 32.2% for (U), 64.2% for (M), and 3.7% for (H). For 1990, these shares changed to 15.7% for (U), 76.6% for (M), and 7.7% for (H). The empirical analysis in this study, being concerned with union wage bargaining, only attempts to explain wages and employment of the two lower skill types (U) and (M) while treating the factor input of (H) as negligible. It is believed that union wage bargaining is less relevant for workers of type (H) who are often also part of management.

Unfortunately, the $I_A BS$ does not include any information on hours worked. However, one can distinguish between full–time and part–time employment. While using employment figures for all workers (male and female, part–time and full–time), this chapter only considers wage trends for full–time working males in order to minimize the impact of participation changes and composition bias. It is assumed that these wages provide a better picture of trends in the price per efficiency unit of labor and, at the same time, they are the focus of wage bargaining. Though somewhat questionable, the underlying assumption is that wages for different types of labor reflect their relative productivities. Put differently, it seems very difficult (and beyond the scope of this study) to implement empirically the model presented in section 6.1 when distinguishing workers by gender and by whether they work part–time or full–time.

6.3 Empirical Analysis

This section describes how the theoretical model developed in section 6.1 is implemented empirically and presents the estimation results.

6.3.1 Implementation

The model outlined in section 6.1 is estimated separately for Manufacturing (MAN) and for Non–Manufacturing (NON–MAN) in West Germany during the time period 1975 to 1990, see tables A.1 and A.2 in the appendix for the industry classification. The analysis omits the sectors agriculture, government, and private households and non–profit organizations. Union membership differs considerably between MAN and NON–MAN (see Fitzenberger, Haggeney, and Ernst, 1998) and collective bargaining appears somewhat more important in MAN compared to NON–MAN. Also employment trends differ considerably, with the employment share of MAN declining continuously, and wage growth appears slightly larger in MAN (Fitzenberger and Franz, 1998). In order to implement the model, I take median wages deflated by the aggregate consumer price index as the measure for average wages and the log difference between the 80%– and the 20%–quantile of wages as the measure for wage dispersion for the two skill groups.

The conventional procedure would be to estimate simultaneously the entire model (output demand, factor demand equations, first–order conditions of the union) as a system of six (without wage dispersion) or eight (with wage dispersion) partly nonlinear equations. Though certainly the asymptotically efficient procedure, I was unable to implement this approach: Estimation often did not converge and, when convergence was achieved, often some of the parameter values took on extreme, highly implausible values.[9] These nu-

[9]The numerical difficulties arise mainly because the first–order conditions involve products of parameter values such that single factors cannot be identified easily and that by themselves the first–order conditions could be brought exactly to zero by setting simultaneously the employment elasticities and the utility weights of all wage arguments to zero. This can become a problem when a GLS–type two–step–estimation procedure is used which reweights the equations based on the estimated variance of the first step

merical difficulties would also have rendered bootstrapping impossible which proves important for robust inference given that the model specification is mostly static, i.e. it is likely to be plagued by autocorrelation.

In light of these problems, I have resorted to a simpler estimation approach which allows for the separate determination of the elasticities of output and of factor demand without invoking the union's first–order conditions. Taking these elasticity estimates as given, only estimation of the union's utility parameters is based on the first–order conditions. Thus, estimation proceeds in two steps: First, output demand and factor demand for given output are estimated. Second, based on the estimated output and labor demand elasticities obtained in the first step, the parameters of the union's utility function are estimated based on the first–order conditions of the union's optimization problem. Both steps are implemented by instrumental variable estimation.

The output and the factor demand equations are estimated as static models in levels (not as a dynamic model) according to the presentation in section 6.1. Output demand is specified with industry specific linear time trends accounting for different output levels and for exogenous taste changes across industries. Each factor demand equation includes sector dummies, which account for differences in technology across industries, and year dummies, which account for further unobservable changes in technology. In addition, the factor demand equations include the capital stock in form of equipment, the capital stock in form of plants, and the share of R&D expenditure in shipments as further quasi–fixed arguments (see the discussion of equation sytem (6.5) in section 6.1). Even though, I only view the factor demand system as a heuristic approximation at the industry level, cost minimization at the firm level is likely to imply that the sum of factor demand elasticities $\eta_{iU} + \eta_{iM} + \eta_{iV}$ is equal to zero for all $i \in \{U, M, V\}$. I will impose this condition on the estimated models and, for a parsimonious specification, I will also use the following cross–equation restrictions on the cross–price elasticities, see Hamermesh (1993, chapter 2). The elasticities of factor demand are estimated under the assumption of constant Allan–Uzawa elasticities of substitution[10], i.e. the empirical model specifies

$$\eta_{j',j} = s_j \cdot \sigma_{j',j} \quad \text{for} \quad j \neq j' \ , \ j, j' \in \{U, M, V\} \qquad (6.7)$$
$$\text{and} \quad \eta_{j,j} = -\sum_{j' \neq j} \eta_{j,j'}$$

where

$$s_U = \frac{w_U L_U}{w_U L_U + w_M L_M + p_V V} \ , \ s_M = \frac{w_M L_M}{w_U L_U + w_M L_M + p_V V} \ ,$$
$$\text{and} \quad s_V = \frac{p_V V}{w_U L_U + w_M L_M + p_V V}$$

residuals.

[10]See Hamermesh (1993, p. 35, equation 2.34), who does not require constant returns to scale of the production function under the definition of the shares s_j used below.

are the shares in total costs. Using these cross-equation restrictions, it is only necessary to estimate the three parameters σ_{UM}, σ_{UV}, and σ_{MV}, since symmetry conditions hold for the substitution elasticities.

The first-order conditions are estimated as specified by equations (6.3) in section 6.1. Using an instrumental variable Method-of-Moments approach, the parameters are estimated such that, on average, a weighted sum of the deviations from the reference levels is set to zero. Since the weights involve the utility weights, the normalization that the utility weights sum to unity is necessary for identification.

At this point, one needs to specify the utility weights and the reference levels for employment and for the wage arguments in the union utility function (see table 6.1 for a summary). The utility weights are specified as a linear function depending upon the deviation of union density from the average union density in MAN or NON–MAN, respectively. As a first-order approximation, this allows to interprete the constants ($\alpha_{U,0}$, $\alpha_{M,0}$, $\alpha_{L,0}$, $\alpha_{dU,0}$, $\alpha_{dM,0}$) as the average utility weight in MAN or NON–MAN, respectively. Utility weights are estimated under the condition that their sum equals unity. This implies that the constants must sum up to unity whereas the slope coefficients ($\alpha_{U,ud}$, $\alpha_{M,ud}$, $\alpha_{L,ud}$, $\alpha_{dU,ud}$, $\alpha_{dM,ud}$) with respect to union density must sum up to zero. Both conditions are imposed on the estimates. There are two reasons (with conflicting empirical implications) why the utility weights could depend upon the union density: First, union density can be interpreted as a proxy for union bargaining power in terms of the Nash–Bargaining problem presented in the introduction. Then larger union density should imply a smaller weight for employment, since employment is a proxy for profits. Second, the larger the union density the more workers are represented by the union. Thus, if the union has the power to influence wages, it is concerned about a larger group of workers when union density is high. This might imply an increasing weight for employment.

Turning to the specification of the reference levels: Due to the numerical difficulties mentionend above, it proves important to choose a parsimonious specification.[11] However, one has to consider the possibility that the reference levels differ by industry and over time. Differences in the size of industries and changes thereof over time should be reflected in the reference levels for employment. Reference levels for wage levels should reflect productivity increases over time (given the productivity orientation of German wage bargaining, see Franz, 1996, p. 279). Even though conventional wage setting equations (extended Phillips curve) use labor productivity as an ar-

[11] Despite being formally identified, I avoid to specify the same arguments (except for an intercept as a level shifter) for the reference levels of employment and of the wage variables. Otherwise, the same variables would appear twice in each first-order condition. For this reason, it makes little sense to test for the consistency of the Stone–Geary specification by checking whether the difference between the arguments of the utility function and their respective reference level is always non-negative. Anyway, violation of this property is not an uncommon finding in the literature (see Pencavel, 1985, p. 221).

gument, I prefer to specify the reference levels for wages as a function of total productivity growth.[12] In addition, the reference levels should depend upon the alternative wage which is influenced by the skill group specific unemployment rate. I avoid putting in an aggregate average wage or replacement ratios for unemployment benefits as further arguments of the alternative wage since the degrees of freedom in the time domain are quite limited (already the unemployment rates and the aggregate productivity growth only vary over time). I also do not allow for sectoral variation of the reference levels for wages since it seems likely that, in this respect, union preferences are uniform across industries. I choose a very parsimonious specification of the reference levels for wage dispersion, only allowing it to depend on an intercept and on the skill group specific unemployment rate. If it is the case that a lack of within-group wage flexibility results in unemployment, it is possible that the union accommodates its distributional goals in the presence of high unemployment. A final aspect of the specification of the reference levels relates to habit persistence in the utility function. Previous estimates of Stone–Geary utility functions (Pencavel and Holmlund, 1988, De la Croix et al., 1996) were allowing reference levels for wages to depend upon their level in the past. In light of the discussion on insider–outsider effects, it is also of interest to investigate whether unions only care about employment changes. Thus, I estimate one set of models without habit persistence in either average wages and employment and another set of models with habit persistence in both. However, I do not allow for habit persistence in wage dispersion. Table 6.1 describes the differences across estimated models. In the model with habit persistence, it turns out empirically that unions tend to care about wage growth. Therefore, in this case, I chose to model the reference level as a function of productivity growth instead of productivity levels. This is done in analogy to a classical Phillips curve specification.

In both steps of the model, instrumental variable estimation is used. While it is clear, that wages, employment, material inputs, prices of material inputs, output, and output prices have to be treated as endogenous, it is not easy to find good instruments. Following the strategy in MaCurdy and Pencavel (1986), where observations differ by their location, identification in this study mainly relies on the use of industry dummies and their interactions with linear and quadratic time trends as instruments. Also, when appropriate, I use the full set of time dummies, the industry specific input of quasi–fixed factors, the predicted industry specific union density among employees (taken from Fitzenberger, Haggeney, and Ernst, 1998) both for MAN and NON–MAN and industry specific import prices in MAN as additional instruments. The set of instruments differs by equation. For output demand, it includes industry specific quadratic time trends (i.e. industry dummies and

[12] This is done for two reasons: First, labor productivity is affected by a change in the skill composition of labor even though technology does not change. Second, measured labor productivity is also affected when capital or material inputs are substituted for labor.

Table 6.1: Specification Details of Estimated Models[a]

Utility Weights	$\alpha_U = \alpha_{U,0} + \alpha_{U,ud}\,(ud_i - \bar{ud}_{MAN/NON-MAN})$ $\alpha_M = \alpha_{M,0} + \alpha_{M,ud}\,(ud_i - \bar{ud}_{MAN/NON-MAN})$ $\alpha_L = \alpha_{L,0} + \alpha_{L,ud}\,(ud_i - \bar{ud}_{MAN/NON-MAN})$ $\alpha_{dU} = \alpha_{dU,0} + \alpha_{dU,ud}\,(ud_i - \bar{ud}_{MAN/NON-MAN})$ $\alpha_{dM} = \alpha_{dM,0} + \alpha_{dM,ud}\,(ud_i - \bar{ud}_{MAN/NON-MAN})$ where ud_i represents union density in industry i and $\bar{ud}_{MAN/NON-MAN}$ the average union density in MAN or NON–MAN, respectively, whichever industry i belongs to
Wage Dispersion	Each model is estimated either with or without the 80% – 20% quantile difference (QD) measure $[d_j = ln(W_j^{80\%}) - ln(W_j^{20\%})$ with $j = U, M]$ for wage dispersion as an argument of labor demand and of union utility
	When wage dispersion is considered, the reference levels are given by: $ln(\bar{d}_U) = \beta_{DU,0} + \beta_{DU,ur}\, ur_U$ $ln(\bar{d}_M) = \beta_{DM,0} + \beta_{DM,ur}\, ur_M$
Without Habit Persistence	Specification of Reference Levels: $ln(\bar{L}) = \sum_i(\beta_{L,i,0} + \beta_{L,i,t}t)DI_i$ $ln(\bar{W}_U) = \beta_{U,0} + \beta_{U,ur}ur_U + \beta_{tfp}^{agg}tfp^{agg} + \beta_{tfp}^{sec}tfp$ $ln(\bar{W}_M) = \beta_{M,0} + \beta_{M,ur}ur_M + \beta_{tfp}^{agg}tfp^{agg} + \beta_{tfp}^{sec}tfp$
With Habit Persistence	Specification of Reference Levels: $ln(\bar{L}) = \sum_i \beta_{L,i,0}DI_i + \gamma_L ln(L_{i,t-1})$ $ln(\bar{W}_U) = \beta_{U,0} + \beta_{U,ur}ur_U + \beta_{tfp}^{agg}\Delta tfp^{agg} + \beta_{tfp}^{sec}\Delta tfp + \gamma_{WU} ln(W_{U,t-1})$ $ln(\bar{W}_M) = \beta_{M,0} + \beta_{M,ur}ur_M + \beta_{tfp}^{agg}\Delta tfp^{agg} + \beta_{tfp}^{sec}\Delta tfp + \gamma_{WM} ln(W_{M,t-1})$

a: For the notation, see the variable and parameter definitions in table 6.2 in the appendix of this chapter.

their interactions with linear and quadratic time trends) and a full set of year dummies (for MAN also import prices). For the factor demand equations, these instruments are augmented by union density and the set of quasi–fixed factor inputs. And for the estimation of the union's first–order conditions, the set of instruments for output demand is augmented by union density.

Given the nonlinearity and the static character of the estimated model and the two step estimation approach, standard errors are estimated by a block bootstrap procedure based on 1000 resamples, where resamples are formed by drawing blocks of observations with replacement from the sample (see Fitzenberger (1998) for the block bootstrap procedure in a pure time series context). Among the resamples, I only consider those for which convergence of the first–order conditions is achieved under the same settings as for the sample estimates. Non–convergence is only a problem for a small number of resamples (less than 5%) and, in such a case, a new resample is drawn instead. This way inference is based on 1000 resamples for which convergence was achieved. The standard errors estimated by the block bootstrap procedure are robust against heteroscedasticity and autocorrelation of fairly general form.[13] In addition, basing the two steps of the estimation procedure on the same resample automatically takes account of the sampling error in the first step parameter estimates, which are predetermined in the second step. This way, one can avoid the necessary correction of the standard errors of the second stage estimates as described in Newey (1984). In the empirical implementation in this chapter, the blocks consist of five adjacent observations over time for a given industry (experimenting for some specifications with a larger block length did not seem to change standard errors in an important way). This allows to accommodate autocorrelation of the error term in each equation and correlation of error terms across equations. The resample size in this chapter is chosen to be twice as large as the sample size in order to mitigate problems with singular samples, i.e. samples for which not all dummy coefficients are identified. According to the asymptotic rate involved, the bootstrap variance–covariance matrix had to be multiplied by two.

Estimation of the model is implemented in the program TSP (see Hall and Cummins, 1997) using the LSQ command with the instrument–option for all equations. All industry–year observations are weighted by total industry employment in the respective year in order to account for the different industry sizes. When more than one equation is involved, two step (nonlinear 3SLS) estimates are obtained using the efficient weighting matrix arising from the contemporaneous correlation of the error terms across equations. Clearly, in terms of obtaining more efficient estimates, this approach neglects the contemporaneous correlation between the three sets of equations (output, factor demand, first–order conditions) but, given the numerical problems mentioned above when estimating the entire model simultaneously, I call into question whether my approach really involves an efficiency loss. In any case, the block

[13]Similar concerns also led MaCurdy and Pencavel (1986, appendix) to construct asymptotic standard error estimates which are robust against heteroscedasticity and autocorrelation for a given observation unit. They used the empirical correlation in the error term to construct a truncated kernel estimate for standard errors taking account of preestimated quantities. Compared to the approach suggested by these authors, the advantages of the block bootstrap method lie in the simplicity of its implementation, in the flexibility to model different correlation structures, while positive definiteness of the variance–covariance matrix is guarenteed, and in the fact, that one automatically obtains appropriate standard errors even though the estimation approach involves preestimated quantities in the second step.

bootstrap approach takes account of contemporaneous (as well as intertemporal) correlation across all equations when estimating standard errors.

6.3.2 Results

Tables 6.3 and 6.4 present the estimation results. The model introduced above is estimated separately for Manufacturing (MAN) and Non–Manufacturing (NON–MAN). In addition, the specifications differ by whether the model only considers average wages or also the measures for wage dispersion and by whether habit persistence in the reference levels of average wages and employment is allowed for, see table 6.1. Before describing the results in detail, it has to be acknowledged that the estimates of some crucial parameters are not robust across specifications. Thus, when evaluating the results, it is important to discuss the appropriateness of the different specifications in light of the empirical results. As a reminder of the discussion in the introduction, it has to be kept in mind, that the estimated union utility represents the complete wage bargaining process where employment is also considered a proxy of employers' profits.

Table 6.3 contains the results for the model without habit persistence where the union cares about the levels of wages and employment irrespective of their values in the past. Since industries are subject to continuous structural change, the reference level for employment allows for an industry specific time trend (it would seem useless for a union to strive for a constant employment level in an industry with ever declining employment). Also wage aspirations grow over time, since workers contrast their wages with average real wages in the economy. Therefore, the reference levels for average wages depend upon total factor productivity growth both at the industry level tfp and at the aggregate level tfp^{agg}. In addition, they also depend upon the skill specific unemployment rates which have an impact on the alternative wage.

The first and the third column in table 6.3 present the model without quantile differences (QD), which only considers the choice of average wages by the union given a set of factor demand functions depending only on average wages. The output demand elasticity η is estimated around -0.3 in MAN and around -0.2 in NON–MAN.[14] Since MAN is more exposed to international competition than NON–MAN, the higher demand elasticity comes as no surprise. Regarding the estimated Allen–Uzawa elasticities of substitution (σ_{UM}, σ_{UV}, σ_{MV}) in MAN, both types of labor (U,M) seem to be substitutes of material inputs but no significant substitution seems to occur between (U) and (M).[15] The situation is different in NON–MAN. There are very strong

[14]Even though profit maximization under monopolistic competition requires η to lie above one at the firm level, the parameter here concerns the industry level as the level at which wage bargaining takes place. A value of η below one at the industry level is not inconsistent with individual firms facing considerably steeper output demand curves.

[15]Though insignificant, the elasticity of substitution between (U) and (M) is about the

substution effects between (U) and (M) (σ_{UM}=3.7). Substitution between (M) and (V) is positive and close to be significant, whereas the elasticity of substitution between (U) and (V) is close to zero and insignificant. Since all cross substitution elasticities in MAN and NON–MAN are positive, it is guaranteed that the own–price elasticities of factor demand are all negative. The output elasticities of factor demand differ across factors. Whereas the output elasticity of demand for material inputs lies above 0.9 both in MAN and NON–MAN and is not significantly different from one, the estimated output elasticities for (U) and (M) are considerably smaller (and significantly smaller than one). Thus, constant returns to scale in production are rejected by the data. Overall, the parameter estimates are consistent with microeconomic theory such that the implied behavorial relationships can reasonably be interpreted as constraints of the union's optimization problem.

Next, the discussion turns to the estimates for the parameters of the union's objective function for the models without QD. Starting with the utility weights, employment exhibits a very high average weight both in MAN and NON–MAN (in NON–MAN, its weight is even not significantly different from one). Both in MAN and NON–MAN, the average weight for wages of (U) is small and not significantly different from zero. This is also the case for wages for (M) in NON–MAN. However, in MAN, the decision makers in wage bargaining seem to care both about total employment and about wages for (M). Whereas in NON–MAN, the impact of union density on the utility weights is nowhere significant, union density proves significant both for wages of (M) and employment in MAN (but not for wages of (U)). Here the results indicate that a higher union density increases the weight of employment, i.e. stronger unions in MAN care more about employment and less about wages. Considering the estimates for the reference levels both for MAN and for NON–MAN, neither the skill specific unemployment rates nor productivity growth rates appear to have a significant influence on the reference levels for wages (the signs of the unemployment rates are even positive, whereas, if anything, one would expect a negative sign).

The second and the fourth column of table 6.3, contain the results for the model with QD. The output demand equation is exactly the same as before (the difference in the estimated standard errors results from the inherent randomness in the bootstrap estimates and the fact that a resample is dismissed when estimation does not converge). Both for MAN and NON–MAN, the coefficients for the factor demand equation already discussed above do not change. In addition, the elasticities of factor demand for (M) with respect to wage dispersion are not significantly different from zero. However, for (U) the results indicate that increasing wage dispersion raises labor demand for workers of this type. Whereas, the effect is only weakly significant in MAN, it is very strong and highly significant in NON–MAN. In contrast to these coefficient estimates, the results for the parameters of union utility appear

same as estimated in Steiner and Wagner (1997).

less satisfactory. Both in MAN and NON–MAN, unions seem to care significantly about all wage arguments in the utility function (also about d_M even though the estimated factor demand elasticity shows no constraint in changing it). In contrast to the results without QD, the employment weight is small and only weakly significant in MAN and it is basically zero for NON–MAN. The effect of union density on utility weights is insignificant in both parts of the economy. Considering the estimates for the reference levels, there are a number of implausibly high, but insignificant estimates for NON–MAN making this specification look very dubious for numerical reasons (note that this is basically a log–linear world). In MAN, one finds a number of large and significant coefficients. Starting with the plausible ones, the reference levels for average wages seem to be positively influenced by aggregate productivity growth and the coefficient is not significantly different from one. Also, the reference level for wage dispersion in skill group (M) seems to be positively affected by higher unemployment in this group, thus, in such a situation the union is willing to accept larger inequality. However, this result is questioned by the fact that wage dispersion for (M) is not a significant determinant of labor demand. Further doubts about the specification for MAN can be raised since unemployment appears to show a large, significantly positive influence on the reference level for average wages.

Summarizing the results for the models without habit persistence, what can be said so far? The models for output demand and factor demand show fairly plausible results with elasticities differing between MAN and NON–MAN. In particular, substitution effects between (U) and (M) seem only very limited in MAN and very strong in NON–MAN. In addition, there is strong evidence for an employment enhancing impact of larger wage dispersion for (U) (both in MAN and NON–MAN) but not for (M). The utility parameters in the model without habit persistence are plausible indicating that decision makers in wage bargaining care strongly about employment. Almost no additional significant parameter can be estimated. The results for the model with QD do not seem convincing. Even though there are some plausible coefficients for MAN, the model yields highly implausible effects for MAN and NON–MAN.

Does the model with habit persistence yield a more satisfactory description of wage bargaining in the light of the model developed in this study? The results can be found in table 6.4. Since the specification of output and of factor demand is the same as for the model without habit persistence, the following discussion is restricted to the estimated parameters of the union's utility function.

Starting with the model without QD in the first and third column, the coefficients related to habit persistence (γ_L, γ_{WU}, γ_{WM}) are highly significant and all very close to one. For wages, however, the coefficients differ significantly from one in three out of four cases. Nevertheless, the data suggest that wage bargaining both in MAN and NON–MAN is basically concerned with year–to–year changes in employment and wages. Similar to the model without habit persistence, the utility weights for employment are fairly high both in MAN and NON–MAN and, only in NON–MAN, the average weights for wages are insignificant. In MAN, unions do care about average wages. The weight of average wages for (U) decreases significantly with rising union density in MAN and union density proves insignificant in NON–MAN. The reference levels for average wages of (U) decrease with a rise in unemployment of this group, however, this effect is only significant for MAN. The unemployment rate for (M) does not exhibit a significant impact on the reference level for average wages for this group. Since the model in habit persistence basically comprises average wage growth as arguments of the union utility function, the reference levels are specified such that they depend upon the growth rate of technical progress (see table 6.1 and the discussion in section 6.3.1 on the productivity orientation of wage bargaining). The results show a significantly positive impact of aggregate productivity growth in MAN and of industry specific productivity growth in NON–MAN with the respective other productivity variable exhibiting no significant impact. Overall, the models with habit persistence and without QD confirm the significant results of the models without habit persistence and without QD and yield further plausible significant parameter estimates. At the same time, habit persistence appears highly significant such that there seems to exist an almost complete orientation on wage and employment changes.

Turning to the results for the model with QD in the second and fourth column of table 6.4, the findings differ considerably between MAN and NON–MAN. For MAN, the coefficients for habit persistence still prove significantly positive and none of them differs significantly from one. The average utility weights are significantly positive for all arguments indicating that the decision makers in wage bargaining care about all arguments considered here (again with the caveat that there does not appear to exist a trade–off for d_M). For NON–MAN, only the coefficient for employment related to habit persistence is still positive and not significantly different from one whereas the coefficient for average wages turn negative but not significantly so. The utility weights for all arguments except employment are significantly positive. However, since the weight for employment appears to be equal to zero, there does not appear to exist a trade–off for wage bargaining in NON–MAN (I take this as an indication that the model does not provide a satisfactory description of wage bargaining in NON–MAN). Also for the impact of union density, the results differ between MAN and NON–MAN: In MAN, the weight for employment rises and the weights for all wage arguments (except for d_M with an insignificant coefficient) decline with increasing union density. In NON–MAN none of the union density coefficients proves significant.

Also, the impact on the reference levels differs between MAN and NON–MAN. For MAN, both skill specific unemployment rates now show a significantly negative influence on the reference levels for average wages. For wage dispersion of (M) there exists a significantly positive influence of the unemployment rate of this group whereas for wage dispersion of (U) the coefficient is positive but not significant. Finally, again only aggregate but not industry specific productivity growth exhibits a significantly positive impact on the reference level for average wages. For NON–MAN, all coefficient estimates describing an impact on the reference levels exhibit implausibly large numbers which, however, prove insignificant.

Summarizing the empirical results, the following points describe what can be learnt reliably from this empirical analysis and what are the weaknesses:

1. Output demand is more elastic in MAN compared to NON–MAN.

2. Whereas substitution of the two types of labor is fairly limited in MAN, the elasticity of substitution is very large (above 3) in NON–MAN. Overall, labor demand for the two skill groups is considerably more elastic in NON–MAN compared to MAN. Both for MAN and NON–MAN, wage dispersion for (U) exhibits a significantly positive coefficient estimate for the demand for (U). This is not the case for (M) implying that there is no trade–off involved for wage dispersion in this group.

3. The objective function of decision makers in wage bargaining is characterized by strong habit persistence both in employment and in average wages. In fact, wage bargaining seems to be only concerned about employment and wage changes. However, this finding is not robust for NON–MAN, when one allows for wage dispersion.

4. Without allowing for wage dispersion, employment carries a very large weight in the objective function. When wage dispersion is introduced, the weight for employment decreases considerably but only in NON–MAN it becomes insignificant. The latter finding implies that the model "does not work" for NON–MAN with wage dispersion.

5. In both parts of the economy, unions seem to care strongly about wage dispersion within groups. However, a well defined trade–off rationalizing this empirical result exists only for (U).

6. In MAN, allowing for habit persistence, unemployment rates for the two types of labor exhibit a negative impact on the reference levels for average wages. There is no such clear result for wage dispersion.

7. In MAN, reference levels for average wages are oriented on aggregate productivity growth whereas sectoral productivity growth plays no role. The situation appears exactly opposite in NON–MAN, but again here the results are much less robust.

6.4 Conclusions

This chapter represents the first attempt to formulate and estimate a structural model for wage bargaining with heterogeneous labor in West Germany. The model accounts for two skill–types of labor. The union's objective function is of Stone–Geary form putting different weights to employment, to average wages across, and to wage dispersion within the two groups of labor. Building on the "right–to–manage" assumption, wage bargaining is constrained by labor demand being determined at the firm level. The empirical analysis is performed separately for Manufacturing and Non–Manufacturing. Unfortunately, the estimated models are not satisfactory in all respect. Maybe, this does not come as a surprise given the complexity of the German wage bargaining system for which the model developed in this study can only consider some important features and given the fact, that this is the first study of this type for West Germany.

Despite the deficiencies of the empirical models, one can draw some robust conclusions about wage bargaining in West Germany: First, there is strong habit persistence such that decision makers in wage bargaining seem to care about changes (not about levels) in average wages and employment. Second, employment changes clearly carry a positive weight in the wage bargaining considerations in Manufacturing and this weight grows with rising union density. The situation is less clear in Non–Manufacturing, but the models without wage dispersion also show a positive weight for employment changes, which is, however, unaffected by union density. In Manufacturing, but not in Non–Manufacturing, wage demands for one skill group are mitigated when unemployment for this group is higher. Third, there is a clear indication (especially for Manufacturing) that unions care about wage dispersion within skill groups even though the estimated models allowing for wage dispersion are not completely satisfactory. Only in Manufacturing, there is a tendency that the wage structure reacts to increasing unemployment rates. Fourth, in Manufacturing, wage demands depend upon aggregate productivity growth whereas sectoral productivity growth plays no role. The situation might exactly be opposite in Non–Manufacturing but the results here are much less robust.

These findings imply that, in the presence of a negative labor demand shock, wage bargaining, in fact, reacts by lowering wage demands temporarily. In Manufacturing, this short–run effect becomes even stronger with higher union density. However, the long–run wage effects of higher unemployment are much smaller in Manufacturing and there seem to be none in Non–Manufacturing. In addition, only in Manufacturing one finds a small reaction of the wage structure (both between and within skill groups) to skill specific imbalances in the labor market.

Clearly, in order to obtain a more satisfactory empirical model of wage bargaining in West Germany with heterogeneous labor, further research is needed, which could address the following issues: First, one could attempt to specify a complete model of Nash bargaining under the right–to–manage assumption, as outlined at the beginning of this chapter. Such a model involves a structural specification of the profit function at the industry level. Second, one could distinguish between contract wages as decision variables of the actual wage bargaining process and effective wages as being determined at the firm level in reaction to contract wages. Third, it could be fruitful to formulate the model as a dynamic bargaining model extending the aggregate analysis by De la Croix et al. (1995) for homogeneous labor.

6.5 Appendix of Chapter 6

6.5.1 Definitions

Table 6.2: Variable and Parameter Definitions

Variable Definitions

Abbreviation	Definition
(U)	Skill group of workers without vocational training degree and without post secondary degree ("ohne abgeschlossene Berufsausbildung und ohne FH/Universitätsabschluß")
(M)	Skill group of workers with vocational training degree and without post secondary degree ("mit abgeschlossener Berufsausbildung und ohne FH/Universitätsabschluß")
(H)	Skill group of workers with post secondary degree ("FH/Universitätsabschluß")
Y	Gross production (shipments) in constant prices
P_Y	Price deflator for shipments
V	Material inputs in constant prices
P_V	Price deflator for material inputs
W_J	Median of annual average daily earnings for skill group J (J=U,M) obtained from social security accounts ("I_ABS"), not including employers' contribution to social insurances, in current prices
L_J	Employees of skill group J (J=U,M) obtained from the I_ABS dataset
KA/KB	Net capital stock in form of equipment/plants obtained from the national accounts, in constant prices
UD	Union density as defined by the share of union members among all employees
$\Gamma[w, L]$	Union utility level depending on wage and employment
Π	Profit level
$\bar{X}$	Reference level in union utility function for $X \in \{L, W_U, W_M, d_U, d_M\}$
$\bar{\Gamma}/\bar{\Pi}$	Reference level for union utility/profit level in general wage bargaining model
DI_i	Dummy variable for industry i
t	Linear time index: 1975 $\equiv$ 0, 1976 $\equiv$ 1, 1977 $\equiv$ 2, ...
tfp^{agg}/tfp	Aggregate/sector specific total factor productivity (with respect to three types of labor and capital) as log difference to 1975 based on 1975 factor shares
ur_j	Aggregate unemployment rate for skill group $j \in \{U, M\}$

Table 6.2: < Continued > Variable and Parameter Definitions

Parameter Definitions

Abbreviation	Definition
α_X	Relative weight in union utility function for $X \in \{L, U, M, dU, dM\}$
$\alpha_{X,j}$	Parameters ($j \in \{0, ud\}$) in the specification of relative weight in union utility function for $X \in \{L, U, M, dU, dM\}$
up	Relative weight (= bargaining power) of union in bargaining process
$\beta_{X,j}$	Parameters in the specification of the reference level for L, W_U, W_M, d_U, or d_M with $X \in \{L, WU, WM, dU, dM\}$ and $j \in \{i\,(\text{industry } i), (i,t), U, M\}$
γ_X	Parameters in the specification of the reference level for L, W_U, or W_M in the presence of habit persistence with $X \in \{L, WU, WM\}$
$\eta_{j1,j2}$	Output constant factor demand elasticities for $j1, j2 \in \{U, M, V\}$
$\eta'_{j1,j2}$	Total factor demand elasticities (including output reactions) for $j1, j2 \in \{U, M, V\}$

- A variable with index i refers to industry i.
- All variables are for West Germany only ("Bundesrepublik Deutschland" before October 3, 1990).

6.5.2 Estimation Results

Table 6.3: Model Without Habit Persistence – Instrumental Variable[a] Estimates of Central Parameters[b] for Manufacturing and Non–Manufacturing (Coefficient Estimates and Block Bootstrap Standard Errors)[c]

	Manufacturing				Non–Manufacturing			
Coefficient	Without QD[d]		With QD[d]		Without QD[d]		With QD[d]	
Name[e]	Coeff.	(s.e.)	Coeff.	(s.e.)	Coeff.	(s.e.)	Coeff.	(s.e.)
η	-.302	(.152)	-.302	(.173)	-.197	(.142)	-.197	(.139)
σ_{UM}	.534	(.965)	.991	(.996)	3.680	(1.64)	3.242	(1.95)
σ_{UV}	.425	(.142)	.418	(.150)	.035	(.167)	.039	(.163)
σ_{MV}	.437	(.055)	.409	(.056)	.198	(.126)	.188	(.125)
η_{UY}	.243	(.095)	.219	(.097)	.367	(.256)	.289	(.265)
η_{MY}	.679	(.082)	.675	(.084)	.085	(.165)	.076	(.177)
η_{VY}	.932	(.048)	.934	(.049)	.940	(.181)	.936	(.182)
$\alpha_{U,0}$	.028	(.024)	.147	(.050)	.005	(.053)	.148	(.076)
$\alpha_{M,0}$	.146	(.034)	.323	(.064)	.015	(.139)	.282	(.156)
$\alpha_{U,ud}$	-.117	(.153)	-.335	(.400)	.007	(.133)	.017	(.098)
$\alpha_{M,ud}$	-.742	(.315)	-.367	(.884)	.214	(.567)	-.012	(.358)
$\beta_{U,ur}$	.244	(.304)	2.552	(.580)	-.088	(1.38)	50.402	(59.0)
$\beta_{M,ur}$	.688	(.454)	5.421	(1.09)	.079	(2.41)	102.927	(80.7)
β^{sec}_{tfp}	.059	(.064)	-.046	(.061)	.237	(.151)	-.890	(.933)
β^{agg}_{tfp}	.221	(.222)	.951	(.279)	-.400	(.760)	12.684	(22.0)
$\alpha_{L,0}$	.826	(.046)	.269	(.183)	.981	(.186)	.012	(.364)
$\alpha_{L,ud}$	.858	(.431)	.798	(1.56)	-.220	(.637)	-.017	(.491)
η_{UdU}	–	–	.461	(.281)	–	–	1.567	(.383)
η_{MdM}	–	–	-.365	(.223)	–	–	.061	(.207)
$\alpha_{dU,0}$	–	–	.113	(.035)	–	–	.201	(.079)
$\alpha_{dM,0}$	–	–	.148	(.083)	–	–	.357	(.207)
$\alpha_{dU,ud}$	–	–	-.344	(.273)	–	–	.020	(.143)
$\alpha_{dM,ud}$	–	–	.249	(.561)	–	–	-.007	(.178)
$\beta_{DU,ur}$	–	–	-1.090	(4.60)	–	–	-9.283	(976.6)
$\beta_{DM,ur}$	–	–	3.225	(.593)	–	–	-221.372	(596.7)

a: The set of instruments for output demand includes sector specific quadratic time trends (i.e. sector dummies and their interactions with linear and quadratic time trends) and a full set of year dummies (for Manufacturing also import prices). For the factor demand equations, these instruments are augmented by union density and the set of quasi–fixed factor inputs. And for the estimation of the first–order conditions, the set of instruments for output demand is augmented by union density.

Table 6.3: <continued>

b: In addition to those presented in this table, this estimated model includes further parameters. Output demand is specified with sector specific linear time trends. Each factor demand equation includes sector dummies and year dummies and the specification for $ln(\bar{L})$ includes sector dummies. See also table 6.1 for the model specification.

c: The coefficient estimates are obtained in two steps. First, the parameters of output demand and labor demand are estimated separately. Then, based on the estimated output and labor demand elasticities, the parameters of the union's utility function are obtained using the first-order conditions of the union's optimization problem. Standard errors are estimated by a block bootstrap procedure based on 1000 resamples, where resamples are formed by drawing blocks of observations with replacement from the sample. The blocks consist of five adjacent observations over time for a given industry. The estimated standard errors are robust against heteroscedasticity and autocorrelation of unknown form. In addition, basing the two steps of the estimation procedure on the same resample automatically takes account of the sampling error in the first step parameter estimates, which the second step is based upon. This way, one can avoid the necessary correction of the standard errors of the second stage estimates as described in Newey (1984).

d: See table 6.1: Model estimated without or with quantile differences (80% − 20%) in log wages as the measure for wage dispersion (in factor demand equations and union utility).

e: See table 6.2 for notation.

Table 6.4: Model with Habit Persistence – Instrumental Variable[a] Estimates of Central Parameters[b] for Manufacturing and Non–Manufacturing (Coefficient Estimates and Block Bootstrap Standard Errors)[c]

	Manufacturing				Non–Manufacturing			
Coefficient	Without QD[d]		With QD[d]		Without QD[d]		With QD[d]	
Name	Coeff.	(s.e.)	Coeff.	(s.e.)	Coeff.	(s.e.)	Coeff.	(s.e.)
η	-.302	(.152)	-.302	(.154)	-.197	(.142)	-.197	(.141)
σ_{UM}	.534	(.970)	.991	(1.01)	3.680	(1.61)	3.242	(1.94)
σ_{UV}	.425	(.142)	.418	(.151)	.035	(.167)	.039	(.168)
σ_{MV}	.437	(.058)	.409	(.055)	.198	(.125)	.188	(.129)
η_{UY}	.243	(.094)	.219	(.097)	.367	(.254)	.289	(.262)
η_{MY}	.679	(.083)	.675	(.085)	.085	(.165)	.076	(.176)
η_{VY}	.932	(.048)	.934	(.050)	.940	(.181)	.936	(.186)
$\alpha_{U,0}$	.051	(.018)	.134	(.026)	.007	(.015)	.253	(.109)
$\alpha_{M,0}$	.115	(.019)	.193	(.040)	.052	(.054)	.255	(.114)
$\alpha_{U,ud}$	-.140	(.070)	-.336	(.142)	-.034	(.058)	.001	(.080)
$\alpha_{M,ud}$	-.054	(.118)	-.436	(.250)	-.075	(.187)	-.001	(.237)
γ_L	.984	(.030)	.982	(.745)	1.029	(.049)	1.016	(.363)
$\beta_{U,ur}$	-.117	(.065)	-.385	(.095)	-.119	(.119)	16.828	(14.1)
$\beta_{M,ur}$	.017	(.116)	-.387	(.143)	.198	(.224)	5.653	(10.7)
γ_{WU}	.933	(.024)	1.045	(.038)	.997	(.025)	-.798	(.548)
γ_{WM}	.960	(.020)	.999	(.030)	.870	(.070)	-.927	(.283)
$\beta^{sec}_{\Delta tfp}$	.029	(.031)	.040	(.041)	.112	(.074)	-4.713	(2.63)
$\beta^{agg}_{\Delta tfp}$	.231	(.119)	.387	(.145)	-.180	(.223)	-2.699	(8.73)
$\alpha_{L,0}$	.834	(.029)	.264	(.117)	.941	(.062)	.002	(.425)
$\alpha_{L,ud}$	.193	(.164)	1.202	(.820)	.109	(.213)	-.003	(.715)
η_{UdU}	–	–	.461	(.276)	–	–	1.567	(.372)
η_{MdM}	–	–	-.365	(.216)	–	–	.061	(.205)
$\alpha_{dU,0}$	–	–	.159	(.037)	–	–	.259	(.138)
$\alpha_{dM,0}$	–	–	.250	(.090)	–	–	.231	(.164)
$\alpha_{dU,ud}$	–	–	-.646	(.261)	–	–	.001	(.278)
$\alpha_{dM,ud}$	–	–	.216	(.514)	–	–	.002	(.528)
$\beta_{DU,ur}$	–	–	.358	(.240)	–	–	-2.420	(293.9)
$\beta_{DM,ur}$	–	–	.687	(.455)	–	–	-2.556	(2.88)

a,b,c,d: See table 6.3.

7 Epilogue

Was ist der langen Rede kurzer Sinn?
F. Schiller, 1798, Wallenstein

This study analyzes wages and employment across skill groups in West Germany during the 70's and 80's. Before discussing the overall conclusions and putting the main results into perspective, I should mention several distinctive features of this study: First, the study attempts a balanced mixture of descriptive evidence and structural estimation. Chapters 2 and 3 provide a comprehensive view on wage trends. Chapter 2 describes also employment trends. Chapter 4 investigates empirical implications of trade theory on the relationship between pertinent endogenous variables. Using instrumental variable techniques, Chapters 5 and 6 estimate structural models of the skill structure of labor demand or of a complete wage bargaining model. Second, all chapters but one take account of wage dispersion both between and within skill groups. Chapters 2 and 3 analyze wage trends for different quantiles in order to encompass both dimensions of wage dispersion. Chapters 5 and 6 suggest a heuristic method to measure the impact of both dimensions on the skill structure of labor demand. And the utility function of the union in chapter 6 is assumed to depend upon both dimensions in order to allow for distributional goals. Third, using three skill groups of labor, the study allows for non-monotonous results across skill groups. In contrast, a considerable part of the international literature is restricted to two skill groups. Fourth, except for the mere descriptive analysis in chapter 2, modelling the specific wage trends for females is beyond the scope of this study. Therefore, the remaining chapters are restricted to wage trends either for males alone or for all workers together. Fifth, inference in chapters 3, 5, and 6 is based on a block bootstrap procedure allowing for heteroskedasticity and fairly general correlation structures in the error term of the estimated relationships. This new inference procedure is introduced in appendix A.2. Sixth, for the empirical analysis, I constructed an industry level dataset merging national accounts data with the IAB–Beschäftigtenstichprobe (an extensive micro dataset on wages and employment which has only become available recently for the time period from 1975 to 1990). In addition, pertinent data from various other sources are added to the basic dataset. In constructing the database, I had to overcome various shortcomings in the data sources (see data appendix A.3).

What are the overall conclusions of this study? What does the study add to the debate on the two–sides–of–the–same–coin hypothesis outlined in chapter 1? The detailed discussions of the specific results can be found at the end of each chapter. Therefore, I restrict myself here to a general discussion of the most important findings.

Above all, and probably not surprising, the study broadly confirms the two–sides–of–the–same–coin hypothesis. I find a skill bias in labor demand trends and that, at the same time, higher wage flexibility (both between and within skill groups) could have alleviated the dispersion in unemployment rates across skill groups. The main cause for the skill bias in labor demand appears to be technological progress, however, the evidence is also consistent with international trade causing a deterioration in the labor market position of low–skilled workers. With regard to wage bargaining, I find some evidence for a moderation of wage demands for a particular skill group in the short run when unemployment increases but little evidence for a long–run reaction when unemployment has become persistent.

In addition, this study provides various findings which were not necessarily to be expected and some of which require a modification of the conventional wisdom about labor market trends in West Germany: First, even though the changes are small in international comparison, the wage structure in West Germany is apparently less stable than commonly believed. Among males, I find wage growth at the median to be higher both for low– and high–skilled workers compared to medium–skilled workers. The wage dispersion within skill groups increases over time for medium–skilled and high–skilled workers but it is stable for low–skilled workers. The wage growth was also higher in Manufacturing compared to Non–Manufacturing industries, in tradable compared to non–tradable goods industries, and in industries subject to little governmental regulations compared to industries subject to major governmental regulations. Even though import competition increased considerably during the 80's, those parts of the economy which depend less upon international trade did, in fact, experience lower wage growth. This is exactly opposite to what one would expect considering that union wage demands are reduced when labor demand becomes more elastic.

Second, as its main contribution, the cohort analysis in chapter 3 shows that a fairly parsimonious characterization of movements in the entire wage distribution for different skill groups is possible. I find a considerable uniformity of wage growth across cohorts thus corresponding to the view that pattern bargaining results in parallel movements of wages in different industries and areas. The descriptive wage trends in chapters 2 and 4 are mostly confirmed by the detailed cohort analysis. The main exception is the following: After controlling for age and cohort effects, wage dispersion within the group of low–skilled workers was increasing and, after a heuristic correction for selection effects due to unemployment, wage growth in the lower part of the wage distribution for low–skilled workers now turned out to be considerably lower than for all other groups. Assuming that unemployment is more likely for low–ability workers earning low wages, it could very well be the case that the disproportionate wage growth observed in the lower part of the empirical wage distribution for low–skilled workers confounds actual wage growth experienced by those who are continuously employed with selection effects.

Third, chapter 5 shows that skill upgrading in employment occurs both in Manufacturing and Non–Manufacturing industries. Labor demand in Non–Manufacturing is considerably more elastic than in Manufacturing and low– and medium–skilled workers are much closer substitutes in Non–Manufacturing compared to Manufacturing. This coincides with the conventional notion that wage restraints for low–skilled workers can be particularly helpful to increase their employment in Non–Manufacturing. The effect of wage flexibility across skill groups is illustrated by the following simulation results based on the estimates obtained in chapter 5: In order to equalize the unemployment rates of the three skill groups in 1990 for given output, the average wage gap between low–skilled and medium–skilled workers would have to increase by around 5 to 6 percent and between low–skilled and high–skilled workers by between 7 and 13 percent based on the level of wages.

In contrast to wage flexibility across skill groups, an overall increase in output growth can only contribute very little to an increase in employment of low–skilled workers. Particularly, since this is also the case for Non–Manufacturing, one cannot hope to improve the labor market position of low–skilled workers by merely engineering (in whatever way this may be done) higher general output growth in this part of the economy. Finally, wage dispersion within skill groups proves important for labor demand in Manufacturing but not in Non–Manufacturing. Put differently, only in Manufacturing, there appears to exist a lack of wage flexibility in this dimension.

Fourth, the structural analysis of wage bargaining finds some short–run and almost no long–run effects of increasing unemployment on wage demands. This is consistent with the finding that unemployment of low–skilled workers has risen disproportionately. Surprisingly, wage flexibility is somewhat larger in Manufacturing compared to Non–Manufacturing industries even though union power and wage growth are lower in Non–Manufacturing. Thus, there exists some evidence that, in the short run, strong unions mitigate their wage demands for a particular group of workers in order to avoid a disproportionate increase of unemployment in that group.

I finish with an obvious caveat: This study cannot address sufficiently all important issues relating to the skill structure of wages and employment in West Germany, and it even raises various new questions. As a few important areas, where further research is needed, let me mention the extension of the analysis to the time period after German unification, the integration of supply and demand of skill types of labor, the modelling of wage dispersion within skill groups in labor demand and in wage bargaining, and the problem of selection effects in empirical wage distributions with changing unemployment.

A Appendix

A.1 The Computation of Censored Quantile Regressions

The computation of the censored quantile regression (CQR) estimate involves minimizing a non–differentiable and non–convex distance function. When introducing the censored least absolute deviation (LAD) regression (i.e. the CQR for the special case of the median), Powell (1984) suggested generic optimization routines, which do not take account of the special characteristics of the problem. Following Powell's suggestion, Horowitz and Neumann (1987) present an empirical application based on the Nelder and Mead (1965) algorithm. Paarsch (1984) even resorted to grid search when evaluating the finite sample properties of censored LAD regression. Womersley (1986) analyzed the numerical properties of censored LAD regression for the first time and suggested an algorithm using a finite direct descent method. However, to my knowledge, his code is not available to applied researchers.

More recently, Buchinsky (1994) suggests an Iterative Linear Programming Algorithm (ILPA) involving an iteration of the Barrodale–Roberts–Algorithm (BRA) first developed for standard LAD regression (or its extension[1] for general quantile regressions). However, ILPA is not guaranteed to converge and, in Fitzenberger (1994), I show that convergence does not guarantee a local minimum of the CQR optimization problem. Koenker and Park (1996) develop a general interior point algorithm for nonlinear quantile regression problems (NLRQ), which they also apply to the CQR case. Again, as I show in Fitzenberger (1997a,b), also NLRQ does not guarantee convergence to a local minimum of the CQR minimization problem. Building on the characterization of the CQR estimate by the interpolation property presented in the following, I develop in Fitzenberger (1994) the algorithm BRCENS as an adaptation of the BRA. In contrast to ILPA and NLRQ, BRCENS guarantees convergence to a local minimum. The simulation studies in Fitzenberger (1994, 1997a,b) show that BRCENS performs best in comparison to ILPA and NLRQ in terms of the frequency that the exact global minimum of the CQR optimization problem is obtained.

[1] Koenker and d'Orey (1987) provide an extension of the BRA to the general quantile regression case.

BRCENS is very competitive in terms of the computation times involved. However, all algorithms perform quite poorly in the presence of a lot of censoring. When trying out different starting values, the performance of BRCENS can be improved considerably at a fairly small computational cost. For the applications in chapters 3 and 5, BRCENS is used with an extensive search across different starting values (also in the bootstrap part).

The purpose of this appendix is to provide a short overview on the computational aspects of CQR's and to describe the algorithm BRCENS developed by the author and applied in chapters 3 and 5.

A.1.1 Censored Quantile Regression and Interpolation Property

Introducing some notation, for a sample of size N, let the dependent variable be the $N \times 1$ vector, $y = (y_1, ..., y_N)$, the design matrix be the $N \times k$ matrix $X = (x_1, ..., x_N)'$, with $x_i = (x_{i,1}, ..., x_{i,k})$, the $N \times 1$ vector of fixed known observation specific censoring values be $yc = (yc_1, ..., yc_N)$, the $N \times 1$ vector of disturbances be $\epsilon = (\epsilon_1, ..., \epsilon_N)'$ and the $k \times 1$ parameter vector be β.

The following discussion considers a censored regression model with censoring from above. For a given quantile $\theta \in (0,1)$, the CQR estimation problem[2] is to minimize the piecewise linear distance function given by

$$\widehat{\beta_\theta} \in \underset{\beta}{\text{argmin}} \sum_{i=1}^{N} sgn_\theta(y_i - min[x_i'\beta, yc_i]) \cdot (y_i - min[x_i'\beta, yc_i]) \ , \qquad (A.1)$$

where the θ–weighted sign function is given by

$$sgn_\theta(\epsilon_i) \equiv \theta I(\epsilon_i > 0) - (1-\theta) I(\epsilon_i < 0)$$

and I(.) denotes the indicator function. The expression $x_i'\beta_\theta$ captures the θ–quantile of the underlying uncensored dependent variable conditional on x_i.

Since the CQR distance function (A.1) is piecewise linear, the CQR minimization problem does not necessarily have a unique solution.[3] Analogous to standard quantile regressions, cf. Koenker and Bassett (1978), the following interpolation property can also be established for CQR's.

Interpolation Property: If the design matrix X has full rank k, then there exists a global minimizer $\widehat{\beta_\theta}$ of the CQR distance function such that $\widehat{\beta_\theta}$ interpolates at least k data points, i.e. there are k observations $\{(y_{i_1}, x_{i_1}), ..., (y_{i_k}, x_{i_k})\}$ with

[2]Fitzenberger (1997a) treats censoring both from above and below and provides the asymptotic distribution of the CQR estimator. The expression "$sgn_\theta(\epsilon_i) \cdot \epsilon_i$" is mostly referred to as "check function" $\rho_\theta(\epsilon_i)$. The notation used here has advantages when studying the asymptotic distribution of the estimator.

[3]Womersley (1986, p. 112) and Fitzenberger (1994) provide a complete characterization of the set of minimizers.

(IP) $y_{i_l} = x_{i_l}'\widehat{\beta_\theta}$ for $l = 1, ..., k$ and the rank of $(x_{i_1}, ..., x_{i_k})'$ equals k.

When evaluating the IP, the following three points deserve attention. First, if the CQR distance function exhibits a unique minimizer, it must satisfy IP. Second, the CQR can interpolate a censoring point where an observation is censored. And third, in contrast to standard quantile regressions (see Koenker and Bassett, 1978), it is not guaranteed that a share of at most θ $[(1-\theta)]$ of the observations lies above [below] the estimated CQR line with an intercept.

The IP is established by analyzing the kinks of the piecewise linear distance function (A.1) for which the directional derivative proves an important tool. The directional derivative evaluated at β in direction $w \in \Re^k$ is given by

$$\begin{aligned} H_\theta'(\beta, w) \;&=\; \sum_{i=1}^{N} [I(x_i'\beta < yc_i) \cdot \qquad\qquad (A.2) \\ \{-sgn_\theta(y_i - x_i'\beta) - I(x_i'\beta = y_i)sgn_\theta(-x_i'w)\} \;&+\; I(x_i'\beta = yc_i) \cdot \\ \{(1-\theta)I(y_i < yc_i, x_i'w < 0) - \theta I(y_i = yc_i, x_i'w < 0)\}] \cdot x_i'w \,. \end{aligned}$$

A.1.2 The Algorithm BRCENS

The algorithm BRCENS is developed in Fitzenberger (1994) as an adaptation of the standard Barrodale–Roberts–Algorithm (BRA) for standard Quantile Regressions to the Censored Quantile Regression case. A standard quantile regression exhibits a linear programming structure. Barrodale and Roberts (1973) notice that the IP allows for a more efficient, condensed simplex approach. Only kinks of the distance function need to be considered for which k (design matrix exhibits full rank) observations are interpolated and for which the rank of the matrix formed by the regressor vectors is equal to k.

Analogous to BRA, the algorithm BRCENS involves two parts. First, the algorithm starts with all coefficients being zero as the set of nonbasic variables (NB).[4] The algorithm proceeds in k steps, where in each step the coefficient from NB changes into a direction for which the directional derivative (A.2) indicates the strongest decline of the objective. This defines a one–dimensional search direction and the coefficient is changed along this direction until the objective starts increasing again. At this point, according to the expression for the directional derivative in (A.2), there exists at least one data point being interpolated. One of these interpolated data points now replaces the coefficient leaving NB. At the end of the first part, the algorithm has reached a situation where IP is satisfied. The second part of BRCENS considers exchanging one of the interpolated observations in NB

[4] In the Simplex setup, the set of nonbasic variables comprises those coefficients and residuals (including the corresponding data points) which are currently zero and for which the Simplex tableau provides the linear representation in terms of the variables in the basis. The variables in the basis (coefficients, data points represented by the corresponding residuals) are typically different from zero.

with a different observation. With all other data points in the NB remaining interpolated, considering one data point defines a one–dimensional search direction. The algorithm keeps moving into the search direction, for which the directional derivative indicates the largest decline of the objective, until the objective cannot be reduced further. At this new point, there exists at least one data point which is added to NB, the set of interpolated data points. The algorithm stops when the directional derivatives for all interpolated data points in NB are non–negative, thus guaranteeing that a local minimum has been achieved. In contrast to the original version of BRCENS used in Fitzenberger (1994, 1997a), the current version referred to in Fitzenberger (1997b) performs the final directional derivative check for all combinations of k interpolated data points with rank k as NB. This check proves necessary to guarantee that a local minimum is reached. The change improves the reported performance of BRCENS relative to the earlier simulation studies.

BRCENS does not guarantee convergence to a global minimum of the CQR objective function. This is caused by the fact that the contribution to the directional derivative becomes zero at data points i, for which the current estimate of the CQR line yields a strictly censored fitted value, i.e. $x_i'\beta > yc_i$ at the current β. Therefore, the estimation exercise in chapters 3 and 5 always tries different starting values and finally takes the estimate yielding the lowest value of the CQR objective function.

A.2 Block Bootstrap Procedure for Robust Inference

Building on Fitzenberger and MaCurdy (1996), this appendix describes the block bootstrap procedure to draw robust inference on the sample mean. Here, the primary goal of robust inference is to estimate consistently the sample variance of the sample mean in order to construct reliable test statistics when estimation is based on grouped data (cells) from time series of cross–sections. The variance estimate should take account of fairly arbitrary heteroskedasticity and correlation of the error term. The correlation structure can involve both autocorrelation over time and correlation in the cross–section dimension, and the correlation can be both within and between cells. Finally, the treatment should allow for different weighting of the groups in the estimation procedure. The setup in Fitzenberger and MaCurdy (1996) used here nests the cases considered in the studies by Deaton (1985) and Moulton (1986, 1990).

Analogous to the treatment in Fitzenberger (1998) for the pure time series case, the asymptotic validity of a block bootstrap procedure for the sample mean extends readily to linear least squares or quantile regression estimation. In fact, the extension mainly relies on the estimator in the linear model being defined by a(n asymptotic) moment condition. Thus, the results presented in the following are likely to extend under appropriate regularity conditions to two–stage least squares estimation and censored quantile regression in the linear model (see Fitzenberger, 1997a, equation (3) for the asymptotic moment condition in the case of censored quantile regression).

In order to ease the exposition, the block bootstrap procedure is discussed here for m–dependent data (exhibiting a rectangular correlation structure) both in the cross–section and time series dimension. However, the results could be easily generalized to the short memory mixing case. In contrast to most of the literature (see Deaton, 1985, or Politis and Romano, 1993), stationarity of the error term is not assumed. Also in contrast to some of the literature, the asymptotics is based on the number of cross–section units, C, being fixed and the number of time periods, T, going to infinity. The data is assumed to be grouped in cells defined by the cross–section unit, c, and the time period, t. A typical example would be a dataset with different birth cohorts observed over time (such as in chapter 3 or in Deaton, 1985). However, also a system of regression equations (as in chapters 5 and 6) with or without cross–equation restrictions, where each equation is based on time series observations, can be cast into the framework suggested here.

In the following, section A.2.1 defines the estimation problem. Using the framework introduced in the previous section, section A.2.2 describes the block bootstrap procedure for inference. The presentation builds on Fitzenberger and MaCurdy (1996). In the latter study, we suggest a set of regularity conditions in order to establish consistency and asymptotic normality of the sample mean. Then, we establish the asymptotic validity of the block bootstrap procedure described here.

A.2.1 Estimation Problem for the Sample Mean

The data consist of individuals i who are grouped into cells defined by the time period t and the cross–sectional unit c of the observation. The number of individual observations in each cell is given by N_{ct}. The data is generated according to the following data generating process

$$y_{c,t,i} = \beta_1 + u_{c,t,i} \tag{A.3}$$

where β_1 denotes the population mean and $u_{c,t,i}$ the random deviation of $y_{c,t,i}$ from the population mean. I allow the error term $u_{c,t,i}$ to be correlated for all individuals within a given cross–section unit c and for a given time period t as well as for correlation across adjacent cross–section units and time periods. Concretely, I assume the error terms to have zero mean

$$Eu_{c,t,i} = 0$$

and to be (m_c,m_t)–dependent

$$Eu_{c_1,t_1,i}\,u_{c_2,t_2,j} = \begin{cases} \gamma(c_1,t_1,i,c_2,t_2,j) & \text{for } |c_1-c_2| \le m_c \\ & \text{and } |t_1-t_2| \le m_t \\ 0 & \text{for } |c_1-c_2| > m_c \\ & \text{or } |t_1-t_2| > m_t \end{cases},$$

irrespective of whether $i = j$ or $i \neq j$ and assuming all error variances to exist. (m_c,m_t)–dependency is defined such that individual error terms are independent when the cross–section units differ by more than m_c or when the time periods of observation differ by more than m_t. This definition yields a rectangular correlation structure in the time and cross–section dimension.

The setup introduced here encompasses various cases, which have been discussed in the literature. First, the case of a random group effect (error components model), Moulton (1986, 1990),

$$u_{c,t,i} = \theta_{c,t} + \epsilon_{c,t,i}$$

where the individual effect $\epsilon_{c,t,i}$ is independent across individuals and over time and the random group effect for each cell $\theta_{c,t}$ is i.i.d. across cells and applies uniformly to all individuals in a given cell (c,t). And second, a standard panel data case, where the error term is m_t–dependent over time but there are no dependencies across individuals.

The observed cell average results as

$$\bar{y}_{c,t} = \beta_1 + \bar{u}_{c,t} \text{ with } \bar{u}_{c,t} = \frac{1}{N_{c,t}} \sum_{i=1}^{N_{c,t}} u_{c,t,i} \tag{A.4}$$

and the total sample mean becomes

$$\bar{y}_{C,T} = \frac{1}{N} \sum_{c=1}^{C} \sum_{t=1}^{T} \sum_{i=1}^{N_{c,t}} y_{c,t,i} = \sum_{c=1}^{C} \sum_{t=1}^{T} g_{c,t}\bar{y}_{c,t} = \beta_1 + \sum_{c=1}^{C} \sum_{t=1}^{T} g_{c,t}\bar{u}_{c,t} \tag{A.5}$$

where $N = \sum_{c=1}^{C} \sum_{t=1}^{T} N_{c,t}$ denotes the total number of observations and $g_{c,t} = \frac{N_{c,t}}{N}$ the cell weight with $\sum_{c=1}^{C} \sum_{t=1}^{T} g_{c,t} = 1$.

Obviously, the distribution of the sample average $\bar{y}_{C,T}$ must be the same, irrespective of whether estimation is based on individual data or on cell means as long as, for the latter case, the weights correspond to the sample weights $g_{c,t} = \frac{N_{c,t}}{N}$ of the cells. It follows

$$E\bar{y}_{C,T} = \beta_1$$

and using the (m_c,m_t)–dependency of the error terms

$$\sigma^2_{C,T} \equiv Var(\bar{y}_{C,T}) = \sum_{c_1=1}^{C} \sum_{t_1=1}^{T} \sum_{c_2=1}^{C} \sum_{t_2=1}^{T} g_{c_1,t_1} g_{c_2,t_2} Cov(\bar{u}_{c_1,t_1}, \bar{u}_{c_2,t_2})$$

$$= \sum_{j_c=-m_c}^{m_c} \sum_{j_t=-m_t}^{m_t} \sum_{c=1+max\{0,-j_c\}}^{C-max\{0,j_c\}} \sum_{t=1+max\{0,-j_t\}}^{T-max\{0,j_t\}} g_{c,t} g_{c+j_c,t+j_t} E\bar{u}_{c,t}\bar{u}_{c+j_c,t+j_t} \ .$$

One should note that with fixed C and T and cell sizes $N_{c,t}$ going to infinity, it is typically not the case that the variances (and covariances) of the cell averages (and therefore for the total mean) converge to zero. As long as there exists a common error component operating for an asymptotically non–negligible portion of observations within a cell, this common effect cannot be "averaged away" by averaging over all individuals within the cell. This is most easily seen for the random group effects model where the cell average is given by

$$\bar{y}_{c,t} = \beta_1 + \theta_{c,t} + \frac{1}{N_{c,t}} \sum_{i=1}^{N_{c,t}} \epsilon_{c,t,i} \ .$$

For $N_{c,t}$ going to infinity $\bar{y}_{c,t}$ converges to $\beta_1 + \theta_{c,t}$. The common component $\theta_{c,t}$ is still present asymptotically.

In Fitzenberger and MaCurdy (1996), we present a set of regularity conditions for which consistency and asympotic normality of the sample mean $\bar{y}_{C,T}$ can be established. Most importantly, the number of cross–section units, C, and the number of individual observations per cell, $N_{c,t}$, are assumed as fixed and the number of time periods, T, goes to infinity.

A.2.2 Block Bootstrap Procedure

This section presents the block bootstrap procedure for inference on the sample mean. Resampling is based on two-dimensional (rectangular) blocks in the cross–section and time series dimension. For the context of the previous section, Theorem 3 in this section establishes that resampling is asymptotically first order correct, i.e. the resample distribution approximates asymptotically the sample distribution at least as good as the asymptotic normal distribution. In particular, the variance of the resample mean estimates consistently the sample variance of the sample mean, thus, asymptotically allowing for robust inference. For this result, I have to assume, as time goes to infinity, that the block length in the time dimension grows to infinity at a small enough rate and that the block length in the cross–section dimension converges to the fixed number of cross-section units.

The block bootstrap procedure considered here is based on resampling from rectangular blocks of sample cell observations[5]

$$B(c,t) = \{(\bar{y}_{c',t'}, N_{c',t'}) : c' = c, ..., c+b_c-1; t' = t, ..., t+b_t-1\} \ ,$$

where $1 \leq b_c \leq C$, $1 \leq b_t \leq T$, $q_c = C - b_c + 1$, $q_t = T - b_t + 1$, $1 \leq c \leq q_c$, and $1 \leq t \leq q_t$. These two–dimensional rectangular blocks are of length b_c in the cross–section dimension and b_t in the time series dimension and they all lie in the interior of the sample $\{c = 1, ...C; t = 1, ..., T\}$. Given (b_c,b_t), let m be the total number of i.i.d. blocks, B_j^*, $j = 1, ..., m$, drawn for the resample and let $l = m \cdot b_c \cdot b_t$ be the total number of cell observations in the resample. The block bootstrap (**BB**) procedure applied in this study is defined as follows:

BB–Procedure: Given (b_c, b_t), resample uniformly with replacement from $B(c,t)$ with $1 \leq c \leq q_c$, and $1 \leq t \leq q_t$, i.e. the blocks of observations forming the resample, B_j^*, $j = 1, 2, 3, ...$, are distributed as $P^*\{B_j^* = B(c,t)\} = \frac{1}{q_c \cdot q_t}$ conditional on the sample observations.

Note that P^* denotes the probability distribution generating the resample conditional on the sample observations.

I use the moving blocks variant of the block bootstrap procedure, Künsch (1988), Liu and Singh (1992), i.e. I allow the blocks to overlap. An alternative would be the Carlstein (1986) rule, where resampling is only based on non–overlapping blocks. Hall, Horowitz, and Jing (1995) show in a stationary time series context that the moving blocks variant enjoys an asymptotic advantage over the Carlstein rule. But they argue that this advantage is hardly present in small samples. I believe the case for the moving blocks variant to be a stronger one in a non–stationary context, since, for a given block size, under the Carlstein rule certain sample correlations between two data points are not taken account of even though the data points differ by less than the block length. This can be the case when the two data points belong to two adjacent Carlstein blocks.

Assuming that the blocksize b_t converges to infinity at a slow enough rate and that b_c converges to C, we establish in Fitzenberger and MaCurdy (1996) that, under the block bootstrap procedure introduced above, the bootstrap

[5] In the regression case, the blocks are given by

$$B(c,t) = \left\{(\bar{y}_{c',t'}, x_{c',t'}, N_{c',t'}) : c' = c, ..., c+b_c-1; t' = t, ..., t+b_t-1\right\} \ ,$$

where $x_{c',t'}$ denotes the regressor vector for cell (c',t').

distribution of the sample mean provides an estimate of the sample distribution which is asymptotically correct to the first order. In particular, the bootstrap variance of the sample mean provides a consistent estimate of its sample variance.

A.3 Details of Data Description

The empirical analysis in this study is based on a number of different data sources for West Germany which had to be combined:

1. National account data from the Federal Statistical Office disaggregated into 2– and 3–digit industries
2. The "IAB–Beschäftigtenstichprobe" ($I_A BS$), a 1% random sample from German Social Security Accounts
3. Skill and age specific trends in employment, unemployment, and participation from the German Microcensus ("Mikrozensus", an annual population survey)
4. Gross union density and predicted net union density among employees taken from Fitzenberger, Haggeney, and Ernst (1998) and extended to the time period from 1975 to 1990
5. Data on research and development expenditure (R&D) in industry (ANBERD) described in OECD (1997)
6. Indices for bargained wages (taken from the Federal Statistical Office)
7. Shares of firms in Manufacturing industries reporting product (PD) or process (PZ) innovations (taken from the ifo Firm Panel described in Schneeweis and Smolny, 1996)
8. Real material inputs from the computer industry and the electrical goods industry (see table A.1 for the industry classification) to the industries in NON–Manufacturing (taken from the Input–Output tables of the Federal Statistical Office)

1. Annual national account data are taken from the "Volkswirtschaftliche Gesamtrechnungen" Fachserie 18, Reihe 1.3 (1970 to 1990) from the Federal Statistical Office (Statistisches Bundesamt). The data source contains a complete accounting system for 58 industries comprising the entire economy. In order to be able to merge the data and to reduce the information on small industries, I aggregate these into 49 industries which are described in table A.1. I omit the industry Housing (No. 62) since it does not comprise any employees. Table A.2 also shows the decomposition of the set of industries into 32 Manufacturing and 14 Non–Manufacturing industries (the latter exclude the Government sector, Agriculture, and Non–Profit Organizations).

The national account data provide import and export series, both in current and constant prices, for groups of goods and services which can be merged with the 36 traded–goods industries (table A.2) in a fairly straight forward manner such that trade is attributed to the industry providing the final value added. Imports and exports for West Germany are only available until 1990.

A limitation of the national accounts lies in the fact that price deflators for material inputs and shipment are only available at a more aggregated level compared to the industry classification in the national accounts. This is not a big problem for Non–Manufacturing, since prices and real values are available for a number of industries and since, where the classification used here is finer, it is assumed that the same price indices apply to all industries for which the aggregate is available. The situation is more serious for Manufacturing. Here, I follow Falk and Koebel (1997) and use production price indices (taken from the commodities' statistics of the Federal Statistical Office) as the price deflator for shipments. Material inputs in constant prices are then calculated as the difference between shipments and value added (both in constant prices). Then, the price index for material inputs is obtained by dividing nominal material inputs (available from national accounts) by the real material inputs constructed above.

2. "IAB–Beschäftigtenstichprobe" (I_ABS): a 1% random sample from German social security accounts during the period from 1975 to 1990 which has only recently been made available by the research institute of the Federal Employment Service ("Institut für Arbeitsmarkt– und Berufsforschung") in Nürnberg. The main features of the data set and a users' guide can be found in Bender et al. (1996). Social security contributions are mandatory for employees who earn more than a minimum wage threshold and who are working regularly. The main exemption are civil servants who do not pay social security contributions at all. Further exclusions from the mandatory contributions are students who work less than 20 hours a week on a regular basis or less than 6 weeks full-time. About 80 percent of the German employees are covered by this mandatory pension system.

The industry classification of the I_ABS differs slightly from the one used in the national account data. The I_ABS industry classification comprises 95 industries which, in most cases, is more detailed than the national account data used here. However, in three cases, namely the industries 35/36 (Wood), 37/38 (Paper), and 60/61 (Banking, Insurances), only information for the union of the two respective industries is available in the I_ABS. For these three cases, I divided the employment and wage information in I_ABS using the employment-weight of each industry in the national accounts.

From the I_ABS dataset, I take wage and employment information by skill groups. The analysis differentiates between workers of the following three skill types:

(U) without a vocational training degree (low–skilled)

(M) with a vocational training degree (medium–skilled)

(H) with a technical college ("Fachhochschule") or university degree (high–skilled)

except for chapter 6 which, being concerned with union wage bargaining, only attempts to explain wages and employment of the two lower skill types (U) and (M) while treating the factor input of (H) as negligible.

The basic information in the $I_A BS$ dataset consists of social security insurance spells comprising the starting point and the end of an employment spell and the average daily gross wage (excluding employers' contributions). The daily gross wage is censored from above and truncated from below. If the wage is above the upper social security threshold ("Beitragsbemessungsgrenze"), the daily social security threshold is reported instead. If the wage is below the lower social security threshold, the employee does not have to pay social security contribution and therefore, does not appear in the dataset. For these reasons, I use quantiles of daily gross wages. An annual wage observation is calculated as the weighted average of the wage observation of the individual for all spells within one year where the spell length is used as the weight. For the subsequent calculations, the annual wage observation is weighted by the total employment spell length within the year relative to the length of the year. These weights are used to calculate various quantiles of wages and raw employment weights for all individuals in cells defined by skill group, industry, age, or year.

For chapter 6, I need the 20%–, 50%–, and 80%–quantiles of wages and raw employment weights for all individuals in one skill group, industry, and year cell. Only in one case (out of $16 \times 49 = 784$ possible cells), the 80%–quantile for (U) and in 45 cases, the 80%–quantile for (M) are censored. To predict the missing value in these cases, the 80%–quantile (in logarithms) is regressed on the median (in logarithms) and a linear time trend for the respective industry. The fitted values replace the missing 80%–quantiles.

Total employment in one industry from the national account data is allocated across skill groups using these employment weights constructed above. With multiple spells (jobs) at the same time, cf. Bender et al. (1996, p. 74), I take the sum of the daily wages across spells as the wage observation. In case of spells originating from different industries, this sum is assigned to each industry as the wage observation together with an employment weight that is the product of the ratio between the respective daily wage and the sum of daily wages times the spell length in years. The latter procedure is based on the assumption that the respective wage share is a good estimate of the relative time spent in the different jobs and that the hourly wage is the same across jobs.

Over time, the income components being subject to the social security tax were extended, cf. Bender et al. (1996, p. 15). In particular, starting in 1984 one–time payments to the employee had to be taxed. Steiner and Wagner (1998) note that this results in a considerable spurious increase in earnings inequality due to the structural break in the data. Because of this structural break in the data, I corrected the wage observations before 1983 in a heuristic way as described in the following. The correction is motivated by the visual impression that only wages above the median in 1984 are affected by the structural break. The underlying assumption for my correction is that only quantiles above the median need to be corrected upwards before 1983. This is operationalized by a linear regression of wage growth between 1983 and 1984 for the 19 quantiles from 5% to 95%, where wage growth up to the median is assumed to be constant. On top of this uniform growth for the lower half of the distribution, wage growth for the quantiles above the median is specified as a linear function in the percentage point difference between the respective quantile and the median. I interpret the linear function in the percentage difference as "excessive" (spurious) wage growth due to the structural break. Wages above the median before 1983 have to be corrected upwards by this spurious wage growth. This correction is implemented for the individual wage observations. First, I determine whether an individual exhibits a wage observation in 1984. If there is more than one employment spell, I take the weighted average. Second, I determine the quantile position of this wage observation in the marginal distribution of wages in 1984. Third, if there is no wage observation in 1984 then I look for a wage observation in 1983 and determine the quantile position in 1983 instead. Fourth, using the quantile position determined either for 1984 or for 1983 I predict spurious wage growth from 1983 to 1984 using the estimate obtained above. Using this fitted values, I multiply all wage observations for this individual before 1984 by this factor. If this leads to a wage observation above the social security threshold value, I censor the wage observation right there. Fifth, for individuals without any wage observations in either 1983 or 1984 no correction is undertaken. Figure A.4 exhibits the marginal distribution of wages after this correction. Comparing it with figure A.3, it can be seen that the correction effectively takes out the spurious rise of the within wage dispersion above the median from 1983 to 1984.

3. Skill specific aggregate unemployment rates: Information from the German microcensus on skill specific employment and unemployment are taken from "Bevölkerung und Erwerbstätigkeit", Fachserie 1, Reihe 4.1.2 from the Federal Statistical Office (Statistisches Bundesamt). These data are available for the years 1976, 1978, 1980, 1982, 1985, 1987, 1989, and 1991. When calculating skill specific unemployment rates for the missing years, I interpolate the data using a regression approach where the aggregate unemployment rate is used to predict the period specific movement. Note that skill specific aggregate or sector specific employment is calculated using national accounts and the $I_A BS$ data as described above.

Skill specific trends in employment, unemployment, and participation: For the years 1976, 1980, 1982, 1985, 1987, and 1989, I obtained the data from a random subsample of the German Microcensus, cf. Statistisches Bundesamt,

Fachserie 1, Reihe 4.1.2.[6] The Microcensus distinguishes between the following three labor market states: Employed ("Erwerbstätig"), Unemployed ("Erwerbslos"), and Non-participating ("Nichterwerbsperson"). The state unemployed does not necessarily correspond to the notion of "registered unemployment" used by the Federal Employment Agency ("Bundesanstalt für Arbeit").[7] When calculating skill specific unemployment rates for the missing years, I interpolate the data using a regression approach where the aggregate unemployment rate and employment in each age–skill cell is used to predict the period specific movement.
For all the Microcensus data used in this paper, I define:

UN number of unemployed persons,
EMP number of employed persons, and
NP number of non-participants.

Then, the size of an age-education group (population) is the sum POP=EMP+ UN+NP. The employment (participation) rate is the ratio EMP/POP and the unemployment rate is given by the ratio UN/(EMP+UN).

4. Gross union density and using the I_ABS to predict net union density: In West Germany, conventional industry specific measures of gross union density (ratio of union members to employment) typically cannot distinguish between working and non–working members (cf. Franz, 1996, chapter 7.2). Also the industry affiliation of the unions does not necessarily correspond to standard industry classifications and some unions cover large groups of industries. The recent study of Fitzenberger, Haggeney, and Ernst (1998) calculates industry specific estimates of gross union density from published union membership information for the time period 1984 to 1990. These measures for gross union density are extended here to the time period 1975 to 1990. In order to obtain net union density, the study of Fitzenberger, Haggeney, and Ernst continues by estimating union membership among employees based on individual data from the German Socioeconomic Panel (GSOEP). The GSOEP provides the membership information for the years 1985, 1989, and 1993. The results of the study show that the econometric specification of union membership is stable across the three available years. One specification of these estimates for the unbalanced panel of observations in the GSOEP contains only variables, which are available in the I_ABS (I only neglect the significant influence of political preferences). This specification is used to predict union membership

[6] I am very grateful to Reinhold Schnabel who calculated these data based on a subsample of the raw Microcensus, which is available at ZUMA, Mannheim, for my definition of skill groups.

[7] Whereas the conventional aggregate unemployment rate refers to registered unemployment and employees during the entire year, the Microcensus only provides data on employment and unemployment in the month of April. In addition, the definitions of unemployment and employment differ slightly. Therefore, the aggregated unemployment rate depicted in figure A.2 does not necessarily correspond to a weighted average of skill specific unemployment rates.

rates among all employed workers in 46 industries for the years 1975 to 1990 (for further details see Fitzenberger, Haggeney, and Ernst, 1998). Given the estimated probit membership function, it proves very important to base the prediction on detailed industry and firm size information, which is provided in the I_ABS. The firm size information is only available after 1976. For the years 1975 and 1976, I take the same size class for each firm as provided for the first observation on the same firm after 1976. If there is no observation for a firm after 1976, I take the lowest firm size class, since firm attrition is likely to be negatively correlated with firm size. The industry classification differs slightly from the one used in the national account data. The I_ABS comprises 95 industries which, in most cases, is finer than the national account classification used for the prediction (see Fitzenberger and Franz, 1998, how to merge the two). It proceeds as follows: First, the I_ABS data for each year is grouped in cells defined by the explanatory variables of the membership functions except for firm size[8] and earnings. Second, for each cell the median wage and the average shares of each firm size category is calculated. Third, based on the cell attributes and the variables calculated in the second step, I predict the union density in the cell by the associated fitted membership probability. Fourth, the union densities across cells are aggregated for each industry in the I_ABS (see table A.1) and for each year by calculating the weighted average across the respective cells where the weights correspond to the employment in each cell. In light of the German wage bargaining institutions, it seems reasonable to refer to industry–specific union density rates at the national level.

5. OECD (1997) provides R&D expenditures by industries for various years between 1975 and 1990 as part of its ANBERD database. Whereas for almost all Manufacturing industries observations in every year are available, this is not the case in Non–Manufacturing. Also, the industry classification of ANBERD is not as detailed as in table A.1, which again is a bigger problem for Non–Manufacturing compared to Manufacturing. When an industry in the ANBERD database comprises more than one industry according to the classification used here, it is assumed that the share of R&D expenditures in total shipments is the same in all industries involved. The resulting R&D shares are then interpolated for the years with missing data on R&D expenditures in the ANBERD database.

6. The Federal Statistical Office ("Statistisches Bundesamt", Fachserie 16) provides indices for bargained wages both for blue–collar workers ("Arbeiter") and white–collar workers ("Angestellte") by industry and sex. For

[8]For two of the eight categories in the I_ABS (see Bender et al., 1996, p. 114), there exists no unique correspondence in the GSOEP. These are the categories 6 (100–499 employees) and 8 (1000 and more employees). For both categories, I assume that the respective employees spent 50% of their employment spell in each of the two categories in the GSOEP with overlap with the respective category in the I_ABS, cf. Fitzenberger, Haggeney, and Ernst (1998, appendix) for details.

blue–collar workers, I use the index for weekly wages and for white–collar workers the index for monthly wages. In the empirical application in chapter 5, these indices are used as instruments. I take the index for all workers and the index for male workers. In some industries, there does not exist a separate index for female workers such that the index for male workers and the index for all workers coincides.

7. The ifo Firm Panel constructed by Schneeweis and Smolny (1996) uses business survey data collected by the ifo Institute in Munich for the years 1980 to 1992. The information is restricted to Manufacturing and I use the shares of firms in each industry reporting product (PD) or process (PZ) innovations as a technology indicator. For the time period before 1980, I impute the value in 1980 for each of the two shares in the two industries.

8. The input–output tables of the Federal Statistical Office ("Statistisches Bundesamt") provide material inputs (both in form of domestic production or in form of imports) from the computer industry and the electrical goods industry (see table A.1 for the industry classification) to the industries in NON–Manufacturing. These data are available for the years 1975, 1978, 1980, 1982, 1985, 1986, 1987, 1988, and 1991. For these years, I calculate the respective ratios of material inputs obtained from each of the two industries to total shipments for each of the NON–Manufacturing industries. For the missing years between 1975 and 1990, I then interpolate these input coefficients.

Figure A.1: Aggregate Skill Specific Employment Trends (1980=100)

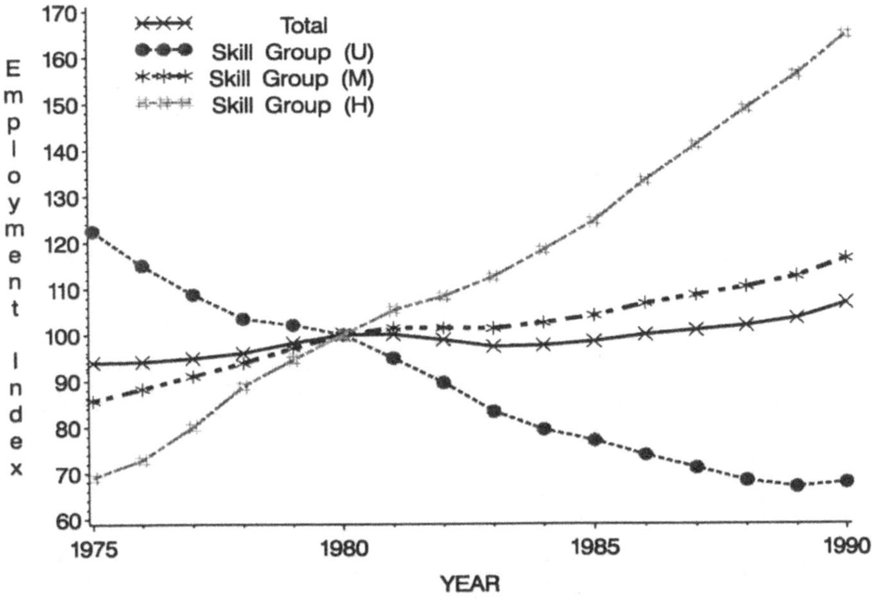

Figure A.2: Trends in Skill Specific Unemployment Rates

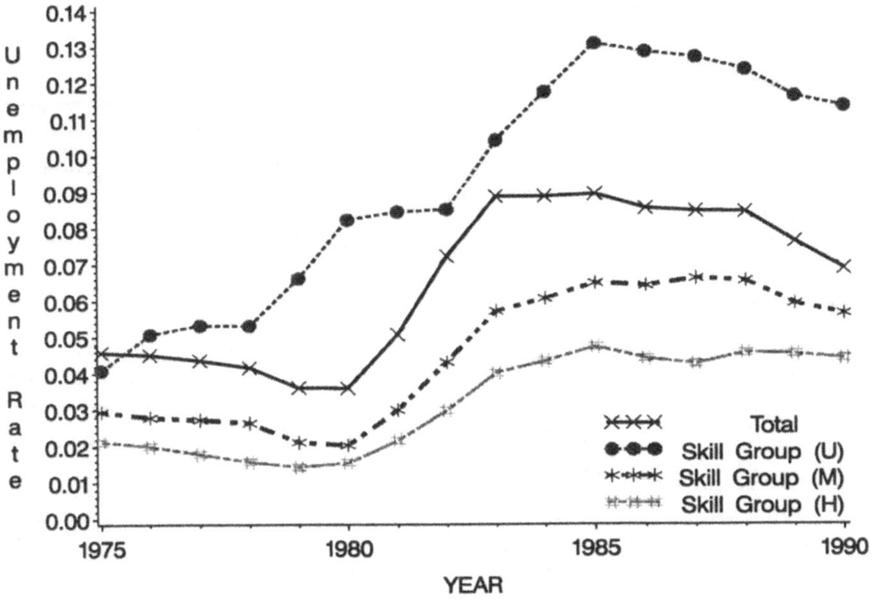

Figure A.3: Distribution of Daily Wages for Full–Time Working Males Before Correction

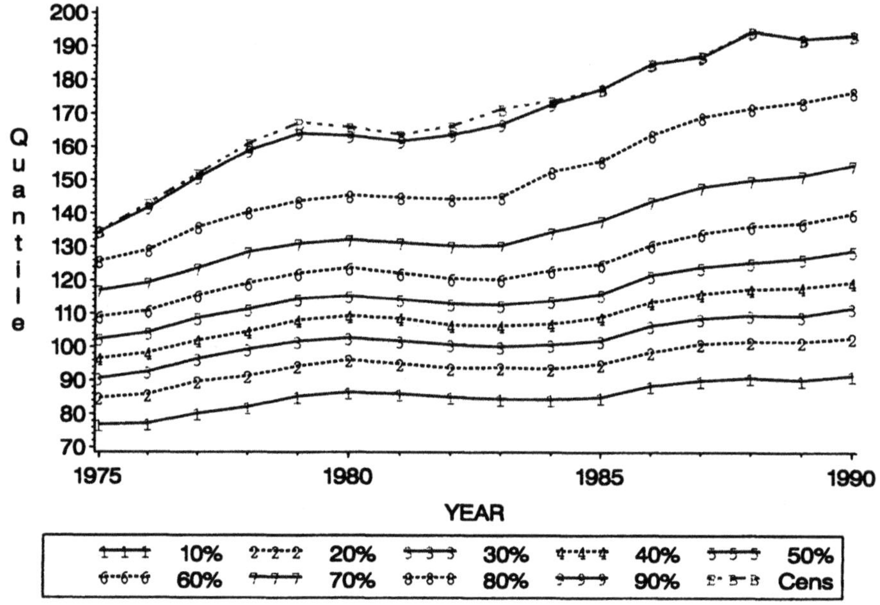

Figure A.4: Distribution of Daily Wages for Full–Time Working Males After Correction

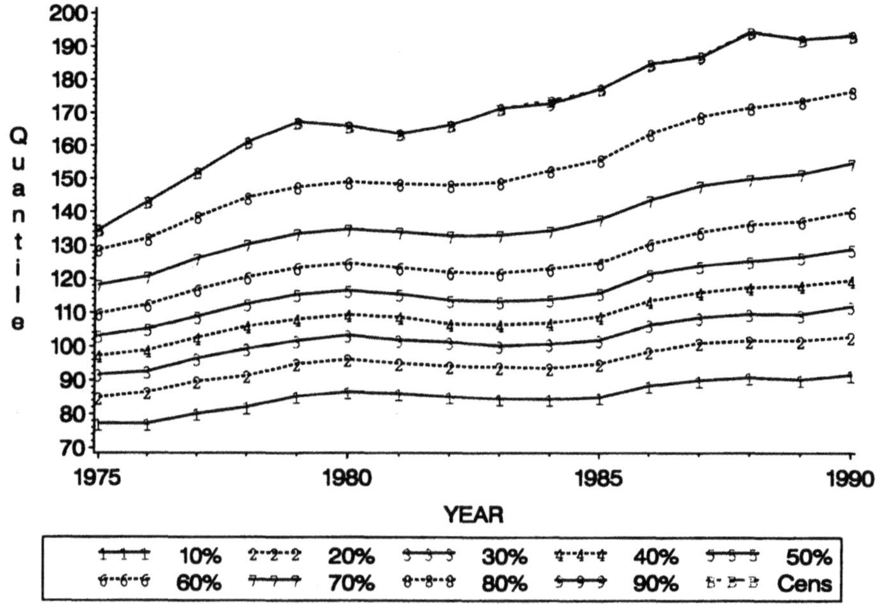

Industry Classification

Table A.1: Industry Classification in National Accounts[a]

StaBu-No.	Industry German	English
01	Land– u. Forstwirtschaft, Fischerei	Agriculture, Forestry and Fisheries
06	Elektrizität–, Gas–, Fernwärme, Wasserversorgung	Electricity, Gas, Heat and Water
10	Bergbau	Mining
14	Chemische Industrie, Herstellung u. Verarbeitung v. Spalt– u. Brutstoffen	Chemical Products
15	Mineralölverarbeitung	Petrolium Processing
16	Herstellung v. Kunststoffwaren	Synthetic Material
17	Gummiverarbeitung	Rubber Products
18	Gewinnung u. Verarbeitung v. Steinen u. Erden	Stone and Earth Products
19	Feinkeramik	Fine Ceramics
20	Herstellung u. Verarbeitung v. Glas	Glass and Products
21	Eisenschaffende Industrie	Iron
22	NE–Metallerzeugung, NE–Metallhalbzeugwerke	Non-Ferrous Metals
23	Giesserei	Foundry
24	Ziehereien, Kaltwalzwerke Stahlverformung usw.	Fabricated Metal Products
25	Stahl– u. Leichtmetall Schienenfahrzeuge	Steel, Light Metal and Tracked Vehicles
26	Maschinenbau	Machinery
27	Herstellung v. Büromaschinen, ADV-Geräten u. -Einrichtungen	Office and Data Processing Machines
28	Strassenfahrzeugbau, Reparatur v. KFZ. usw.	Vehicles and Repairs
29	Schiffbau	Shipbuilding
30	Luft– u. Raumfahrzeugbau	Air and Space
31	Elektrotechnik, Reparatur v. Haushaltsgeräten	Electric Appliances and Repairs
32	Feinmechanik, Optik, Herstellung v. Uhren	Precision and Optical Instruments
33	Herstellung v. Eisen–, Blech– u. Metallwaren	Iron, Sheet Metal and Metal Products

< Table continues on next page >

Table A.1: < Continued > Industry Classification in National Accounts[a]

StaBu- No.	Industry < continued > German	English
34	Herstellung v. Musikinstrumenten, Spielwaren, Füllhaltern usw.	Musical Instruments, Toys, Fountain Pens
35	Holzbearbeitung	Woodwork
36	Holzverarbeitung	Wood Processing
37	Zellstoff–, Holzschliff–, Papier– u. Papperzeugung	Pulp, Paper and Board
38	Papier– u. Pappeverarbeitung	Paper and Products
39	Druckerei, Vervielfältigung	Printing and Publishing
40	Ledergewerbe	Leather
41	Textilgewerbe	Textiles
42	Bekleidungsgewerbe	Apparel
43	Ernährungsgewerbe (ohne Getränkeherstellung)	Food
44	Getränkeherstellung	Beverages
45	Tabakverarbeitung	Tobacco
46	Baugewerbe	Construction
50	Handel	Trade
54	Eisenbahnen	Railways
55	Schiffahrt, Wasserstraßen, Häfen	Ship Traffic, Waterways,
56	Deutsche Bundespost	German Postal Services
57	Übriger Verkehr	Other Transportation
60	Kreditinstitute	Credit Institutions
61	Versicherungsunternehmen	Insurance Companies
64	Gastgewerbe, Heime	Catering and Hotels
65	Bildung, Wissenschaft, Kultur usw., Verlagswesen	Educations, Research, and Culture
66	Gesundheits– u. Veterinärwesen	Health and Veterinary
67	Übrige Dienst-leistungsunternehmen	Other Services
70	Staat	Government
73	Private Haushalte, Private Organisationen ohne Erwerbscharakter	Private Households and Private Non–Profit Organizations
76	Alle Wirtschaftsbereiche	Total

a: The industry classification used in this study builds upon the classification in the National Accounts of the German Statistical Office ("Statistisches Bundesamt", FS 18, R 1.3). The numbers refer to the classification numbers used by the Statistical Office.

Table A.2: Industry Correspondence List

StaBu–No.[a]	I_ABS–No.[b]	Manu–[c] facturing	Non–Manu–[c] facturing	Trad–able	Regu–[d] lated
01	00–03			*	*
06	04		*		*
10	05–08		*	*	*
14	09/10	*		*	
15	11	*		*	
16	12	*		*	
17	13	*		*	
18	14	*		*	
19	15	*		*	
20	16	*		*	
21	17	*		*	
22	18	*		*	
23	19	*		*	
24	20–22	*		*	
25	23–25	*		*	
26	26/27	*		*	
27	33	*		*	
28	28–30	*		*	
29	31	*		*	
30	32	*		*	
31	34	*		*	
32	35/36	*		*	
33	37	*		*	
34	38/39	*		*	
35	40–42	*		*	
36	40–42	*		*	
37	43	*		*	
38	43	*		*	
39	44	*		*	
40	45/46	*		*	
41	47–51/53	*		*	
42	52	*		*	
43	54–56	*		*	
44	57	*		*	

< Table continues on next page >

Table A.2: < Continued > Industry Correspondence List

StaBu-No.[a]	$\mathrm{I_A}$BS-No.[b]	Manu-[c] facturing	Non-Manu-[c] facturing	Trad- able	Regu-[d] lated
45	58	*		*	
46	59–61		*		
50	62		*		
54	63		*		*
55	66		*		*
56	64		*		*
57	65/67/68		*		*
60	69		*	*	*
61	69		*	*	*
64	70/71		*		
65	75–77		*		
66	78		*		*
67	72/73/79–86		*		
70	74/91–94				*
73	87–90				

a: The numbers of industry classification used in the National Accounts of the German Statistical Office ("Statistisches Bundesamt", FS 18, R 1.3).

b: The numbers of industry classification used by the Federal Labor Office ("Bundesanstalt für Arbeit") for the $\mathrm{I_A}$BS dataset, see Bender et al. (1996, pp. 129–130).

c: Industries characterized as Non–Manufacturing comprise all industries not characterized as Manufacturing except for the Government sector, Agriculture, and Non–Profit Organizations.

d: Industries characterized as "regulated" comprise the government sector itself and those industries with considerable government control of market access or subsidization of the domestic production.

List of Figures

List of Tables

Bibliography

Abraham, K.G. and S.N. Houseman (1995). Earnings Inequality in Germany. In: Freeman, R.B. and L. Katz (Eds.), *Differences and Changes in Wage Structures* (pp. 371–403). University of Chicago Press: NBER.

Anderson, G.J. and R.W. Blundell (1982). Estimation and Hypothesis Testing in Dynamic Singular Equation Systems. *Econometrica*, 50, 1559–1571.

Anderson, T. W. and C. Hsiao (1981). Estimation of Dynamic Models With Error Components. *Journal of the American Statistical Association*, 76, 598–606.

Arellano, M. and S. Bond (1991). Some Tests of Specification for Panel Data: Monte Carlo Evidence and an Application to Employment Equations. *Review of Economic Studies*, 58, 277–297.

Baldwin, R.E. (1995). The effect of trade and forgein direct investment on employment and relative wages. *National Bureau of Economic Research, Working Paper*, 5037.

Baldwin, R.E. and G.G. Cain (1997). Shifts in U.S. Relative Wages: The Role of Trade, Technology and Factor Endowments. *National Bureau of Economic Research, Working Paper*, 5934.

Beißinger, T. and J. Möller (1998). Wage Inequality and Employment Performance: A Microdata Analysis of Different Age–Education Groups for Germany. *Discussion Paper, University of Regensburg*, 307.

Bender, S., Hilzendegen, J., Rohwer, G., and H. Rudolph (1996). Die IAB–Beschäftigtenstichprobe 1975–1990. Beiträge zur Arbeitsmarkt– und Berufsforschung, 197, Institut für Arbeitsmarkt- und Berufsforschung der Bundesanstalt für Arbeit (IAB), Nürnberg.

Bergström, V. and E.E. Panas (1992). How Robust is the Capital–Skill Complementarity Hypothesis? *Review of Economics and Statistics*, 74, 540–552.

Berman, E., J. Bound, and Z. Griliches (1994). Changes in the Demand for Skilled Labor Within U.S. Manufacturing: Evidence from the Annual Survey of Manufactures. *Quarterly Journal of Economics*, 109, 367–397.

Berndt, E.R. (1991). The Practice of Econometrics: Classic and Contemporary. Addison–Wesley Publishing Company.

Betts, J.R. (1997). The Skill Bias of Technological Change in Canadian Manufacturing Industries. *Review of Economics and Statistics*, 79, 146–150.

Blau, F. and L.M. Kahn (1996). International Differences in Male Wage Inequality: Institutions versus Market Forces. *Journal of Political Economy*, 104, 791–837.

Borjas, G.J. (1994). The Economics of Immigration. *Journal of Economic Literature*, 32, 1667–1717.

Borjas, G.J. and V.A. Ramey (1995). Foreign Competition, Market Power, and Wage Inequality. *Quarterly Journal of Economics*, 110, 1075–1110.

Bound, J. and G. Johnson (1992). Changes in the Structure of Wages during the 1980's: An Evaluation of Alternative Explanations. *American Economic Review*, 82(3), 371–392.

Card, D., Kramarz, F., and T. Lemieux (1996). Changes in the relative Structure of Wages and Employment: A Comparison of the United States, Canada, and France. *National Bureau of Economic Research, Working Paper*, 5487.

Carlstein, E. (1986). The Use of Subseries Values for Estimating the Variance of a General Statistic from a Stationary Sequence. *Annals of Statistics*, 14, 1171–1179.

Chamberlain, G. (1994). Quantile Regression, Censoring, and the Structure of Wages. In: C. Sims (Ed.), *Advances in Econometrics: Sixth World Congress*. Volume 1: Econometric Society Monograph.

De la Croix, D., Palm, F.C., and G.A. Pfann (1996). A Dynamic Contracting Model for Wages and Employment in Three European Economies. *European Economic Review*, 40, 429–448.

Deaton, A. (1985). Panel Data from a Time–Series of Cross–Sections. *Journal of Econometrics*, 30, 109–126.

DeNew, J.P. and C.M. Schmidt (1994). The Industrial Structure of German Earnings 1980–1990. *Allgemeines Statistisches Archiv*, 78, 141–159.

Deutsche Bundesbank (1995). Das Produktionspotential in Deutschland und seine Bestimmungsfaktoren. *Monatsberichte*, 47(8), 41–56.

Dixit, A. and V. Norman (1986). Theory of International Trade. 2nd edition. Cambridge University Press, Cambridge.

Eicker, F. (1967). Limit Theorems for Regressions with Unequal and Dependant Errors. In: L. Lecam and J. Neyman (Eds.), *Proceedings of the Fifth Berkeley Symposium on Mathematical Statistics and Probability, Volume I* (pp. 59–82). University of California: Berkeley.

Entorf, H. (1996). Strukturelle Arbeitslosigkeit in Deutschland: Mismatch, Mobilität und technologischer Wandel. In: Gahlen, B., Hesse, H., and Ramser, H.J. (Eds.), *Arbeitslosigkeit und Möglichkeiten ihrer Überwindung* (pp. 139–168). Schriftenreihe des Wirtschaftswissenschaftlichen Seminars Ottobeuren, Band 25: J.C.B. Mohr (Paul Siebeck) Tübingen.

Falk, M. and B. Koebel (1997). The Demand for Heterogeneous Labour in Germany: Non–Traded versus Traded Goods Sectors. *Centre for European Economic Research (ZEW), Mannheim, Discussion Paper*, 97–28.

Falk, M. and F. Pfeiffer (1997). Skill–Biased Technological Change in Germany 1977–94. *Centre for European Economic Research (ZEW), Mannheim, Paper presented at the "DFG–Schwerpunktprogramm Industrieökonomik und Inputmärkte" in Heidelberg, 8. May 1997.*

Fitzenberger, B. (1994). A Note on Estimating Censored Quantile Regressions. *Center for International Labor Economics, Discussion Paper Nr. 14, University of Konstanz.*

Fitzenberger, B. (1997a). A Guide to Censored Quantile Regressions. In: Maddala, G.S. and C. Rao (Eds.), *Handbook of Statistics, Volume 15: Robust Inference* (pp. 405–437). Amsterdam: North–Holland.

Fitzenberger, B. (1997b). Computational Aspects of Censored Quantile Regression. In: Dodge, Y. (Ed.), *Proceedings of The 3rd International Conference on Statistical Data Analysis based on the L_1-Norm and Related Methods* (pp. 171–186). Volume 31, Hayword, California: Institute of Mathematical Statistics Lecture Notes–Monograph Series.

Fitzenberger, B. (1998). The Moving Blocks Bootstrap and Robust Inference for Linear Least Squares and Quantile Regressions. *Journal of Econometrics*, 82, 235–287.

Fitzenberger, B. and W. Franz (1998). Flexibilität der qualifikatorischen Lohnstruktur und Lastverteilung der Arbeitslosigkeit: Eine ökonometrische Analyse für Westdeutschland. In: Gahlen, B., Hesse, H., and Ramser, H.J. (Eds.), *Zunehmende Ungleichheit? – Erklärungen und Konsequenzen* – (pp. 47–79). Schriftenreihe des Wirtschaftswissenschaftlichen Seminars Ottobeuren, Band 27: J.C.B. Mohr (Paul Siebeck) Tübingen.

Fitzenberger, B., Haggeney, I., and M. Ernst (1998). Wer ist noch Mitglied in Gewerkschaften? Eine Panelanalyse für Westdeutschland. *Centre for European Economic Research (ZEW), Mannheim, Discussion Paper*, 98-11.

Fitzenberger, B., R. Hujer, T.E. MaCurdy, and R. Schnabel (1995). The Dynamic Structure of Wages in Germany 1976–1984, A Cohort Analysis. *Center for International Labor Economics, Discussion Paper Nr. 22, University of Konstanz.*

Fitzenberger, B. and C. Kurz (1997). New Insights on Earnings Trends across Skill Groups and Industries in West Germany. *Center for International Labor Economics, Discussion Paper Nr. 38, University of Konstanz.*

Fitzenberger, B. and T.E. MaCurdy (1996). Block Bootstrap Procedures for Robust Inference on Regression Estimates based on Grouped Data from Time Series of Cross–sections: Theoretical Results. *Unpublished Manuscript, University of Konstanz and Stanford University.*

FitzRoy, F. and M. Funke (1994). Capital–Skill Complementarity in West German Manufacturing. *Empirical Economics*, 20, 651–665.

FitzRoy, F. and M. Funke (1996). Wages and International Price Competitiveness: Germany vs U.K. *Unpublished Manuscript, University of St. Andrews and Universität Hamburg.*

Flaig, G. and V. Steiner (1993). Searching for the Productivity Slowdown: Some Surprising Findings from West German Manufacturing. *Review of Economics and Statistics*, 75, 57–65.

Franz, W. (1995). Die Lohnfindung in Deutschland in einer internationalen Perspektive: Ist das deutsche System der Lohnfindung ein Auslaufmodell? *Beihefte der Konjunkturpolitik, Zeitschrift für angewandte Wirtschaftsforschung*, 43, 31–57.

Franz, W. (1996). Arbeitsmarktökonomik. 3rd Edition, Springer–Verlag, Berlin, Heidelberg.

Freeman, R.B. (1995). Are Your Wages Set in Bejing? *Journal of Economic Perspectives*, 9(3), 15–32.

Freeman, R.B. (1997). Divergent Performances: Job Creation and Income Determination in the EU and the US. *Paper presented at the conference of the German–American–Academic Council (DAAK/GAAC) on "Labor Markets in the USA and Germany", Bonn.*

Gärtner, M. (1989). Arbeitskonflikte in der Bundesrepublik Deutschland. Eine empirische Untersuchung ihrer markroökonomischen Ursachen und Konsequenzen. Springer–Verlag, Berlin, Heidelberg.

German Council of Economic Experts (SVR) (1994). Strengthening the Recovery – Creating new Jobs. Annual Report 1994/95 (Sachverständigenrat zur Begutachtung der gesamtwirtschaftlichen Entwicklung). Metzler–Poeschel. Stuttgart.

German Council of Economic Experts (SVR) (1995). Facing Global Competition. Annual Report 1995/96 (Sachverständigenrat zur Begutachtung der gesamtwirtschaftlichen Entwicklung). Metzler–Poeschel. Stuttgart.

German Council of Economic Experts (SVR) (1996). Pushing Forward with Reforms. Annual Report 1996/97 (Sachverständigenrat zur Begutachtung der gesamtwirtschaftlichen Entwicklung). Metzler-Poeschel. Stuttgart.

Gosling, A., S. Machin, and C. Meghir (1994). What Has Happened to Men's Wages since the Mid-1960s? *Fiscal Studies*, 15, 63–87.

Gosling, A., Machin, S., and C. Meghir (1996). The Changing Distribution of Male Wages in the UK. *Department of Economics, University College London, Unpublished Manuscript.*

Haisken–DeNew, J.P. and K.F. Zimmermann (1995). Wage and Mobility Effects of Trade and Migration. *Discussion Paper, University of Munich*, 95-24.

Hall, B.H. and C. Cummins (1997). Time Series Processor, Version 4.4, User's Guide. Palo Alto.

Hall, P., Horowitz, J.L., and B.Y. Jing (1995). On blocking rules for the bootstrap with dependent data. *Biometrika*, 82, 561–574.

Hall, R.E. and D.M. Lilien (1979). Efficient Wage Bargains under Uncertain Supply and Demand. *American Economic Review*, 69, No.5, 868–879.

Hamermesh, D.S. (1993). Labor demand. Princeton University Press, Princeton, NJ.

Heckman, J.J. and R. Robb (1985). Using Longitudinal Data to Estimate Age, Period and Cohort Effects in Earnings Equations. In: W. Mason and S. Fienberg (Eds.), *Cohort Analysis in Social Reasearch* (pp. 138–150). New York: Academic Press.

Hesse, H. (1996). Internationale Konkurrenz: Ursache von Arbeitslosigkeit und Lohnungleichheit? In: Gahlen, B., Hesse, H., and Ramser, H.J. (Eds.), *Arbeitslosigkeit und Möglichkeiten ihrer Überwindung* (pp. 331–358). Schriftenreihe des Wirtschaftswissenschaftlichen Seminars Ottobeuren, Band 25: J.C.B. Mohr (Paul Siebeck) Tübingen.

Horowitz, J. and G. Neumann (1987). Semiparametric Estimation of Employment Duration Models. *Econometric Reviews*, 6, 5–40.

Jaeger, K. (1996). Gewerkschaftsverhalten und Arbeitslosigkeit. In: Gahlen, B., Hesse, H., and Ramser, H.J. (Eds.), *Arbeitslosigkeit und Möglichkeiten ihrer Überwindung* (pp. 179–209). Schriftenreihe des Wirtschaftswissenschaftlichen Seminars Ottobeuren, Band 25: J.C.B. Mohr (Paul Siebeck) Tübingen.

Jerger, J. and A. Spermann (1997). Wege aus der Arbeitslosenfalle - ein Vergleich alternativer Lösungskonzepte. *Zeitschrift für Wirtschaftspolitik*, 46, 51–73.

Jones, R.W. (1995). Trade and Wages: Comments on Theoretical Issues. *Unpublished Manuscript, Department of Economics, University of Rochester.*

Juhn, C., K.M. Murphy, and B. Pierce (1993). Wage Inequality and the Rise in Returns to Skill. *Journal of Political Economy*, 101, 410–442.

Koenker, R. and G. Bassett (1978). Regression Quantiles. *Econometrica*, 46, 33–50.

Koenker, R. and V. D'Orey (1987). Algorithm AS 229: Computing Regression Quantiles. *Applied Statistics*, 36, 383–393.

Koenker, R. and B.J. Park (1996). An Interior Point Algorithm for Nonlinear Quantile Regression. *Journal of Econometrics*, 71, 265–283.

Kraft, K. (1994). Wage Differentials Between Skilled and Unskilled Workers. *Weltwirtschaftliches Archiv*, 130, 329–347.

Krueger, A.B. and L.H. Summers (1988). Efficiency Wages and the Inter-Industry Wage Structure. *Econometrica*, 56, 259–293.

Krugman, P. (1994). Past and Prospective Causes of High Unemployment. *in: Federal Reserve Bank of Kansas City (Hrsg.), Reducing Unemployment: Current Issues and Policy Options, Proceedings of a Symposium in Jackson Hole, WY, Kansas City, MO*, (pp. 68–81).

Krugman, P. (1995). Growing World Trade: Causes and Consequences. *Brookings Papers on Economic Activity*, 1, 327–362.

Krusell, P., Ohanian, L., Ríos–Rull, J.–V., and G.L. Violante (1997). Capital–Skill Complementarity and Inequality: A Macroeconomic Analysis. *Unpublished Manuscript, University of Pennsylvania.*

Kugler, P., Müller, U., and G. Sheldon (1989). Struktur der Arbeitsnachfrage im technologischen Wandel – eine empirische Analyse für die Bundesrepublik Deutschland. *Weltwirtschaftliches Archiv*, 124, 490–500.

Künsch, H.R. (1989). The Jackknife and the Bootstrap for General Stationary Observations. *Annals of Statistics*, 17, 1217–1241.

Landmann, O. and M. Pflüger (1996). Arbeitsmärkte im Spannungsfeld von Globalisierung und technologischem Wandel. In: Külp, B. (Ed.), *Arbeitsmarkt und Arbeitslosigkeit* (pp. 173–230). Freiburg: Haufe-Verlag.

Lawrence, R.Z. (1994). Trade, Multinationals & Labor. *National Bureau of Economic Research, Working Paper*, 4836.

Lawrence, R.Z. and M.J. Slaughter (1993). International Trade and American Wages in the 1980s: Giant Sucking Sound or Small Hiccup? *Brookings Papers on Economic Activity*, (pp. 161–226).

Layard, R., S. Nickell, and R. Jackman (1991). Unemployment – Macroeconomic Performance and the Labour Market. Oxford University Press, Oxford.

Leamer, E.E. (1996). In Search of Stolper–Samuelson Effects on U.S. Wages. In: S. Collins (Ed.), *Imports, Exports and the American Worker.* Washington, D.C.: The Brookings Institution.

Lindquist, K.G. (1995). The Existence of Factor Substitution in the Primary Aluminium Industry: A Multivariate Error–Correction Approach using Norwegian Data Panel. *Empirical Economics*, 20, 361–383.

Liu, R.Y. and K. Singh (1992). Moving Blocks Jackknife and Bootstrap Capture Weak Dependance. In: R. Lepage and L. Billard (Eds.), *Exploring the Limits of Bootstrap* (pp. 225–248). New York: Wiley.

Lücke, M. (1997). European Trade with Lower–Income Countries and the Relative Wages of the Unskilled – An Exploratory Analysis for West Germany and the UK. *Working Paper, Kiel Institute of World Economics*, 819.

Machin, S., Ryan, A., and J. Van Reenen (1996). Technology and Changes in Skill Structure: Evidence from an International Panel of Industries. *Discussion Paper, CEPR, London*, 1434.

Machin, S. and J. Van Reenen (1997). Technology and Changes in Skill Structure: Evidence from Seven OECD Countries. *Discussion Paper, University College London.*

MaCurdy, T.E. and T. Mroz (1995). Measuring Macroeconomic Shifts in Wages from Cohort Specifications. *Unpublished Manuscript, Stanford University and University of North Carolina.*

MaCurdy, T.E. and J.H. Pencavel (1986). Testing between Competing Models of Wage and Employment Determination in Unionized Markets. *Journal of Political Economy*, 94 (3, suppl.2), 3–39.

Marsaglia, G. (1986). A Current View of Random Number Generators. *Computer Science and Statistics: Proc. 16th Symposium Interface in Atlanta. March 1984.*

Meyer, W. (1995). Is Pattern Bargaining Dead? An Empirical Investigation with Micro Data for West Germany. *Konjunkturpolitik*, 41, 228–243.

Möller, J. (1990). Das Hysteresis–Phänomen in Arbeitslosigkeit–Inflations–Modellen: Theorie, Empirische Relevanz und wirtschaftspolitische Konsequenzen. Habilitationsschrift, Universität Konstanz.

Möller, J. (1996). Technological Change, Unemployment, and Recent Trends in Human Capital Formation – Did the German Wage Structure Respond to these Impulses? *Discussion Paper, University of Regensburg*, 280.

Möller, J. (1997). Trends in the German Wage Structure. *Paper presented at the ZEW/IAB–Conference on the IAB–Beschäftigtenstichprobe, February 7/8 1997*.

Möller, J. and L. Bellmann (1996). Qualifikations– und industriespezifische Lohnunterschiede in der Bundesrepublik Deutschland – Eine Untersuchung für das Verarbeitende Gewerbe auf Basis der IAB–Beschäftigtenstichprobe. *ifo Studien – Zeitschrift für empirische Wirtschaftsforschung*, 42, 235–272.

Moulton, B.R. (1986). Random Group Effects and the Precision of Regression Estimates. *Journal of Econometrics*, 32, 385–397.

Moulton, B.R. (1990). An Illustration of a Pitfall in Estimating the Effects of Aggregate Variables on Micro Units. *Review of Economics and Statistics*, 72, 334–338.

Nadiri, M.I. and I.R. Prucha (1996). Estimation of the Depreciation Rate of Physical and R&D Capital in the U.S. Total Manufacturing Sector. *Economic Inquiry*, XXXIV, 43–56.

Nelder, J.A. and R. Mead (1965). A Simplex Method for Function Minimization. *Computer Journal*, 7, 308–313.

Neven, D. and C. Wyplosz (1996). Relative Prices, Trade and Restructuring in European Industry. *Working Paper, Centre for Economic Policy Research, London*, 1451.

Newey, W.K. (1984). A Method of Moments Interpretation of Sequential Estimators. *Economics Letters*, 14, 201–206.

Nickell, S.J. (1997). Unemployment and Labor Market Rigidities: Europe versus North America. *Journal of Economic Perspectives*, 11, 55–74.

Nickell, S.J. and B. Bell (1995). The Collapse in Demand for the Unskilled and Unemployment across OECD Countries. *Oxford Review of Economic Policy*, 11, 40–62.

Nickell, S.J. and B. Bell (1996). Changes in the Distribution of Wages and Unemployment in OECD Countries. *American Economic Association, Papers and Proceedings*, 86(2), 302–314.

Nissim, J. (1984). The Price Responsiveness of the Demand for Labour by Skill: British Mechanical Engineering: 1963–1978. *Economic Journal*, 94, 812–825.

OECD (1993). Economic Outlook – Earnings Inequality: Changes in the 1980s. *Paris*, Chapter 5, 157–184.

OECD (1996). Employment Outlook – Earnings Inequality, low–paid Employment and Earnings Mobility. *Paris*, Chapter 3, 59–108.

OECD (1997). Research and Development Expenditure in Industry. Report on the BERD and ANBERD Database, Directorate for Science, Technology and Industry. Paris.

Oswald, A.J. (1985). The Economic Theory of Trade Unions: An Introductory Survey. *Scandinavian Journal of Economics*, 87, 160–193.

Paarsch, H. (1984). A Monte Carlo Comparison of Estimators for Censored Regression Modells. *Journal of Econometrics*, 24, 197–213.

Papaconstantinou, G., Sakurai, N., and A. Wyckoff (1996). Embodied Technology Diffusion: An Empirical Analysis for 10 OECD Countries. *OECD Science Technology and Industry Working Papers*, 1.

Paqué, K.–H. (1995). Structural Unemployment and Real Wage Rigidity in Germany. Habilitationsschrift, Kiel.

Paqué, K.–H. (1998). Internationaler Handel, technischer Fortschritt und Lohndifferenzierung. Ein Blick in die empirische Literatur. In: Gahlen, B., Hesse, H., and Ramser, H.J. (Eds.), *Zunehmende Ungleichheit? – Erklärungen und Konsequenzen* – (pp. 359–379). Schriftenreihe des Wirtschaftswissenschaftlichen Seminars Ottobeuren, Band 27: J.C.B. Mohr (Paul Siebeck) Tübingen.

Pencavel, J.H. (1985). Wages and Employment under Trade Unionism: Microeconomic Models and Macroeconomic Applications. *Scandinavian Journal of Economics*, 87, 197–225.

Pencavel, J.H. (1991). Labor Markets under Trade Unionism. Basil Blackwell, Oxford.

Pencavel, J.H. and B. Holmlund (1988). The Determination of Wages, Employment, and Work Hours in an Economy with Centralised Wage-Setting: Sweden, 1950–83. *Economic Journal*, 98, 1105–1126.

Pischke, J.–S. (1998). Ausbildung und Lohnstruktur: Deutschland und die USA in den 80er Jahren. In: Gahlen, B., Hesse, H., and Ramser, H.J. (Eds.), *Zunehmende Ungleichheit? – Erklärungen und Konsequenzen* – (pp. 95–117). Schriftenreihe des Wirtschaftswissenschaftlichen Seminars Ottobeuren, Band 27: J.C.B. Mohr (Paul Siebeck) Tübingen.

Politis, D.N. and J.P. Romano (1993). Nonparametric Resampling for Homogeneous Strong Mixing Random Fields. *Journal of Multivariate Analysis*, 47, 301–328.

Powell, J.L. (1984). Least Absolute Deviations Estimation for the Censored Regression Model. *Journal of Econometrics*, 25, 303–325.

Powell, J.L. (1986). Censored Regression Quantiles. *Journal of Econometrics*, 32, 143–155.

Richardson, J.D. (1995). Income Inequality and Trade: How to Think, What to Conclude. *Journal of Economic Perspectives*, 9(3), 33–56.

Ronning, G. (1986). Ökonometrische Analyse dynamischer Anteilsgleichungen. *Zeitschrift für Wirtschafts- und Sozialwissenschaften*, 106, 605–621.

Ronning; G. (1992). Share Equations in Econometrics: A Story of Repression, Frustration and Dead Ends. *Statistical Papers*, 33, 307–334.

Sachs, J.D. and H.J. Shatz (1994). Trade and Jobs in U.S. Manufacturing. *Brookings Papers on Economic Activity*, 1, 1–84.

Schettkat, R. (1992). The Labor Market Dynamics of Economic Restructuring. The United States and Germany in Transition. *New York (Praeger).*

Schnabel, C. (1994). Die Übertarifliche Bezahlung: Ausmaß, Entwicklung und Bestimmungsgründe. *Beiträge zur Wirtschafts- und Sozialpolitik, Institut der deutschen Wirtschaft, Köln*, 217.

Schneeweis, T. and W. Smolny (1996). Das ifo Unternehmenspanel 1980–92 – Einige Ergebnisse einer Verknüpfung der Umfragen des ifo Instituts. *Discussion Paper, Center for International Labor Economics (CILE), University of Konstanz*, 32.

Schulte zur Surlage, R. (1985). Qualifikationsstruktur der Arbeitsnachfrage. Campus Verlag, Frankfurt/Main.

Siebert, H. (1995a). Geht den Deutschen die Arbeit aus? Wege zu mehr Beschäftigung. *München (Goldmann).*

Siebert, H. (1995b). Vier Forderungen an die Arbeitsmarktökonomie. *Das Wirtschaftsstudium*, 4, 255–256.

Siebert, H. (1997). Labor Market Rigidities: At the Root of Unemployment in Europe. *Journal of Economic Perspectives*, 11, 37–54.

Slaughter, M.J. and P. Swagel (1997). The Effect of Globalization on Wages in the Advanced Economies. *Working Paper of the International Monetary Fund.*

Steiner, V. and K. Wagner (1997). Relative Earnings and the Demand for Unskilled Labor in West German Manufacturing. *Centre for European Economic Research (ZEW), Mannheim, Discussion Paper*, 97–17.

Steiner, V. and K. Wagner (1998). Has Earnings Inequality in Germany Changed in the 1980's? *Zeitschrift für Wirtschafts- und Sozialwissenschaften*, 118(1), 29–59.

Stolper, W. and P.A. Samuelson (1941). Protection and Real Wages. *Review of Economic Studies*, 9, 58–73.

White, H. (1980). A Heteroskedasticity–Consistent Covariance Matrix Estimator and a Direct Test for Heteroskedasticity. *Econometrica*, 48, 817–838.

Winker, P. (1998). Efficient Labour Contracts: Impediments and How to Circumvent Them. *Unpublished Manuscript, University of Mannheim.*

Wood, A. (1995). How Trade Hurt Unskilled Workers. *Journal of Economic Perspectives*, 9(3), 57–80.

GPSR Compliance

The European Union's (EU) General Product Safety Regulation (GPSR) is a set of rules that requires consumer products to be safe and our obligations to ensure this.

If you have any concerns about our products, you can contact us on ProductSafety@springernature.com

In case Publisher is established outside the EU, the EU authorized representative is:

Springer Nature Customer Service Center GmbH
Europaplatz 3
69115 Heidelberg, Germany

Batch number: 10725973

Printed by Printforce, the Netherlands